FAILURE IN

THE

SADDLE

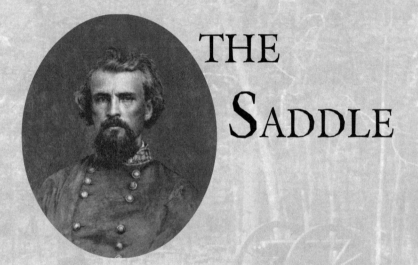

FAILURE IN
THE
SADDLE

David A. Powell

Nathan Bedford Forrest, Joseph Wheeler, and the Confederate Cavalry in the Chickamauga Campaign

Oliver's Alabama Battery (also known as the Eufala Artillery) along Battleline Road facing Kelly's Field. *Photo by Lee White*

SB

Savas Beatie
New York and California

Cataloging-in-Publication Data is available from the Library of Congress.

ISBN 978-1-932714-87-6

05 04 03 02   5 4 3 2
Second edition, first printing

SB

Published by
Savas Beatie LLC
521 Fifth Avenue, Suite 1700
New York, NY 10175

Editorial Offices:

Savas Beatie LLC
P.O. Box 4527
El Dorado Hills, CA 95762
Phone: 916-941-6896
(E-mail) sales@savasbeatie.com

Savas Beatie titles are available at special discounts for bulk purchases in the United States by corporations, institutions, and other organizations. For more details, please contact Special Sales, P.O. Box 4527, El Dorado Hills, CA 95762, or you may e-mail us at sales@savasbeatie.com, or visit our website at www.savasbeatie.com for additional information.

To my parents, for all they've given me

The Fight at Reed's Bridge

Harper's Weekly

Contents

Contents (continued)

Contents (continued)

Maps

Maps (continued)

Introduction

In 1998 I wrote an article for Gettysburg Magazine that examined J.E.B. Stuart's famous (or infamous) ride around the Union army in June 1863. Despite the wide variety of literature that existed on the subject, I had some questions of my own to answer about that event. For me, the best way to find answers to my questions has always been to research the topic and write about it. I thoroughly enjoyed the process of analyzing the choices and movements of the men involved in that difficult operation. Along the way I also refined some ideas about the mounted arm.

Civil War cavalry has long been the stuff of romance, though often at the expense of a more hard-headed and realistic appraisal of its place in military affairs. This has become less true in more recent times, as a number of talented historians turn their attention to the importance of cavalry to Civil War campaigns. This is good news for readers of military history because cavalry played a critical role in 19th century operational art, and it needs to be better understood.

In a field dominated by tactical monographs on the various battles of the war, the mounted arm tends to get shoved to the sidelines (or relegated to footnotes), its role in most major battles treated peripherally if at all. The glory and the ink are reserved for the infantry (and to a lesser extent, the artillery). The horsemen "guard the flanks," "escort wagons," "conduct raids," or are "held in reserve." Sometimes they fight enemy cavalry or wage rearguard actions, but rarely is cavalry portrayed as critical to the evolution or the outcome of any campaign. This is not only unfortunate but has resulted in an imperfect understanding of the evolution of campaigns and in how we judge operational effectiveness at the army level.

The value and importance of cavalry is demonstrated before battle is joined. Indeed, it is invariably the cavalry that dictates how a campaign unfolds and plays out. William Woods Averell, a Union cavalry general who spent his Civil War years fighting in the Eastern Theater, defined the role this way:

> Reliable information on the enemy's position or movements, which is absolutely necessary to the commander of an army to successfully conduct a campaign, must be largely furnished by the cavalry. The duty of the cavalry when an engagement is imminent is specially imperative—to keep in touch with the enemy and observe and carefully note, with time of day or night, every slightest indication and report it promptly. . . . On the march, cavalry forms in advance, flank, and rear guards, and supplies escorts, couriers and guides. Cavalry should extend well away from the main body on the march like antennae to mask its movements and discover any movement of the enemy. Without this kind of work, strategy is impossible.[1]

Averell captured perfectly the essentials of the cavalry mission: to scout and screen, to probe and cover. Without effective cavalry, even a talented army commander can suddenly appear operationally incompetent.

In 2009 Savas Beatie published my first book (with David A. Friedrichs) entitled *The Maps of Chickamauga: An Atlas of the Chickamauga Campaign, Including the Tullahoma Operations, June 22-September 23, 1863.* My first Chickamauga manuscript, however, was finished in 2004 and is the book you are now holding. The more I studied the sources and walked the terrain, the more I realized the important role cavalry played in the fall 1863 campaign to capture Chattanooga. For three weeks that September Federal Maj. Gen. William Rosecrans and Confederate Gen. Braxton Bragg played cat and mouse in the mountains of North Georgia, each seeking opportunities to damage and ultimately turn and destroy the other. The mounted arm influenced high command decisions and shaped the course and the outcome of the fighting.

This was especially true for Confederate cavalry. Despite being led by such legendary commanders as Nathan Bedford Forrest and Joseph Wheeler, it did

---

1   Edward J Eckert and Nicholas J. Amato, *Ten Years in The Saddle, The Memoir of William Woods Averell, 1851-1862* (San Raphael CA: Presidio Press, 1978), p. 328.

not perform well from the outset. Mounted miscues, mistakes, and outright refusals to follow orders hamstrung the Rebels as Rosecrans turned Bragg's flank and nearly severed his supply line. These stunning lapses in the saddle by experienced cavalrymen led directly to Bragg's loss of Chattanooga—a critically important logistical and manufacturing hub—without a major engagement. When Bragg finally regrouped and decided to turn the tables on his opponent, the Army of the Cumberland was not where he believed it to be. The result was the confusing and bloody two-day battle of Chickamauga. Although a tactical success, the fighting was a hollow Confederate victory. Most of the Union army slipped away from the field on the night of September 20-21, 1863, and by doing so avoided destruction. Chattanooga remained in Federal hands and was reinforced. Two months later in November the Southern army was routed from the surrounding hills and shoved back into North Georgia. Bragg, as the commander of the Rebel Army of Tennessee, has traditionally received the blame for these failures. The more I studied the campaign, however, the more I moved away from the simplistic view that it was "all Bragg's fault."

Failure in the Saddle is the result of this evolution of thought. My intent was to pen an operational analysis grounded in an honest and complete assessment of the role played by Confederate cavalry. My primary focus, therefore, is on mounted operations at the expense of other aspects of the maneuvering and fighting. (A similar study from the Union point of view would offer a fascinating counterpoint to this work, and perhaps one day someone will undertake it.)

My hope is that you come away from this work with a challenged—and even changed—perspective of the Chickamauga Campaign and the men who waged it and, perhaps, a few new questions of your own.

Acknowledgments

First and foremost I would like to thank my good friend Eric Wittenberg for his generosity in helping me get this book published with Savas Beatie. Eric is an award-winning author and noted cavalry historian in his own right, and the idea for *Failure in the Saddle* is based at least in part on some of his writings about cavalry in the Gettysburg Campaign. Eric is both a fine historian and a gentleman, and I continue to read eagerly everything he writes. If this book rises to the standard he has set with his own work, I will be content.

I would also like to thank Sam Elliott, who was the first to read the manuscript and offer comments. Every first time writer has to let someone see his work eventually, and Sam was very kind to this literary virgin. His comments helped shape and improve the project. Although it has continued to evolve since 2004, Sam's initial input was invaluable.

Since this project shares so many ties with *The Maps of Chickamauga*, many of the same friends deserve credit here as well. Dave Friedrichs' outstanding cartography appears here again and includes several new original creations not found in our previous work. Zack Waltz and John Reed—your long-term support is always appreciated. Greg Biggs read over an early draft of the manuscript and offered helpful suggestions, especially concerning Forrest.

Special thanks to Scott Day and Lee White. Scott proofed the driving tour portion by following my directions and making sure I wasn't going to get anyone lost in the process. Lee is responsible for many of the photographs in the book. Living as I do 600 miles from the battlefield, I can't just hop in the car and take a quick trip when I realize I need something. Having a friend like Lee who works at the park and is always willing to help is a great blessing.

Chickamauga Park Historian Jim Ogden once advised me that I would need to enter a witness protection program if my work is too critical of Forrest. I hope that won't be necessary. In any case, I first visited many of the sites discussed in this book with either Jim or with noted author Dr. Glenn Robertson of the Combat Studies Institute. Both men are responsible for encouraging me to think not just about the battle but the campaign as a whole. Being allowed to tag along on one of Dr. Robertson's staff rides was a great privilege, and one I hope to repeat some day. Jim's ongoing support for the Chickamauga Study Group every March has been indispensable. Special thanks to Harvey Scarborough for his last-minute photography.

Authors don't get very far without publishers, and I would like to thank everyone at Savas Beatie for their efforts, not just editorially but also on the marketing and sales end. Theodore P. Savas helped craft this manuscript into a much improved final product. Sarah Keeney, Veronica Kane, Kim Rouse, and Helene Dodier have worked equally hard to make sure it reaches as wide an audience as possible. Their help in lining up events and getting the word out has opened unexpected doors, for which I am excited and grateful.

The deepest thanks of all, of course, go to my wife Anne. Between my day job, necessary to keep hearth and home together, and the time devoted to these writing projects, I am a very busy person. Anne's unstinting support in allowing me to pursue my avocation is beyond price.

David A. Powell

Dramatis Personae

The Commander of the Army of Tennessee

A native of Warrenton, North Carolina, Gen. **Braxton Bragg** spends his early years there before entering West Point in 1833. Like William Rosecrans, he graduates 5th in his class (of fifty) four years later. There are several notable future Civil War generals in his class, including Jubal Early, William H. French, John Sedgwick, Joe Hooker, and John C. Pemberton.

Bragg enters the artillery branch, fights the Seminoles Indians in Florida, and performs distinguished service in the Mexican War (three brevets). His handling of artillery at the battle of Buena Vista in 1847 against a numerically superior enemy is particularly noteworthy and seals the victory. This success helps catapult Jefferson Davis, an infantry officer, out of the ranks of the anonymous.

The common wisdom is that Bragg and Davis became close friends as a result of their shared Mexican War experiences, and that is why Davis later refused to remove Bragg from command during the Civil War. While Davis bears no serious animosity toward Bragg, he is also not a particularly close friend. In fact, Davis plays a major role in Bragg's resignation from the Army in 1856.

Bragg is upset over the disbanding of horse artillery batteries after the Mexican War. When Davis is appointed secretary of war in the Franklin Pierce administration, Bragg writes to Davis and urges changes that will restore the batteries and make other modifications to the artillery arm to improve its overall

Braxton Bragg

National Archives

efficiency. Davis rejects his suggestions outright and orders Bragg's battery to the Texas frontier—a move that infuriates Bragg and convinces him the order is retaliatory in nature. Bragg resigns from the Army. Both he and his wife view Davis as personally hostile. At a dinner party with William Sherman in 1860, Elise Bragg tells the future Union general that her husband is "no particular favorite" of Davis'.

Bragg is tending to a plantation in Louisiana when that state leaves the union. After being given command of the Louisiana army he is promoted to brigadier general in the Confederate Army in March 1861 and accepts a Gulf Coast command that includes Pensacola, Florida, and Mobile, Alabama. That September Bragg is promoted to major general but remains in Pensacola, a backwater of the war. Bragg convinces himself that Davis keeps him there out of sheer spite. Davis is not being petty or vengeful. In fact, he has a favorable opinion of Bragg's abilities. In early 1862 when Bragg offers to take his troops north to Corinth, Mississippi, Davis readily agrees. There, Bragg assists Gen. Albert S. Johnston in organizing a motley command that will eventually become the Army of Tennessee.

Bragg's first major combat in the Civil War is at Shiloh in April of 1862, where he directs a corps and serves capably. Although the Confederates lose the battle (and Johnston loses his life) and retreat into Mississippi, Bragg is promoted to full general less than one week later. When Gen. P. G. T. Beauregard proves unable to fulfill his role as army commander, Bragg is elevated as his successor. That August he leads what was then called the Army of Mississippi north into Tennessee and Kentucky, triggering several combats including the large but indecisive battle at Perryville on October 8. The manner in which he conducts the campaign results in harsh criticism from his subordinates and lays the seeds for future discord within the South's primary Western field command.

On December 31 Bragg moves to meet a Union advance southeast of Nashville near Murfreesboro, where his attack nearly destroys William Rosecrans' army. The next day, January 1, 1863, the combatants remain largely (and curiously) inactive. Bragg renews the attack on January 2 but is repulsed with heavy loss. Although the battle is a tactical draw, Bragg gives up Middle Tennessee by withdrawing south, a move that opens the door to another round of divisiveness within the army's ranks. His corps commanders openly express a lack of confidence in his ability to lead the army and ask President Davis to relieve Bragg.

Davis sends Gen. Joseph E. Johnston to inspect Bragg's army and report on the state of affairs, including the dangerous problems within the officer corps. Davis gives Johnston the authority to relieve Bragg, if he deems it necessary. Johnston is worried about how it would look if he relieves Bragg and assumes command himself, so he gives Davis an unrealistically favorable report concerning Bragg and the army. In fact, it was so favorable that Davis cannot relieve Bragg without completely disregarding Johnston's advice.

Ben Cheatham, one of Bragg's division commanders, vows to never serve under Bragg again, and John C. Breckinridge, whose division was cut to pieces by the Union artillery in a nearly suicidal attack on January 2, challenges Bragg to a duel. These and other major confrontations are left unresolved when the summer of 1863 arrives, and with it the Tullahoma Campaign and subsequent maneuvering that will trigger the bloodshed at Chickamauga.

Not every officer is at odds with Bragg. Joe Wheeler, the young West Pointer who had risen to command Bragg's mounted arm, is appalled at the discord roiling the army. Wheeler's strong sense of duty and outward respect for command authority leads him to firmly support his embattled commanding officer. This sense of loyalty is reciprocated by Bragg, who expands Wheeler's responsibilities during the summer of 1863. Wheeler's own missteps in Kentucky, at Murfreesboro, and during Tullahoma suggest that expanded duties might be too much for the young officer. Bragg, however, has few friends within the ranks of his own senior officers, so loyalty continues to trump competence.

Bragg also expands the duties of cavalryman Nathan Bedford Forrest. Prior to the summer of 1863 Forrest operated as an independent-minded brigade commander with a talent for raiding and partisan-style activities. Bragg promotes him to command a mounted corps and assigns a host of traditional cavalry duties. Commanding a brigade of partisan raiders has not prepared Forrest for these activities. With no prior military experience to draw upon, and with no chance to hone his skills at lower levels of traditional responsibility, Forrest is expected to seamlessly assume the complex duties of managing a far-flung corps of cavalry almost overnight.

Bragg in 1863 is a walking contradiction. Unlike Joe Johnston, he is perfectly willing to commit his army to decisive combat, but his uniquely unhealthy relationship with not only his chief lieutenants but a good percentage of the men in his army make it doubly difficult for him to plan and execute a successful campaign. These serious difficulties will surely be compounded if his cavalry—the army's vital first line of defense—is not completely reliable.

Corps Commanders and Rivals

Brigadier General **Nathan Bedford Forrest** is a man in his prime in 1863. Forty-two years old, more than six feet tall and 180 pounds, he is physically and mentally imposing. The native Tennessean is not a gentleman, though he strives to behave like one most of the time. Forrest was born into a pioneer family and

Nathan Bedford Forrest

National Archives

retains much of the attitude of a frontiersman, but by his fifth decade he is a self-made millionaire, a slave-trader, and planter prominent in prewar Memphis business and social circles. He is never far from physical violence. His first gunfight at twenty-four left his uncle and two opponents dead or mortally wounded on the streets of Hernando, Mississippi. He excels at physical combat, willingly invites it every chance he gets, and has killed many opponents on the battlefield (and suffered several wounds). This proclivity for violence is not limited to the enemy. In June 1863, Forrest stabs and kills one of his own lieutenants after that enraged officer shoots the general. A relentless and instinctive warrior, Forrest is both canny and aggressive. Thus far these attributes have served him well. In his wake are successful raids, thousands of captured Federals, millions in destroyed Union war materiel. His star is rising.

Legendary is his temper; subtlety when dealing with other commanders and superiors is not part of his repertoire. After a botched attack against the Federals at Dover, Tennessee, he publicly refused to take orders from Maj. Gen. Joseph Wheeler, the Army of Tennessee's chief of cavalry. "I will be in my coffin before I again fight under your command," Forrest told Wheeler to his face. Wheeler lodges no complaint and takes no retaliatory action, but efforts to keep the two high-spirited cavalrymen apart has so far resulted in a disjointed chain of command. An accusation by Maj. Gen. Earl Van Dorn in the wake of a Confederate victory at Thompson's Station in March of 1863 prompts another angry confrontation. Van Dorn charges that Forrest kept too many captured supplies for his own command's use, and that the Tennessean exaggerated his own role in the victory (at Van Dorn's expense, naturally). In a face-to-face meeting the pair unsheathe their swords and a deadly duel nearly ensues. The feud might have come to more if Forrest had not been sent the next day to chase a Union raiding column into Alabama. By the time he returns to the army Van Dorn is dead.

One of Forrest's strengths becomes a weakness that complicates his ability to command at higher levels: he must always see things for himself. Leaders must strike a balance between leading from the front and being far enough removed from the swirling combat to grasp the larger picture. Forrest loves too much the forefront of the fight. This is less a problem when riding at the head of a regiment or even a brigade.

The defense of Chattanooga, Tennessee, offers Forrest new horizons and increased duties. He is no longer the independent raider but a corps commander tied to an army and saddled with all the responsibilities his new assignment requires for success.

*   *   *

Major General **Joseph Wheeler** is twenty-six years old in the summer of 1863. He is not physically imposing. Confederate soldier Charles F. McCay was less than impressed when he met Wheeler the first time, describing him as "a

Joseph Wheeler

USAMHI

very small man . . . [who] looks just like a monkey or an ape." In a confusing postscript McKay added, "not withstanding his apish look [Wheeler] is a very fine looking man."[1]

---

1   Charles F. McCay to "dear Mother" Atlanta History Center, Atlanta, GA.

Wheeler is a professional soldier and alumni of West Point, entering the Academy in 1854 as part of the Class of 1859—the first class instructed under the new five-year curriculum, which placed a greater emphasis on tactical instruction than in previous years. Attending West Point has been a single-minded goal. Born in Augusta, Georgia, in 1836, Wheeler focuses on a military life from an early age and wins an appointment from New York (where he was living with relatives) in 1853.

Wheeler graduates last in his class in cavalry tactics in 1859 and is commissioned in the 1st Dragoons. Despite his low standing in mounted tactics he spends a year at the cavalry school of instruction in Carlisle, Pennsylvania, drilling new recruits, a not uncommon assignment for newly-minted officers. For the first time he gets the chance to drill and maneuver larger bodies of troops, something not always possible in the remote posts of the frontier. The experience provides him with a theoretical grounding in the skills of a cavalryman.

In 1860, young Lieutenant Wheeler leaves the world of theory for harsh reality when he is assigned to a company of the 1st Mounted Rifles in the Southwest. He faces Apaches in several small encounters, but most of his tour is marked by more boredom and drill than real combat. With the outbreak of civil war Wheeler resigns to follow Georgia out of the Union. Commissioned in the state forces, he soon accepts another in the fledging Confederate Regular Army. Service in Pensacola follows, as does his first contact with Braxton Bragg. In dire need of trained officers, Bragg aids Wheeler in obtaining a position as colonel of the 19th Alabama Infantry. Trapped in a military backwater, neither Bragg nor Wheeler see combat until April 1862 after joining Albert Sidney Johnston in time to fight at Shiloh. Wheeler leads his Alabamians there with distinction.

In July 1862, Wheeler abruptly moves from infantry command to the head of a brigade of cavalry, again at Bragg's doing. In the wake of Shiloh, with Johnston dead and Beauregard relieved of command, Bragg assumes command of what will soon be the Army of Tennessee, then stationed at Tupelo, Mississippi. The army's various cavalry units are in disarray, lack a cohesive command structure, and are in desperate need of drill and discipline. Wheeler's previous experience with horse soldiers makes him a logical choice for this duty.

Early service with that branch proves disappointing. The invasion into Kentucky went awry in part because of poor information-gathering on the part of Rebel cavalry. This failure of intelligence induces Bragg to attack a force three times his size under the mistaken belief that he is dealing with a Federal diversionary column. Similar lapses at Stone's River in December 1862 and again at Tullahoma in June 1863 misinform Bragg and lead to unpleasant surprises. In each case Wheeler is at fault. It is possible Wheeler desires the role of partisan more than regular cavalryman since popular attention seems drawn more to the flashy exploits of men like Forrest and John Hunt Morgan than to workhorse cavalry operations. Several times Wheeler proposes grandiose independent cavalry raids or engages in lone wolf acts at inopportune moments. At Murfreesboro, for example, he departs Bragg's front for twenty-four hours to ride around William Rosecrans' Federal army. These missteps trouble Bragg, who repeatedly reproaches Wheeler for his inattention to the army's needs. Thus far the army commander has not expressed a desire to demote or replace the young cavalryman.

Other problems plague Wheeler. His commands are infamous for their lack of drill and discipline, a most unusual deficit for a West Pointer and former cavalry drillmaster. Tales of looting and thievery follow his troopers wherever they roam. Staff officers complain of failures to follow procedure. Insubordination often passes unchallenged. Forrest's blunt language after the Dover fiasco, for example, meets with no reprisal or official reprimand. Perhaps the bantam Wheeler is simply intimidated by the older and more physically imposing Forrest. Whatever the reason, Wheeler's unwillingness to confront discipline problems leaves matters to fester—to the detriment of the Army of Tennessee.

The Division Commanders

Brigadier General **Frank C. Armstrong** is another young man. At twenty-seven he's only a year older than Joe Wheeler. He is also a prewar cavalryman, though not a West Pointer. Both his father and stepfather (his mother remarried upon Frank W. Armstrong's death in 1839) were serving officers. Instead of attending West Point Armstrong attends Holy Cross in Massachusetts. An inspection trip with his stepfather across Texas offers the young Frank an opportunity to distinguish himself in a fight with Indians. He is commissioned a Second Lieutenant in the Second Dragoons on June 7, 1855. Service with his regiment includes the Mormon expedition in 1859. Armstrong fights for the Union at First Bull Run but resigns on August 13, 1861 to accept a position in the Confederate army.

His energy and effectiveness as a staff officer in Missouri and Arkansas win him promotion to line command, first as colonel of the 3rd Louisiana Infantry

Frank Armstrong

Tennessee State Library and Archives

and then as commander of Maj. Gen. Sterling Price's cavalry. In the late fall of 1862 Armstrong heads up the Confederate rearguard in the wake of the defeat at Corinth. His efforts garner the attention and praise of Earl Van Dorn. A promotion to brigadier general follows and his star continues to rise through the spring of 1863. Armstrong fights his brigade (part of Brig. Gen. William H. Jackson's Division) conspicuously and successfully at Thompson's Station alongside General Forrest's command.

Armstrong is an aggressive and able outpost officer with widespread experience skirmishing with Federal forces on a regular basis. Serving under Forrest, he performs well during the summer 1863 disaster that is Tullahoma. Forrest's elevation to corps command at the beginning of September kicks Armstrong up another rung of the command ladder to lead a division, and a most important one at that. His new command includes not only his former brigade but also Forrest's celebrated brigade. Will these troopers fight as well under Armstrong as they did under Forrest?

* * *

Brigadier General **John Pegram** is thirty-one in 1863 and the product of Virginia society. Born in Petersburg he grew up in Richmond, where his father worked as a banker, politician, and state militia general and his mother enjoyed life as a Virginia socialite. John has always moved in the best circles. After the death of his father the family suffers for lack of funds and his mother opens a school for young ladies. West Point offered a solid education at no cost, and in 1850 John has little trouble securing a nomination from congressman and future Confederate Secretary of War James A. Seddon. Pegram graduates in 1854 a respectable tenth out of forty-six. During his time along the Hudson River John becomes friendly and even flirtatious with Superintendent Robert E. Lee's daughters.

Pegram spends several years on the frontier where combat experience eludes him. He serves in both the 1st and 2nd Dragoons and takes part in the Mormon expedition, but most of his time elapses in garrison. In 1859 he travels to Europe, nominally to observe a war in Italy but witnesses no action. Pegram returns in 1860 and is ordered back to the Dragoons, where he sees his only hostile action against the Navaho in New Mexico. When word of secession reaches his remote corner of the world in January 1861 Pegram resigns his commission, only to withdraw the resignation one week later. In March he reverses himself yet again and offers himself to Virginia even though he is still a Federal officer. He accepts multiple appointments that April, first as a cavalry captain in the Confederate Regular Army and then as an artillery lieutenant in Virginia's forces. Almost immediately he applies for a third commission as either an engineer or as a cavalryman. The following month his career track stabilizes with an appointment as a lieutenant colonel in the 20th Virginia infantry Regiment. Do these abrupt course changes and moments of indecision reflect a character flaw?

Pegram's field service begins in the fall of 1861 in what for the South is the ultimately unsuccessful Western Virginia campaign. He does not distinguish himself. A recent biographer concluded, Pegram "did not win his command's confidence because of his constant vacillation."[2] Caught up in the defeat at Rich Mountain, Pegram ends the campaign a Union prisoner, out of the war until his exchange in the spring of 1862. In the general reorganization of the

---

2   Walter S. Griggs, Jr. *General John Pegram, C.S.A.* (H. E. Howard, 1993), p. 37.

John Pegram

Museum of the Confederacy

Confederate army that spring his former 20th regiment votes in an entirely new slate of officers.[3] When Gen. P. G. T. Beauregard seeks an engineer for his staff in Mississippi, General Lee recommends Pegram. For the next seven months Pegram serves under Beauregard, Braxton Bragg, and finally Kirby Smith, riding into Kentucky with the latter commander.

Staff duty ends with his appointment to brigadier general and a return to cavalry duty at the head of a brigade under Joe Wheeler in November 1862. Ten months of sometimes troubled service follow. His relationships with his subordinates are not harmonious, and his decisions are fraught with error. In the spring of 1863 Pegram leaves the Army of Tennessee to assume command of the cavalry in the Department of East Tennessee, with similar results. With a

---

3   In early 1862, in order to induce men to re-enlist for the duration of the war, the Confederate government let regiments hold new elections for officers.

new campaign about to open he is back with Bragg's army. His lackluster record notwithstanding, Pegram returns to lead a division of cavalry under the exacting and often-difficult Forrest.

*　*　*

At forty years old in 1863, Brig. Gen. **William T. Martin** is not a young man. A Kentuckian by birth but raised largely in Mississippi, Martin is a successful lawyer and businessman in Natchez when secession sweeps the land. Despite his Whig politics and anti-secessionist political leanings, this member of Mississippi society both by birth and marriage quickly raises a cavalry company recruited from "The best families" in town.[4] His company is incorporated into a battalion known as the Jeff Davis Legion and shifts to the seat of war in Virginia. Service under J.E.B. Stuart follows, as does a promotion to lieutenant colonel and a reputation as a talented horse soldier. Martin leads his command in the Seven Days' Battles and that fall rides with the Army of Northern Virginia into Maryland. At Sharpsburg he serves for a time on General Robert E. Lee's staff. His solid accomplishments earn him a promotion to brigadier general in December 1862 and a trip to the Western Theater.

Many Confederates in the Western Theater feel with some justification that the government in Richmond slights their departments in terms of both troops and talent, so the arrival of a rising star from the Virginia theater of war is greeted with elation. By January 1863 Martin is commanding a division, first under Earl Van Dorn and then under Joe Wheeler. Both generals are happy to see him. Martin lives up to his billing, earning laurels at Thompson's Station and other actions. At Tullahoma he plays a lesser role when Wheeler tags his division for a raid and pulls Martin's troops off screening duties on Bragg's right flank—just as Rosecrans begins moving to turn the Confederate flank.

As fall approaches Martin is given a pair of key assignments. His first charge is to send two of his regiments after deserters. In the wake of the retreat from Middle Tennessee, the Army of Tennessee's morale has deteriorated and men are leaving the ranks in large numbers. Bragg needs every man available for field duty, and enforcing the draft and returning absentees to their units requires

---

4　Stuart W. Sanders, "Major General William Thompson Martin," *Kentuckians In Gray* (University Press of Kentucky, 2008), p. 195.

William T. Martin

Generals in Gray

armed force. Martin is also ordered to patrol the south bank of the Tennessee River from Chattanooga down into Alabama in an effort to catch Rebel deserters trying to reach home in Tennessee and, of course, to watch for Federal troops crossing the river in the opposite direction. Martin's command is now the smallest of the four cavalry divisions in Bragg's army. Fulfilling both missions at once will be difficult. Martin leaves only two more regiments, barely 500 troopers, to patrol the winding river.

* * *

In 1863 Brig. Gen. **John A. Wharton** leads a division under Joe Wheeler. In Wharton's opinion their roles should be reversed. At thirty-five Wharton is considerably older than Wheeler. He is also one of the wealthiest men in his adopted state of Texas, well-educated and well placed in society. Unlike Wheeler he is not a military man.

John A. Wharton

National Archives

Wharton's sole experience in martial affairs comes from his experiences in the current struggle. After helping raise the 8th Texas Cavalry (also known as "Terry's Texas Rangers," one of the more famous cavalry units in the Confederate army) he serves as its commander in early 1862. He is wounded at Shiloh but misses little active service, fights under Forrest in the Murfreesboro raid of July 1862, and marches with Bragg in the invasion of Kentucky that autumn to lead his Texans brilliantly at Perryville. His finest moment of the war thus far comes at Murfreesboro on December 31, 1862. Promoted to brigade command only a month before, he leads his men as part of the Rebel assault against Rosecrans' unsuspecting right wing and helps rout a Union corps. Wharton takes prisoners and trophies, including cannon, and drives the Federals for nearly a mile.

When his stellar performance fails to earn him a promotion to major general Wharton becomes frustrated. Recognition of his capabilities is not coming fast enough. When the coveted promotion falls instead to Wheeler,

Wharton does not voice disgruntlement—at least not publicly. Wheeler organizes the corps that March and gives Wharton a division. In the infantry divisions are commanded by major generals. Despite the elevation in responsibility, no promotion is forthcoming. Ill feelings exacerbate when Wharton takes part in the abortive raid on Dover in February 1863 and witnesses the same failings and foibles in Wheeler that so enrage Forrest.

Wharton has friends in Congress, notably fellow Texan Senator Louis T. Wigfall. Wharton tries to use his influence to gain the promotion he seeks and a chance to transfer to the Trans-Mississippi, where he and the 8th Texas can serve closer to home. That same political influence makes Wharton a dangerous rival for Wheeler, who is aware of the rumors of Wharton's rising star and desire for higher rank. Will that knowledge and bitter rivalry affect Wheeler's command decisions?

The Brigade Commanders

Colonel **C. C. Crews**, thirty-four years old, commands Wharton's First Brigade. Although a physician, he eschews the medical profession for a combat command. He serves as a lieutenant and then captain of Company C of the 2nd

Georgia Cavalry in 1862 before being elevated to regimental command in November. He is captured at Glasgow Kentucky on September 30, 1862, during the Perryville Campaign and wounded in the hip at Dover. Despite his extensive service Crews is largely a cipher. Rarely is he mentioned, and then only within the context of his duties. From all accounts the doctor is a competent commander and

Charles C. Crews

USAMHI

will remain with Wheeler to the end, commanding an all-Georgia brigade in 1864 and 1865. Chickamauga will test his abilities.

* * *

Harnessed with C. C. Crews at the head of John Wharton's Second Brigade is Col. **Thomas Harrison**. A lawyer and not a soldier by training, Harrison serves under Jefferson Davis in the 1st Mississippi Rifles during the Mexican War. Like Wharton, Harrison is another product of the 8th Texas Cavalry. He assumes command of that regiment when Wharton is promoted, and takes up command of the brigade by dint of seniority when Wharton rises to lead the division.

Harrison is a rather strict disciplinarian and so he is not popular among the rank and file. At forty years of age he is also one of the oldest officers in the Confederate cavalry corps. One contemporary describes him as "a small, nervous, irascible man." He is also a hard drinker. A Texan who serves with him sourly noted that "Harrison is addicted to getting drunk & does it when battle is pending & has thus lost the confidence of his men & injured our effectiveness against the enemy."[5] If the observation is true, the drinking has not cost him Wheeler's confidence, for the Army of Tennessee's cavalry commander later promotes Harrison to brigadier general.

Thomas Harrison

USAMHI

5 See "Handbook of Texas Online, http://www.tshaonline.org/handbook/online/articles/HH/fhaaf.html, accessed 2/17/2010.

John T. Morgan

USAMHI

Colonel **John T. Morgan** is another lawyer and Tennessee native and heads Martin's First Brigade. He received his only formal education in a small pioneer school before moving with his family to Alabama. He practices law in Tuskegee and as a member of the state's secession convention votes to pull out of the union.

Morgan enlists as a private in the 5th Alabama Infantry and is elected major in May 1861. By the following year he is a lieutenant colonel and returns to Alabama to raise a cavalry regiment. He and his new 51st Alabama Partisan Rangers spend time protecting railroads in Tennessee before joining General Forrest's command later in the fall of 1862. When Bragg's army returns from its Kentucky raid Morgan serves well under Joe Wheeler, fights under him at Murfreesboro, and is promoted to brigadier general in June 1863. Thirty-nine years old that summer and well respected, Morgan turns down a promotion and offer to return to Virginia to take command of Robert E. Rodes' Brigade when that officer is elevated to divisional command in January 1863. Morgan will remain in the Western Theater with the cavalry.

* * *

Colonel **Alfred A. Russell** is another doctor-turned-soldier. Thirty-six at the opening of the Chickamauga Campaign, Russell leaves a medical practice in Stevenson, Alabama, to join the 7th Alabama Infantry as its major in 1861. After Shiloh he departs the 7th to raise a battalion of Tennessee cavalry that consolidates into the 4th Alabama Cavalry, which Russell commands. He gains considerable attention at Parker's Crossroads in December 1862 under Forrest and in August of 1863 leads Martin's Second Brigade. Described as "cool in action" and "a man of fine judgment," Russell has one peculiar tic under fire: he repeatedly unbuttons and re-buttons his coat. [6] Another Mexican War veteran, Russell brings an air of solid competence to command. He will need it in the broken terrain of North Georgia.

*   *   *

Yet another Mexican War veteran leading Confederate cavalry is Col. **James T. Wheeler.** The well-to-do Giles County, Tennessee, farmer enlists as a private in 1861 but is soon elected to company command. In the summer of 1862 he ascends to colonel of the 1st (6th) Tennessee Cavalry, formed by the merger of two independent battalions. Wounded at Holly Springs that December, Wheeler has only returned to active service in May 1863. At that time his regiment is serving in Armstrong's Brigade. The expansion of Forrest's Division into a cavalry corps at the end of August elevates Wheeler via seniority into Armstrong's place. He is thirty-seven in the fall of 1863, and at six feet four inches a giant of a man.[7]

*   *   *

Colonel **George G. Dibrell** is Frank Armstrong's other brigade commander and another gentleman

George G. Dibrelll

USAMHI

6   Bruce S. Allardice, *Confederate Colonels: A Biographical Register* (University of Missouri Press, 2008), p. 330.

7   *Ibid.*, p. 391.

farmer from Tennessee. Dibrell has very tough shoes to fill because he commands "Forrest's Old Brigade." In addition to being measured against that cavalry legend, Dibrell has recently replaced Col. James W. Starnes, who was mortally wounded during the disastrous Tullahoma Campaign that turned the Confederate army out of Middle Tennessee. Starnes was one of Forrest's favorite officers and would have assumed command of the brigade had he lived.

Dibrell has already made a name as a fighter. Initially a Union man, he follows his state when Tennessee secedes and enlists in the 25th Tennessee Infantry, fighting well at Mill Springs while in command of the outpost line. His first moment of prominence comes at Corinth, Mississippi, in May 1862, where he again has charge of the outposts and holds off ten times his number of Federals for most of a day. With solid recommendations in hand he departs the infantry service and rides to the eastern and central part of the state—behind Union lines—to raise the 8th Tennessee Cavalry. The talented and capable officer is forty-one in 1863, and ready for the tough assignments.

*   *   *

Short of Joe Wheeler himself, Brig. Gen. **Henry B. Davidson** has the best military lineage of any of the commanders in the two cavalry corps. At

thirty-two he is both the youngest of the brigade commanders and the newest. Davidson enlisted to fight in the Mexican War at just fifteen, where his service garnered attention and an appointment to West Point in 1848 as a member of the Class of 1853. Like Wheeler, after a stint at Carlisle Davidson spends some time on the frontier performing outpost duty and seeing some action.

Henry B. Davidson

Museum of the Confederacy

Despite his prewar credentials he has thus far served the Confederacy only in a staff capacity, including time with Gen. Albert Sidney Johnston. Davidson's chance at line command arrives on August 18, 1863, at Staunton, Virginia, where he is plucked from that rear depot, given a general's wreath, and ordered to join the Army of Tennessee to head up John Pegram's former brigade. The decaying state of the Confederacy's rail net makes it problematic as to whether Davidson will arrive in time to fight at Chickamauga.

*   *   *

Colonel **John S. Scott**, thirty-six years old, is a wealthy Louisiana planter. His only martial experience consists of a few months in the Louisiana militia during the Mexican War. His money and his prominence allow him to recruit the 1st Louisiana Cavalry in 1861, its ranks loaded with the social elite of planter society. Scott begins well, gaining attention from no less a figure than Albert Sidney Johnston, who describes him "the best cavalry officer I know of." That

reputation is replaced quickly by a less complimentary one.[8]

Scott is headstrong and quarrels with other officers. He lacks military skills and doesn't take orders well, especially from younger or less socially prominent superiors. He feuds often with Pegram and reached the Tennessee army blemished. Another failure may well end his career.

John T. Scott

National Archives

8   *Ibid.*, 335.

Chapter 1

Turned out of Middle Tennessee:
The Tullahoma Prelude

"I HAVE ARRIVED HERE and assumed command. My forces are on picket from this place to Chattanooga."[1] With this communiqué from Kingston Tennessee on July 30, 1863, Brig. Gen. Nathan Bedford Forrest informed Maj. Gen. Simon Bolivar Buckner that his cavalry division had completed its retreat from Middle Tennessee and had assumed responsibility for patrolling the south bank of the Tennessee River between Kingston and the mouth of the Hiwassee River. It also marked an official end to one campaign and, after a short pause, the beginning of another.

The campaign just ended was Tullahoma. Five weeks earlier, Gen. Braxton Bragg's Confederate Army of Tennessee was camped 100 miles closer to Nashville at the southern edge of the Highland Rim, the geographical divide surrounding the Tennessee capital. Major General William S. Rosecrans' Union Army of the Cumberland opposed Bragg from its camps around Murfreesboro. Both armies had gone into winter quarters there after the savage late December 1862 and early January 1863 fighting at Stones River just outside Murfreesboro. Both sides had spent the following six months training and drilling, and

---

1 *The War of the Rebellion: A Compilation of the Official Records of the Union and Confederate Armies,* 128 Volumes (Washington, D.C.: United States Government Printing Office, 1889), Series 1, vol. 23, pt. 2, 940, hereinafter *OR.* All further references are to Series 1 unless otherwise noted.

resupplying. Although his superiors wanted him to act, Rosecrans had reasons for patience—foremost among them his need to stockpile supplies. Moving southeast from Nashville against Bragg meant crossing land known as "the Barrens." Forage there was scarce. Rosecrans also needed to enhance his cavalry strength. And so the months slipped past.

This lull ended at the end of June 1863, when Rosecrans launched a flanking movement designed to cut off Bragg's Confederates from their rail supply line leading back to Chattanooga. Rosecrans set out with a battle in mind because he believed that any large-scale combat would be waged on his terms. If his flanking operation was successful, Rosecrans would have the initiative and Bragg would be out of position. In addition, the Union army significantly outnumbered its Confederate opponent.[2]

While the Tullahoma operation did not turn out to be the Army of Tennessee's final stand—though only by a narrow margin—Rosecrans' effort to deceive Bragg worked brilliantly. He feinted with his own cavalry and two infantry divisions against the Confederate left near Triune in order to convince Bragg that the threat would come from this direction, while the bulk of the Federal infantry (nearly 40,000 men) moved against the Rebel right. The feint fooled Maj. Gen. Joseph Wheeler, the leader of Bragg's cavalry. Wheeler's command was already in the process of transferring from the Rebel army's right flank, riding west from Manchester and McMinnville to Shelbyville in response to an order from Bragg to concentrate for the coming campaign. Bragg intended that Wheeler, together with Brig. Gen. Nathan Bedford Forrest's cavalry division, already in place on Bragg's left, either oppose the expected Union advance (the feint) or launch a raid against Rosecrans' long line of communications that stretched back into Kentucky. Thus, when the Federal feint got underway, Wheeler was riding west to join Forrest at Spring Hill,

---

2   OR 23, pt. 1, 402-9 discusses Rosecrans' intentions and operations in detail. The Federal Army numbered about 70,000 men, including 10,000 cavalry, after deducting the forces he would need to leave behind to securely defend Nashville, while Bragg's force numbered only 40,000 men, of which 12,000 were cavalry. Thus, in infantry and artillery Bragg was outnumbered fully two to one. Bragg's army was weakened significantly that summer by the need to send reinforcements to try and help relieve Vicksburg. See OR 23, pt. 2, 572-9, for Union strengths, and *ibid.*, 846 for Confederate numbers. For strategic and tactical maps of the Tullahoma operation, with accompanying text and a detailed order of battle, see David A. Powell and David A. Friedrichs, *The Maps of Chickamauga: An Atlas of the Chickamauga Campaign, including the Tullahoma Operation, June 22 – September 23, 1863* (New York and California: Savas Beatie 2009).

where he would assume command of the united force and await Bragg's next set of instructions.

Knowing that Wheeler's departure would leave his own right flank denuded of mounted troops, Bragg intended to move Brig. Gen. John Hunt Morgan's cavalry division from Sparta to McMinnville. Wheeler left behind a small cavalry force to screen Bragg's right until Morgan arrived. Morgan, however, had other plans.[3]

An inveterate risk-taker, for some time Morgan had envisioned a daring raid across the Ohio River onto Union soil. In Virginia early that June, Gen. Robert E. Lee began moving his Confederate Army of Northern Virginia north with the intention of clearing Federal troops from the Shenandoah Valley in preparation for a thrust into Maryland and beyond. Swept up in his own enthusiasm, Morgan told his subordinates—but somehow failed to inform Bragg—that perhaps they could meet Lee or remain in Illinois or Indiana for an extended period of time. The idea was entirely unfeasible, but Morgan could not be dissuaded from undertaking the raid.

Knowing he could not gain approval for such an impractical and dangerous operation, Morgan deliberately deceived his superiors by scaling back his ambitions. He asked Wheeler instead for permission to take a smaller force north and attack Louisville. On June 14, Wheeler pitched the idea to Bragg. This less ambitious plan appealed to both men because both wanted to strike at Rosecrans' lengthy supply lines stretching between Louisville and Nashville. Bragg approved a raiding force of one brigade, or about 1,500 men. Morgan wheedled Wheeler into upping that number to 2,000 troopers, all the while knowing he had no intention of moving with anything less than his entire command. On June 20, his duplicitous approval in hand, Morgan crossed the Cumberland River with three brigades of cavalry, about 2,500 men. His move carried the gray troopers into Kentucky—and out of the rest of the campaign.[4]

Rosecrans' movement began in the midst of all this shuffling of Rebel mounted troops. Wheeler reported to Bragg that the Triune movement was the

3 OR 23, pt. 2, 866-7 outlines Bragg's intentions for Wheeler and Morgan as early as June 6, 1863. Dodson, W. C. Ed., *Campaigns of Wheeler & His Cavalry, 1862-1865 and The Santiago Campaign, Cuba 1898* (Memphis: Williams and Fox, 1997), 85-6 documents Wheeler's move to Shelbyville and suggests that a raid was the goal.

4 James A. Ramage, *Rebel Raider: The Life Of General John Hunt Morgan* (Lexington, KY, The University Press of Kentucky, 1986), 158-162.

primary Union advance. At the same time, a lack of cavalry on the Rebel right flank meant the Confederates failed to notice Rosecrans' main effort at all. Wheeler's men were rding hard to finish their redeployment to Shelbyville when the first Union troops appeared near Manchester and seized the gaps through the Highland Rim. When Union infantry in strength appeared seemingly out of nowhere at Liberty and Hoover's gaps, the terrible truth of what was unfolding struck Bragg. Rosecrans was turning his right flank, and the unexpected move threatened to envelop and destroy his badly outnumbered army. Bragg had no choice but to order a rapid retreat.

Federal and Confederate cavalry collided at Shelbyville on June 27 in a fight that rang an ominous note for future Confederate cavalry operations. Shelbyville, an important depot for Bragg's army, was being evacuated and wagon trains were rolling south across the Duck River as fast as they could. To protect them, Wheeler's troopers deployed behind breastworks north of town, where they hoped to delay the enemy advance. Forrest's division was still riding toward town when the first Union cavalry arrived at Shelbyville. The fight that followed, spearheaded by Col. Robert H. G. Minty's Federal brigade, was not one the Rebels would celebrate around campfires or in song. Minty's troopers overran Wheeler's breastworks and thundered into the village, where a desperate street fight ensued. Wheeler had no choice but to hold on for as long as possible to make sure Forrest was not cut off and trapped north of the rain-swollen river. At one point Wheeler was forced across the river to the south bank, but when he heard from one of Forrest's staff officers that the column was approaching Shelbyville, Wheeler called for volunteers and charged his way back across the bridge in a desperate effort to keep the route open for Forrest's men.[5] The two columns, however, never linked up. Instead, Forrest's troopers found a crossing several miles outside of town and made their way successfully to the far side of the river. Forrest, however, neglected to send a messenger to inform Wheeler of his change in plans.[6] Wheeler's men were overwhelmed, several hundred were taken prisoner, and many barely escaped with their lives when they were forced to swim across the Duck. Shelbyville was a stunning triumph for the well-handled Union horsemen. Wheeler's Rebel cavalry were routed and large amounts of supplies captured. The battle was similar in one

---

5   John Watson Morton, *The Artillery Of Nathan Bedford Forrest's Cavalry* (Marietta, Georgia: R. Bemis Publishing, 1995), 107, and Dodson, *Campaigns of Wheeler*, 89-90.

6   Jack Hurst, *Nathan Bedford Forrest: A Biography* (New York: Alfred A. Knopf, 1993), 131.

important respect to the larger and bloodier June 9 cavalry battle at Brandy Station, Virginia, where Jeb Stuart was surprised and nearly routed by Alfred Pleasonton's command. Both signified that the Union mounted arm was emerging as a powerful combat force.[7] "Altogether it was the greatest cavalry disaster of the war," concluded a Rebel officer caught up in the whole mess, "and I can attribute it to nothing but bad management. Gen. Wheeler was not himself at all."[8]

By the beginning of July, the Southern army was concentrated at Tullahoma, where some months before Bragg had prepared entrenchments in anticipation of just this kind of fight. What Bragg could never have planned for was the need to send significant numbers of men to Mississippi, where Maj. Gen. Ulysses S. Grant's army had trapped the Confederates inside the city of Vicksburg. Once those troops were siphoned away, Bragg was too shorthanded to stand and wage a pitched battle against the Army of the Cumberland. After a day's deliberation, Bragg abandoned Tullahoma and fled to Chattanooga where, with the Tennessee River acting as a barrier, Bragg hoped to recover his equilibrium. Rosecrans pursued the withdrawing Army of Tennessee, but heavy rains and the need to use secondary roads to bypass and outrun the retreating Confederate columns prevented him from catching Bragg. Despite Bragg's ultimate escape, Rosecrans' Tullahoma Campaign was a very important—and largely overlooked—success. The well-planned and executed operation cleared a large swath of Tennessee from Confederate control at minimal cost. The unexpected abandonment of so much acreage demoralized both those soldiers who served inside the Army of Tennessee and the Southern civilian population living in the abandoned region. The fact that the news came quickly on the heels of the twin Confederate defeats at Gettysburg and Vicksburg only added to the growing despair.

Arguably, Bragg's failure to divine Rosecrans' intentions immediately was an ironic stroke of good fortune. Had Wheeler figured out early what the enemy intended, Bragg may have stood and fought his heavily outnumbered and off-balance Army of Tennessee with a pair of rain-swollen rivers (the Duck and

---

7   Michael R. Bradley, *Tullahoma: The 1863 Campaign for the Control of Middle Tennessee* (Shippensburg, PA: Burd Street Press, 2000), 76-9. Bradley discusses the fight at Shelbyville in some detail.

8   George Knox Miller Letter, July 10th, 1863. Southern Historical Collection, University of North Carolina, Chapel Hill, NC.

Elk) behind him. The failure of Rebel cavalry to provide Bragg with the intelligence he needed made his retreat and strategic defeat all but certain. Some reasons for the deficiency in Bragg's mounted arm are obvious, but others are more obscure and worth exploring.

Cavalry was a Civil War-era army's primary source for the gathering of intelligence, especially day-by-day tactical movements. Its many tasks included the screening of friendly forces, the shadowing of the enemy, and the transmission of timely and accurate reports. An effective screen kept friendly movements hidden, while the penetration of an opposing screen revealed enemy movements and plans. In this game of cut and thrust, the army with the fewest effective mounted troops usually operated at a disadvantage.

Keenly aware of the importance of cavalry to his Tullahoma plans, Rosecrans made strenuous efforts to increase both its effectiveness and the raw numbers of his mounted arm. During the six long months between the fighting at Stone's River and his advance on Tullahoma, Rosecrans bombarded his superiors in Washington with requests for more horses, more cavalry regiments, and better weapons. Despite pressing needs on every front, the War Department sent him several thousand horses. When those animals did not prove sufficient for his needs, Rosecrans authorized several infantry regiments to press local animals into service, and then converted them into mounted infantry. Colonel John T. Wilder's brigade of five regiments was the principal beneficiary of these round-ups. By June, 2,500 mounted infantry were added to Rosecrans' horse cavalry strength. The firepower of the Federal cavalry was also significantly increased when the War Department sent Rosecrans several thousand Colt revolving rifles and breech loading carbines. Despising bureaucratic red tape, Wilder and his men arranged privately for the purchase of nearly 2,000 seven-shot, breech loading Spencer repeating rifles, which gave the brigade enough firepower to take on an enemy division.[9] These significant improvements gave Rosecrans a sense of at least mounted parity with the Southern horsemen.

Bragg was at a considerable disadvantage in overall numbers, but he possessed a much larger contingent of mounted men than did Rosecrans. In

---

9   Richard A. Baumgartner, *Blue Lightning: Wilder's Mounted Infantry Brigade in the Battle of Chickamauga* (Huntington, WV: Blue Acorn Press, 1997), 33-34. Wilder's men unanimously voted to so arm themselves. Wilder took out a personal loan and each man signed and pledged $35.00 for their rifle. The move embarrassed even Washington, which appropriated the money to pay for the firepower before the men in the ranks could pay for it themselves.

May 1863, Bragg fielded some 17,000 horsemen in five divisions—half again as many as his opponent. By the end of June, transfers to Mississippi and Morgan's raid into Ohio had diminished Bragg's cavalry arm by 5,000 men. Still, the 12,000 troopers remaining left him on par with Federal mounted strength.[10] The Rebels could not match the Federals weapon for weapon, of course. Most of Bragg's troopers still carried muzzle-loading long-arms, at best an infantry weapon, and perhaps one-quarter of those were antiquated smoothbore muskets.[11] Scouting and screening, however, involved less stand-up combat than a pitched battle, minimizing this deficiency.

For the approaching campaign around Chattanooga, however, the Rebel cavalry was reinforced by another 5,000 men from East Tennessee. This new force largely offset both the earlier detachments and the losses suffered during Tullahoma, returning Bragg's mounted strength to about 16,000 men. His troopers were led by cavalry generals of large reputation, including Joseph Wheeler and Nathan Bedford Forrest. How these leaders would do with the material at hand was yet to be determined.

10 OR 23, pt. 2, 941, 957; *ibid.*, 30, pt. 4, 518 for Rebel numbers in July and August. In May, Bragg was ordered to send one cavalry division to Mississippi and as noted earlier John Hunt Morgan left with his entire division and crossed the Ohio River onto Northern soil. Most of his command was captured or dispersed there, making the entire raid a complete waste of 2,500 men.

11   OR 23, pt. 2, 762, documents the armament of part of Bragg's cavalry as of the end of March, 1863.

C hapter 2

Army of Tennessee: The Cavalry

B y the mid-summer of 1863, Braxton Bragg's cavalry strength was imposing—at least on paper. Despite the loss of two divisions to other missions, on June 10 the Army of Tennessee's mounted arm numbered 13,868 officers and men present for duty.[1] Another 500 troopers were acting as escorts for the various corps and army headquarters. Unfortunately, Confederate cavalry commanders maintained less than accurate records. This fact irritated Bragg's chief of staff W. W. Mackall, who rarely missed an opportunity to remind his boss.[2] Even allowing for sloppy record keeping, Bragg had at least 12,000 troopers present in the ranks.[3]

---

1 *OR* 23, pt. 2, p. 873. This figure does not include John Hunt Morgan's command.

2 In an effort to fix this problem, Bragg sent out blank forms and detailed instructions on July 15 to his corps commanders and Nathan Forrest's independent cavalry division, ordering them to submit returns every ten days. Bragg Papers, Army Correspondence, Series I, Folder 7, Palmer Collection, Western Reserve Historical Society.

3 Men in the Confederate army were responsible for procuring their own mounts. As a result, cavalry numbers fluctuated significantly due to casualties and lost animals. On June 10, Bragg's cavalry was reported at nearly 14,000, despite major transfers elsewhere. On July 20, as the Tullahoma Campaign was winding down, his cavalry numbers were reported as 9,357 present for duty, suggesting a loss of some 4,500 men during this five-week period. On July 31, with the return of stragglers, the same force was reported as 10,529, an increase of 1,200 men in just ten days. August also witnessed similar rapid strength increases. That August, Union horsemen, including the mounted infantry units, totaled about 14,000 men. For Confederate strengths, see *OR* 23, pt. 2, pp. 873, 941, 957, and for Union strengths, see *ibid.*, p. 574.

Unlike the Federals, Bragg's large mounted arm was not organized as one unified cohesive command. Prior to the summer detachments, the Southern army functioned with a pair of cavalry corps under Maj. Gens. Joseph Wheeler and Earl Van Dorn. Each officer was tasked with watching one of the army's flanks.

The first of these officers, Joe Wheeler, had been serving as General Bragg's chief of cavalry since July 1862. The native Georgian was a bantam of a man. In fact, he barely met the West Point height requirement when he was appointed to the academy in 1854. At just 26, he was also young. Although Wheeler was born on September 10, 1836, outside Augusta, he spent most of his youth far to the north in Connecticut and New York and secured his academy appointment from the latter state. After he graduated near the bottom of his 1859 class—nineteenth out of twenty-two—Wheeler was commissioned a brevet 2nd lieutenant in the 1st United States Dragoons and assumed his first duty post at Carlisle Barracks in Pennsylvania. In 1860, Wheeler transferred to the Regiment of Mounted Rifles and headed west to the New Mexico Territory and Fort Craig, where he was promoted to 1st lieutenant that September. "Fighting Joe" was forever affixed to the young soldier during a skirmish with Indians.[4]

Despite his years spent above the Mason Dixon Line, Wheeler considered himself a Southerner. After his home state left the Union, the Georgian submitted his resignation and accepted a commission in March 1861 as a lieutenant with a Georgia artillery unit. Fort Sumter fell the next month, and a week later Wheeler was dispatched to Pensacola, Florida, where his initial service under Braxton Bragg began. Wheeler began his Confederate career as colonel of the 19th Alabama Infantry that September, moving north to Huntsville, Alabama, and then south again to Mobile, where his regiment was assigned to Brig. Gen. Jones Withers' command. Events elsewhere, including the fall of Forts Henry and Donelson in Tennessee in February 1862, dictated a concentration of Confederate forces at Corinth, Mississippi. As part of Brig. Gen. John K. Jackson's brigade, Wheeler led his infantry with distinction at Shiloh, fighting for control of the Hornet's Nest on April 6 and helping to protect the retreat the following day. In the Corinth Campaign that followed Wheeler once again demonstrated his bravery in the face of the enemy by

---

4 Edwin C. Bearss, "Joseph Wheeler," in William C. Davis, editor, *The Confederate General*, 6 vols. (Harrisburg: National Historical Society, 1991), vol. 6, p. 125.

waging a series of sharp skirmishes before helping to cover yet another withdrawal after yet another Southern defeat.[5]

When the command structure was reorganized that summer, Bragg was given control of the Army of Mississippi and Wheeler transferred to cavalry service. On paper, Wheeler appeared to be the ideal cavalryman: a West Point degree, pre-war service in the Mounted Rifles, combat experience against Indians, and command experience with infantry in two different large-scale campaigns. In addition, Wheeler authored a manual of cavalry tactics published in the late spring of 1863. Bragg's mounted arm, it seemed, was in capable hands. His initial operations substantiated that opinion.[6]

In July, Fighting Joe led a raid into West Tennessee that met and defeated several enemy efforts to stop him and destroyed railroad bridges and other enemy supplies. A much longer operation into Kentucky followed when Bragg invaded the state in the fall of 1862. For nearly two months Wheeler screened for the roving army, fought dozens of skirmishes, and participated in the only large-scale pitched battle at Perryville. During the Murfreesboro Campaign at the end of December, Wheeler's troopers rode around Rosecrans' Army of the Cumberland, attacking and destroying wagon trains and large numbers of prisoners. His exploits continued when the calendar turned to 1863 with additional raids that destroyed steamboats and created more havoc behind enemy lines. On January 20, Wheeler was promoted to major general.

By the time Bragg had been forced to fall back from Tullahoma during the summer of 1863, Wheeler's two division commanders were also experienced leaders. Brigadier General John A. Wharton had served in Terry's Texas Rangers and was hailed as "gallant" by General Hardee after his performance at Shiloh, where he was wounded. Service under Nathan Bedford Forrest followed. Wharton was wounded again outside Murfreesboro in July, and fought in the Kentucky Campaign, after which he was promoted to brigadier general in November. Wheeler's second division leader, Brig. Gen. William T. Martin, had served under the storied Maj. Gen. James (Jeb) Stuart in Virginia, where he participated in the famous "Ride Around McClellan," the Seven Days' Battles, and at Sharpsburg that fall. On December 2, Martin was promoted to

---

5 *Ibid*; Edward G. Longacre, *A Soldier to the Last: Maj. Gen. Joseph Wheeler in Blue and Gray* (Washington DC, Potomac Books, 2007), pp. 36-7.

6 Wheeler's resignation from the United States Army was not formally accepted until April 22, 1861.

brigadier general and sent to the Western Theater. There, he served under Wheeler at the head of a two-brigade division during the Tullahoma operations. When he assumed the reins of cavalry command for Bragg in July 1863, both Wharton and Martin had been serving at the heads of divisions, and each boasted extensive experience at the brigade and regimental level.[7]

Wheeler had carved out a solid resume as an accomplished cavalry commander, but below the surface the swirling and troubled waters of personality clashes threatened to impinge on future operations. Friction between Wheeler and John Wharton ensued after the ambitious subordinate's solid performance at Murfreesboro. There, Wharton had joined in the Rebel attack against the Union right flank, routing it and taking many prisoners. He hoped his success would help win him promotion to major general. It did not. Instead, the urging of Braxton Bragg led to the thanks of the Confederate Congress and a promotion to that rank of Joe Wheeler on January 20, 1863.[8] Although Wharton reached divisional command later that spring he remained a brigadier, a rank that was not commensurate with his new responsibilities.

Deeper personality clashes with more important generals, coupled with questions about Wheeler's leadership, were also breaking into the army's consciousness. In February 1863, Wheeler led an attack against the Union garrison at Dover, Tennessee. The assault, which included 2,000 of Wharton's men and another 800 men from Nathan Bedford Forrest's brigade ended in defeat, confusion, and recrimination. Ammunition was in short supply, and neither Forrest nor Wharton much liked the idea of cavalry assaulting fortified Union infantry, even if the enemy only numbered a few hundred. The attack itself was mismanaged and driven off with about 300 killed, wounded, and missing. One of Wharton's troopers in the 8th Texas described the effort as "a rash and senseless fight."[9] Adding to the misery was the bitter cold weather,

---

7   Ezra J. Warner, *Generals in Gray* (Louisiana State University Press), pp. 331-2 for a summary of Wharton's career, and pp. 214-5 for Martin's biography; Ramage, *Rebel Raider*, p. 160. As noted earlier, another cavalry division available to Bragg under Brig. Gen. John H. Morgan embarked on a raid on June 20 just before Rosecrans opened his Tullahoma offensive. Morgan's absence was not an uncommon event, for his command was often detached on similar missions. The bulk of the traditional cavalry duties fell to Martin's and Wharton's men.

8   Edward G. Longacre, *A Soldier to the Last: Maj. Gen. Joseph Wheeler in Blue and Gray* (Potomac Books, 2007), p. 90.

9   H. J. H. Rugley, *Batchelor-Turner Letters 1861-64: Written by Two of Terry's Texas Rangers* (Steck Co. 1961). p. 46

which made the retreat pure misery for man and beast alike. The whole sad affair infuriated Forrest. Wharton, though not as outspoken as Forrest, was also unhappy with the outcome. In his official report, Wheeler deliberately underreported his losses in an attempt to polish the event with a shine of success. Although others may have been fooled, he could not hide the truth from his men.[10]

Growing dissension amongst the generals was bad enough, but the ill-discipline found within the ranks only added to the growing ineffectiveness of Bragg's mounted arm. Temporary absences were frequent and usually unrecorded. Significant discrepancies existed between the number of men Wheeler was supposed to have on hand (as shown on his returns), and the number he carried into battle (as he reported in his official reports). At Chickamauga, for example, Wheeler offered the vague claim that his force "never exceeded 2,000 men," with the balance assigned as flank guards or for foraging.[11] Wheeler went on to note that he had less than one-third of the men shown on his rolls through August, when his tri-monthly strength returns averaged about 7,000 men. Wheeler's boastful nature accounts for some of this discrepancy. By excluding any commands on the field that were not actively engaged ("guarding flanks," as he wrote) Wheeler minimized his strength and magnified his results. Even this numerical slight-of-hand could not account for the substantial discrepancy. The sad fact was that poor discipline meant that men came and went largely as they pleased.

On January 22, 1863, one of Wheeler's own pronouncements outlined the scope of the problem. "The disgraceful state of discipline which exists in certain portions of this command has rendered them worse than useless appendages to the Brigade," grumbled the commander. "Companies muster for duty not more than one-fourth or one-fifth of their strength, and . . . are allowed to scatter so as to be of little or no use. . . . This disgraceful state of things is caused by the gross neglect of duty on the part of Regimental and Company commanders . . ."[12]

Cavalry reports and records for the Army of Tennessee's mounted arm are particularly sparse for the fall of 1863. This makes it difficult to obtain a complete picture of the status of Bragg's cavalry organizations. Other records

10 Longacre, *A Soldier to the Last*, pp. 92-3.

11 *OR* 30, pt. 2, p. 522.

12 "Confederate circular regarding discipline issued after the Battle of Stone's River," Forrest Papers, Gilder Lehrman Institute, New York.

help round out the picture. An important source for evaluating the army's cavalry is a comprehensive inspection report dated January 1865. Wheeler's men shadowed Maj. Gen. William T. Sherman's armies as they rampaged across Georgia in late 1864. Public outcry and serious questions raised by both senior military commanders and civilian officials alike about their discipline problems created considerable controversy. In response, department commander Gen. P. G. T. Beauregard ordered one of his officers, Lt. Col. Alfred Roman, to conduct a detailed assessment of the state of Wheeler's command. Roman's findings were damning, especially with regard to drill, discipline, and training. His words echo Wheeler's own from 1863 and suggest that little had changed in the interim. The main occupation of the troopers seemed to be horse racing. On the subject of discipline, Roman reported, "too much familiarity exists between officers and men. Discipline is thereby impaired. It has become loose, uncertain, wavering. Orders are not promptly obeyed. Inspection of arms and ammunition are carelessly attended to by company commanders. They are made weekly and often not at all, when a standing order from Corps Headquarters requires that they should be made daily." The matter of roll calls and morning reports, infuriated Roman. "In many cases officers would be at a loss to find a list of their men. The appointment of regimental and field officers of the day is very much neglected." He added, "There seems to be an independent careless way about most of the officers and men which plainly indicates how little they value the details of army regulations and tactics in general."[13] While Roman's inspection was made twenty-four months after Wheeler's order and fourteen months after the Chickamauga Campaign, it demonstrates that very little had changed under Wheeler's stewardship. Certainly the state of affairs reflected the overall decline in fortunes of the Confederacy, but the comparison is illuminating nonetheless. After years in the army, the basic routines of drill, discipline, and inspections should have been second nature to these organizations. According to Roman's thorough report, each of these attributes was absent or wanting.

A natural offshoot of lax discipline was straggling and looting, and both were present in spades within Wheeler's ranks. The cavalry had become accustomed to living off the country even in friendly territory, and the troops often wandered off in search of supplies. These unofficial expeditions brought howls of protest from local citizens, but little was done to put a stop to it. The

---

13 Roman report, pp. 2-14, Papers of Alfred Roman, Library of Congress.

Daily Sun, published in Columbus, Georgia, reported on the sack of Cleveland, Tennessee, by an entire regiment of Rebel cavalry from Forrest's command in September 1863. The Confederates did more than look for food. They broke into the county courthouse and destroyed county records, robbed stores and private dwellings, and subjected the residents to "every conceivable outrage." They even broke into the bank intent on relieving it of its funds, but discovered the vault empty. "We have denounced our enemies for their fiend-like crimes," editorialized the newspaper, "but here we have men claiming to be Southern soldiers, disgracing themselves, the flag under which they fight, and the cause which they pretend to uphold."[14]

August 1863 was a period of rest and recuperation for most of Wheeler's men, an interlude between the just-finished Tullahoma Campaign and the active operations about to get underway. That month Wheeler left only a handful of cavalry to guard the Tennessee River and moved his two divisions well to the rear. Wharton's Division was dispatched to Rome, Georgia, and spent the entire month there. This was familiar ground for Wharton, who had spent time there at the home of his brother-in-law while recovering from a wound. Few civilians welcomed the division's arrival with open arms. "Wharton's Cavalry, who were stationed here for the month of August and September," explained local Rueben S. Morton, "committed all sorts of depredations into King County, stealing everything they could find in the way of provisions and carrying off Horses. When they left a few weeks since, a lot of stragglers remained behind who formed a regular Set of Horse Thieves, stealing horses and robbing all over the County."[15] A number of these Southern stragglers formed the equivalent of outlaw bands; even months later they had not rejoined their units. Some continued terrorizing northwest Georgia well into 1864.[16]

When Wheeler took his command on a raid into Tennessee in October 1863, the newspapers reported similar crimes. "[Wheeler's] men . . . are furthermore said to have committed many depredations upon the citizens,

14 "Infamous if True – What Would Gen. Bragg Say?" *Columbus Daily Sun*, September 24, 1863.

15 Rueben S. Morton Diary Entry for October, 1863, John H. Tower Papers, Naval Historical Foundation, Library of Congress.

16 Daniel E. Sutherland, *A Savage Conflict: The Decisive Role of Guerrillas in the American Civil War* (Chapel Hill, University of North Carolina Press, 2009), pp. 186-7.

taking whatever pleased their fancy, whether from friend or foe."[17] A member of one of Wheeler's regiments, offering a view from within the ranks, had similar complaints. "It would surprise you how our own Soldiers act towards the Citizen," he wrote on October 8, 1863. "They take everything, they go into his yard take his chickens, hogs, potatoes, and everything else and do not think of offering to pay. . . . Our regimental and Company officers are not near as strict as they should be about Such Things."[18] In the immediate aftermath of his October raid, even Wheeler complained about the state of affairs that had degenerated so far that "many men were allowed by their officers to throw away their arms to enable them to bring out private plunder." It was a damning admission for a commander to level about his own men—especially to superiors in an official report.[19]

General Forrest's comments about a unit transferred to his command are equally revealing. That August, Lt. Col. Oliver P. Hamilton's Tennessee Cavalry Battalion was sent to join Col. George Dibrell's brigade of Tennesseans. On the 13th, when he learned that Hamilton's men would come under his purview, Forrest replied, "I would take them if desired, [but] from the numerous complaints against them . . . they appear emphatically to be 'Wild Cavalry' and ought to be placed under restraint and control."[20] Forrest also complained that officers from Hamilton's battalion sent to Middle Tennessee to recover men absent without leave behind enemy lines were inducing men still attached to the unit to desert and join their own guerrilla bands. Unless these officers were arrested and brought to trial, Forrest concluded, he would "lose half the men" still in the ranks.[21]

These complaints foreshadowed the scope and scale of the problems that would plague Wheeler's movements across eastern Georgia and into the Carolinas one year later. Wherever his troopers rode they generated a torrent of

---

17 "Wheeler's Reconnaissance," *Columbus Daily Sun*, October 22, 1863.

18 William Robert Stevenson, "Robert Alexander Smith: A Southern Son," *Alabama Historical Quarterly*, Volume XX, (1958), p. 49.

19 *OR* 30, pt. 2, p. 666.

20 Forrest to Wheeler, August 13, 1863, Forrest File, Chickamauga-Chattanooga National Military Park. (hereinafter CCNMP). Hamilton's Division was recruited the year before as a home guard force, and entered Confederate service in April 1863. Initially, it served with Morgan's division, but did not go along on the Ohio raid.

21 *Ibid.*

complaints from Southern citizens. Many objected to Wheeler's orders to destroy property the Federals could find a way to use, but many more complaints were for excesses and blatant looting. Colonel Roman also addressed these charges in his report, and while he concluded that "bad men [and] stragglers form but a small portion of Wheeler's Corps," he also admitted that "their alleged depredations and straggling propensities, and their reported brutal interference with private property have become common by-words in every county where it has been their misfortune to pass." Roman acknowledged that "much truth is hidden under some of the rumors thus brought into circulation."[22]

Braxton Bragg was aware of some of these vexing issues, but he was not fully apprised of just how ill-disciplined Joe Wheeler's command was after the army retreated south from Tullahoma. Straggling was a serious problem throughout the army, especially after the demoralizing retreat from Middle Tennessee, and Bragg worked hard to counteract its ill effects. He issued several orders to address the crisis and assigned two of Wheeler's regiments to provost duty in the rear to collect men absent without leave and send them back to their commands. Bragg also ordered Wheeler to patrol each ford across the Tennessee River in an effort to prevent deserters from escaping north.[23] Wheeler's lack of candor about the true state of affairs within his command, however, remained hidden from the embattled army commander. After nearly a full month spent resting and refitting, Bragg's chief of staff wrote to another corps commander that "inspection of Wheeler's Cavalry shows it even worse than we thought."[24]

The second cavalry corps operating independently with Bragg's Army of Tennessee in the early summer of 1863 was even more unsettled than Wheeler's command—primarily because Maj. Gen. Earl Van Dorn was no longer leading it. The West Point graduate and Mexican War veteran, together with four recently organized brigades of cavalry, was dispatched from Mississippi earlier that year by Gen. Joseph E. Johnston to reinforce Bragg. Forrest's brigade was attached (but not integrated) into Van Dorn's Corps. The arrangement proved unsatisfactory to both officers, especially when Forrest and Van Dorn clashed

---

22 Roman Report, pp. 15-16.

23 *OR* 30, pt. 4, p. 502.

24 *Ibid.*, p. 561.

over credit for the battle of Brentwood in March and again in April, when swords were drawn but not utilized.[25]

On May 7, 1863, Van Dorn was sitting at his desk at the Martin Cheairs house in Spring Hill when a civilian doctor named James Peters shot and killed him because of an affair the general was carrying on with his wife. Van Dorn's untimely demise triggered a rapid series of leadership changes and infused confusion into an organization that was already rife with it. A month before Van Dorn's murder, Nathan Bedford Forrest was a brigade commander leading several West Tennessee cavalry regiments. Forrest's men were not traditional cavalry but an independent raiding force of partisans used primarily for operations behind Union lines. In late April 1863, Forrest was sent to northern Alabama to defeat a Union raid led by Col. Abel D. Streight. The raiding mission was two-fold: distract Rebel attention away from Maj. Gen. Ulysses S. Grant's efforts against Vicksburg, and cut the Army of Tennessee's supply line at Rome, Georgia. Streight intended to slip into northern Alabama and ride east to reach the rail line somewhere in northwest Georgia. Forrest dealt with the threat in an exemplary fashion. Working with his own men and local cavalry under Col. Philip D. Roddy, Forrest pursued Streight's Yankees relentlessly and captured the entire force, despite being outnumbered heavily.[26]

With his stunning success behind him, Forrest returned to the Army of Tennessee to discover that Van Dorn had been killed during his absence.[27] Nine days after Van Dorn's murder, Forrest assumed command of the leaderless cavalry corps at Spring Hill. The outwardly simple solution to elevate Forrest proved anything but, and the ripple effects created confusion that would return to haunt the Tennessee army. With Forrest now leading a corps, his brigade was united with another command under Brig. Gen. Frank Armstrong to form a new cavalry division. A few days later, however, one-half

25 Forrest and John Hunt Morgan, who was similarly assigned to Wheeler's Corps, were not integrated into existing divisions because they were not considered "regular" cavalry. See also Edwin C. Bearss, "Earl Van Dorn," in Davis, *The Confederate General*, 6, p. 75.

26 Thomas Jordan, and J.P. Pryor, *The Campaigns of General Nathan Bedford Forrest and of Forrest's Cavalry* (Da Capo Press, 1996), pp. 252-278. This chapter has a detailed discussion of Streight's raid.

27 Robert G. Hartje, *Van Dorn: The Life and Times of a Confederate General* (Vanderbilt University Press, 1994), pp. 307-327. The commonly accepted story is that Van Dorn was shot by Dr. Peters at Spring Hill, supposedly for trifling with his wife. An alternate theory supposes that Peters was a Federal agent.

of Forrest's new corps (a division under Brig. Gen. William Hicks "Red" Jackson) was recalled to Mississippi. Because Forrest remained behind in Tennessee, all he had left to command was Armstrong's single division, an uncomfortable situation at best. Armstrong was unofficially bumped back down to brigade command. In the space of a single week Forrest had jumped from leading a brigade to corps command, and then back down to division command.[28]

Lost in the mix was the fact that for the first time in his career, Forrest was expected to assume traditional cavalry duties. His new mission was to screen Bragg's left flank and scout for any Union advance. Without any formal training other than field experience under his belt, Forrest was now expected to perform regular cavalry duties. When the Tullahoma Campaign opened in late June, Forrest had a mere month's experience leading an organization larger than a brigade.

An option open to Bragg at this time was to place Forrest's division in Wheeler's Corps in order to streamline the chain of command. Personal considerations made this impossible because of the earlier botched attack on Dover. The affair remained a festering wound for both men. Forrest's reaction to Dover was both fiery and characteristic. His brigade, which had led the assault, lost about one-quarter of its strength. In his usual outspoken manner, Forrest exchanged a series of hot retorts with Wheeler that finally reached a crescendo when the brigade commander stated unequivocally that he would never again serve under Wheeler's command.[29] Wheeler ignored the insult and accepted all responsibility for the failure, but in an effort to avoid aggravating an already tense situation, Bragg decided to keep Forrest's men independent of Wheeler from that time forward. The fight at Shelbyville along the Duck River during the Tullahoma Campaign, however, served as an apt demonstration that divided command solved nothing and in fact created additional problems when confusion over Forrest's intentions left Wheeler to make a desperate fight to hold open an escape route that Forrest had no intention of using.

---

28 Jordan and Pryor, *Campaigns of Forrest*, pp. 283-4. The confused state of Forrest's command levels can be summarized as follows: In May 1863, Forrest is a brigade commander; in June, he is jumped to assume command of Van Dorn's Corps; That same month, he is effectively dropped back down to division command; in September, he will once again lead a corps; at the beginning of October, his men will be assigned to Joe Wheeler, and Forrest will ask for a transfer.

29 Morton, *The Artillery of Nathan Bedford Forrest's Cavalry*, p. 77.

Forrest's weakened physical state complicated matters. Lieutenant Andrew W. Gould had lost two artillery pieces during the fighting with Streight's Federals. Once back in Spring Hill, Forrest arranged to transfer Gould out of his command. Embarrassed and humiliated by Forrest's stance, Gould confronted him at his headquarters on June 13. The ensuing argument grew so heated that Gould drew a pistol and shot Forrest, the ball lodging in the muscle of his hip. The wounded Forrest drew his pen-knife and stabbed Gould, who later died. Although doctors informed Forrest that he would be able to resume active duty in a few days, his injury was not fully healed when Rosecrans' Federals began moving on June 24.[30]

A final concern about the new situation in Van Dorn's former cavalry corps was the question of Forrest's own ambition and desires. Despite his recent promotion to division command, the Tennessean found service in the Army of Tennessee unsatisfactory. On August 9, after the close of the Tullahoma operations, Forrest sent a letter to Bragg requesting that he be relieved of command and sent to West Tennessee. He wanted an independent command there along the Mississippi River running all the way from Kentucky to Vicksburg. He sought only one battery of artillery, his own personal escort company, and one cavalry battalion, intending to raise a new force behind enemy lines. Since the territory was firmly in Union hands, Forrest was still thinking in terms of partisan warfare and hit-and-run tactics.[31] Bragg refused the request on the grounds that Forrest could not be spared from the Army of Tennessee.

Rebuffed, Forrest forwarded a copy of the letter over Bragg's head to Confederate President Jefferson Davis, who kicked it back down the chain of command and asked Bragg to comment. On August 14 Bragg wrote, "it would deprive this army of one of its greatest elements of strength to remove General Forrest." That honest reply tabled Forrest's request for the time being, but his application was most unusual coming from a man who had so recently been given greater command authority. Perhaps Forrest felt the pull of his home city of Memphis, now under Union occupation, and that he could do the most damage against the enemy in a region he knew well. Most likely, however, is that Forrest was used to independent command, often had difficult relationships

---

30 Brian Steel Wills, *A Battle From the Start: The Life of Nathan Bedford Forrest* (HarperCollins, 1992), pp. 122-25, offers an excellent account of this incident.

31 *OR* 30, pt. 4, pp. 508-9.

with superiors, and simply did not want the added responsibilities his new role under Bragg demanded.[32]

For his part, Bragg valued and trusted Forrest. Colonel George W. Brent, who served on Bragg's staff as assistant adjutant general, described Forrest as "the best of our cavalry commanders. He has been uniformly successful: Kept his men in good order. . . . He is brave & active & a man of excellent judgment. Had he been educated & cultivated he would have made a higher reputation."[33]

In the wake of the Tullahoma Campaign, Bragg's sphere of influence was extended to include Maj. Gen. Simon B. Buckner's small Department of East Tennessee. The decision to merge Buckner's command added a new division of some 5,000 men under John Pegram to the Tennessee army's cavalry. The addition once again gave Bragg a clear numerical advantage in the mounted arm, pitting nearly 16,000 Rebel cavalrymen against Rosecrans' 11,000 Federal troopers.[34] Forrest was assigned the new division on an ad-hoc basis, and the relationship was formalized with the creation of a second cavalry corps on September 3.[35] Forrest's enhanced command remained on the army's right, northeast of Bragg's headquarters at Chattanooga, linking the Army of Tennessee with Buckner's command coming down from Knoxville.

Forrest's new corps numbered almost 8,000 men. On paper it appeared well organized. Each division had two brigades, and each brigade numbered between 1,500 and 2,000 troopers and included a battery of artillery. There is much more to an effective military command, however, than a well-drawn organizational chart. A number of problems plagued the new corps, beginning

---

32 *Ibid.*, p. 509.

33 Brent Journal, September 3, 1863, Bragg Papers.

34 Federal numbers are taken from the Cavalry and Wilder's Brigade monthly returns for August 1863, found in NARA, RG 94. They show 7,751 men present for duty in the Cavalry Corps, and another 2,378 in Wilder's Brigade of mounted infantry, for 10,129 men. Roughly another 1,000 were present serving with the army as provosts, on various courier duties, or with the 39th Indiana Mounted Infantry. Confederate numbers are more difficult to determine. On August 20, 1863, Wheeler reported 7,142 men present for duty in his corps, while Forrest reported 3,876 on the same date, a total of 11,018 men. OR 23, pt. 2, p. 941. Bragg had also recently added most of the mounted forces from the Department of East Tennessee, which had 5,757 mounted men present for duty on August 10, 1863. *Ibid.*, p. 962. Only about 70% of the companies present in East Tennessee actually joined Bragg, or about 4,000 men. Finally, another eleven companies of cavalry were serving with the various infantry corps as escorts and couriers, adding another 600-700 men. All told, Bragg had between 15,500 and 16,000 cavalry operating with the army.

35 OR 30, pt. 4, p. 591.

with Forrest himself. Still new to division command, Forrest had no experience operating at the corps level during an active field campaign except for his brief flirtation with replacing Van Dorn. Whether he could think and operate on a higher and broader level, rather than as a brigade commander reacting to the immediate situation, remained to be seen.

Other problems included the poor quality of some of the corps' units and their leaders. Only about one-half of his cavalry corps had reliable and experienced leadership. When he assumed command of the new corps, Forrest turned his own mounted division back over to the senior brigade commander, Frank Armstrong, which in turn elevated its senior colonel, James T. Wheeler of the 6th Tennessee, to brigade command. Armstrong was a pre-war Regular Army officer and an experienced cavalry leader with extensive time in brigade command. He would prove to be an excellent choice to lead a division. Wheeler (no relation to Joseph Wheeler, the other corps commander in Bragg's army) was a pre-war farmer with experience in the Mexican War and similarly seasoned as a regimental commander, so bumping him up to lead a brigade was also a solid choice. These promotions did not disrupt the smooth functioning of the division.[36]

The same could not be said for the troopers from East Tennessee. That division, under the leadership of Brig. Gen. John Pegram, had been recently created out of a collection of disparate mounted forces from Simon Buckner's department.[37] Pegram's Division was comprised of two brigades, Pegram's own

---

36 Warner, *Generals in Gray*, pp. 12-13, and Bruce S. Allardice, *Confederate Colonels: A Biographical Register* (University of Missouri Press, 2008), p. 391.

37 John Pegram was formally given division command on August 24, 1863. See *OR* 30, pt. 4, p. 546. Before that date, Pegram's "division" did not exist. On July 31, there were nine regiments, six battalions, two squadrons, and two independent companies of cavalry serving in Simon Buckner's Department of East Tennessee. Of those units, eight regiments and two battalions were serving in two independent cavalry brigades commanded by John Pegram and John S. Scott. In late August of 1863, those two brigades were combined to create a mounted division. At the same time, several regiments were transferred between the brigades, and the two battalions were merged to form the new 6th North Carolina Cavalry. Placed under Pegram, the ranking officer, this newly designated division was dispatched to join General Forrest. Of the roughly 137 companies comprising the cavalry in the Department of East Tennessee, 96 companies merged to form Pegram's new division, or roughly 70% of the existing mounted force. The remainder (40 companies) remained behind to help defend southwestern Virginia. For more information, see the organizational chart for the Department of East Tennessee, July 31, 1863, in *OR* 23, pt. 2, pp. 945-6, and compare to organization of Pegram's Division, *ibid.*, 30, pt. 2, p. 20. See also Appendix 1, "Confederate Cavalry Strength and Losses," for specific organizational details during the Chickamauga Campaign.

and another under Col. John S. Scott.[38] Pegram had led a cavalry brigade before, although not always successfully. In the fighting during the Murfreesboro Campaign on December 30, 1862, he provided General Bragg with the critical intelligence of the Union army's crossing of Stones River early that morning, which in turn convinced Bragg to hold an entire infantry division out of the day's fighting. What Pegram failed to report, however, was that when Bragg launched his attack, these same Federals almost immediately recrossed the river. In other words, they were no longer a threat. That second bit of undelivered intelligence was vital because it would have allowed Bragg to use the withheld division to support his main attack on the west bank.[39] Both Bragg and Pegram's division commander, Maj. Gen. John C. Breckinridge, were critical of the cavalry leader's actions in their after-action reports. When Bragg consolidated his mounted arm by forming Joe Wheeler's cavalry corps in January of 1863, Pegram left the Army of Tennessee to assume command of the scattered cavalry forces operating in Buckner's Department of East Tennessee.[40]

Problems with the new East Tennessee division did not end there. Pegram and John Scott, the latter a native of Louisiana, did not like one another. Pegram arrested and court-martialed the fiery Scott in April 1863 for insubordination when Scott was a regimental commander serving under Pegram in Buckner's East Tennessee department. The two officers quarreled over an improperly delivered order during an action at Somerset, Kentucky, on March 30, 1863, and Scott lost his temper. A courts-martial was convened and found Scott guilty as charged and referred him to General Buckner for punishment. To Pegram's disgust, the department commander did nothing more than issue a verbal reprimand to Scott before returning him to duty.[41]

---

38 Technically, this division had a third brigade under Col. George B. Hodge comprised of Tennessee troopers, but this brigade did not serve with John Pegram's command during the Chickamauga Campaign. It operated independently in East Tennessee after Buckner's withdrawal from that department, and has not been included in this discussion. *Ibid.*, pt. 4, p. 569.

39 Walter S. Griggs, Jr., *General John Pegram, C.S.A.* (H. E. Howard, 1993), p. 61.

40 *OR* 20, pt. 2, p. 503. The order transferring John Pegram has not yet been located. However, the January 20, 1863, returns for both the Army of Tennessee and the Department of East Tennessee show Pegram serving in the latter command.

41 Nelson Gremillion, *Company G, 1st Louisiana Cavalry, CSA. A Narrative* (University of Southwestern Louisiana, 1986), p. 30.

Relations remained distant between the two officers. Independent command did nothing to soothe their relations or increase their effectiveness. In June 1863, Scott was given his own brigade, which he led on an unsuccessful raid through East Tennessee. The expedition did little harm to the Federals but cost many Southern casualties, including a significant number of desertions. Morale within the ranks of the brigade plummeted. "My loss will not, I think, exceed 350 men, very few of whom were killed," reported Scott. "The straggling of men to their homes is, however, very great, as it was impossible for me to protect the rear and at the same time guard the front, owing to the very small assistance I received from field and company officers of the several commands."[42]

Part of the problem facing both Pegram and Scott was a lack of cohesion. Both brigades underwent a number of structural changes during this period when units and officers were shuffled from command to command. Pegram's own brigade was not firmly reorganized until July 1863. The static and scattered nature of service in the Department of East Tennessee, coupled with the regular but not always predictable organizational changes, meant that the various regiments had little experience working with one another in the field. These problems were further compounded because some of the units were locally raised mountaineers who were unhappy about leaving their homes and not committed strongly to the larger Confederate cause. As a result, a new wave of desertions plagued many of Buckner's units, both infantry and cavalry, when they left Knoxville and marched and rode southwest for Chattanooga that August. Captain Thomas B. Hampton of Company B, 63rd Virginia Infantry, recorded the many problems that existed in his regiment. On September 14, he confirmed that "there is a considerable desertion in our Regt. at present," although he hoped the worst was past. However, two days later, Hampton added, "our Regt has deserted at a tremendous rate. . . . I am heartily ashamed of such cowards."[43]

Simon Buckner's mounted units experienced similar problems. On September 11, 1863, John W. Cotton, a member of the 10th Confederate Cavalry, wrote that "there is a heap of soldiers deserting, more Tennesseans than any body else." Cotton continued, adding that "there is 15 of our company

---

42 OR 23, pt. 2, p. 842.

43 "Camp near Fayette Georgia, September 14, 1863," Thomas B. Hampton Letters, Center for American History, University of Texas at Austin.

deserted," leaving only ten men . . . present for duty.[44] Writing from the ranks of the 6th North Carolina Cavalry, Capt. Julius Gash of Company D revealed his own frustrations with the state of affairs. The 6th was newly formed, an amalgamation of the pre-existing 5th and 7th North Carolina cavalry battalions, and had thus far seen hard times. In August, the Tar Heels narrowly escaped being trapped at Cumberland Gap, where they lost most of their regimental papers and a good deal of enthusiasm for the war. On September 5, Gash wrote home:

> My company papers, receipts, muster rolls, and all gave up. I don't care a D—n. My company has about gone up too. All deserted or at home without leave. Twenty-five men of our regiment started home about a week ago, but were nearly all apprehended! . . . General Buckner says he intends shooting every man of them, and I hope to God he will. . . . I have learned during this war that there is no confidence to be placed in white men. I'll swear men have deserted my company who I had the most implicit confidence in and men too who have been for near twelve months good soldiers as was in the Confederate army.[45]

A number of the cavalry units in Pegram's and Scott's brigades were locally raised from Kentucky, North Carolina, Tennessee, and Virginia, similar in composition to the men in the 10th and the 6th regiments. These men were less than fervently committed to the idea of secession, disillusioned by steady defeat and not at all happy to be abandoning their home region to a Union army advancing on Knoxville to go defend another state. As a result, most of these units suffered significant losses during the ride southwest from East Tennessee to Chattanooga.[46]

Pegram's elevation to divisional command also meant that another brigadier was needed to lead his former brigade. Instead of promoting a regimental commander from its ranks, a new man was plucked from another

44 Lucille Griffith, ed. *Yours Till Death: Civil War Letters of John W. Cotton* (University of Alabama Press, 1951), p. 83.

45 Christopher M. Watford, *The Civil War in North Carolina: Soldiers and Civilians' Letters and Diaries, 1861-1865* (McFarland & Co., 2003), pp. 122-3.

46 Ella Lonn, *Desertion During the Civil War* (University of Nebraska Press, 1998), pp. 4, 16.

assignment and inserted into the troubled organization. Brigadier General Henry B. Davidson was new to both the cavalry and brigade command. He had spent most of the war as a staff officer, and was serving as commander of the depot at Staunton, Virginia, when called upon to lead a brigade in Bragg's army. On August 18, 1863, Davidson was given a general's wreath and ordered to take command of Pegram's former brigade. Given his current duty post in Virginia, it would take the new general some time to reach the army and assume his new command.

Instead of handing off the subordinate task to a senior colonel, Pegram remained in command of both the brigade and the division. Trying to fill both jobs at once proved difficult, and Pegram spent most of his time directing his former brigade, which in turn left no one supervising Colonel Scott. Pegram was so deeply identified with his former command that some members of his brigade were barely aware that Davidson had been assigned to lead it—even after the campaign ended. Years later J. W. Minnich, who served in the brigade, wrote that "although we called ourselves Davidson's Brigade, we often forgot that it was no longer Pegram's. . . . After [Chickamauga] we saw Davidson rarely."[47]

*   *   *

And so it was that when William Rosecrans prepared to move against Braxton Bragg in late August, the Confederate cavalry was in a state of flux and confusion. Some of Joe Wheeler's subordinates did not have confidence in him, notably senior division commander John Wharton, who believed that he deserved Wheeler's job. Discipline problems and a lack of training permeated the corps' rank and file—problems that would fester throughout the war.[48] Casual absenteeism reduced manpower, especially when active campaigning began.

---

47 J. W. Minnich, "Reminiscences of J. W. Minnich, 6th Ga. Cavalry," *Northwest Georgia Historical and Genealogical Society Quarterly*, Volume 29, No. 3, (Summer, 1997), p. 21. Minnich wrote extensively about Chickamauga and various versions of his accounts appear in many places. Since each account has details not found in the others, I have been careful to cite the specific source for each one. No reports survive from Brig. Gen. Henry B. Davidson, and reports by other commanders refer to him only in passing. He left very little imprint on the brigade or the fighting at Chickamauga.

48   See Appendix 3, "Colonel Alfred Roman's Inspection Report of Joe Wheeler's Cavalry Corps," for a damning indictment of Wheeler and his command.

Nathan Bedford Forrest was new to corps command (and apparently unhappy with it). John Pegram had not excelled at brigade command, John Scott was a questionable choice to lead a brigade given his summer raiding performance, and Scott and Pegram were on miserable terms and barely communicated for most of the campaign. Whether Henry Davidson—a stranger to both the brigade and his superiors—would even make it in time to participate in any fighting remained unknown. Finally, some of the units themselves were dispirited and plagued by problems of rampant desertion.

C hapter 3

Chattanooga: Union Intentions

T he wide envelopment was a hallmark of William Rosecrans' generalship. His first army-sized envelopment maneuver in December 1862 departed from Nashville and culminated in the Battle of Stones River, a tactical stalemate that ripened into a de facto Union victory when Bragg retreated a few days later. He utilized a much larger and more successful envelopment during the Tullahoma operation.

Part of the reason for Rosecrans' Tullahoma success was the sheer scope of the movement itself. The advance to Stones River was limited to a front stretching some twenty-five miles wide, during which Rosecrans' separate columns were never more than twenty miles apart. While the tight frontage reduced the Federal army's risk of being defeated in detail, it also limited Rosecrans' chances of catching Bragg out of position and inflicting the same sort of defeat on him. Tullahoma was a much more ambitious effort. Launched on June 23, 1863, the advance carried the Army of the Cumberland nearly fifty miles closer to Chattanooga. During the wide movement, the Federal columns were separated by as much as forty miles. Marching on such a broad front expanded Roscrans' risk, but confused Bragg about his ultimate objective.[1]

---

1 Steven E. Woodworth *Six Armies in Tennessee* (University of Nebraska Press, 1998), pp. 26-29. Woodworth provides a good overview of Bragg's confusion and the reasons for it.

Rosecrans' new mission was to capture Chattanooga, one of the most important logistical and industrial cities in the Confederacy, and if possible advance beyond it into Georgia to threaten Atlanta. It was "old Rosy's" toughest task yet. His first obstacle was the Tennessee River, too wide and deep to ford at most places. Bragg destroyed all the bridges and any boats he could find during his retreat. Rosecrans would have to force a crossing with his own pontoons. Chattanooga was buried in the southern end of the Appalachian Mountain chain. Long imposing ridges running generally southwest to northeast, one behind the other ran perpendicular to Rosecrans' intended avenue of advance. Once across the Tennessee River, the Army of the Cumberland would have to climb each of these ridges in turn. Nor could the mountains be scaled easily. Eons of erosion translated into heights marked by nearly vertical palisades that all but precluded passage. Only a limited number of gaps pierced the mountain walls. The gaps dictated a wide separation between the advancing columns of blue, and guaranteed only limited access to lateral communication roads should the need to concentrate quickly arise.

Despite these and other concerns, Rosecrans decided on another wide envelopment. This time, a Federal command under Maj. Gen. Ambrose E. Burnside would join Rosecrans to help further the deception. Charged with capturing Knoxville and East Tennessee, the Kentucky-based Burnside had some 30,000 men at his disposal to do so. A move against Knoxville by Burnside and Rosecrans against Chattanooga would place Bragg on the horns of a serious dilemma. The Confederates were not strong enough to oppose both advances, and a serious threat against both would force them to choose which city to defend. In order to derive maximum mutual benefit, however, both Federal armies needed to advance simultaneously.[2]

On paper, it made sense for Rosecrans to approach Chattanooga first by moving due east, and then marching south on the city. This would allow him to remain closer to Burnside, and make it possible for either Federal army to move swiftly to the other's aid if needed. For logistical reasons, however, a move into that part of Tennessee was impossible for an army that large. First, no rail line ran east to carry the supplies it would require to sustain itself. Second, the region immediately east of Manchester was called "The Barrens" for a very good reason. The sparsely settled area of rough hills and forest, with few roads and narrow valleys, provided little chance for the Federals to live off the land.

---

2   *OR* 30, pt. 2, pp. 545-552.

Finally, beyond The Barrens was the sparsely settled Cumberland Plateau complete with difficult mountain crossings.

The natural gateway into Chattanooga was not east but south into Alabama and then east, following the course of the Tennessee River Valley. This is the same course the Nashvile and Chattanooga Railroad followed through Stevenson, Alabama, before crossing the river at Bridgeport. While this route also incorporated difficult terrain and presented limited opportunities for forage, the railroad would allow Rosecrans to stockpile supplies and establish advanced depots. Both Stevenson and Bridgeport were on the north bank of the Tennessee River, roughly thirty miles downstream from Chattanooga.[3]

Rosecrans understood his options and decided to feint north with infantry and cavalry to fool Bragg into thinking the main Federal army would move in conjunction with Burnside. After a few days of conspicuous activity to bait the trap, three infantry corps would slip across the Tennessee River between Chattanooga and Stevenson. The Union XXI Corps, under Maj. Gen. Thomas L. Crittenden, would move for Chattanooga. Rosecrans' other two corps, the XIV under Maj. Gen. George H. Thomas, and the XX under Maj. Gen. Alexander McDowell McCook would march directly across the mountains into northern Georgia with the intention of cutting the railroad between Chattanooga and Atlanta somewhere east of Rome, Georgia.[4] If successful, the movement would at least force Bragg to retreat once again, since he could not survive in Chattanooga without his rail connection. If everything went according to plan and Bragg delayed too long, his army might be trapped in the mountains and destroyed. Rosecrans' new plan was a mirror image of the Tullahoma operation. There, Rosecrans had feinted right and moved left. Now, he was feinting left and moving right. The Chattanooga operation was also his most ambitious to date. At their most distant point, the right and left flank elements of the Army of the Cumberland would be almost sixty miles apart.

A tremendous amount of preparation was required for a move of this magnitude. At the conclusion of the Tullahoma Campaign, Union forces occupied both Stevenson and Bridgeport, Alabama. On July 29, a Union infantry division under Maj. Gen. Philip H. Sheridan of McCook's XX Corps

---

3 Good descriptions of this terrain can be found in both Rosecrans' official report, *OR* 30, 1, pp. 48-9, and Thomas Lawrence Connelly, *Autumn of Glory* (Louisiana State University Press, 1986), pp. 138-145.

4 John Fitch, *Annals of the Army of the Cumberland* (Stackpole Books, 2003), p. 458.

occupied both towns.[5] At the same time, Rosecrans ordered the railroad back to Nashville fully repaired. Once the line was back in working order, supply depots were established at both Stevenson and Bridgeport to accumulate the tons of supplies needed for the undertaking. The stockpiling would take weeks, but it would not take that long for locals and spies to pass the word to Bragg.

Knowing he could not keep the preparations for a river crossing below Chattanooga entirely secret, Rosecrans relied on a combination of stealth and misdirection to deceive his opponent. One method involved planting false stories with spies and Confederate prisoners. For example, a captured Rebel lieutenant who had slipped across to the north bank of the Tennessee River to visit his family near Winchester was taken to Union headquarters. Rosecrans offered to release the Southern officer—provided he told Bragg everything he saw and heard while in Federal hands. In other words, the lieutenant was to report that Rosecrans was stockpiling supplies for a crossing at Bridgeport. Rosecrans also contrived to let the Rebel "overhear" a conversation in which Rosecrans ordered the establishment of a depot at McMinnville, Tennessee, with 100,000 rations "immediately [once] the road is in order."[6]

By revealing parts of the real plan to the gullible young Confederate, Rosecrans hoped Bragg would assume it to be an obvious trick, while the cover story of the depot at McMinnville would appear a careless error that, hopefully, Bragg would assume to be legitimate. A spur of the Nashville Railroad ran to McMinnville, and any move toward Knoxville or the upper Tennessee crossings would have to depart from there. By such stratagems, Rosecrans hoped to keep Bragg guessing about which threat was real and which was the feint. Advancing on a broad front would preserve this uncertainty for as long as possible. On August 15, Rosecrans issued the orders that would define the initial part of the campaign, and concentrate his army on the banks of the Tennessee River.[7]

To further enhance the deception, Rosecrans intended to use McMinnville as a departure point for Crittenden's XXI Corps, which would march east from McMinnville into the Sequatchie Valley. The seizure of this terrain would

---

5   Philip H. Sheridan, *Personal Memoirs of P. H. Sheridan, in Two Volumes* (Broadfoot Publishing, 1992), Vol. II, p. 272.

6   William Starke Rosecrans, "Rosecrans' Accounts of Tullahoma and Chickamauga" *National Tribune,* March 25, 1882.

7   OR 30, pt. 2, pp. 35-8.

provide Rosecrans with a strategic advantage. The valley was a long narrow gorge that, from its origin point on the north bank of the Tennessee River near Jasper, ran northeast for about sixty miles with a width alternating between two and four miles. Walden Ridge formed the southeastern wall, separated the valley from Chattanooga, and—like the rest of the terrain in the region—could only be traversed at a few points. Control of the Sequatchie Valley would provide Federal troops with an easy lateral route across Bragg's front, while the seizure of the handful of gaps cutting across Walden Ridge would prevent Rebel cavalry from observing their activities. If the early stages of the operation unfolded as planned, Bragg would only catch fleeting glimpses of enemy troops when they crossed Walden Ridge as needed to appear in front of the Rebel army strung out along the river. Each of the three divisions in Crittenden's XXI Corps would enhance the deception by advancing on a different axis, entering the valley at three widely scattered points.

A few odds and ends remained that would have to be dealt with before the main operation could get underway. Part of a Rebel cavalry brigade under Col. George G. Dibrell occupied the area around Sparta, Tennessee, sent there to recruit and keep an eye on the Yankees. For the time being Rosecrans was content to let them be; their reports of extensive Union activity at McMinnville served only to reinforce Rosecrans' ruse. Brigadier General Robert H. G. Minty's Federal cavalry brigade was tasked to drive Dibrell's men away ahead of Crittenden's marching infantry before the Southern cavalry could discern the XXI Corps' routes and objectives.[8]

Since Alexander McCook already had one of his XX Corps divisions at Stevenson (Phil Sheridan's men were guarding the river there and keeping unwanted Rebel scouts on the far bank), the rest of his corps would join Sheridan and cross there. McCook moved his headquarters to Stevenson. His last two divisions would move there as quietly as possible. Their orders required them to "select a convenient camp, concealed from the observation of the enemy," and prepare to cross once Bragg had taken the bait.[9]

The XIV Corps, Rosecrans' largest command and in the hands of his most trusted subordinate, Maj. Gen. George H. Thomas, was the fulcrum of the entire advance. Rosecrans intended for Thomas to cross the river with his four divisions between Stevenson and Jasper at the lower end of the Sequatchie

8   *Ibid.*, p. 36.

9   *Ibid.*, p. 37.

Valley. From there, Thomas' men could either move north up the valley to support Crittenden, or southwest along the Tennessee River to reach McCook. In either case, if Crittenden's columns were not to become bottled up in the narrow confines of the Sequatchie, Union control of Jasper was critical. Rosecrans wanted, indeed needed, these movements accomplished quickly. His orders, issued on August 15, called for Thomas to complete his part of the operation by Wednesday, August 19.[10]

As the generals readied their commands and the supply depots began to fill, the matter of how much the men would carry with them was sorted out. Rosecrans realized he had to carry as much food, forage, and ammunition as possible during the initial days of the advance until he could reach more densely settled country. Crittenden's men, whose march would take them the farthest from the railroad, were ordered to each carry ten days of rations and eight days of forage into the Sequatchie Valley. Thomas' troops, with better access to the advanced depot at Bridgeport, were ordered to take eight days' rations and five days of forage. McCook's XX Corps, who would be advancing along the railroad, could draw on both Stevenson and Bridgeport. In order to support the needs of three corps, thousands of carloads of supplies would have to be hauled forward to those points in order to make sure rations were available in sufficient quantities once the entire army was relying on their stocks.[11]

Once these preliminary movements were complete, Rosecrans could undertake his crossing of the deep and winding Tennessee River. If intelligence reports and reconnaissance suggested that Bragg had not shifted his forces to resist a crossing below Chattanooga, Rosecrans could begin the next stage of his plan. The XXI Corps would move southwest, marching down the Sequatchie and join Thomas' men near Jasper, while sending a limited force across Walden Ridge to continue the deception plan. Conversely, if Bragg anticipated this move, Rosecrans could still funnel troops and supplies up the Sequatchie and let Crittenden seek a crossing north of Chattanooga in conjunction with Burnside's offensive. While this was clearly the less desirable choice, based on available logistics, it was a useful option to leave open. Depending upon Bragg's response, it might offer a viable alternative for occupying the city.

In either case, after a second pause of a few days to accumulate more rations in forward depots, Rosecrans would be ready to enter Georgia.

10 *Ibid.*, pp. 35-6.

11 *Ibid.*

C hapter 4

Crossing the Tennessee: August 22 to September 6, 1863

N athan Bedford Forrest confirmed the arrival of his division in Kingston, Tennessee, with a telegraph to Simon Bolivar Buckner on July 30. The move reflected Bragg's ongoing concern for Knoxville's safety, as well as his desire to unite with Buckner's command. Kingston was seventy miles northeast of Chattanooga but only thirty-five miles from Knoxville. The telegraph connected all three and ensured Bragg could remain in contact with both officers, but concentrating the commands would consume several days.

Forrest's arrival did little to relieve Buckner's growing concerns. If Burnside and/or Rosecrans moved against him, where would he turn for assistance? Bragg's Army of Tennessee was the only sizable Rebel force within a reasonable supporting distance. Bragg, however, could not move northeast to join Buckner without exposing Chattanooga to capture, an unacceptable option both militarily and politically. The loss of Chattanooga and the absence of the Confederate army would also open the way south through Georgia to Atlanta and beyond. Buckner's own options were limited. His army of some 15,000 was too small to defend East Tennessee by itself, but joined with Bragg would provide the Rebels near parity with Rosecrans on the Chattanooga front.[1]

---

1   OR 23, pt. 2, p. 945.

On August 22, as both Burnside and Rosecrans opened their campaigns, Buckner outlined his plans to a subordinate. "Burnside is evidently moving on East Tennessee in force. Rosecrans is also moving upon General Bragg. The necessity of combining with General Bragg," Buckner continued, "compels me to draw most of my troops to this [southwest] end of the district. The impossibility of opposing the enemy's advance at all points leads me to concentrate on his right."[2]

Buckner may have been confident about Union movements, but the disposition of Bragg's forces demonstrated exactly the opposite. His army was stretched along an extended front of more than 150 miles. On Bragg's right, Forrest's troopers screened the crossings on the Tennessee River between Kingston and the mouth of the Hiwassee River, thirty miles upstream from Chattanooga. Between the Hiwassee and Bridgeport, Alabama, Bragg relied on his infantry to patrol the south bank of the Tennessee. Farther downstream on his left, Joe Wheeler's cavalry was deployed as far south as Gadsden, Alabama, nearly eighty miles to the southwest. The attenuated nature of his command reflected Bragg's uncertainty about where the Federals would appear. The long mountain ridges only exacerbated his problem. Major General Daniel Harvey Hill, writing years later, described Bragg as being "bewildered by the 'popping out of the rats from so many holes.'"[3] Confederate infantry alone was spread along more then 50 miles of riverbank. This wide deployment was dangerous because it precluded rapid concentration at any one point, and exhausting because roving patrols were required to constantly monitor the extended frontage. In addition, many small detachments of troops and couriers were stationed at likely crossing points.

Forrest understood his assignment from the start. In addition to maintaining patrols along the river and staying in touch with both Bragg and Buckner, he sent Col. George G. Dibrell and his regiment, the 8th Tennessee Cavalry, to Sparta. The seat of White County, Sparta was located on the East Tennessee Turnpike that connected Knoxville to Nashville. The route also ran directly through Forrest's headquarters at Kingston, and so provided a useful avenue of communication between the two men. Dibrell and the 8th Tennessee were intimately familiar with White County. Company D was raised in Sparta,

---

2 *Ibid.*, 30, 4, p. 537.

3 D. H. Hill, "Chickamauga—Great Battle Of The West," *Battles and Leaders of the Civil War* (Thomas Yoseloff, 1956), vol. 3, p. 644.

while the other companies had come from the environs as well as adjacent Putnam and Overton counties.[4] Dibrell enjoyed a prominent pre-war career as a merchant and farmer in the region.[5] In early August, all or parts of two other regiments reinforced Dibrell's command to a demi-brigade numbering more than 1,000 men.[6] Many of these men promptly left the ranks or were furloughed to visit home, gather supplies, and recruit. The informality of military protocol among Rebel cavalry units—or lack of discipline or respect for the authority of their officers—was once again causing problems.

Dibrell reported that fully one-half of his regiment was absent, filling the surrounding countryside with roving bands of Rebel troopers home on leave or seeking to re-equip themselves.[7] Ironically, these furloughs created the impression in Federal command circles of a much larger Confederate force operating in Middle Tennessee. According to these rumors, up to four brigades of Confederate cavalry and Forrest himself were on the loose.[8] While this decision helped fool the Federals as to the size of Dibrell's command, it also sent hundreds of his men beyond immediate recall as they fanned out to visit homesteads across a wide region.

Dibrell's presence in Sparta quickly attracted Union attention. Any Union advance from McMinnville into the upper Sequatchie Valley at Pikeville had to pass directly through Sparta. Union Col. Robert H. G. Minty probed Dibrell's camps early that August, provoking several significant skirmishes. On August 4, Minty and several regiments numbering 1,096 troopers tried to ambush Dibrell's Tennessee regiment near Rock Island Ferry, but the move misfired and only succeeded in capturing a handful of Rebel pickets.[9]

Another effort five days later pitted about 800 Federals against Dibrell's command. This time, the fighting was of a more significant nature. The action

4   Civil War Centennial Commission, *Tennesseans in the Civil War* (Nashville, 1964), pp. 62-3.

5   Warner, *Generals in Gray,* p. 7.

6   Technically, since Pegram's Division had not yet been attached to Forrest, Dibrell was still a regimental commander in Armstrong's Brigade, and Forrest was still divisional commander. *OR* 30, pt. 2, p. 527.

7   Betty Jane Dudney, *Civil War in White County Tennessee* (Master's Thesis, Tennessee Technological University, 1985), p. 23.

8   *OR* 30, pt. 3, p. 56.

9   D. L. Haines. "Record of the Fourth Michigan Cavalry" Michigan Historical Collections, Bentley Historical Library, University of Michigan, Ann Arbor, MI.

began when Minty encountered Company D of the 8th Tennessee posted as pickets about four miles south of Sparta. The Rebels fell back through town in a running fight until they reached the main Confederate camp north of town in a pasture at the junction of the Calfkiller River and Wildcat Creek. The land happened to be part of Dibrell's own property, so he knew the ground intimately.[10] Alerted by the retreat of his pickets, Dibrell sent company B to reinforce Company D while the rest of the regiment deployed on the north bank of Wildcat Creek. Here, Dibrell was further reinforced by a company of local men under guerilla commander Capt. Champ Ferguson, who was also loitering in the area and who now rushed to aid the embattled 8th regiment. Steep banks and the pond at Fisk's Mill rendered Wildcat Creek an almost unassailable position, and only a single bridge spanned the waterway. Minty's first charge was repulsed handily. A second effort, this time dismounted, also met with failure. Determined to get at Dibrell, Minty opted to move upstream and outflank him. The Tennessean's knowledge of the land convinced him to retreat a mile farther north and take up yet another strong position behind Blue Spring Creek. After a limited exchange of fire at this new location, Minty withdrew.[11]

The fight lasted a couple of hours, but losses were light on both sides. Minty claimed a victory, writing on August 11, "Of course I whipped Dibrell. His men were scattered about the country like blackberries. I think it doubtful that they will return to Sparta," Both claims were premature. While Minty was reporting his success to headquarters, Dibrell was already occupying his former camp, where his men enjoyed a breakfast prepared by local women. Dibrell would remain ensconced there for the next week.[12]

On August 15 Minty's troopers returned to Sparta with new orders to ride for Pikeville—the opening move of the larger campaign.[13] Minty's mission was to drive George Dibrell's Rebels out of Sparta once and for all, and then

10 Coral Williams, "Legends and Stories of White County, Tennessee" (Master's Thesis, George Peabody College for Teachers, 1930), Chapter V. You can read this online at: www.danielhaston.com/history/tn-history/white-county/legends-whiteco5.htm.

11 *Ibid.*; OR 23, pt. 1, p. 848.

12 OR 52, 1, p. 437. By this time, many of Dibrell's men were indeed "scattered like blackberries," having gone home on furloughs, formal or otherwise, though Minty's troopers had little to do with it.

13 *Ibid.*, 30, pt. 2, p. 35.

securely occupy the northern end of the Sequatchie Valley. This time Minty sent the 7th Pennsylvania and 4th Michigan cavalry regiments riding up the east bank of the Calfkiller River in search of another route to outflank Dibrell. The Rebels were alerted to the danger, however, and met the Yankees at a crossroads called Sperry's Mills. There, the Federal regiments drove Dibrell's troopers back across the river toward their camp. At the same time, Minty dispatched his remaining two horse regiments, the 3rd Indiana and 4th U.S. Regulars, up the west bank of the river in an effort to cut off the Confederate retreat. This trap also failed, primarily because of Dibrell's familiarity with the neighborhood. The Rebels, reported a frustrated Minty, "had no difficulty in escaping."[14]

Minty's men followed the Tennesseans for several miles before turning back to Sparta for the night.[15] The aggressive Dibrell was not ready to abandon the fight, however, and circled around to ambush the head of the Union column. Moving back along Calfkiller Creek, Robert Burns of Minty's staff described the attack: "We were riding carelessly along at the head of the column when suddenly an infernal fire was opened upon us from the opposite side [of the creek] where the 4th Mich. and 7th Pa. had been half an hour previously. The Rebels where wholly concealed by the bushes, which lined our side of the creek."[16]

The ambush wounded about fifteen Federals, but this time the Union cavalry was not turning back. Minty ordered regiments across the creek and the Confederates fell back to their former position at Fisk's Mill, joined there on their left flank by Col. William S. McLemore's newly arrived 4th Tennessee Cavalry at Meredith's Mill.[17] Minty's men dismounted and the new fight lasted from about 4:00 p.m. until dark. Realizing that he was overmatched, Dibrell retreated later that night to the top of Cumberland Mountain. Several days later he joined Forrest at Kingston to report that a major enemy movement was underway. Forrest passed the intelligence on to Bragg's headquarters on the 21st.[18]

14 *Ibid.*, 1, p. 920.

15 Haines, *Record of the Fourth Michigan Cavalry.*

16 Robert Burns Letter, August 25, 1863, Minnesota Historical Society, St. Paul, Minn.

17 Williams, *Legends and Stories*, Chapter V.

18 Entry for August 21, 1863, Brent Journal.

After successfully driving off Dibrell's Confederates, Minty turned south to Pikeville and rode into the Sequatchie Valley, ready to link up with the Federal XXI Corps. Once again both sides claimed a victory, but this time Dibrell's retreat was so abrupt he left many of his furloughed men behind. Some eventually made their way back to their regiments, but many remained absent for months. Others joined local guerrilla bands and helped fuel an ongoing guerrilla war in the region. Their absence left Dibrell's ranks depleted of hundreds of troopers just as one of the most important campaigns of the war was opening.[19]

While Minty was riding to Pikeville, Union Col. John T. Wilder's brigade of mounted infantry and two infantry divisions was moving to secure the rest of the Sequatchie Valley. Wilder was the vanguard piercing into the central valley at Dunlap, and the southern end of the valley at Jasper, Tennessee. Once Dibrell withdrew to Kingston, no organized Confederate force remained north of the Tennessee River to contest this vital corridor. Consequently, the Rebels were completely blind to subsequent Union movements.

Dibrell's dispatches, combined with other vague reports, gave Bragg some intimation that Rosecrans was stirring, but he lacked the specifics to act. The Confederate army commander didn't really need Forrest to forward the message from Dibrell to alert him to the unfolding danger. A more dramatic warning arrived on August 21 when Wilder's Yankees arrived on Stringer's Ridge across the river from Chattanooga and opened fire. Artillery rounds exploding in the city streets threw the townsfolk into a panic. Many were at church when the iron shells jolted them from their worship. The interruption shocked the Southern high command. Major General Daniel H. Hill wrote, "our pickets and scouts, if any were out, had given no warning of the Yankee approach."[20]

The appearance of Yankees opposite the city alarmed many, but no enemy troops had crossed the Tennessee River above or below Chattanooga. In Bragg's headquarters, one glaring absence was the lack of any reports from Wheeler, whose men were picketing downstream. Colonel George Brent on

---

19 Dudney, *Civil War In White County,* p. 23, and John Barrien Lindsley, *Military Annals of Tennessee* (Broadfoot Publishing Company, 1995), vol. 2, p. 659. See also Jordan and Pryor, *Forrest's Cavalry,* p. 298. Approximately 200 of Dibrell's men were left behind.

20 *OR* 30, pt. 2, p. 136. D. H. Hill's report records his complete surprise when Wilder's troops first showed up across the Tennessee River from Chattanooga. D. H. Hill, "Chickamauga—Great Battle of the West," pp. 639-40.

Bragg's staff recorded the mounting uncertainty and sense of growing frustration. "Our scouts bring in but little definite or reliable intelligence," he complained on August 22. "Our secret service corps gives us nothing tangible."[21]

The same day Brent lodged a complaint in his journal, Simon Buckner received chilling news from his scouts in Kentucky that Burnside's army was also on the move. The Federal general was heading for Knoxville in what looked like the second arm of a giant pincer movement against his Department of East Tennessee. Knowing he was not strong enough to fight for the city, Buckner ordered John Pegram's new cavalry division to ride to Kingston and join Forrest; his infantry would follow. Bragg and the authorities in Richmond received the news of Burnside's approach and Buckner's decision that same day.[22] The report reinforced the overall impression that Rosecrans was moving north of Chattanooga in conjunction with Burnside.

Buckner dispatched to Bragg a steady stream of reports about the growing threat to Knoxville, but Col. Brent did not record a single report from Wheeler.[23] What, if anything, was happening downstream from Chattanooga? A full week elapsed before a civilian brought word on August 28 that Rosecrans had established his headquarters at Jasper, Tennessee, twenty miles west of Chattanooga as the crow flies.[24] That information seemed to contradict the idea that Rosecrans was moving north and east. Bragg clung to the belief that Rosecrans would not "sever himself from Burnside."[25]

Wheeler's silence during the last week in August frustrated Bragg. A month earlier on July 9, he spelled out in no uncertain terms what he expected from the Army of Tennessee's senior cavalryman: "It is of vital importance that we should know the positions and movements of Rosecrans. The General desires you to send a small force and many scouts on his right flank to get information. Forrest is doing the same on his left. Please report every item as fast as learned."[26] Wheeler took the "small force" suggestion too literally.

---

21 Entry for August 22, 1863, Brent Journal.

22 *OR* 30, 4, p. 526.

23 *Ibid.*

24 *Ibid.*, p. 561.

25 Entry for August 28, 1863, Brent Journal.

26 *OR* 23, pt. 2, p. 904.

After the retreat from Tennessee following the Tullahoma operations, Wheeler established his headquarters at Gadsden, Alabama, nearly eighty miles southwest of Chattanooga, where he concentrated more on refitting his cavalry than on patrolling the Tennessee River. He detailed only two regiments to watch the river, and only one of those units, the 3rd Confederate Cavalry, was assigned the vital fifty-mile stretch between Bridgeport and Guntersville.[27] The 8th Confederate Cavalry was assigned the next forty miles of riverbank from Guntersville to Decatur, Alabama.[28] All told, Wheeler assigned barely 500 men to patrol ninety miles of riverbank. The army's senior cavalry leader sent the balance of his command to the rear.

John Wharton's cavalry division was ordered to Rome, Georgia, where it spent the month of August in comparative comfort, holding barbeques and "living high on Peach Pie."[29] Wharton's men were still there when the final days of August arrived, fifty miles due south of Chattanooga and at least that far from the river they were supposed to be patrolling. They were in no position to watch for or contest a Union crossing. William T. Martin's division was even more out of position. Martin's camps were near Alexandria, in Calhoun County, Alabama.[30] Alexandria was almost 100 miles southwest of Chattanooga, forty-five miles southeast of the nearest point on the Tennessee River at Guntersville, and some sixty miles from Stevenson. Seemingly oblivious to the potential threat Rosecrans' Army of the Cumberland posed, Wheeler had yet to order either command to the front. Wheeler's careless dispositions effectively rendered Bragg blind to enemy threats on his left, and Bragg wasn't even aware that Wheeler had failed him.

Bragg had stationed infantry brigades as far west as Taylor's Store, opposite Bridgeport (about twenty-five miles west of Chattanooga), but withdrew them on August 21 when Wilder's men dropped shells into the city. Now, only small infantry pickets watched the various ferries between Bridgeport and

---

27 OR 23, pt. 2, pp. 912, 930, mention the cavalry regiment at Bridgeport, and later identify it as the 3rd Confederate Cavalry.

28 *Ibid.*, p. 923, and George Knox Miller letter, September 15, 1863.

29 John McGrath Papers, Louisiana State University, Baton Rouge. See also J. K. P. Blackburn, L. B. Giles, and E. S. Dowd, *Terry Texas Ranger Trilogy* (State House Press, 1996), p. 208. See also Rueben S. Morton Diary concerning depredations committed by Wharton's men at this time.

30 I. B. Ulmer Reminiscences, 3rd Alabama Cavalry file, Alabama Department of Archives and History, Montgomery, Alabama (hereafter ADAH).

Chattanooga. On the 22nd, Union troops appeared at Bridgeport and Shellmound, the latter on the north bank near Jasper. The Federals erected a pontoon bridge across the river at Shellmound and small bodies of infantry and cavalry crossed to skirmish with Confederate pickets. The mission was both deception and reconnaissance: to fool Bragg into thinking the crossing was merely a feint, and to determine the strength of the Rebels in the area available to oppose the main crossings once they began.[31]

The simple answer to the latter reconnaissance question was "not much." Having demonstrated in front of Chattanooga for more than a week, Rosecrans turned to implement the next part of his plan. On August 29, Federals began crossing in larger numbers using both boats and pontoon bridges. That same day, the Union commander wired the War Department, "Bridge across at Caperton's Ferry [near Stevenson, Alabama.] Two brigades over. Cavalry forded at two places. [Brigadier General John M.] Brannan's advance crossed at Battle Creek. [Major General Joseph J.] Reynolds' advance at Shellmound. Reports not in yet, but suppose we have 100 prisoners. No fighting to amount to anything."[32]

The lack of significant resistance to these crossings surprised Rosecrans. Some of the crossings were completely unguarded, while Confederate pickets manning the others were captured or dispersed handily. Brannan crossed at Battle Creek with two infantry companies via flatboat. Their crossing and landing was completely unopposed. The rest of the brigade began crossing as scouting parties fanned out two miles inland without finding a single Rebel.[33] Neither was there resistance at Caperton's Ferry farther downstream, where Union infantry secured another bridgehead without firing a shot. As soon as the far banks were in Union hands, engineers commenced throwing pontoon bridges across the river. In each case the Federals were both surprised and delighted with the lack of opposition, and moved rapidly to cross over the rest of the army. During the next week, seven infantry divisions and the bulk of the cavalry corps and supply trains streamed across the Tennessee River.

During the first few days of the massive operation, Bragg received only limited word of the enemy activity below Chattanooga. Colonel Brent noted

---

31 OR 30, pt. 4, p. 534; W. S. Rosecrans, "The Chattanooga Campaign," *National Tribune*, March 25, 1882.

32 *Ibid.*, 3, p. 213.

33 *Ibid.*, p. 214.

that word of the crossings at Shellmound and Bridgeport arrived at headquarters on August 29, but the report was dismissed as "a feint."[34] At 1:00 p.m. that same day, Col. William N. Estes, commander of the overmatched 3rd Confederate Cavalry, dispatched a hasty report of the crossing at Caperton's Ferry, followed by the news that his command was "gradually falling back on Trenton [Georgia]." Because the intelligence was routed to Wheeler at Rome, Estes' message did not reach Bragg's headquarters until later that day or early on August 30, and it wasn't until 2:00 a.m. on September 1 that Bragg dispatched a party of engineers to investigate.[35]

Even if he had had more details of the enemy crossings, Bragg might not have reacted to them much differently. The small parties of Federals slipping across the Tennessee River between Shellmound and Stevenson since the 22nd and sparring with Rebel outposts had already been dismissed as deception, so the latest reports would probably have been interpreted as more of the same. Bragg's attention remained fixed on his right flank, upstream from Chattanooga toward Knoxville. Brent's casual dismissal of the Bridgeport crossing as a feint confirms that Rosecrans' diversions deceived Bragg completely. D. H. Hill, whose infantry corps defended the upstream portion of the river, concurred with Bragg. In fact, Hill insisted adamantly that the main crossings would come on his front between the mouth of Chickamauga Creek and Harrison, Tennessee.

On August 29, Bragg belatedly instructed Wheeler to bring his entire corps forward, realizing at last that the Rebel screen was dangerously inadequate. The order, however, reflected how fixated army headquarters was with Hill's front. Rather than demand that the river downstream be properly defended, Bragg ordered exactly the opposite. He was so convinced that the real threat loomed to the northeast that he ordered Wheeler to split his corps and send Wharton's cavalry division to help screen Hill's position instead of reinforcing the downstream force.[36]

Bragg's decision to shift Wharton to join Hill concentrated three of his four available mounted divisions on the Confederate right flank. This imbalance left Wheeler's smallest division under Brigadier General Martin to cover

---

34 Entry for August 29, 1863, Brent Journal. The reports were from Captain P. H. Rice, Confederate Signal Corps, commanding a detachment atop Lookout Mountain.

35 *OR* 30, pt. 4, p. 564, 579.

36 Entry for August 29, 1863, Brent Journal; *OR* 30, pt. 4, pp. 563-4.

Bridgeport, Shellmound, and Stevenson. Martin had only six regiments, barely 2,500 troopers, to face nearly the entire Union army.[37] Bragg's order, more than any other issued during this period, clarifies the imbalance in Confederate dispositions and Bragg's lack of actual concern about his left flank.

In an effort to supplement the nearly non-existent cavalry screen, Bragg attempted to reinforce his infantry pickets, at least within a few miles of Chattanooga. On August 26, 100 men of the 19th Tennessee Infantry, part of Brig. Gen. Otho Strahl's Brigade, were sent west of Lookout Mountain to picket the roads from Trenton and Bridgeport. The 19th was hand-picked because two of its companies were from the region. When the detachment marched through Chattanooga, citizens greeted their sons and neighbors in an impromptu parade. The first few days of this duty passed uneventfully, but at midnight on August 30, infantry from the Union XIV Corps and 375 men of Col. Daniel M. Ray's 2nd Tennessee Cavalry (U.S.) collided with the 19th's picket guard.[38] Brent's diary confirms that the flare-up did little to alter the thinking at army headquarters. The staff officer speculated that the Federal force responsible was "probably not large." Still, Bragg could not afford to ignore these signs any longer. [39] On August 30, Bragg diverted Wharton's cavalry, then en route to join Hill, to ride instead to Lafayette, Georgia.[40] He also ordered Lt. Gen. Leonidas Polk to send a full infantry brigade to reinforce the 19th Tennessee.[41]

Farther downstream, with the bulk of Martin's troopers spread across a wide swath of Alabama, no immediate help was available for Colonel Estes' 3rd Confederate Cavalry. The 3rd was the only body of Confederate troops directly impeding the main Federal advance. On August 30, while Bragg was trying to decipher what, if anything, the dust-up with the 19th Tennessee west of Lookout Mountain portended, Wheeler made a stopgap effort to aid Estes by ordering another of Martin's regiments to make a forced march north.

37 David A. Powell, *Strengths and Losses of the Union and Confederate Armies at Chickamauga*, unpublished manuscript, CCNMP, pp. 62-63, discusses the strength of Martin's Division.

38 S. J. A. Frazier, "Reminiscences of Chickamauga," clipping from *The Lookout*, May 20, 1909, Hamilton County Library, Chattanooga Tennessee. See also *OR* 30, pt. 1, pp. 469, 911.

39 Entry for August 30, 1863, Brent Journal.

40 *Ibid.*

41 Entry for August 30, 1863, Alfred T. Fielder Diary, 12th Tennessee Infantry, Tennessee State Library and Archives, Nashville, Tennessee.

Lieutenant Colonel T. H. Mauldin's 3rd Alabama Cavalry, 300 strong, was still forty-five miles away and would not arrive for some time.[42]

Once below the Tennessee River, the next natural obstacle Rosecrans would face was Sand Mountain. The high ground rose abruptly from the banks of the Tennessee, with almost no valley floor between the south bank and the mountain slopes. The top is a relatively flat plateau, lower in elevation but wider than Lookout Mountain. Between Sand and Lookout mountains is Wills Valley, which stretches southwest deep into Alabama. Control of Sand Mountain would allow Rosecrans to protect his crossing sites and prevent Bragg from discovering his strength and dispositions. Seizure of the high ground would also allow the Federal to send forays into Wills Valley to keep track of the Rebels on their front. All of this and much more was in the minds of Union commanders as they poured troops across the river and scaled the heights to establish secure bridgeheads for the rest of the Army of the Cumberland. By 8:00 a.m. on August 31, the most successful crossing had occurred at Caperton's Ferry, where most of McCook's XX Corps was already on the south bank of the river.[43] The pontoon bridge at Bridgeport was still under construction, but part of Maj. Gen. Philip H. Sheridan's division (XX Corps) had crossed using individual pontoon boats. At Shellmound, a division of Thomas' XIV Corps was already on the south bank and a second was crossing at a rate of 400 men an hour.[44] By nightfall on August 31, Union troops controlled Sand Mountain, rendering Bragg blind to the extent of the crossings.

Given the strength of the Federals in his front, Colonel Estes' cavalry regiment could do nothing to prevent what was taking place. His men, scattered about in small patrols, were swept easily aside. Reports that did reach Bragg were confused and vague. On August 31, Mauldin's 3rd Alabama reached Trenton, about twelve miles southeast of Shellmound. The dispatches fired off by the stunned colonel revealed, for the first time, the potential danger confronting Bragg's army. Mauldin's mission was to reinforce Estes' battered 3rd Confederate Cavalry, but as he quickly discovered, there was no organized force to support. In his first message to headquarters, the Alabama officer reported that "the command [Colonel Estes'] that was picketing on the river

---

42 *OR* 30, pt. 4, p. 574.

43 *Ibid.*, pt. 1, p. 485.

44 *Ibid.*, pt. 3, p. 251.

have been scattered and the whole line is open."[45] Mauldin attempted to reestablish his pickets atop Sand Mountain, but was driven back by the Federals already occupying the high ground. By nightfall, Mauldin reported his position as "picketing on the [east] side of Sand Mountain, endeavoring to protect my command."[46] Worse still was news that Union cavalry was now operating in the valley around Trenton, with some enemy horsemen ranging as far east as Lookout Mountain. The news gave Mauldin good reason to worry about his line of retreat. The next day, the colonel abandoned the forward struggle and fell back to establish a new extended picket line atop Lookout Mountain stretching from Chattanooga all the way to Trenton.[47]

Joe Wheeler, riding with Wharton's troopers, thundered into Lafayette, Georgia, about 5:00 p.m. on September 1. Destined to become the focal point of Union and Confederate movements during the next two weeks, Lafayette was twenty-one miles due south of Chattanooga and about eighteen miles southeast of Trenton on the other side of Lookout Mountain. From Lafayette, Wharton could send troops west through McLemore's Cove to reinforce Mauldin's thin line of Alabama pickets atop Lookout Mountain. Martin's Division, however, would not arrive for several more days.[48]

Bragg finally grasped the fact that Rosecrans had crossed in some strength over the Tennessee River between Bridgeport and Stevenson, and notified Richmond on September 2.[49] The paucity of information with which Bragg had to act, however, was made clear in a tersely worded message to Joe Wheeler. "Dear General: I am uneasy about the state of affairs," wrote Bragg's chief of staff Brig. Gen. W. W. Mackall. "It is so vitally important that the General [Bragg] should have full and correct information. One misstep in the movement of this army would possibly be fatal. Your line of pickets now occupy on Lookout Mountain about the same advantages they possessed on the

---

45 *Ibid.*, pt. 4, p. 574.

46 *Ibid.*

47 Holt, W. T. Army of Tennessee Scout Book, Museum of the Confederacy, Richmond, VA. Entry for September 4 includes the report of S. G. Ballard. Handfuls of independent scouts and scattered local home guards remained behind Union lines, but they were unable to make regular contact with Bragg's army. At best, any information they were able to provide was days late, and at worst, wildly inaccurate. The were a poor substitute for a proper cavalry screen.

48 Entry for September 1, 1863, W. B. Corbitt Diary, Emory University, Atlanta, Georgia.

49 *OR*, 30, pt. 4, pp. 583-4.

river or Sand Mountain. The passage at Caperton's Ferry broke the line," chastised Mackall, "and a week has passed and we don't know whether or not an army has passed."[50]

Despite lingering uncertainty about Rosecrans' intentions, Bragg seemed to now grasp that the real threat was not against Knoxville but Chattanooga and his own army. On September 1, he ordered Forrest and Buckner to join the main army at Chattanooga. Buckner had already reached Loudon, Tennessee, on August 30, with his rearguard at Lenoir Station. Knoxville would have to be abandoned. Even the strategic Cumberland Gap was left in the hands of a token force of four regiments that had orders to withdraw rather than be encircled and destroyed. The following day, Buckner covered half the distance and reached Charleston, evacuating Knoxville more smoothly perhaps than could have been expected given the circumstance. Some supplies and a few troops moved by rail, but the bulk of the men marched, covering the wagon trains hauling supplies Buckner was loathe to leave behind or destroy. The next day, September 3, Forrest was formally given command of Pegram's Division, a move that effectively restored him to corps command.[51]

The same day Forrest resumed corps command Bragg began exploring the possibility of striking back. His initial plan was to find a way to get at Rosecrans' forces while they were scattered along the north bank of the Tennessee River, with Forrest and his new corps playing a critical role in the attacks. Realizing that at least two Union corps had crossed downriver beyond his effective left flank, Bragg proposed sending a column across the river north of Chattanooga to attack the Yankees demonstrating in Sequatchie Valley. With the bulk of Rosecrans' army miles away, an opportunity beckoned to damage the smaller portion left behind. The problem was getting a large force quickly across the river. Bragg had but one pontoon bridge in place at Chattanooga, but not enough transportation to take it up and move it elsewhere. Using the bridge already in place to cross at Chattanooga was not possible because, without the element of surprise, the Federals could defend their side of the bridge easily. Always willing to support a bold attack, Forrest promised to locate fords across

---

50 *Ibid.*, p. 584.

51 *Ibid.*, p. 591. The reader will recall that Forrest stepped down to divisional command after one of the two divisions in Earl Van Dorn's former Corps under William Hicks "Red" Jackson was sent to Mississippi in June. The order formally assigning Pegram's Division to Forrest once again put Forrest in command of a full corps of cavalry, and not just his own division. See Chapter 2 for a more detailed discussion of the cavalry command structure.

the river and volunteered to use his horsemen to help the infantry get across. Bragg selected D. H. Hill's Corps for the operation, but the infantry commanders worried about their ability to cross over artillery, especially since the Federals had erected earthworks at various places along the north bank of the river. As it turned out, events unfolding elsewhere shelved Bragg's bold and aggressive plan.[52]

While Bragg was busy planning Hill's offensive above the Tennessee River, a series of alarming reports arrived at headquarters. On September 2, Martin's cavalry division stopped at Summerville, Georgia, a small hamlet twenty miles south of Lafayette. There, Martin's men heard reports of Union troops operating within just four miles of the village. Word was passed quickly up the chain of command to Chattanooga.[53] The next day, September 3, Col. Brent also recorded a message from Wharton that placed Federals at Cash's Store on Sand Mountain, an alarming eighteen miles southwest of Trenton. If these reports were accurate, Rosecrans was making a much wider swing than just a direct flanking attack against Chattanooga.[54] Worse yet was the fact that Summerville was east of Lookout Mountain, which suggested that the Federals had already—in a strength yet to be determined—crossed that formidable barrier. If so, they were much closer to Bragg's critical lifeline, the Western and Atlantic Railroad, than previously supposed. In fact, the Federals had not yet crossed to the east side of Lookout Mountain in strength, but they were very close to doing so.[55]

On September 5, a new report reached Bragg's headquarters corroborating the earlier information. This dispatch placed Crittenden's Union XXI Corps in Wills Valley with "10,000 [troops,] reported about 14 [miles] below Trenton."[56]

---

52 *Ibid.* The dispatch from Bragg to Hill, dated 10:00 a.m. September 4, 1863, outlines Bragg's plan, the problems with the crossings, and Forrest's promise to find suitable fords.

53 Stevenson, "Robert Alexander Smith: A Southern Son," p. 43. See also report of Union Brig. Gen. Robert B. Mitchell, in *OR* 30, pt. 3, p. 332. Mitchell identifies Martin's men at Alpine on September 2, 1863.

54 Entry for September 3, 1863, Brent Journal.

55 Rosecrans left the small force of men north of the river not to invite attack, but so Bragg would be confused by his actions and remain in Chattanooga for as long as possible, or even move toward Knoxville. I don't think he expected Bragg to strike north of the Tennessee River, but Rosecrans would have been delighted if he had attempted such a thing. So in that sense, and with the Union feint to the north, what was dangled before Bragg was a trap of sorts.

56 Entry for September 5, 1863, Holt, Army of Tennessee Scout Book.

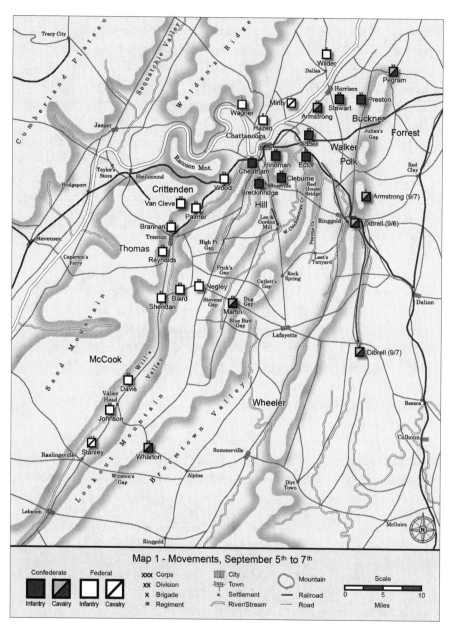

Map 1 - Movements, September 5th to 7th

Confederate	Federal			
		XXX Corps	City	Mountain
		XX Division	Town	
		X Brigade	Settlement	Railroad
Infantry Cavalry	Infantry Cavalry	III Regiment	River/Stream	Road

Scale
0   5   10
Miles

This map demonstrates just how far out of position Braxton Bragg's Army of Tennessee was at the end of the first week of September 1863. Except for Martin's and Wharton's cavalry divisions, all of Bragg's army is at, or northeast of, Chattanooga, while virtually all of Rosecrans' Army of the Cumberland is across the Tennessee River and closing in on Bragg's left-rear.

With these details in hand and Martin's cavalry at Lafayette, Bragg had no choice but to make a dramatic shift in course, beginning with the disposition of Wheeler's troopers. The army commander ordered Wheeler to send Wharton and his division to Alpine, just six miles from Summerville at the eastern foot of Lookout Mountain, and block the pass there to prevent deeper Union incursions.[57] The next day, September 6, an independent scout named "Davenport" reached Bragg and confirmed the enemy was in strength in Wills Valley at Valley Head a few miles west of Alpine across Lookout Mountain.[58]

Towering as it does above Chattanooga along the southern bank of the Tennessee River, the northern end of Lookout Mountain makes for a perfect vantage point. Bragg established a signal station atop the crest manned by Captain P. H. Rice and a detachment of the Confederate Signal Corps. Rice relayed his observations into the city via flags and, after dark, by torch. On September 6, Rice's signalmen observed Union columns approaching both Trenton and Chattanooga from the west. From north of the city, Col. John Scott sent word that leading elements of Ambrose Burnside's Union cavalry had reached the Hiwassee River and were approaching from Knoxville.[59] Chattanooga was in danger of being surrounded. This news, coupled with reports of powerful Union columns operating nearly forty miles in his left rear, convinced Bragg that crossing to the north bank of the Tennessee River was no longer a viable option, and that his position at Chattanooga was now untenable.[60]

If Bragg had known the true state of Rosecrans' dispositions, he would have been even more alarmed for the safety of the city and the army defending it. By September 2, Brig. Gen. Jefferson C. Davis' infantry division, which was spearheading McCook's XX Corps, had nearly reached Winston's Spring at Valley Head.[61] The next day, Thomas' powerful XIV Corps converged on

---

57 Entry for September 5, 1863, Brent Journal.

58 Entry for September 6, 1863, Holt, Army of Tennessee Scout Book, titled "Davenport's scout." Davenport was probably Mountraville Davenport, a home guard captain and local terror to Unionist area farmers. As noted, however, his information was several days late because Union troops reached Valley Head on September 2.

59 Entry for September 6, 1863, Brent Journal.

60 *Ibid.* Entries for September 5-7 reflect the growing awareness of the threat from the southwest and Bragg's decision to abandon Chattanooga.

61 *OR* 30, pt. 3, p. 302.

Trenton from two directions. Also on September 3—the same day Bragg began contemplating an attack against what he believed was the main body of Crittenden's XXI Corps north of the Tennessee River—Rosecrans ordered Crittenden to begin moving the bulk of his corps south of the river at Shellmound.[62] The earliest Bragg could have organized and executed his attack north of the Tennessee was September 4 or 5. By that time, the only Federals left there to strike were two brigades of infantry under Brig. Gens. William B. Hazen and George D. Wagner, Wilder's mounted infantry brigade (less one regiment sent to join Thomas), and Minty's brigade of Federal cavalry.[63] Moving forward with his plan would have plunged Bragg headlong into a trap. A sizable chunk of his army would be farther north (and on the wrong side of the river) just as Rosecrans was turning east to cut the Western and Atlantic Railroad, upon which the Army of Tennessee depended for food and other supplies. In addition, Bragg risked being pinned against that river or caught in the act of crossing.

Above the Tennessee, meanwhile, Hazen and Wagner maintained a highly successful façade of an invasion force. As Hazen later described it, this display consisted of the infantry "practicing a series of show-marches, camps with fires, and martial music of fifteen regiments" in order to confound Bragg's observers on the southern bank and convince the Rebels that a much larger Union force was massing there.[64] Even after Bragg realized that Rosecrans' deception was just that, the feint still achieved a measure of secondary success. By now Bragg knew the main Federal effort was not upstream against his right flank. Yet, he still believed Crittenden's entire XXI Corps opposed him at Chattanooga. A lone enemy corps was a tempting target worth trying to attack and destroy in its own right. The idea of attacking Crittenden held the attention of the commander of the Army of Tennessee for several critical days.

In reality, the Federals still above the river numbered barely 7,500 men, and were much too nimble to be caught and destroyed by the right hook Bragg was proposing to throw. Wilder's men patrolled aggressively the banks of the Tennessee opposite Chattanooga on horseback. They were alert to even minute

---

62 *Ibid.*, p. 328.

63 *Ibid.*, p. 323. Hazen was originally in command of this force, but Wagner was later placed in charge after it was discovered that Wagner was his senior by date of rank.

64 William B. Hazen to Benson H. Lossing, August 23, 1866, William P. Palmer Collection, Western Reserve Historical Society, Cleveland, Ohio.

changes in Confederate dispositions, as the steady stream of reports flowing into Rosecrans' headquarters aptly demonstrates. Wilder ensured his men paid special attention to the Rebel pontoon bridge at Chattanooga. They pounded it with artillery and watched for any sign the Confederates were going to swing it out into place to cross the river. Minty's men were responsible for watching the river as far upstream as Hiwassee, with roving patrols all the way to Kingston. It is highly unlikely that Bragg could have affected a crossing fast enough and strong enough to take any of these Federals by surprise.[65] Bragg wasted the first several days of September chasing a phantom opportunity.

Between September 2 and 5, Rosecrans' main body made little forward progress. Instead, the Yankees concentrated on crossing their cavalry, the rest of their infantry, and the massive supply columns needed to carry a month's worth of basic rations into the wilds of northern Georgia. Aside from the river itself, scaling Sand and Lookout mountains also proved to be more difficult on the ground than it looked on a map. Each column required at least a day to ascend the west face of each mountain, another day's march to reach the eastern summit, and then a third day to descend into the next valley. The painfully slow progress was compounded by the limited number of gaps, which created bottlenecks as the infantry and artillery waited their turn to climb or descend the high ground. As a result, the lead elements of the XIV and XX corps experienced several days of inactivity waiting for the bulk of the army to catch up. During that time, they searched out bushwhackers, recruited a number of Unionist locals as guides, and destroyed anything useful to the Southern war effort, including tanning yards and nitre works.[66]

By September 5, Rosecrans' columns were closed up and ready to resume their advance. Generally speaking, McCook's XX Corps and the Union cavalry were stationed around Valley Head ready to cross Lookout Mountain and Broomtown Valley for a move on Alpine; Thomas' XIV Corps was concentrated farther north in Wills Valley around Trenton, Georgia, heading for Lafayette; and Crittenden's XXI Corps was in Lookout Valley headed for Chattanooga.[67]

---

65 Minty's and Wilder's daily reports are detailed in "Summaries of the news reaching Headquarters of General W. S. Rosecrans, 1863-64," RG 393, part 1, entry 986, NARA.

66 OR 30, pt. 3, p. 302; and John W. Rowell, *Yankee Cavalrymen: Through the Civil War With the Ninth Pennsylvania Cavalry* (University of Tennessee Press, 1971), p. 141.

67 OR 30, pt. 1, p. 52.

Chapter 5

The Right Flank: Evacuation of Chattanooga and Retreat to Lafayette

(September 6-13, 1863)

By September 6, Braxton Bragg was sure of three things: Rosecrans had fooled him, his army was in peril, and Chattanooga—one of the most important cities in the Southern Confederacy—was lost.

And nary had a shot been fired.

Outflanked and thus out of position, the commander of the Army of Tennessee decided to abandon Chattanooga without a major battle and move south. By retreating, he would be moving toward additional reinforcements because troops from other parts of the Confederacy were arriving to join his army. Two infantry divisions, about 6,000 men, were on their way from Mississippi, en route to Dalton, Georgia, on the Western and Atlantic Railroad. The aggressive Bragg still hoped to attack Rosecrans, and looked for an opportunity to pounce on one of the Army of the Cumberland's widely separated columns as they snaked their way across Lookout Mountain and moved into the valley beyond. Bragg turned to Forrest and his cavalry to protect the potentially dangerous retreat. The army's infantry began evacuating Chattanooga as early as September 7. By the following day the logistical and industrial center was largely devoid of Southern troops.

Forrest's assignment was two-fold: screen the rear of the infantry as they pulled out, and provide at least one brigade to lead their progress south. Bragg ordered the army to concentrate twenty-one miles south of Chattanooga around Lafayette. Forrest was ordered to take at least Dibrell's Brigade ahead to secure the location and link up with Wheeler's cavalry.[1]

In preparation for this movement, and to begin fulfilling the first part of his assignment, Forrest ordered Pegram's troopers on September 6 to burn the bridge spanning the Hiwassee River at Charleston and ride south to Philadelphia, Tennessee.[2] The next day they moved farther south to Graysville, Georgia, a small village on the state line. There they remained for the next two days, acting as the army's rear guard while the infantry trekked past. On September 9, Forrest directed Scott's Brigade to move another dozen miles south along the railroad and secure Ringgold, Georgia. That left only one of Pegram's regiments, Rucker's Tennessee Legion under Col. E. W. Rucker, garrisoning Chattanooga. Seventy-five men from Lieutenant Colonel Mauldin's detachment of the 3rd Alabama Cavalry still manned the northern tip of Lookout Mountain. These two units represented the final vestige of Confederate strength in the city.[3]

Forrest personally supervised the other half of his mission. Instead of sending just Dibrell's cavalry brigade to Lafayette, Forrest moved with Frank Armstrong's entire division. Dibrell's troopers led the way with instructions to establish contact with Wheeler's cavalry. Forrest, Armstrong, and Armstrong's remaining brigade under Col. James T. Wheeler of the 6th Tennessee Cavalry followed Dibrell's men south. Instead of stopping in Lafayette as previously ordered Forrest pushed his command southward to Summerville, about forty miles below Chattanooga, which the troopers reached on September 8. Their goal was now Alpine, about ten miles farther southwest. The change in Forrest's orders came about because Joe Wheeler could or would not follow Bragg's.

---

1   OR 30, pt. 4, p. 611.

2   Jeffrey C. Weaver, *The Confederate Regimental History Series: The 5th and 7th Battalions North Carolina Cavalry and the 6th North Carolina Cavalry (65th North Carolina State Troops)* (n.p. 1995), p. 103.

3   OR 30, pt. 2, p. 523; Entry for September 8, 1863, Brent Journal; Gustave Huwald Letter, October 7, 1866, Leroy Moncure Nutt Papers, Southern Historical Collection, Wilson Library, University of North Carolina, Chapel Hill. Rucker's Legion was formed by the temporary merger of the 12th and 16th Tennessee cavalry battalions in June 1863. They were separated again in February 1864, when Colonel Rucker transferred to Mississippi to join his former commander (Forrest). While the legion (also known as the 1st East Tennessee Legion) was never officially designated as a cavalry regiment, it functioned as one throughout the campaign.

The army commander needed to uncover Union intentions in Wills Valley, and had been pressing Wheeler hard to make a strong reconnaissance there, to no avail. Instead, Wheeler offered a series of excuses about why such a scouting was unnecessary. By September 8, Bragg had had enough, and decided to use Forrest instead.[4]

That afternoon, when he discovered that Forrest now had responsibility for the Wills Valley mission, Wheeler reversed himself. Instead of steadfast inaction, he ordered Wharton to take 300 handpicked men from his own division and meet Forrest at Alpine, where Federal cavalry and infantry were rumored to be approaching in force. The next morning, this combined force of some 1,200 troopers departed from Alpine for a reconnaissance across Lookout Mountain.[5]

The major concentration of cavalry at Alpine might have triggered a significant fight the next day on September 9 had not Forrest's orders changed abruptly later that night. Bragg changed his mind and ordered the cavalry leader to ride back north to Lafayette.[6] Chattanooga was in Union hands, Federals were pursuing Bragg's rear guard aggressively, and John Pegram's troopers were having a difficult time holding them at bay.

Forrest was still riding south when the Army of Tennessee's headquarters left Chattanooga at 6:00 a.m. on September 8 on what proved to be a hot and dusty nine-mile trek to Lee and Gordon's Mills.[7] Bragg halted there to contemplate his next move. Given their dispersed nature, the individual Federal columns offered significant opportunities for a counterstroke. Despite the loss of Chattanooga and his ongoing intelligence problems, Bragg retained enough optimism and aggressiveness to think offensively. When the army finished concentrating at Lafayette, he would be in a position to strike in a number of different directions.

Also on the 8th, a Union patrol from Col. Smith D. Atkins' 92nd Illinois Mounted Infantry, part of John Wilder's mounted infantry brigade, slipped past Mauldin's Alabama screen and climbed to the northern summit of Lookout Mountain. From there, the Illinois troops enjoyed a breathtaking view of the

---

4   This curious episode is discussed in more detail in Chapter 6.

5   *OR* 30, pt. 4, p. 615 and pp. 627-8.

6   Jordan and Pryor, *Campaigns of Forrest*, pp. 305-6.

7   Entry for September 8, 1863, Brent Journal.

retreating Confederate columns. Rosecrans ordered the city occupied in force the next morning.[8] Early on September 9, the Atkins' 92nd Illinois led Maj. Gen. Thomas J. Wood's division of Crittenden's XXI Corps into Chattanooga after a short but sharp fight with the 3rd Alabama. Mauldin only mustered 75 men for the action, which cost him three killed and ten wounded. Both the Alabamians and Rucker's Tennessee Legion were chased out of town at a brisk trot.[9]

By 10:00 a.m., the flag of the 92nd Illinois floated proudly from the roof of the Crutchfield House, Chattanooga's finest hotel. The banner triggered a wave of cheers from the rest of Wilder's men, who were still on the far bank. That same afternoon Atkins' Illinois troops screened the advance of Maj. Gen. John M. Palmer's infantry division to Rossville, just a few miles south of Chattanooga. The infantry halted there, but the Illinois troops weren't yet done for the day. The 92nd rode back north to the Tennessee River, where they helped guide the balance of Wilder's brigade across to the south bank near the mouth of Chickamauga Creek. Their exhausting labors finally complete, the mounted infantry of the 92nd bivouacked that evening in a grape arbor, where the soldiers discovered their just reward: thirty full barrels of Catawba wine. The alcohol was promptly confiscated for the Union cause.[10] More important than the confiscated alcohol was the relocation of troops: all of John Wilder's powerful mounted command was now on the Confederate side of the Tennessee River.[11]

Following Wilder's lead, Hazen's and Wagner's infantry crossed the river at Frier's Island and occupied Chattanooga. Hazen's men rejoined their parent division under John Palmer (XXI Corps), while Wagner's troops assumed the role of permanent Federal garrison of the city. Minty's troopers tried to cross about twenty miles upstream at the mouth of Sale Creek, but the presence of unidentified Rebel cavalry aborted that effort. After waiting a day to make sure the enemy cavalry was not the head of a larger threat, on September 11 Minty

---

8   *Ninety-Second Illinois Volunteers* (Freeport, Illinois. Journal Steam Publishing House and Bookbindery, 1875), pp. 100-101.

9   *OR* 30, pt. 2, p. 71.

10   *Ninety-Second Illinois Volunteers*, p. 102. In the 19th Century, Catawba wine was one of the more popular varieties in the United States, so much so that in 1854, Henry Wadsworth Longfellow wrote an 11-stanza ode to the grape.

11   *OR* 30, pt. 1, p. 446.

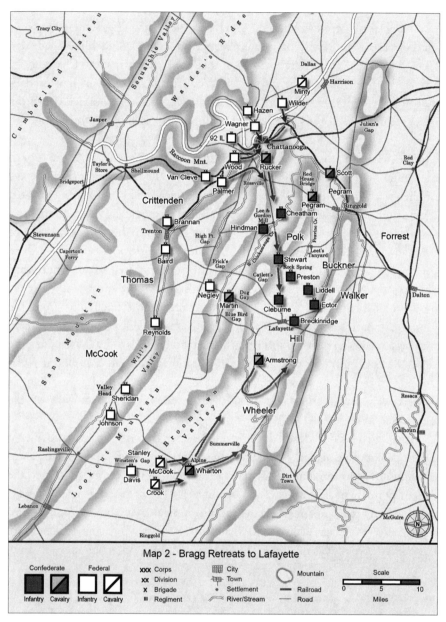

Map 2 - Bragg Retreats to Lafayette

Confederate		Federal				
▪	◪	☐	◫	XXX Corps	▦ City	Scale
Infantry	Cavalry	Infantry	Cavalry	XX Division	⊞ Town	0 5 10
				X Brigade	• Settlement	— Railroad	Miles
				lll Regiment	≈ River/Stream	— Road	

○ Mountain

By the beginning of the second week of September, Bragg has withdrawn from Chattanooga to Lafayette. Once again his army is out of position. Three of his four cavalry divisions are south of Lafayette facing the Federal threat from Alpine; only Pegram's and Scott's brigades are in position to protect the railroad running through Ringgold to Dalton. Without that line Bragg cannot supply his army, and defending it will become critically important over the next few days. Bragg realizes his vulnerability by September 9 and orders Armstrong's Division to reverse course back north.

rode down to Chattanooga and the next day crossed his command at Frier's Island.[12]

It was this rapid Union occupation of Chattanooga that convinced Bragg he needed to bolster his rear guard. Forrest would have to be recalled. Late on the 8th, Bragg sent the cavalry leader new orders to dispatch Armstrong's Division back to Lafayette while Forrest reported to Bragg personally at Lee and Gordon's Mills. The cavalryman wasted no time in effecting Bragg's orders. The troopers reversed course immediately. When the corps leader arrived, Bragg directed Forrest "to repair northward [and] ascertain definitely the movements of the enemy in the direction of Chattanooga."[13]

Once again the Tennessean complied promptly. By the morning of the 9th Forrest was at Dalton, where he established his corps headquarters and set about assuming control of Pegram's scattered forces. Armstrong's men would come on as best they could. Even a man of Forrest's legendary endurance must have been sorely taxed by this constant activity. He'd been in the saddle for most of the last twenty-four hours, and had ridden more than sixty miles. Armstrong's troopers had covered almost as much territory. The ride to Summerville and backtracking to Lafayette spanned at least forty miles. These abrupt changes of orders reveal Bragg's uncertain grasp of events, which translated into undue strain on both horses and men.

Forrest's new mission called for him to reinforce Pegram's Division and establish a cavalry screen between Chattanooga and Bragg's concentrating army. As Forrest soon discovered, the direct road south from Chattanooga to Lafayette lacked a cavalry screen. Pegram's men were already spread thin guarding the railroad from Graysville to Ringgold, and he did not have enough men to stretch a credible line that far west. Lieutenant General Leonidas Polk's infantry corps at Lee and Gordon's Mills blocked that route south, but Polk needed horsemen to screen his own front. Forrest ordered Armstrong's Division to report to Polk.

Armstrong's men had already reported to Polk that morning, and all the marching and countermarching triggered no little consternation in the ranks. On September 8, Pvt. Thomas W. Davis of the 6th Tennessee recalled the miserable ride back to Lafayette and of the need to leave the horses "saddled all

12 *Ibid.*, p. 925.

13 Jordan and Pryor, *Campaigns of Forrest*, p. 306.

night. I slept very cold." The next day brought with it a terrible realization, as Thomas confided in his diary:

> Gen. Bragg dispatches for a good brigade [and] Armstrong's is sent. The Gen.
> goes forward—pass Gen. Hill's corps of infantry. It is much jaded by the
> recent march. I learn from them that Chattanooga has been evacuated—it
> evolves a mingled emotion of disappointment & vexation. Found Gen. Brag
> on the Chickamauga at Lee & Gordon's Mill—Rosecranz has achieved a great
> victory without the loss of a man. It will cause a thrill of joy to vibrate through
> the entire Yankee nation.[14]

Forrest's men had returned not a moment too soon. The next day, with nearly the entire Federal Army of the Cumberland firmly established south of the Tennessee River and Chattanooga secured, Rosecrans ordered Crittenden's XXI Corps to resume its advance. Early on September 10, a Union infantry brigade under Brig. Gen. Charles Cruft left Rossville and marched southeast on the Federal Road for Ringgold, about ten miles distant. Cruft's brigade was but the advance guard of Palmer's entire division. Behind Palmer marched Brig. Gen. Horatio Van Cleve's division in support. Combined, Palmer and Van Cleve totaled 10,000 infantry, all aimed directly at Ringgold and the Western and Atlantic Railroad, Bragg's lifeline to Atlanta. By mid-morning the Yankee column was at Graysville, about half way to their objective.[15]

Pegram's Confederate brigade was stretched thin in an effort to watch multiple avenues of advance, so only the 6th Georgia Cavalry and the 6th North Carolina Cavalry were available to oppose the thrust against Ringgold. The troopers did as best they could, triggering a brisk skirmish outside Graysville. The firing brought Cruft's vanguard to a halt. Unsure of what he faced, the brigadier deployed the bulk of his command on a ridge overlooking Peavine Creek and sent the Union 1st Kentucky Infantry and two companies of cavalry forward across the stream to reconnoiter. The Federal horseman formed a mounted skirmish line and led the advance, while the 1st Kentucky remained

---

14 Entries for September 8th and 9th, "The Civil War Diary (June - November, 1863) of Thomas W. Davis," Chattanooga Public Library, Chattanooga, TN.

15 Rosecrans wanted to cut the Western and Atlantic Railroad to deny its use to Bragg. That line, however, was not useable for the Federals because their railhead was still back at Bridgeport, where the railroad bridge spanning the Tennessee River had been destroyed.

formed in column on the road as support. While Cruft was deploying and tentatively creeping forward, Pegram used an unfinished railroad bed, not shown on Federal maps, to move the two Rebel regiments from Graysville to the Peavine Creek Bridge. Most of his command was dismounted and deployed in a skirmish line astride the Ringgold Road, but part of the 6th Georgia remained horsed and in reserve. Pegram sent two companies of Georgians charging down the unfinished railroad bed to strike the 1st Kentucky in the flank. The result was more than he could have hoped for: an entire company of bluecoats, fifty-eight men, was captured with scarcely a shot fired.[16] The rest of the Federals retreated as fast as they could across Peavine Creek. Forrest arrived at the tail end of the action, just in time to see the Union prisoners being herded south. "Shortly after, Gen. Forrest came up," recalled a Rebel gunner, "and being told of the taking of the prisoners, he only regretted, in his blunt way, that they had not been killed in the fight."[17]

Later that day, Cruft made one more effort to cross the creek, this time with a much larger force. After bringing up a second Union brigade to watch the Graysville flank, several of Cruft's regiments waded the stream and advanced in skirmish order. The reconnaissance flushed out few Rebels, and the advance halted about one mile east of the creek. The Federal column turned about and returned to Rossville that night. Despite blunting the move toward Ringgold and the Western and Atlantic Railroad, Pegram realized he was heavily outnumbered and decided not to loiter any longer at Graysville. The Confederates fell back, riding south to Rock Springs Church, about halfway to Lafayette and several miles southwest of Ringgold. Pegram rendezvoused there with Rucker's Legion and established contact with Frank Armstrong's cavalry, taking up a new position astride the Lafayette Road.[18]

Forrest hurried reports of the day's events and enemy movements to both Polk and Bragg. The offensive-minded cavalry leader, who believed that two of Crittenden's XXI Corps divisions were just south of Graysville at Red House

16 OR 30, pt. 1, pp. 23-5. James H. Ogden, Park Historian, Chickamauga-Chattanooga National Military Park, first alerted me to the presence of the unfinished railroad bed and its significance to this skirmish. Cruft was furious at the capture, and clearly felt that the men of the 1st Kentucky had given up without a fight. Among other things, he demanded, "how could 58 men be captured by cavalry without sabers in a narrow road with thick underbrush on each side?"

17 Huwald Letter, October 7, 1866.

18 OR 30, pt. 2, p. 72.

Bridge, and a third division was at Rossville six miles to the rear, saw an opportunity to strike.[19] In reality, all three Union divisions camped that night along the old Federal Road between West Chickamauga Creek and Peavine Creek only two miles apart. Crittenden's corps, however, was nine miles south of Chattanooga and more than twenty miles from any other Union troops. When midnight arrived without a reply, Forrest rode to Lee and Gordon's Mills hoping to find someone with enough seniority to act. Both Bragg and Polk were gone by the time Forrest arrived. Polk departed with orders to move his infantry to Lafayette, and Bragg left for a midnight meeting with D. H. Hill. Only Armstrong's cavalry remained in the vicinity.

Armstrong had already provided Polk with helpful assistance. On the morning of the 10th, wrote Lt. W. B. Richmond, alarming reports from Colonel Rucker threw Polk's headquarters into confusion. "Rucker was full retreat," wrote Richmond, "and the enemy only three quarters of a mile away, and advancing. The whole staff were at once mounted, a number ordered to the various brigade headquarters, and the whole of Cheatham's division placed under arms. . . . The whole camp excited, and all through the stampeding report of the cavalry."[20]

When Polk called upon Armstrong for assistance, the cavalry commander rode north and established a screen across the Lafayette Road. Armstrong arrived at the McDonald house, a substantial dwelling about four miles north of Lee and Gordon's Mills, about 2:30 p.m. There, he found Rucker's regiment intact—reports of its rout exaggerated. Rucker informed Armstrong of Pegram's location and the Union probe toward Graysville, though he did not know where Pegram's other brigade under Colonel Scott was currently stationed. Throughout the rest of the afternoon and evening, Armstrong kept Polk informed about his screening arrangements, the fight at Graysville, his various reconnaissance missions, and his contacts with Pegram's men. The steady stream of detailed messages painted a picture of a competent professional pitching in with a will, which Polk's headquarters staff digested with relief.[21]

---

19 Jordan and Pryor, *Campaigns of Forrest*, p. 306.

20 *OR* 30, pt. 2, p. 72.

21 *Ibid.*, pp. 72-73. Colonel Rucker's lack of knowledge about the rest of the division is Pegram's fault. Pegram was in contact with Rucker and had sent Scott to hold Ringgold, but apparently did not inform Rucker about Scott's deployment.

New threats against Ringgold developed the following day: Wilder's mounted infantry brigade was back. After crossing below the Tennessee River the previous day, Crittenden shoved Wilder in front to lead the advance of the XXI Corps. Wilder dispatched a small scouting party to investigate the rumor that two Rebel regiments were holding Ringgold. In fact, the village was defended by Scott's entire cavalry brigade. Somehow, Wilder's men missed seeing them and reported Ringgold unoccupied. According to current intelligence reports, no Rebels were closer than Dalton, fifteen miles southeast on the Western and Atlantic Railroad.[22]

Wilder's mounted infantry may have missed Scott's men, but the Southern troopers were more than aware of Wilder's presence. Forrest was on hand early and deployed the Louisianan's troopers to defend Ringgold.[23] The fluid day-long affair that followed drove Scott's men nearly half way to Dalton. The problem, explained Lt. W. G. Allen of the 5th Tennessee Cavalry, was that "His [Wilder's] brigade would flank our right and we would fall back and fight until we were flanked again."[24] Scott was both heavily outnumbered and outgunned. Wilder entered the fight with about 2,500 men, while Scott counted only 1,200, and the Union mounted infantry was armed with Spencer seven-shot repeating rifles, which gave them a significant edge in firepower. These advantages allowed Wilder to overlap and turn Scott's line again and again. By late afternoon, the outmatched Rebels retired to a final line about one-half mile south of Tunnel Hill, Georgia, five miles south of Ringgold. Just before dark, Dibrell's Brigade and Capt. John W. Morton's artillery battery, both of Armstrong's Division, arrived to reinforce Scott's exhausted command.[25]

---

22 *OR* 30, 3, pp. 512-3.

23 After midnight, Forrest's movements are hard to trace. If he left Lee and Gordon's Mills to ride to his headquarters in Dalton, the trip of about fifteen miles would have left him little time to sleep. It is more likely that he either spent the night at Armstrong's camp or with Pegram's men. Scott's accounts make it clear that Forrest was on hand at Ringgold very early on September 11, and directed the fighting there the entire day. See Forrest's Report, *OR* 30, pt. 2, p. 524, and Scott's report, *ibid.*, p. 530.

24 William G. Allen Memoirs, 5th Tennessee Cavalry, Tennessee State Library and Archives.

25 Where Dibrell's men came from or if they came to Scott's aid by design or by accident is unclear. Morton, *The Artillery of Nathan Bedford Forrest's Cavalry*, p. 113, infers he was with Forrest and Scott most of the day, though without actually providing much detail on how he got there. Cotten, *The Williamson County Cavalry*, p. 127, claims that Dibrell's men were returning from a scouting mission around Dalton and, hearing the firing, rushed to Scott's aid on their own. Jordan and Pryor, *Campaigns of Forrest*, p. 307, merely state that Dibrell came up "after his

Additional help in the form of men from Pegram's command threatened to flank Wilder from their position near Peavine Church. This combination of stiffening resistance, coupled with a threat to his flank, stopped Wilder for the night.

September 11 had been a difficult day for Forrest's troopers. John Scott's retreat had triggered a general withdrawal of the entire Confederate cavalry line. At dawn on the 11th, Armstrong's headquarters was still at the McDonald house. Armstrong had already given up one brigade under Colonel Dibrell for a scouting mission around Dalton. This left Armstrong with only one other brigade—Col. James Wheeler's—under his immediate command. The first inkling Armstrong received regarding a threat to his right flank was when Pegram's troopers fell back about 7:30 a.m. Pegram's retreat was triggered by Scott's withdrawal after Wilder turned him out of Ringgold, which in turn exposed Armstrong's eastern (right) flank. With Federal infantry from Brig. Gen. Thomas J. Wood's division pressing him from Rossville, Armstrong withdrew to Lee and Gordon's Mills, where he struggled to protect the Lafayette Road while maintaining a connection with Pegram.[26] Wood's Federals promptly followed Armstrong. By that afternoon, Armstrong had little choice but to abandon the Mills for a less exposed position a couple miles south at Rock Springs Church. Leonidas Polk's newly established headquarters at Dr. Anderson's house was nearby. The Federals halted at Lee and Gordon's Mills, content with their gains.

Determined to try and figure out what the enemy was up to, Forrest set out that night on a hazardous personal reconnaissance. He was personally brave to a fault and possessed a flair for the dramatic, but the undertaking demonstrated that he was still thinking and operating like a captain rather than a corps commander. Leading his personal escort company, Forrest reached the picket line of the 5th Tennessee Cavalry. Despite the best efforts of 5th Tennessee's Lieutenant Allen, who had orders to let no one pass, Forrest brushed the officer aside and he and his men spurred their mounts north into Tunnel Hill, which was currently hosting Wilder's brigade. The reconnaissance triggered a brisk but short skirmish that left the corps leader and two from his escort wounded. One of Forrest's staff officers, Lt. Mattew Cortner, was captured by the 98th Illinois

---

reconnaissance" to Dalton. Why Dibrell was not with Armstrong, and whether Forrest ordered Dibrell to the front, remain unanswered questions.

26 *OR* 30, pt. 2, p. 74.

Mounted Infantry.[27] The episode rankled Lieutenant Allen, who confessed, "I formed an unfavorable opinion of him [Forrest] because he rode rough shod over me while on duty."[28]

Fortunately for the Confederate cause, Forrest's wound was minor and did not render him unfit for duty. The only detailed description of the injury—which was described as "painful, but not dangerous"—claims the bullet struck him near the spine within one inch of a similar wound he received at Shiloh. The wound seems not to have slowed down the vigorous cavalryman, as his movements over the next few days clearly demonstrate. The reconnaissance, however, revealed nothing of importance and risked the life of one of Bragg's best officers. The effort was a risk no corps leader should ever have undertaken.[29]

September 12 dawned with Forrest's corps scattered and Armstrong's Division divided. Armstrong was operating with Colonel Wheeler's Brigade near Rock Springs, guarding the Lafayette Road. Dibrell's Brigade was miles away near Tunnel Hill, along with Scott's Brigade. Both Scott and Dibrell were apparently taking orders directly from Forrest, bypassing their respective division commanders. Pegram and his former brigade were still at Peavine Church.[30] The situation demonstrates the convoluted nature of the Southern cavalry command structure. Both division commanders were doing little more than directing their former brigades. The tactically capable Forrest was not making effective use of his chain of command.

Like the preceding two days, September 12 also promised to be busy. Crittenden's XXI Corps was now more divided than ever. Van Cleve's and Palmer's divisions had followed Wilder as far as Ringgold, where they camped on the evening of the 11th. Thomas Wood's division, which had shoved Armstrong's troopers south along Lafayette Road, halted at Lee and Gordon's

---

27 Entry for September 11, 1863, Edward Kitchell Diary, Lincoln Library, Springfield, IL. Kitchell recorded Cortner's name as Lieutenant Cortue. Confederate documents show that Lt. Matthew Cortner was captured just before Chickamauga and later paroled and exchanged. Discussion with Historian Michael R. Bradley, May 10, 2005.

28 William G. Allen Memoirs, Tennessee State Library and Archives.

29 By a Confederate, *The Grayjackets: And How They Lived, Fought, And Died, For Dixie* (Jones, Brothers and co., n.d.), pp. 356-7. See also Jordan and Pryor, *Campaigns of Forrest*, p. 308, who claimed Forrest was "little disturbed" by the injury.

30 It will be recalled that the Henry B. Davidson, elevated to brigadier general, was on his way to assume command of Pegram's former brigade, but had not yet arrived.

Mills.[31] Advancing Van Cleve and Palmer toward Dalton would further partition Crittenden's already divided command and increase the distance between his already isolated corps and the rest of the Federal army operating many miles to the southwest on Lookout Mountain and the valleys it overlooked. Accordingly, Crittenden decided on the morning of the 12th to concentrate all three of his divisions (Van Cleve, Palmer, and Wood) at Lee and Gordon's Mills. The left flank of the Union movement would be covered by the ubiquitous Wilder and his rapid-firing mounted infantry.[32] The movement of heavy Federal columns across his front provoked alarm at General Polk's headquarters. Lieutenant Richmond recorded that three Union divisions were converging on Rock Springs (a few miles below the Mills), a natural assumption given the routes of march.

Wilder's men left Tunnel Hill at first light and headed back toward Ringgold. There, Wilder sent the 92nd Illinois to Rossville in response to reports of Rebel cavalry operating in his rear, while the rest of the brigade turned south on a side road west of Taylor's Ridge leading to Leet's Spring and Tanyard.[33] Riding at the head of his former brigade, Pegram was also up early that morning. He led his men east from Peavine Church toward the same destination. Because they had less distance to travel, Pegram's troopers arrived first. He stopped his men there to rest. Some bathed in the spring or did their laundry, hanging it out to dry in the warm morning sun, while others gathered fodder for the horses.[34] Pegram wisely dispatched fifteen men to scout the road in the direction of Ringgold, but the patrol blundered into Wilder's Yankees. Every man was killed or captured before any warning could be sent.[35] As a result, when the rest of Pegram's men saddled up and headed up Ringgold Road, they were unaware of the danger awaiting them. The first hint of trouble arrived when the lead regiment, the 6th Georgia Cavalry, discovered a line of horsemen in the woods atop a ridge on their flank. A fight developed within a

---

31 For the locations of Crittenden's divisions on the morning of the 12th, see Entries for September 11 and 12, "Summaries of the news reaching Headquarters of General W. S. Rosecrans, 1863-64" NARA; *OR* 30, pt. 3, pp. 574-5; *ibid.*, pt. 1, p. 604.

32 *OR* 30, pt. 2, p. 76.

33 *Ninety-Second Illinois Volunteers*, p. 103.

34 J. W. Minnich, "Unique Experiences in the Chickamauga Campaign" *Confederate Veteran*, Vol. 30, issue #6 (June, 1922), p. 222.

35 Huwald Letter, October 7, 1866.

few minutes and the Georgians fell back in some disorder to the clearing at Leet's.

There, the 6th North Carolina Cavalry and one of Capt. Gustave Huwald's guns were deployed on a ridge overlooking the spring in an effort to hold off the Yankees while Pegram tried to form the rest of the brigade in line about one-half mile south.[36] Wilder, meanwhile, dismounted the 17th and 72nd Indiana Mounted Infantry regiments and sent them forward against the North Carolinians. A brisk fight developed. Rather than risk a frontal attack, Wilder shifted four companies of the 72nd Indiana to the east to flank the shorter Rebel line.[37] This move prompted the 6th North Carolina to retreat to Pegram's second line.

Even armed with Spencer repeating rifles, Wilder's men approached this new line with caution. The 17th and 72nd Indiana still led the way, with the 98th Illinois moving behind them in support. Once again, Col. Abram Miller of the 72nd eschewed a frontal attack for another flanking attempt against Pegram's right with the same four companies of Hoosiers.[38] This time, the 120 or so men of the flanking party shifted into the woods on the left of the 72nd only to discover they were confronting both the 6th Georgia and Rucker's Tennessee Legion. With some 600 men deployed and ready, the Confederate line was longer and stronger than the Indianans expected. Instead of turning the Rebel flank, they found their own left overlapped by Rucker's men.[39] The fighting that followed, recalled John Bernard of the 72nd, "proved disastrous for some of our boys."[40] Within minutes the four companies lost sixteen killed and wounded and withdrew.

The sudden change in circumstance gave even the aggressive Wilder reason for concern. Advancing against strong Confederate opposition would be a costly proposition, and troubling information was coming in from the flanks.

36 Minnich, "Unique Experiences," p. 222, and OR 30, pt. 2, p. 528. Pegram claimed that his new line was only 400 yards to the rear, but Minnich disputes that distance. I have concluded that Minnich is more likely correct.

37 Entry for September 12, 1863, William H. Records Diary, Indiana State Library. Indianapolis, IN.

38 OR 30, pt. 1, p. 451.

39 For the strength of the Confederate units, see Powell, *Strengths and Losses*, CCNMP.

40 John M. Bernard to his wife and children, September 15, 1863, William Henry Smith Memorial Library, Indiana Historical Society, Indianapolis, IN.

Scott's Confederates had followed the mounted enemy infantry from Tunnel Hill and reoccupied Ringgold. Instead of stopping there, they continued along the road Wilder's men had just traversed and were now pressing his rear guard, the 123rd Illinois Mounted Infantry. Word also arrived from the 92nd Illinois that another 600 Rebel troopers were operating near Rossville, where they attacked a Union wagon train. Only the 92nd's timely arrival had saved the wagons.[41] Read together, these reports suggested that Wilder's "Lightning Brigade" was nearly surrounded. Wilder decided that the wisest course was a retreat northwest to Rossville, where he expected to find Union infantry.

Darkness was approaching when Wilder broke contact with Pegram and retreated northwest toward Peavine Church. The wily Union commander moved only a couple of miles before setting up a decoy camp in the dark. His men built a wide swath of campfires and arranged picket lines as if intending to halt for the night. Once it was dark enough to mask movement, however, they slipped away.[42] The ruse so fooled the Confederates that Pegram even asked for infantry support for a dawn attack against the non-existent Union camp. The request was answered in the form of Maj. Gen. Benjamin F. Cheatham's Division of Polk's Corps, which had just arrived at Rock Springs Church from Lafayette. Cheatham moved forward about two miles and deployed in battle line, his men spending the night awaiting an order to attack that never arrived.[43] Pegram's troopers rushed the "camp" at first light only to discover it devoid of any enemy. Wilder's men were already at Lee and Gordon's Mills, which they reached about midnight after a difficult, tiring, but ultimately uneventful eight-mile ride.[44]

By the morning of September 13, Crittenden's XXI Corps, Wilder's brigade, and Minty's cavalry, just sent down from Chattanooga, were deployed at the Mills. They were still isolated from the rest of the army, but they now were far less vulnerable to any attack Bragg might be able to muster against them.

---

41 OR 30, pt. 1, p. 455. This unknown regiment was one of Armstrong's units.

42 Entry for September 12, 1863, Records Diary.

43 Entry for September 13, 1863, William Sylvester Dillon Diary, Georgia Department of Archives and History.

44 Entry for September 12, 1863, Records Diary.

C hapter 6

The Left Flank:
Bragg Resumes the Offensive
(September 6-15, 1863)

T he limited and often contradictory intelligence reports Braxton Bragg received while his army was still holding Chattanooga suggested William Rosecrans's Army of the Cumberland was dispersed across a wide front. If true, these Federal dispositions presented an opportunity to attack and destroy the enemy in detail.[1] The question remained: Where to strike?

The intelligence flowing into Bragg's headquarters was insufficient for him to determine which enemy columns comprised the main body and which represented feints. On September 5, as he abandoned the idea of attacking north of the Tennessee River with D. H. Hill's infantry, Bragg once again prodded senior cavalry commander Joe Wheeler to assume a more aggressive posture.

At this time, Wheeler's two divisions were deployed atop Lookout Mountain, extending Colonel Mauldin's original picket line of Alabamians much farther south. Mauldin's line ended near Trenton, but when reports placed Federals far beyond that location, Wheeler deployed troopers another

---

1 *OR* 20, pt. 2, pp. 27-28. Bragg's report discusses his reasons for withdrawing from Chattanooga, and that in pursuing, the enemy "thus exposed himself in detail."

forty miles south, establishing a new line running from Lafayette all the way to Blue Pond Gap, Alabama. Wheeler posted detachments at each gap and mountain crossing, but few if any Rebels ventured across Lookout Mountain and down into Wills Valley, which by this time was filling up with Federals.[2]

Late on September 5, Bragg sent Wheeler an unequivocal directive to push a reconnaissance into Wills Valley: "The General commanding directs that you will, without delay, move with your command into the valley, drive in the enemy's pickets, and assail him so as to develop his designs, strength, and position. This must be done even at the sacrifice of troops. The General expects a rapid movement and prompt report."[3] Bragg's urgency was understandable. Federals that far south were closer to Bragg's railroad lifeline than his own army, and if they were present in significant strength they could easily cut Bragg off from Atlanta before he could react. On the face of it, there seemed little room for argument or interpretation.

Wheeler, however, provided only excuses. In a lengthy missive dispatched the next afternoon, Wheeler ticked off a laundry list of reasons why he could not obey Bragg's order. His troops were scattered across a front some forty miles long, he explained, and felled trees blocked the gaps. The information Bragg wanted, he chastised, could be discovered by "other means," and Wheeler assumed Bragg "would not desire great risks run or almost insuperable difficulties overcome."[4] Bragg's order to carry out the mission even if it cost the lives of men—"This must be done even at the sacrifice of troops"—was an explicit example that Bragg indeed expected his cavalryman to run "great risks" if necessary to gain the information the army required so desperately. Wheeler, though, appears to have treated that passage as mere rhetoric. Wheeler's litany continued. He would not find out anything even if he did as directed, he insisted, and riding into Wills Valley would render his horses unserviceable. The move would leave Rome, Georgia, exposed to the enemy, and he would have to fight his way into the valley because Federals picketed the gaps on their side of the mountain. The most damning sentence in Wheeler's September 6 reply reveals a great deal about what Wheeler regarded as the proper role of cavalry

2 *Ibid.*, 30, pt. 4, pp. 585-6, details Wheeler's dispositions. Blue Pond Gap is near present-day Cedar Bluff, Alabama, on the shores of Weiss Lake Reservoir in northwest Alabama. Wheeler's "line" stretched some 45 to 50 miles.

3 *Ibid.*, p. 602.

4 *Ibid.*, p. 614.

on campaign, and where his understanding of his role diverged from Bragg's: "I thought if General Rosecrans' Army was commencing a vigorous campaign upon us, it was of the first importance that our cavalry be kept in as good a condition as possible, as it would be indispensable to protect our lines of communication."[5]

Wheeler was wrong. It was of the first importance that his men discover what Rosecrans was up to and promptly inform Bragg so the Confederate army could act accordingly. Defending lines of communication was only a secondary mission at this point of the campaign. The exchange reveals just how far apart Bragg's and Wheeler's expectations were regarding the role of cavalry.

In short, Wheeler was not about to do what Bragg ordered be done. Instead, he continued to forward intelligence of limited value, painting Union dispositions in sketchy terms. For example, on September 4 Wheeler informed Bragg that the Federals in Wills Valley amounted to 4,000 or 5,000 troops; in his September 6 response, the cavalryman suggested that number had been reinforced to corps strength.[6] If the former were true, there was probably no more than a division of cavalry in the valley—suggesting the move there was a feint. If the latter were correct, however, it suggested the move into Wills Valley was a main thrust and thus a very real threat against both Bragg's army and his line of communications with Atlanta. Apparently, Wheeler's "other means" of discovering enemy designs were unable to tell the difference. In fact, the Federal force was indeed substantial. By September 6, the little settlement at Valley Head, Alabama (site of Winston's Spring, a major water source for upper Wills Valley), hosted 15,000 Yankees, including not only four brigades of Union cavalry but also two infantry divisions of McCook's XX Corps, with another infantry division not far away.[7]

Wheeler's insubordinate refusal to scout into Wills Valley almost compelled Bragg to send Forrest to do the job. As described previously, Forrest moved Armstrong's Division to Lafayette on September 8. Bragg ordered him

5 *Ibid.*, p. 615.

6 *Ibid.*, p. 614.

7 These four Union cavalry brigades, about 6,000 strong, comprised the main body of Rosecrans' Cavalry Corps, while the two infantry divisions of McCook's XX Corps numbered about 4,500 men each. The third division, when it joined the corps, would add another 4,000 men. NARA, RG 94, Returns for XX Corps and Cavalry Corps, Army of the Cumberland, September 10, 1863. For the actual Union dispositions, see *OR* 30, pt. 2, p. 485, and S. H. Stevens, "Second Division Itinerary" CCNMP.

to continue immediately southwest to Alpine. Bragg's initial instructions to Forrest were to slow the expected Union advance on Rome.[8] With Forrest on hand, Wheeler ordered John Wharton to detail 300 hand-picked men to unite with Forrest and the latter's leading brigade, some 900 men of Col. Dibrell's command, for a reconnaissance west of Lookout Mountain. Wharton's men, instructed Wheeler, should "include those officers and men, who, having already scouted the mountain, are familiar with that section of the country."[9] The expedition was to depart from Alpine at 9:00 a.m. on September 9. What prompted Wheeler to reverse course and prepare a major expedition into Wills Valley is not clear, except that now, perhaps, he reasoned that the bulk of the risks would be borne by Forrest's men instead of his own.

Nothing came of this expedition. On the night of September 8, Bragg abruptly recalled Forrest back to Lafayette, and from there back to Ringgold to bolster Pegram's crumbling rearguard. With Forrest now unavailable for any scouting missions into Wills Valley, the probe was cancelled. Without Forrest's reinforcements, Wheeler reverted to form and called off Wharton's role in the mission as well.

* * *

Wheeler was content to let well enough alone in Wills Valley, but Rosecrans was not. Like Bragg, the Federal commander was also unhappy about how parts of his army had performed thus far. McCook's XX Corps and his Cavalry Corps had spent three largely inactive days around Valley Head. It was time to get moving. Rosecrans pressured both McCook and Maj. Gen. David S. Stanley, his cavalry commander, to drive ahead.[10]

Unlike Joe Wheeler, Stanley got the message. On September 8, he ordered Brig. Gen. George Crook to push the cavalry across Lookout Mountain to Alpine, clearing the way for the infantry to follow. That night, the Federals climbed Lookout Mountain and camped, intending to descend the eastern side the next morning. Finding the main road blocked with recently felled trees, the column detoured to a second road, which was similarly blockaded. These

---

8 *OR* 30, pt. 4, p. 628.

9 *Ibid.*, p. 627.

10 *Ibid.*, pt. 3, pp. 397-8, 412.

obstacles, which Wheeler claimed presented an "almost insuperable difficulty" for his own troopers, were removed in short order by the Yankees. "Before we left camp," wrote an officer in the 4th Ohio, "20 men were detailed from each Reg't with axes & they did their work so well that the column was delayed only a short time."[11] By noon the Yankee cavalry had reached the eastern foot of Lookout Mountain and were skirmishing with the Rebels.[12] Elements of two of Wharton's regiments, the 8th Texas and 4th Georgia Cavalry, held the pass for a while but were unable to stop a full enemy brigade. That night, Wharton's men retreated northeast to Summerville, about one-half the distance to Lafayette. The skirmishing cost the 1st Ohio Cavalry alone 30 killed and wounded. Confederate losses are unknown.[13]

Wharton assumed a blocking position around Summerville, but much of his scattered division was still being recalled from the various gaps it had been sent to watch. Moreover, to Bragg's continued discomfort, accurate information on Federal numbers remained elusive. On the 9th, Wharton forwarded on messages to headquarters estimating Union opposition between 4,000 and 40,000 men—which was no help at all.[14]

The Federal horsemen occupied Alpine, and McCook's infantry soon followed. One division camped atop Lookout Mountain that night, taking possession of the gaps leading down the east side of the escarpment. By September 10, McCook had established his corps headquarters in Alpine. Two of his three infantry divisions were camped there, while the third, under Philip H. Sheridan, marched up to Valley Head.[15]

From Alpine, the XX Corps was well positioned to march on Lafayette from the south up another long and narrow mountain valley. Broomtown, as the valley was called locally, was geographically similar to Sequatchie and Wills valleys. About three miles wide, well watered and with plenty of forage,

---

11 Entry for September 8, 1863, Lieutenant James Thompson Diary, 4th Ohio Cavalry file, CCNMP.

12 Entry for September 8, 1863, Captain William E. Crane Diary, 4th Ohio Cavalry, General Thomas' Papers, RG 94, NARA.

13 *Proceedings of the Thirtieth Annual Reunion, 1st O.V.V.C.* (Columbus, OH, n.p. 1909), p. 16. Confederate participants barely mention the action or their subsequent retreat. Had General Forrest not been recalled northward the day before, this might have been a more substantial action because the 900 men of Dibrell's Brigade would also have been present.

14 *OR* 30, pt. 4, p. 630.

15 *Ibid.*, pt. 1, p. 486.

Broomtown Valley was bounded by Lookout Mountain on the west and Taylor's Ridge on the east. Most significantly, Lafayette was only fifteen miles to the north with no rough terrain intervening. On September 10, McCook expected to find George Thomas' XIV Corps either occupying Lafayette or poised to capture it. The Federals needed the town to control the rest of Broomtown Valley and to reestablish direct communications between all three of Rosecrans' infantry corps. With McCook and Thomas at Lafayette, the wings of the Army of the Cumberland would be no more than thirty miles apart on good valley roads that provided excellent lateral communications between each corps. With Lafayette in enemy hands, McCook could only communicate with the rest of the army by sending dispatch riders back over the same torturous mountain roads by which he had come, a trip of some sixty miles.

Two pieces of information that reached McCook at Alpine brought his advance to an abrupt halt. The first bit of news was the result of a cavalry reconnaissance toward Lafayette. Instead of conducting a deep retreat, Bragg was concentrating the Rebel army around Lafayette.[16] The second report arrived the next day from Thomas: his Federals would not reach Lafayette until September 12 at the earliest.[17] If McCook advanced before Thomas arrived, the XX Corps would be in serious jeopardy of being crushed by Bragg's entire army.

Command problems were not unique to Bragg's Army of the Tennessee. Stanley was so sick he could no longer ride a horse. He left the front and entered a field hospital at Stevenson on the 17th. His second in command, Brig. Gen. Robert B. Mitchell, was a Kansas politician in whom Stanley had no confidence.[18] No one expected aggressive or competent action from Mitchell. With Stanley's loss and Mitchell's elevation, McCook felt more isolated than ever.

On the day the Union horsemen entered Alpine, George Thomas' leading division under Maj. Gen. James S. Negley also descended the eastern face of

---

16 Summaries of News Received at Rosecrans Headquarters, RG 393, NARA.

17 *OR* 30, pt. 3, p. 538.

18 David S. Stanley, *Personal Memoirs Of Major General D. S. Stanley, U.S.A.* (Harvard University Press, 1917), pp. 134-5, 158. Robert B. Mitchell was a pre-war lawyer who served in the Mexican War before moving to Kansas. He was wounded at Wilson's Creek, and led an infantry division at Perryville. His field service ended with Chickamauga. After that battle, he was ordered to Washington to sit on a courts-martial board, and ended his wartime career heading up the departments of Nebraska and Kansas.

Lookout Mountain.[19] Negley eased into the wedge-shaped valley of McLemore's Cove, formed by an angled offshoot of Lookout called Pigeon Mountain. Lafayette and Broomtown Valley were a short distance east of Pigeon Mountain. Although Negley led the advance of Thomas' corps, he did so alone. Except for a company or two of his own escort, he had no cavalry and so no mounted screen worthy of the name to protect his front. Thomas' remaining divisions were still struggling through the choked passes on Lookout Mountain. Eyeing Pigeon Mountain as an additional obstacle between his division and Lafayette, and without proper cavalry pickets and a ready reserve to call upon, Negley advanced cautiously.

With McCook at Alpine, Negley in McLemore's Cove, and Crittenden at Lee and Gordon's Mills, Bragg found himself facing serious threats from several directions. On the morning of September 9, he ordered Joe Wheeler to send all of William Martin's small cavalry division into McLemore's Cove to oppose Negley's advance.[20] Martin and one of his regiments, the 51st Alabama Cavalry, were already in the cove reporting on the Federal activity, but Bragg wanted a stronger Rebel presence there. The Confederates had been picking and prodding at the Union column from horseback. The troopers pestered the Yankees into something of a game by galloping suddenly into full view of the enemy to provoke a chase. At one point overconfidence crept in and three young Rebels strayed a little too close. A dozen Federals from Negley's escort took off after them in pursuit, hauling in one of the trio within half a mile. The young Rebel left a memoir after the war about a conversation he claimed to have conducted with Negley himself: "[Negley's] first words were, 'Well, Johnny, are you not tired of fighting?' 'I am not, General,' I replied. 'Well, it seems to me,' he continued, 'that it would be policy for a rat to leave a sinking ship.' 'It might be policy, General, but not principle,' I replied. 'I am going down with the ship.'"[21]

Negley's division, about 5,000 strong, camped that night at the foot of Stevens' Gap. His men were only about ten miles from Lafayette, and did not expect the town to be held in strength. Thus, far, the reports that had reached Thomas' headquarters placed the main Rebel army at Dalton, a good fifteen

19 Robert G. Athearn, ed. *Soldier in the West: The Civil War Letters of Alfred Lacey Hough* (University of Pennsylvania Press, 1957), p. 137.

20 *OR* 30, pt. 4, p. 629.

21 William Cary Dodson Memoir, Emory University, Atlanta GA.

miles farther east.[22] Even so, Thomas dispatched another division under Brig. Gen. Absalom Baird to support Negley, just in case he ran into trouble.[23]

Trouble was exactly what Bragg had in mind. General Martin's reports convinced Bragg there was a chance to crush Negley's column, which intelligence estimated correctly at between 4,000 and 5,000 strong, at the foot of Stevens' Gap. Bragg had already ordered that Martin be reinforced with the rest of his cavalry brigade. If Negley's destruction was the goal, infantry would be needed to carry out that task. Bragg called upon Leonidas Polk to send Maj. Gen. Thomas C. Hindman and his division into the cove to spearhead the attack. That afternoon, Bragg issued verbal orders to Hindman to assault Negley and rode toward Lafayette. Written orders confirming the attack reached Hindman's camp near Lee and Gordon's Mills later that night.[24] Hindman would not have to attack alone. D. H. Hill's Corps was already concentrated at Lafayette, and Bragg ordered Hill to send a division to support Hindman's effort.

More of Martin's Rebel cavalry arrived that evening. From the north, Colonel Mauldin's 3rd Alabama Cavalry abandoned its outposts atop Lookout Mountain and reached the cove around midday. Martin's remaining regiments were riding up from Summerville, where they had been under Wheeler's control. By dawn on September 10, Martin's command was reassembled.[25]

The division leader set his men to work blockading the gaps in Pigeon Mountain, intending to fall back to those defenses if pressed. As early as the 8th, however, he warned Bragg that his cavalry could not hold back enemy infantry for very long. Wagons and artillery had to pass through the gaps, but foot soldiers could climb the ridge almost anywhere and easily outflank static defenses. The best Bragg could hope for was that Martin's men could delay the Union advance for a day or two.[26]

---

22 *OR* 30, pt. 3, pp. 509-10.

23 John C. Starkweather, "Report of Stevens' Gap," General Thomas' Papers, RG 94, NARA.

24 *OR* 30, pt. 2, p. 28, discusses Bragg's actions and orders during this period.

25 Martin's entire division numbered only six regiments in two brigades and one small battery of two guns. Two regiments of his command were still operating with the provost marshal, hunting deserters. All told, Martin had no more than 2,500 men on the 10th, and was the smallest of the four cavalry divisions serving with the Army of Tennessee. Powell, *Numbers and Losses*, CCNMP.

26 *OR* 30, pt. 2, p. 522.

William Martin was doing a fine job. He kept a steady flow of accurate information moving to Bragg and duplicate reports to D. H. Hill, whose men were now in position to back up the Rebel cavalry. When Negley's Federals set off for Lafayette about 8:00 a.m. on September 10, Martin saw to it that they did not get far. Negley marched via Bailey's Crossroads to the Widow Davis house, and from there started toward Dug Gap. From the start, heavy skirmishing slowed his advance. The Federals consumed most of the day to reach the Davis house, from which they could see Martin's Rebels working on barricades in Dug Gap. Skirmishers threatened both flanks, adding to their discomfort.[27]

Negley called a halt at 3:00 p.m. In addition to his own difficulties, information reached him that instead of falling back to Dalton, much of the Confederate army now occupied Lafayette. An indiscreet young Rebel lieutenant was the first to give the game away. He was captured that morning on the picket line. He "was so defiant in his manner and boasted so loudly" that the Yankees were walking into a trap, recalled one soldier, that Negley took heed of the warning.[28] A little later, a young child strayed into the Union lines and revealed that a large number of Confederates were at his home, just one mile away.[29] The information froze the Union advance in its tracks. Negley informed Thomas of his predicament, called for reinforcements, and prepared to pull back.[30]

While most of Bragg's attention on the 10th was focused on the developing situation in McLemore's Cove, he was still concerned with the threat to the southwest from Alpine. At 10:30 a.m., he sent Wheeler a very specific set of orders concerning that peril. The army commander directed Wheeler to move via the Summerville Road and discover "the designs, movements, strength, and positions of the enemy." The orders were so specific they dictated which roads Wheeler was to cover with scouts, that he was to watch for a move toward Rome, and should recall some of his scattered pickets in order to increase his fighting strength.[31] The fact that Bragg's order to his senior cavalry commander addressed basic, even rudimentary, tasks that should have been accomplished

27 William D. Ward Diary and Papers, DePauw University, Greencastle Indiana.

28 Athearn, *Soldier in the West*, pp. 138-9.

29 *Ibid.*

30 *OR* 30, pt. 3, pp. 534-5.

31 *Ibid.*, pt. 4, p. 634.

as a matter of course by any experienced cavalryman spoke volumes. Simply put, by now Bragg lacked the confidence to let Wheeler use his own discretion in such matters, and wanted to ensure that there would be no surprise from the south while he organized a heavy blow westward against Negley.

Bragg spent the next two days designing plans to destroy an isolated piece of the Army of the Cumberland in McLemore's Cove. He mustered for the effort nearly 22,000 men: Hindman's Division of 6,500, plus Maj. Gen. Patrick Cleburne's Division (Hill's Corps), about 5,500 strong, and Maj. Gen. Simon B. Buckner's Corps of 10,000. To resist the assault, the Federals could field some 11,000 men in the form of Negley's division, reinforced by Baird's division.[32] Bragg called a midnight conference at his headquarters to discuss the attack that was now planned for the following day. To his surprise, D. H. Hill, who was to move in from the east and support Hindman in his move southward, voiced reluctance about the idea. Bragg and Hill were discussing the operation when a courier named Maj. James Nocquet arrived carrying an important dispatch and other information. The dispatch was from Hindman and, read together with other information as relayed by the major, must surely have perplexed Bragg: Hindman did not want to launch the assault against Negley.[33]

According to the dispatch, which asked about the Federal presence in Stevens' Gap, Hindman was concerned that the enemy would attack his rear while he was operating in the cove. An impassioned discussion ensued, during which Nocquet set forth other concerns Hindman harbored. The Federals at Davis' Crossroads, he asserted, were merely a diversion. Indeed, most of Thomas' XIV Corps was at Alpine with McCook's XX Corps, which constituted the real threat to Lafayette. If he entered the cove to attack Negley,

---

32 The details of McLemore's Cove have been studied and addressed many times, and need not be told again here except in outline form (see also footnote 37 for a few more details). The best in-depth treatments of this abortive affair are found in Connelly, *Autumn of Glory*, pp. 174-186, and William Glenn Robertson, "The Chickamauga Campaign: McLemore's Cove," *Blue & Gray Magazine*, Vol. XXIII, No. 6 (Spring, 2007), pp. 7-24, 42-50.

33 Connelly, *Autumn of Glory*, p. 183. Major Nocquet was well known to Bragg. The Frenchman spoke only limited English, and had served all of one month on Bragg's staff before being dismissed for incompetence. Thereafter, he joined Simon Buckner's staff as an engineer and, when Buckner reinforced Hindman, was chosen by those two officers to communicate Hindman's concerns to Bragg. Why Nocquet enjoyed Buckner's confidence after his earlier dismissal by Bragg is unclear, but that confidence was indeed misplaced. A few months later, Nocquet disappeared with $150,000 in army construction funds and was never heard from again. His selection as the man to explain Buckner's and Hindman's concerns to Bragg about the attack in McLemore's Cove was remarkably inept.

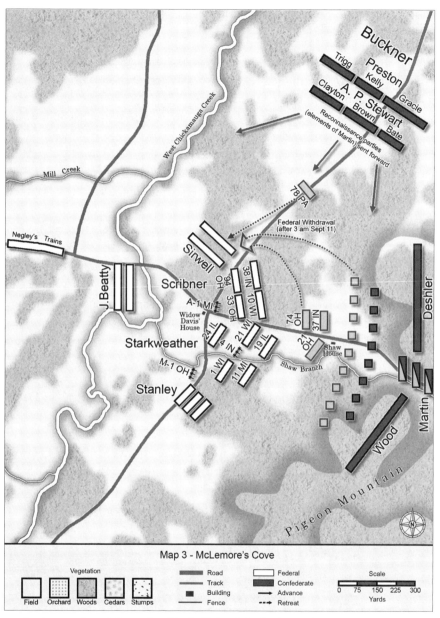

Map 3 - McLemore's Cove

Vegetation

| Field | Orchard | Woods | Cedars | Stumps |

Road — Federal
Track — Confederate
Building
Fence — Advance / Retreat

Scale
0   75   150   225   300
Yards

By the morning of September 11, six Union brigades have taken up a semi-circular defensive line around the Widow Davis house, hoping to stave off a looming Rebel attack until Union trains can withdraw safely back to Lookout Mountain. Bragg ordered an attack, and elements from three Rebel infantry corps are poised to strike, but the blow never lands.

argued Nocquet, these other Federal columns would trap him. Cavalry division commander William Martin, who was also present for the war conference, contradicted Major Nocquet on every significant point. There was no immediate threat to Hindman's rear, Martin asserted, and Thomas' XIV Corps was not at Alpine, but in McLemore's Cove.[34]

When the frustrating exchange ended, an unconvinced Bragg sent Nocquet back to Hindman with orders to attack as early as possible the next day, as originally directed. Hill would be in position east of the crossroads to support him. On the morning of September 11, Bragg, Hill, and Cleburne made their way through Dug Gap to confront the Federals and join in Hindman's attack. They waited in vain for any sounds of combat.[35]

Martin, who was given full discretion by Bragg to help wherever he was needed, joined Hindman in time for the attack in McLemore's Cove and for what proved to be a very long and frustrating day. The adept cavalryman deployed his troopers on Hindman's front and flanks and provided a constant flow of information detailing Federal positions and activity. Hindman, though he moved out early and by 6:00 a.m. was within four miles of Negley's position, stopped. Hindman believed he was about to be flanked and that his own route of retreat would be blocked. Hill made contact with Hindman and offered several excuses about why he could not support him. "Hours were lost in consultation," Martin complained. When Hindman halted just north of Davis' Crossroads (and Hill frozen to the east), the cavalry leader thought "the delay was inexplicable."[36] It was also a gift to the Yankees. Negley, now reinforced by Baird, needed time to allow his trains to move back through Stevens' Gap and out of danger. The isolated Federals spent the entire day waiting anxiously for the Rebel blow to fall, but it never came. By late that afternoon, the wagons were safely away and the Union infantry fell back in good order.[37]

---

34 Robertson, "McLemore's Cove," pp. 42-3.

35 Entry for September 11, 1863, Taylor Beatty Diary, UNC.

36 William T. Martin, "A Defense of General Bragg at Chickamauga," *Confederate Veteran*, Volume XI, No. 4 (April, 1883) p. 205. See also Martin Papers, Center for American History, University of Texas at Austin.

37 With both Hindman and Hill unwilling to act, Bragg—out of frustration and in an attempt to salvage the situation—ordered two divisions from Simon Buckner's Corps to assume the offensive. It took Buckner until about noon to reach Hindman's position, meaning half of the day was already lost. Hindman made matters worse by letting Buckner's infantry take the lead, a clumsy and time-consuming decision. Once in front of Hindman, Buckner deployed Brig. Gen.

Like Martin, Bragg found Hindman's delays simply inexplicable. When Martin met him after the enemy escape, the commanding general was "indignant and excited" over Hindman's "utter disregard of . . . orders."[38] The final act of the dismal operation was a brief cavalry charge, launched more out of frustration than good tactics. Martin, with about 150 Alabama cavalrymen, attacked the Union rearguard and was repulsed by a volley from the 19th Illinois.

Thomas' decision to pull Negley back to Lookout Mountain left the Federals to the south at Alpine more exposed than ever, though McCook did not hear of Thomas' withdrawal immediately. The day after Negley retreated, McCook ordered Brig. Gen. George Crook to move the cavalry to Lafayette and find Bragg's army. Crook sent two brigades eastward via Summerville, and another two up the direct road to Lafayette.[39] Wheeler's cavalry fell back before the Federal troopers, and that evening Crook's columns reached within seven miles of Lafayette, where they halted and spent a tense night in battle line, their horses fully saddled and ready for action.[40]

The next morning Crook brought the two brigades over from the Summerville Road and united the two columns. They had encountered a strong Rebel force the night before, and Crook wanted as many men as possible in case a larger action developed.[41] With all four brigades on the Lafayette Road, Crook resumed his advance. John Wharton's Confederate cavalry had been spread thin, deployed in an arc north and east of Alpine watching for a Union advance and skirmishing each day with Federal patrols. Wharton concentrated his men to meet Crook's advance.

On September 13, Wharton's dismounted division engaged in a running fight for several miles as the Federals pressed him steadily north toward

---

A. P. Stewart's Division with Brig. Gen. William Preston's Division behind him. More hours slipped away. Late that afternoon, Hindman, Buckner, and the other officers met for a council of war and voted to retreat. When they received news that the Federals had beaten them to it and were themselves withdrawing, they changed their minds and Stewart finally advanced on Davis' Crossroads at 5:00 p.m. By then it was too late. Connelly, *Autumn of Glory*, pp. 174-186, and Robertson, "The Chickamauga Campaign: McLemore's Cove," pp. 7-24, 42-50.

38 Martin, "A Defense of General Bragg at Chickamauga," p. 205.

39 *OR* 30, pt. 1, p. 918.

40 *Proceedings of the Thirtieth Annual Reunion*, p. 17.

41 *OR* 30, pt. 1, p. 892.

Lafayette.[42] Wharton finally received help when he fell back to within three miles of the town. As enemy resistance stiffened, Crook ordered the 9th Pennsylvania Cavalry to make a mounted charge and clear the road. In a cloud of obscuring dust, a squadron of the 9th set spurs and thundered ahead, capturing eighteen Rebel skirmishers, losing several men and eight horses of their own in the effort.[43] The dust was still settling when the prisoners revealed disquieting news. They belonged to Brig. Gen. Daniel Adams' infantry brigade, part of Maj. Gen. John C. Breckinridge's Division of D. H. Hill's Corps.[44] Another brigade from the same division extended Adams' line farther west. The news grew progressively worse the longer the prisoners talked. Not only was Hill's entire corps in Lafayette, but Bragg and two other infantry corps were also present. This news confirmed that, far from retreating, the Army of Tennessee was dangerously close, concentrated, and coiled to strike.

Crook retired to Alpine that afternoon, the bearer of bad news to McCook. Once he realized that he was sticking his head into a viper's nest, the XX Corps commander decided that his only option was to retreat, and he sent word to Rosecrans of his decision. The ramparts of Lookout Mountain offered a greater degree of security and would better allow McCook to defend the passes. Late the next day (September 14), Rosecrans affirmed McCook's decision to withdraw and, in orders relayed through Thomas, ordered the XX Corps to first fall back west to Lookout Mountain, and then hurry north to rejoin the rest of the army. Thomas' latest dispatch also informed McCook that McLemore's Cove was now enemy territory. This, too, was bad news. Instead of using Dougherty's Gap to move quickly to join Thomas, the XX Corps would have to cross all the way to the other side of Lookout Mountain and use Wills Valley, an exhausting and time-consuming march.[45]

With the recall of McCook's corps, Rosecrans lost the initiative. He was no longer trying to trap Bragg's army, but save his own.

---

42 John Randolph Poole, *Cracker Cavaliers: The 2nd Georgia Cavalry under Wheeler and Forrest* (Mercer University Press, 2000), p. 86.

43 *OR* 30, pt. 1, p. 904.

44 Entry for September 14, 1863, Samuel Pasco Diary, 3rd Florida File, CCNMP.

45 *OR* 30, pt. 3, pp. 627-9.

C hapter 7

Rosecrans Retreats, Bragg Pursues

(September 13-15, 1863)

G eorge Thomas' brush with disaster in McLemore's Cove, coupled with mounting evidence of large numbers of Rebels at Lafayette, convinced William Rosecrans it was time to reunite his scattered command. By the evening of September 14, both Thomas' XIV Corps and McCook's XX Corps were retreating westward to the relative security of Lookout Mountain, where they were much less vulnerable to converging Confederate attacks. The XXI Corps under Crittenden, however, deployed near Lee and Gordon's Mills and within just a few miles of Bragg's army, remained exposed.

As previously described, on the night of September 10 Forrest searched for Bragg to report the vulnerable nature of the XXI Corps' scattered disposition. He arrived at Polk's headquarters only to discover that Bragg had already departed for Lafayette. The Southern army commander determined to strike at Negley first in McLemore's Cove, and his attention was focused on that operation. Forrest returned to his command, frustrated at Bragg's apparent lack of interest in the opportunity to pluck what he supposed was the ripe and low-lying fruit of Crittenden's XXI Corps.[1] Now, two days later the opportunity beckoned once again—and Bragg was interested. He set his next plan in motion that night after receiving a dispatch from John Pegram.

---

1 Jordan and Pryor, *Forrest's Cavalry*, p. 308.

On September 12, Simon Buckner's, D. H. Hill's, and Maj. Gen. William H. T. Walker's newly arrived corps were gathered at Lafayette.[2] Ben Cheatham's Division of Polk's Corps was camped just a few miles north of Lafayette at Rock Springs Church. After the fizzled fiasco in McLemore's Cove, Thomas Hindman's Division was marching back through Lafayette with orders to rejoin Polk. Joe Wheeler, with John Wharton's cavalry division, was still screening for Union threats emanating from Alpine, while Wheeler's other division under William Martin kept an eye on Negley's departing Yankees. Nathan Bedford Forrest's troops were spread out covering Bragg's northern flank between Dalton on the Western and Atlantic Railroad and Rock Springs Church five miles below Lee and Gordon's Mills.[3]

Leonidas Polk, suitably reinforced, would attack the Union forces at Lee and Gordon's Mills. Hindman's Division, together with Walker's Corps, would march through the night and be in position to join the attack at dawn. Justifiably worried about another tactical miscarriage, Bragg bombarded Polk with orders. The first was sent at 6:00 p.m. Two hours later, Bragg sent a second, more detailed missive explaining the supposed Union position. With the approach of midnight Bragg threw out a third dispatch, reminding Polk that the Federals were trying to close up from the south and that the "attack in the morning should be quick and decided." If that was not clear enough, Bragg concluded with a five-word coda: "Let no time be lost."[4]

Bishop Polk was not so sure. At 11:00 p.m., he informed Bragg by courier that he was outnumbered, needed reinforcements, and that he was taking up a defensive position in the interim. One need not wonder too deeply how the news struck Bragg, who penned and sent out a fourth order insisting that Polk was "already numerically superior to the enemy," and that his "success depended upon the promptness and rapidity of his movements." To further reassure his wavering subordinate, Bragg added that "Buckner's corps would be moved within supporting distance the next morning."[5]

---

2 W. H. T. Walker's men were sent from Mississippi in response to the Chattanooga crisis. They were first assigned to defend Rome, Georgia, on September 4, 1863, and later ordered to Lafayette. Walker's Corps was a small one, and with only four brigades present was roughly the size of one of Bragg's other divisions. See *OR* 30, pt. 4, p. 595.

3 Entries for September 11 and 12, 1863, Brent Journal.

4 All three orders can be found in *OR* 30, pt. 2, p. 30.

5 *Ibid.*, pp. 30-31.

Bragg was mistaken about the dispositions of the Federals confronting him to the north, and the fault lay with John Pegram. During the past twenty-four hours, Pegram's dispatches included a number of details about the enemy positions that suggested the various organizations were still widely scattered. It was this intelligence that prompted Bragg's flurry of orders to Polk. The cavalryman told Bragg initially that one Union division was still at Ringgold, which was followed up with a report of a Union infantry division "three quarters of a mile beyond [north of] Peavine Church on the road to Graysville from Lafayette."[6] These reports suggested to Bragg that the Federals had a division each at Ringgold, Peavine Church, and Lee and Gordon's Mills (each separated from the others by several miles), or alternatively, Pegram was tracking a lone Union division on its way to Ringgold several miles from the Mills. Either option offered tantalizing possibilities.

The reality was quite different. By September 12, Crittenden had already decided to unify his command at Lee and Gordon's Mills, and by that same afternoon all three divisions were concentrated there. No Union force was moving back toward Ringgold. Pegram rightly identified a Union organization near Peavine Church as Wilder's mounted infantry, but he also reported the presence of Maj. Gen. John M. Palmer's infantry division, which was not there.[7] Pegram had been fighting Wilder all day and getting the worst of it, and perhaps he was feeling heavily outnumbered. Even Wilder's location was a false trail by then because his command had abandoned its decoy camp that night to slip away to Lee and Gordon's Mills. Far from being scattered across a dozen miles, the Federal XXI Corps was concentrated in decent defensive positions behind West Chickamauga Creek, itself a formidable obstacle to any attack. Like any army commander, Bragg was relying upon his cavalry to supply him with intelligence he could then act upon to advantage. Unfortunately, Pegram's grasp of the situation was very wrong.

Bragg was also mistaken with regard to relative numbers. With the addition of Wilder, Crittenden had available some 15,000 men, nearly all of whom were well rested and strongly posted. Minty's cavalry brigade, brought down from Chattanooga, strengthened the XXI Corps position with an additional 1,500 troopers. Polk, by contrast, had only Ben Cheatham's 6,500 men on hand. Hindman and Walker would have to march through the night to be in position

6   *Ibid.*, p. 30.

7   Entry for September 12, 1863, Brent Journal.

by dawn. Even then, Polk could count on no more than 20,000 infantry and much of it would be exhausted. He also had available about 5,000 cavalry, including parts of both Armstrong's and Pegram's divisions, but unlike Wilder's Spencer-armed Federals or even Minty's well-equipped troopers, these under-armed Rebel horsemen would be of little use in an infantry attack.[8]

The addition of Buckner's Corps would add another 10,000 bayonets to Polk's assault, but it was impossible for Buckner to have his men in position and ready to support Polk by dawn. Orders did not reach Buckner until just a few hours before sunrise, and his men did not leave Lafayette until daylight.[9] Polk was right when he sent his 11:00 p.m. dispatch to Bragg: his attacking column was not nearly strong enough to overwhelm Crittenden's corps. None of the promised reinforcements had even arrived, so he could only count on Cheatham's 6,500 to face 15,000 Federals. Bragg made a rudimentary mistake by including Hindman, Walker, and Buckner in his calculations without allowing for the fact that while orders had been issued, they could not react fast enough or be in position in time to realistically help Polk.

At 5:00 a.m. the next morning, September 13, Bragg left Lafayette to ride yet again to the scene of an expected Confederate assault. Instead of witnessing an offensive, he found Polk awaiting an enemy attack and still trying to bring Hindman's and Walker's commands into line.[10] At 9:00 a.m., with Bragg looking on, Polk issued a communiqué asking every subordinate commander to inform him when they had deployed so the general advance could begin.[11] The Federals, however, knocked away that timetable by seizing the initiative themselves.

About mid-morning, Crittenden sent Brig. Gen. Horatio P. Van Cleve's division forward to make a reconnaissance toward Rock Springs.[12] By 11:00 a.m. the leading brigade ran into Rebel pickets on the Lafayette Road. The Southern troops belonged to James T. Wheeler's Brigade, part of Armstrong's

---

8 Powell, *Strengths and Losses*, CCNMP. Rebel cavalry in the Western Theater usually fought dismounted and were not afraid of confronting enemy infantry, as the fighting at Dover demonstrated, but they were usually not a match for enemy infantry, especially if entrenched.

9 Entry for September 12, 1863, Brent Journal.

10 *Ibid.*, entry for September 13, 1863.

11 OR 30, pt. 2, p. 76.

12 Horatio P. Van Cleve to Wife, September 14, 1863, Horatio P. Van Cleve Papers, Minnesota Historical Society, Minneapolis, MN.

Division, and included both the 3rd Arkansas and 6th Tennessee cavalry regiments. Small clashes between the opposing skirmish lines had been going on for days but this one was different. "[T]he skirmishing today has been heavier than on any previous day," observed Tennessee Private Davis of the 6th regiment.[13] The 3rd Arkansas lost at least one man of Company A killed as well as several horses in the sharp clash.[14] The Union patrol achieved some success, driving the Rebel screen back about a mile and a half, but the thrust ended when it hit General Polk's main line of battle.[15] A limited action ensued while the Federals carefully felt out the line's strength, determined the Confederates were present in large numbers, and fell back to Lee and Gordon's Mills. Once again a major attack planned and expected by Bragg sputtered into little more than a skirmish.

The operation was underway when Bragg received two dispatches that convinced him to once again change his strategy. The first, from Pegram, reported belatedly that Union troops had disappeared from both the Ringgold and Peavine roads, suggesting that the Federals were now concentrated at Lee and Gordon's Mills.[16] The second message was D. H. Hill's report of the skirmishing south of Lafayette that morning, where John C. Breckinridge's infantry had moved to reinforce Joe Wheeler's cavalry fending off the Union advance from Alpine.[17]

Bragg had no way of knowing that this encounter convinced McCook to retreat as soon as practicable. From Bragg's perspective, it appeared as though the Federals were still pushing aggressively up from the south, threatening Lafayette from two directions. That settled it: the entire army must return to Lafayette. Bragg turned Buckner's men around and sent them back to Lafayette, thus returning them to the point of their dawn departure. Polk and Walker were to follow Bucker by the evening of the 13th. [18] After a day's (and in some instances, a night's) hard marching, most of the Rebel army was right back where it started.

13 Entry for September 13, 1863, Davis Diary.

14 OR *Supplement*, pt. 2, vol. 2, pp. 215-225.

15 Entry for September 13, 1863, Jason Hurd Diary, Combat Studies Institute.

16 OR 30, pt. 4, p. 647.

17 Entry for September 13, 1863, Brent Journal.

18 *Ibid.*

The confusing circumstances and faulty intelligence had kept Bragg's men in motion in and around Lafayette for several days, all to no avail. They needed rest and food while the army's trains were sent back to a more secure location. Additionally, Bragg had to take into account that reinforcements for his army were now en route by rail from Lee's army in Virginia. They were due to arrive at either Ringgold or Dalton, a good day's march from Lafayette. The leading elements of these reinforcements were already in Atlanta, and would soon be up to join the fight. Bragg needed a new plan to properly integrate them into his army.

The Confederates spent the next two days observing, refitting, and discussing their options. By the afternoon of September 14, Polk's troops were back in camp around Lafayette. The corps commander offered Bragg an explanation for his failure to attack the day before, which was essentially a rehash of his reasons from the 11:00 p.m. September 12 note, supported by the direct testimony of his subordinates. At Bragg's headquarters, meanwhile, uncertainty prevailed about the exact dispositions of the various Federal forces. McCook was thought to still be at Alpine, while Crittenden's command was certainly deployed between Lee and Gordon's Mills and Crawfish Springs. Information on Thomas' XIV Corps, however, was at best sketchy. His men had withdrawn from McLemore's Cove, but their current location was unknown.[19]

More information trickled in on September 15. At 1:00 a.m. Joe Wheeler dispatched some of Wharton's troopers on a probe toward Alpine. From that point the cavalrymen reported at dawn that the Yankees had departed, moving back west up and over Lookout Mountain before turning north toward Chattanooga.[20] Forrest dispatched one of Colonel Scott's regiments east to Cleveland, Tennessee, to see if Rosecrans and Burnside were making any attempt to join up their respective commands. The 5th Tennessee Cavalry arrived in Cleveland just in time to charge the town and break up what Rebel trooper William Sloan called a "Lincolnite . . . jollification meeting," but no Federal troops were spotted. They did manage to confiscate a number of horses and enough whiskey to intoxicate many of the men who "became very boisterous on [the] return trip," forcing the command to halt prematurely

---

19 *Ibid.*, entry for September 14, 1863.

20 Entry for September 15, 1863, W. B. Corbitt Diary.

before returning to Ringgold.[21] The remaining Rebel cavalry had a quieter time: Martin's men continued picketing the passes over Pigeon Mountain and observing the now-empty McLemore's Cove, Armstrong's troops watched Crittenden's Federals, and Pegram's men screened Ringgold Depot and the railroad.

Later that September 15th morning, Bragg called a conference. D. H. Hill, Polk, Walker, and Buckner were all present when the army commander outlined his determination to resume the attack. Despite his resolute words, the events of the last few weeks had taken a toll on Bragg. To staff officer Colonel Brent, his boss appeared "sick and feeble."[22] Regardless of Bragg's appearance, the assembled officers agreed that taking the offensive was still a good idea, and worked to cobble together a new plan of attack aimed at cutting Rosecrans off from Chattanooga.

Thousands of reinforcements were due to arrive on the Western and Atlantic Railroad in Ringgold over the coming days, so the rail stop was the natural departure point for Bragg's next move. Brigadier General Bushrod Johnson's Brigade had been detached from Buckner's Corps a few days earlier and sent to Ringgold to help protect the depot. By the 15th, the famous Texas Brigade from Lee's Army of Northern Virginia joined them there. Two more brigades under Brig. Gens. John Gregg and Evander McNair, fresh from Mississippi, also arrived and were added to this gathering to create a provisional division under Johnson's command.[23]

Later, Johnson's ad-hoc organization would be integrated with Lt. Gen. James Longstreet's First Corps reinforcements as they arrived over the next few days. Until Longstreet or his division commanders reached Ringgold, however, Johnson would command this new column. Bragg further strengthened this force by ordering Brig. Gen. States Rights Gist's mixed brigade of Georgians and South Carolinians to Ringgold. Gist's men had been strung out along the

---

21 Entry for September 15, 1863, William E. Sloan Diary, Tennessee State Library and Archives.

22 Entry for September 15, 1863, Brent Journal.

23 *Ibid.* The brigades under Gregg and McNair were sent from Mississippi by Gen. Joe Johnston to help defend Atlanta, but were not supposed to move north of that city. Johnston's intent was to loan (rather than transfer) them to another army, and expected them to be returned promptly once other troops arrived. He did not expect them to be sent into battle as part of the Army of Tennessee, and in fact protested to both Bragg and President Jefferson Davis when Bragg ignored Johnston's wishes and incorporated them into his attack plans.

railroad between Dalton and Rome, dispatched there when the Union threat from Alpine loomed large. Now that the Yankee threat had abated, these troops could be moved north in preparation for Bragg's next planned offensive.[24]

24 Special Orders, Sept 15, 1863, Army Correspondence, Bragg Papers. Gist's troops were also reinforcements from Joe Johnston. Gist arrived at Rome earlier in the month to protect that place from a potential thrust by the Federals. Once on the field with the Army of Tennessee, Gist and his men were assigned to W. H. T. Walker's Corps, where Gist's seniority set off yet another round of command re-shuffling. As the senior man, Gist assumed command of a division, and Col. Peyton H. Colquitt was put in charge of Gist's Brigade.

Chapter 8

Bragg's Fitful Advance to Battle
(September 16-18, 1863)

Given the several missteps he had thus far experienced in the young campaign, Bragg's steadfast determination to wrest the initiative away from his counterpart and go over on the offensive offers a clear demonstration of his aggressive generalship. His decision to use Ringgold as his locus for further operations shifted the main burden of responsibility for screening and scouting onto the shoulders of another aggressive officer: Nathan Bedford Forrest. Both of Forrest's divisions were ideally situated for a move north, while Joe Wheeler's troopers, still well to the south and west of Lafayette, would bring up the rear of the army. Bragg's operational plan entrusted Forrest with broad responsibilities.

With Rosecrans' scattered infantry corps rapidly concentrating, the chance of crushing one before the others could march to its assistance diminished daily. All three, however, were still well south of Chattanooga and Bragg realized the extraordinary opportunity that fact presented to him. If he could thrust his army—or at least a substantial part of it—between Rosecrans and Chattanooga, the Union commander would have to make a very unpalatable choice: retreat across the mountains toward Bridgeport and Stevenson, try and force his way through Bragg's men to the relative security of Chattanooga, or retreat south away from his logistical supply line into the wilderness of McLemore's Cove in North Georgia. The Army of the Cumberland was still in great peril.

Convinced the large-scale turning movement had merit, Bragg issued an order on the night of September 16 that would frame Confederate operations for the next week. Simon Buckner's, W. H. T. Walker's, and Leonidas Polk's infantry would move north into line around Rock Springs, Peavine Church, and Leet's Tanyard, generally opposite Glass Mill on West Chickamauga Creek. Forrest was ordered to "cover the front and flank of those movements" and, more specifically, in anticipation of the Rebel infantry using those crossings, seize "Reed's Bridge, Bryam's [Lambert's] Ford, Alexander's Bridge, and the fords next above."[1] Responsibility for the bridges and covering Buckner and Walker fell to John Pegram's Division because of its location. Armstrong would shield Polk's movement. To make sure the Federals did not suddenly reverse course and make a surprise lunge for Lafayette, Bragg ordered D. H. Hill's Corps back to block the gaps in Pigeon Mountain. Bragg instructed Wheeler to leave a small force to guard the approaches from Alpine and with the rest of his command follow the Union retreat, admonishing him to "press the enemy, secure some prisoners if possible and join our flank near Glass Mill."[2] Bushrod Johnson's new division (less Henry Benning's Brigade from the Army of Northern Virginia, which was guarding the depot), would march from Ringgold to Leet's Tanyard.[3]

After issuing these orders the night before they were set to be implemented early on the 17th, Bragg cut new orders postponing the movement of his infantry for twenty-four hours. Buckner, Walker, Polk, and Johnson received these suspension orders, and an advisory of what was transpiring reached Wheeler. An order regarding this significant change in plans, however, was not drafted for Forrest.[4]

There were good reasons behind Bragg's decision to have his infantry wait one day before moving. Armstrong's Division was scattered south of Rock

---

1   *OR* 30, pt. 4, p. 657.

2   *Ibid.*

3   *Ibid.*, pt. 2, p. 31. Although Bragg's order referred to Bryam's Ford, the more common name seems to have been Lambert's Ford, which I have utilized in the text on the maps.

4   The suspension orders can be found in *OR* 30, 4, pp. 660-62, for all the commanders except Forrest. No record of Forrest's suspension order has been located, even in Bragg's Letterbook. Although not definitive, it is reasonable to conclude that Bragg intended for his infantry commanders to wait while Forrest continued with his instructions to seize the crossings over Chickamauga Creek a day early, which would clear the way when the general advance resumed the next day.

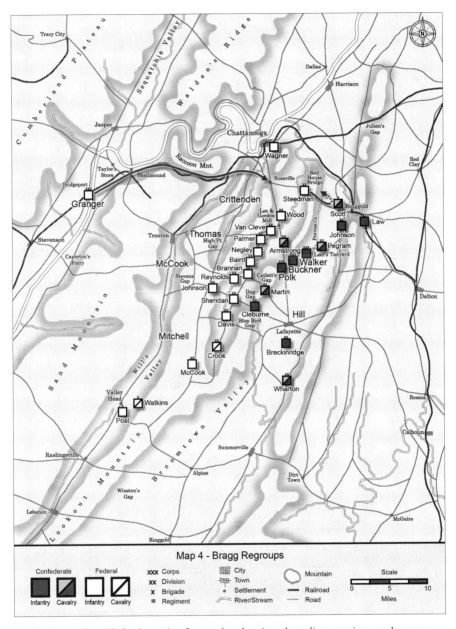

Map 4 - Bragg Regroups

Confederate	Federal					
Infantry Cavalry	Infantry Cavalry	XXX Corps XX Division X Brigade III Regiment	City Town Settlement River/Stream	Mountain Railroad Road	Scale 0 5 10 Miles	

By September 17, both armies face each other in a long line running northeast to southwest from Chattanooga deep into North Georgia, divided largely by West Chickamauga Creek. Bragg has saved his army from entrapment, but has not managed to spring any of the counter-traps he hoped to realize in the mountain coves around Lafayette. Now, with his strength growing near Ringgold, Bragg devises a new plan.

Springs watching Owen's Ford and Glass Mill, and the delay would allow Armstrong to concentrate his cavalry for the coming advance. The pause would also give Forrest more time to capture the specified crossings over Chickamauga Creek and ensure that Pegram's cavalry established contact with Walker and Buckner. Johnson, too, needed another day at Ringgold to collect all the troops now headed there, which would increase his strength to about 5,000 infantry. Finally, Hill's infantry, still below Lafayette, were too far south to cover the intended distance in a single march. The Federals, however, refused to sit and wait patiently for Bragg's plans to unfold.

While Bragg's headquarters was issuing delaying orders on the morning of the 17th, a Union column of six regiments and an artillery battery under Brig. Gen. James B. Steedman, commander of the First Division of the Union Reserve Corps, surprised the Confederates in Ringgold.[5] Steedman's column, which held the left flank of Rosecran's Army of the Cumberland, brushed aside a handful of "the enemy's pickets" and reached "the crest of the ridge commanding the town." Just three-quarters of a mile distant were the Ringgold railroad depot and Rebel camps. The battery unlimbered and shelled the targets unopposed for a while until the rounds stirred up enough excitement for Steedman to see the dust trails of Rebel troops converging on him from several directions. He ordered the guns limbered and withdrew.[6]

Although relatively harmless, the artillery barrage came as a surprise to the occupants of Ringgold. The embarrassment and consequent responsibility for the shelling rested solely at the feet of Col. John Scott. His cavalry brigade had been in Ringgold for three days, and it was his job to protect the growing and critically important depot. His troopers should have discovered Steedman's movement much sooner—certainly in time for Rebel infantry at Ringgold to form up and defend the depot. Scott's report of this affair failed to mention that the attack came as a surprise to anyone. Instead, he wrote disingenuously that when the enemy advanced on Ringgold, "I marched out to meet them and drove them back."[7] Some of the newly arrived Confederate infantrymen recalled the matter differently. Captain William H. Harder of the 23rd

---

5   General John C. Smith, *Oration at the Unveiling of the Monument Erected to The Memory of Maj. Gen. James B. Steedman* (Knight and Leonard, 188), p. 17. See also Entry for September 17, 1863, Bushrod Johnson Diary, Record Group 109, NARA.

6   *OR* 30, pt. 1, p. 859.

7   *Ibid.*, pt. 2, p. 531.

Tennessee described meeting "our scouts and teamsters in a wild flight, having been set on by Federal cavalry."[8] (What Harder did not know was that they were thrown into a panic by Steadman's surprise bombardment.) Frank T. Ryan of the 1st Arkansas Mounted Rifles, part of Brig. Gen. Evander McNair's Brigade, was busy scrounging for vegetables when he and several comrades found themselves the recipients of the unexpected barrage. The Arkansans hurried back to their unit, where they found the brigade in line of battle facing the hill upon which the Yankee cannon were planted.[9] Scott also made much of his pursuit of Steedman and engagement later that night, claiming he "surprised their camp, throwing their whole force into confusion. After a sharp fight," he continued, "I retired to my camp at Ringgold." By his own account, Scott had with him just one small regiment of cavalry. Steedman's version of the night encounter is quite different. "At 11 p.m., the enemy having followed us, threw 6 shells into my camp, and then, under the cover of darkness, speedily retired."[10]

The affair itself was inconsequential, but its effects were not. Bragg knew he could not let Ringgold fall into enemy hands, and that if it were captured, his plans would be ruined. His immediate response was to direct Pegram to send reinforcements "at once" into Ringgold and drive out the enemy, if they were still present.[11] The affair also convinced Bragg to modify his overall plan. In the September 16 orders, Johnson's destination was Leet's Tanyard, about a dozen miles southwest of Ringgold and roughly the same distance southeast of Lee and Gordon's Mills. Instead, Bragg issued new orders dispatching Johnson due west to cross the Chickamauga at Reed's Bridge several miles north of the mills and much closer to Rossville. Bragg expected Johnson's infantry would be well beyond (north of) the Union left flank when he crossed Chickamauga Creek. As a result, Johnson's command was now the guiding element of Bragg's revised offensive plan. All other Confederate columns would begin moving when Johnson's men reached them.[12]

---

8 William Henry Harder Reminiscences, 23rd Tennessee Infantry file, Combat Studies Institute.

9 Frank T. Ryan Reminiscences, Civil War Miscellany file, Georgia Department of Archives and history. Atlanta, GA. The 1st Arkansas Mounted Rifles were dismounted and serving as infantry.

10 *OR* 30, pt. 1, p. 859.

11 Orders, September 15, 1863, Bragg Papers.

12 *OR* 30, pt. 2, p. 31.

There was one other important reason for Bragg to both postpone his original orders of September 16 and modify his strategy. While Bragg was aware of the decision to transfer James Longstreet's First Corps from the Army of Northern Virginia west to reinforce him, the uncertain state of Confederate railroads in 1863 made it impossible to know when those troops would become available to him. In the early hours of September 17, however, details about the First Corps' pending arrival emerged with the appearance of Maj. Osmun Latrobe of Longstreet's own staff, coupled with the first infantry from Virginia. Latrobe informed Bragg that at least one division would reach Ringgold and be ready for action by the morning of the 18th.[13]

On September 18, Bragg once again set his army in motion. Johnson's Division, now at full strength with about 5,000 men, would cross Chickamauga Creek and "sweep down" toward Lee and Gordon's Mills from the northeast, striking Rosecran's left and rear. Walker's and Buckner's corps, crossing at Alexander's Bridge and Thedford's Ford, respectively, would fill in behind Johnson to lend weight to the attack. Walker's command added 7,000 more infantry (less one brigade not yet present), and Buckner just more than 9,000 men. Polk's Corps, another 13,500 men, was shifted north from Glass Mill to the crossing opposite Lee and Gordon's Mills, and from there was expected to follow Buckner to Thedford's Ford, thereby adding even more strength to the attacking column rolling southwest.[14] If all went as planned, Bragg's massive right hook would send 34,500 infantry beyond and behind Rosecrans left flank and drive it southwest away from Chattanooga and into the mountainous terrain of north Georgia.

Forrest's role was only marginally revised for the coming attack: "cover the march . . . from Ringgold in front and on right flank."[15] These general instructions were similar to Bragg's intentions of the 16th: lead the columns, find the enemy, help seize the crossings, and support the infantry. To accomplish his mission, Forrest had Scott's Brigade at Ringgold and Pegram's former brigade (Henry Davidson was still en route and so had not yet assumed

13 Entry for September 17, Osmun Latrobe Diary, Maryland Historical Society. See also, William Glenn Robertson, "The Chickamauga Campaign: The Armies Collide," *Blue & Gray Magazine*, XXIV, No. 3 (Fall, 2007), p. 40.

14 Brig. Gen. States Rights Gist's Brigade was bucking the congested rail system. The detachment of Bushrod Johnson's Brigade to form the provisional division reduced Buckner's strength.

15 Orders, September 16, 1863, Bragg Papers.

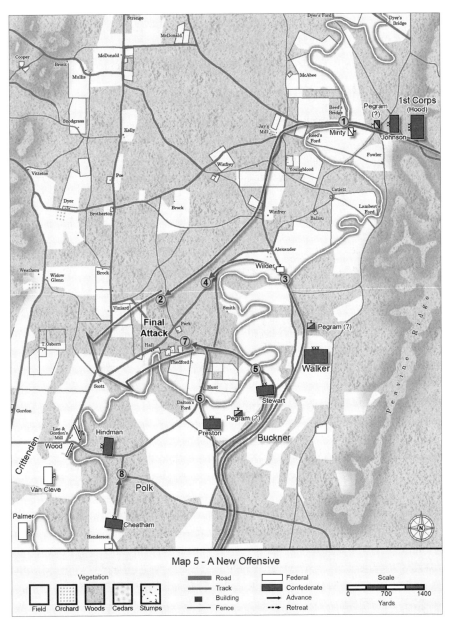

Map 5 - A New Offensive

The final version of Bragg's newest offensive plan was drawn up while his army was resting around Lafayette. It involved a large turning movement around Rosecrans' right flank, and another thrust farther south at Lee and Gordon's Mills to drive the Federals away from Chattanooga and their logistical lifeline. The critical mission of leading this attack fell to John Pegram's troopers.

command) in the vicinity of Peavine Church. Armstrong's two brigades were still operating with Polk, but were expected to be released soon once Wheeler relieved them. Even without Armstrong, Scott and Pegram were well-placed to execute these tasks.

The plan went awry almost immediately. Bushrod Johnson, whose division was setting the tempo for the entire assault, left Ringgold without any cavalry screening his advance or guiding him to his final destination. Nor would he see any horsemen for much of the day. A more immediate problem was the fact that Johnson had yet to receive the new orders directing him to Reed's Bridge instead of Leet's Tanyard. As a result, he followed the outdated September 17 plan and marched three miles toward Leet's before someone discovered the mistake and army headquarters dispatched a courier to put the errant division back on the right course. Johnson turned his brigades back toward Ringgold and marched onto the road to Reed's Bridge, but the mistake consumed most of the morning.

Once Johnson was back on the right road, the consequence of the cavalry's absence resulted in unexpected opposition. Late that morning, about one mile east of Reed's Bridge near Peeler's Mill, Federal horsemen from Col. Robert H. Minty's brigade atop Peavine Ridge opened fire on the head of Johnson's column. Minty had joined Crittenden's XXI Corps at Lee and Gordon's Mills on the 13th, moved into the Reed's Bridge area on the 15th, and had been picketing the Chickamauga Creek crossings for the past three days.[16] They were familiar with the area and deployed to make a stand. Johnson had never seen the terrain, was uncertain what he was up against, and contrary to his expectations, had a fight on his hands. He deployed his infantry and slowly began to work his way westward.

Buckner and Walker fared no better than Johnson. Pegram's troopers accompanied their combined infantry column initially, but were called away sometime that afternoon to join Forrest farther north. In the meantime, his cavalry provided only limited information to the trailing infantry. At some point Pegram informed Walker that the Federals held Alexander's Bridge, though without much elaboration as to strength or position. This vague report was the only intelligence either Walker or Buckner received from any Confederate cavalry during the entire day. Walker's leading brigade, Mississippians

16 Robert G. Minty, "Minty's Saber Brigade: The Part They Took in the Chickamauga Campaign, Part One," *National Tribune*, February 25, 1892.

commanded by Brig. Gen. Edward C. Walthall, confirmed the veracity of the message when they approached the bridge about 1:00 p.m. and were met and repulsed by a furious fire from Wilder's men and their Spencers.[17] Walthall deployed his regiments and settled in for a protracted fight. Walker's setback at Alexander's Bridge delayed both Buckner and Polk, who had beed ordered to wait until Walker was well across Chickamauga Creek before joining him on the west bank.

Forrest never explained why he failed to follow Bragg's orders. An examination of how he utilized his two available brigades, however, is useful for understanding what Forrest may have been thinking. Scott's command began the day at Ringgold. Instead of accompanying Johnson, Scott's entire brigade was sent to guard the Old Federal Road leading to Rossville. The decision to block this road with a strong force probably stemmed from the nasty surprise Steedman gave the Rebels the day before. Embarrassed once, Forrest was determined not to let it happen again. Pegram was ordered to dispatch Scott to cover that approach.[18] Still, the three regiments comprising Scott's command (1st Louisiana, 2nd and 5th Tennessee) totaled about 1,100 men—more than were needed to picket the road. Some of them could have been spared for Johnson in accordance with Bragg's orders to Forrest.

Several miles short of Rossville at Red House Bridge, Scott ran into a Union infantry brigade on a similar assignment and halted for the rest of the day.[19] According to Scott's campaign report, his command "proceeded to Red House . . . and drove in the advance of the enemy's Reserve Corps."[20] Nimrod Porter of the 2nd Tennessee Cavalry, part of John Scott's Brigade, remembered that he came off picket duty and "found the brigade in line at Red House Bridge, on Chickamauga. They have been fighting the enemy all day."[21]

The Federals opposing Scott saw things quite differently. Union Brig. Gen. Walter C. Whitaker reported that on September 18, Granger ordered him to "move and occupy [Red House] bridge . . . if it could be done without bringing on a general engagement." Whitaker further noted that "in crossing Spring

17 "The Late Battle—Walthall's Brigade," *Memphis Daily Appeal*, October 1, 1863.

18 OR 30, pt. 1, p. 859.

19 Entry for September 18, 1863, William E. Sloan Diary.

20 *OR* 30, pt. 2, p. 531.

21 Entry for September 18, Nimrod Porter Diary, Tennessee State Library and Archives.

Creek [we] had a skirmish, which resulted in driving back the enemy, with the loss of 1 killed and 3 wounded."[22] Captain William A. Boyd of the 84th Indiana, one of the Union regiments involved in the affair, recalled a limited advance through thick timber, under a spirited if not very effective fire, until they reached an open field, where both opened fire with artillery, again without much loss.[23] Neither side was much interested in a larger fight. Both commanders had fulfilled their orders as they understood them.

Pegram's activities on September 18 are more obscure. His former brigade—which he insisted on commanding—numbered roughly 1,900 men and began the day near Rock Springs. His men had been in Taylor's Valley since their encounter with Wilder at Leet's Tanyard six days earlier, and so were well rested. As J. W. Minnich of the 6th Georgia later recalled, the men were recovering "from our rather strenuous campaigning" of the past couple of weeks. The brigade was well situated to assign regiments to lead both Walker's and Buckner's columns. Neither Forrest's nor Pegram's reports provide even a cursory description of Pegram's activities or instructions for all of September 18, nor do any other sources from the brigade. As a result, his movements and actions can only be speculated upon by using other sources, both Union and Confederate. [24]

The infantry under Walker and Buckner commenced their movement around 6:00 a.m., and almost immediately ran into delays. Walker, Buckner, and Pegram were all trying to use the same road simultaneously, which resulted in a considerable traffic jam. Buckner charitably described the mess as having "somewhat retarded" his progress.[25] Pegram, presumably at the front with his cavalry, rode ahead of the fitfully moving infantry.

---

22 *OR* 30, pt. 1, p. 864. Spring Creek was a small stream just east of Rossville.

23 William A. Boyd Journal, Bancroft Library, University of California at Berkeley.

24 J. W. Minnich, "Unique Experiences in the Chickamauga Campaign," *Confederate Veteran*, Vol. 30, No. 10 (October, 1922), p. 381. John Pegram's relationship with his former brigade serves as a microcosm of the confused command issues in not just Bragg's cavalry but many of his infantry organizations as well. Pegram retained direct command of his former brigade (why the senior colonel did not assume command is unknown), even though he was supposed to lead a division. In effect, Pegram was leading both, and neither. Nor did Pegram, as division commander, provide much in the way of instruction to Col. John Scott, who led the other brigade in his division. For all practical purposes, Pegram and Scott operated independently, with the latter officer taking his orders directly from Gen. Forrest. Pegram's decision to hold down both roles at once was unwise.

25 *OR* 30, pt. 2, p. 357.

Walker, who was tasked with crossing the creek at Alexander's Bridge, was not sure whether the crossing was even in Rebel hands. According to Bragg's previous orders, Forrest's men would seize it well ahead of Walker's arrival. Walker's report reflected his uncertainty. A month after the battle at Chickamauga, he outlined his instructions as he understood them: "I was ordered by the commanding general to cross the Chickamauga at Alexander's Bridge if practicable. If not, to cross at Byram's Ford, about 1 and 1/2 miles below." Before Walker even reached the bridge "I was informed that I would have to fight for it, as it was held by the enemy."[26] Walker didn't state who provided this information, but it almost certainly came from Pegram.

The fight for possession of Alexander's Bridge escalated into a sharp and protracted affair. The far bank of the creek was defended by Wilder's Mounted Infantry, who had arrived there the day before. Members of the 72nd Indiana located good foraging across the bridge on the east bank on the evening of the 17th, and another party set out that morning on a similar mission. They returned hastily, recalled Hoosier Sgt. Benjamin McGee, chased by Pegram's Rebel horsemen. In their urgency, some of the foragers skipped the bridge altogether and plunged into the creek. Others of Company A, 72nd Indiana, opened fire on the approaching Confederates, who made a half-hearted effort to charge the bridge before being driven off.[27] The cavalry had to be some of Pegram's men, but no Rebel source mentions the fight at all. Word of the encounter, however, snaked its way up the Confederate chain of command.

At 2:00 p.m., Walker's leading division under Brig. Gen. St. John Liddell reached the high ground overlooking the bridge from the south. Aware of how much Bragg's schedule was slipping off its timetable, Walker ordered Liddell to attack immediately. "The reconnaissance I made," Liddell reported, "was a very hasty and imperfect one . . . relying chiefly on information . . . obtained from . . . General Pegram . . . I [ordered] . . . an attack."[28] The assault was made by Walthall's Mississippi brigade, whose members discovered two important pieces of information by doing so: the 72nd Indiana had torn up the bridge planking to make a small lunette in the road about 100 yards north of the creek, and the Yankees were armed with seven-shot Spencer repeaters. The heavy rate

26 *Ibid.*, p. 239.

27 B. F. McGee, *History of the 72d Indiana Volunteer Infantry of the Mounted Lightning Brigade* (S. Vater & Co., 1882), p. 167.

28 *OR* 30, pt. 2, p. 251.

of gunfire tore through Walthall's ranks and drove them back. Stymied at the bridge after a protracted fight of about one hour, Walker decided to move his corps downstream a mile or so and use the alternate crossing at Lambert's Ford, where he crossed over by nightfall.

Pegram's men were present for at least part of this fight, though only as spectators. Private J. W. Minnich of the 6th Georgia Cavalry, Pegram's former brigade, wrote exhaustively about his experiences at Chickamauga, documenting in detail every action his brigade was involved in from September 10th through the 23rd. The important events of September 18 he discussed only in passing. "We found ourselves on the right and rear of Liddell's Division, when Walthall's Mississippi Brigade was trying to force a crossing of Alexander's Bridge," penned Minnich. "We were not engaged, though under fire both from rifle fire and a few shells that whistled by, but apparently all passed over us." Minnich added that Pegram's command (in response to a summons from Forrest) also moved downstream, crossing the Chickamauga at Fowler's Ford "late in the afternoon." [29]

*   *   *

Forrest started his day at Dalton, fourteen miles south of Ringgold and roughly the same distance east of Pegram. With him was a limited mounted force consisting of his escort (a hand-picked detachment of about 100 men he often used as an elite force, to be committed at the critical moment), and a scratch battalion identified in the records as "Martin's Detachment" of John Hunt Morgan's command.

Martin's men were all Kentuckians, the survivors and escapees from Morgan's disastrous raid into Kentucky earlier that summer. Some had made their way back from Ohio, evading Union troops the entire distance, while others had been left behind when the raid started because of their own poor health or the lack of a horse. When Morgan's division was cut off and mostly captured at Buffington Island, these survivors were left without a formal command and became the focus of an administrative tug-of-war. Bragg wanted them all dismounted and formed into another infantry regiment, a dismaying prospect to the men in question. Fellow Kentuckian and corps commander Simon Buckner also objected to the idea. In the end, they were reformed as a

---

29 Minnich, "Unique Experiences in the Chickamauga Campaign," p. 381.

cavalry regiment in August 1863. Their commander was Col. Adam Johnson, who had served under Forrest as a scout, earned promotion as a partisan commander in 1862, and led nearly 350 survivors of Morgan's men safely out of Ohio. He was a perfect choice for command, and by the middle of September nearly 1,200 Kentuckians had joined him, including 500 mounted men.[30] Within days, the mounted portion of the new unit was transferred to Forrest's command.

When they reached the Army of Tennessee and Bragg first caught sight of them, the Kentuckians faced again the real prospect of becoming a dismounted command. Lacking proper equipment and short of saddles—and with bark rope substituting for bridles and stirrup leathers—Colonel Johnson's new command hardly looked like soldiers, mounted or otherwise. Bragg again suggested they could better serve the army's need as infantry. This time it was Forrest who intervened. When Bragg relented, Forrest placed Lt. Col. Robert M. Martin in command. Martin, a fellow Kentuckian admired for his reckless courage on the battlefield, had recently recovered from a serious wound and was just the kind of hell-for-leather trooper Forrest respected. Still, their numbers were small: Martin's new command numbered only some 240 men fit for duty when it accompanied Forrest out of Dalton on September 18.[31]

Forrest's escort and Martin's men were the only Southern cavalry to see prolonged action on September 18. They accompanied Forrest when he belatedly reached Bushrod Johnson at around 11:00 a.m. After completing their counter-march Johnson's infantry halted east of Peavine Ridge to explore Minty's disposition and prepared to attack.[32] Although he was five hours late, Forrest spurred his mount for the front to assume command of the advance.

---

30 Dee Alexander Brown, *The Bold Cavaliers* (J. B. Lippincott Company, 1959), p. 248.

31 Colonel Johnson remained in command of the overall force of survivors, including the dismounted men, and was responsible for re-equipping them. They were functioning administratively, or even on temporary leave trying to get new horses. Some were with the supply trains and others perhaps at depots like Ringgold. This was one of the major problems with Confederate cavalry. Martin led that portion of the command fit for field service. Adam Rankin Johnson, *The Partisan Rangers of the Confederate States Army* (Austin, TX, State House Press, 1995), pp. 155-6.

32 *OR* 30, pt. 2, pp. 451-2.

C hapter 9

The Fight at Reed's Bridge
(September 18, 1863)

W illiam Rosecrans was well aware he had lost the initiative and that his army was vulnerable to attack. His primary concern was the sizable gap between his left flank at Lee and Gordon's Mill and his main supply base at Chattanooga.

On September 15, XXI Corps commander Thomas Crittenden ordered Brigadier General Minty and his cavalry brigade to Peavine Valley north of Leet's Tanyard to establish a picket line monitoring Rebel movements in the area. Minty departed at midday and, via Reed's Bridge, reached Peeler's Mill that afternoon. Minty was only five miles from Ringgold and the Western and Atlantic Railroad. From this new camp, the Irish-born Federal cavalryman sent scouts out in a wide arc toward Graysville, Ringgold, Leet's Mill, and Rock Spring.[1] The patrols returned that night with alarming news: infantry belonging to Lt. Gen. James Longstreet of the Army of Northern Virginia occupied Dalton, and Simon Buckner's infantry from East Tennessee had reached Rock Springs. Crittenden flatly refused to believe the reports—especially that Longstreet had arrived from Virginia.[2] The news did not change much over the

---

1   OR 30, pt. 1, p. 922.

2   *Ibid.* In his campaign report, Minty noted his communication with Crittenden about the presence of various Confederate columns and Longstreet's arrival, and followed it with an

next two days (September 16 and 17). Each day, Minty reported strong enemy cavalry and infantry patrols skirmishing with his pickets and a growing Rebel presence around Ringgold. Union Brig. Gen. James B. Steadman's reconnaissance to Ringgold on the 17th confirmed the buildup. The information was dutifully passed up the chain of command.

Despite his doubts, Crittenden could not ignore the accumulating evidence. At midday on the 17th, even before news of Steadman's Ringgold foray reached him, the XXI Corps commander took the extra precaution of sending John Wilder's brigade to guard Alexander's Bridge just south of Minty's position. That afternoon, Wilder's men made camp on the Alexander farm, a picturesque setting on a gentle rise of land overlooking a bridge bearing the same name. Wilder and Minty quickly established contact. Together, they formed a solid cavalry screen directly astride the routes Bragg intended to use to flank Rosecrans. They also controlled the critical creek crossings, especially Alexander's and Reed's bridges.[3] Believing his position at Peeler's Mill was too exposed, Minty shifted his main camp about one mile westward to Reed's Bridge.[4]

Minty expected trouble. Even before the sun rose on the morning of September 18, he dispatched two large patrols to scout his front. A battalion of the 4th U.S. Cavalry, 100 strong, rode southeast toward Leet's Tanyard, while a mixed force of similar size drawn from the 4th Michigan and 7th Pennsylvania rode due east toward Ringgold. The rest of the brigade stood to arms at dawn. When a few hours passed without incident, the men in camp went about their regular morning fatigue duties. "Stable Call" was sounded, and the horses were fed and watered. According to the 4th U.S. Cavalry's Sgt. James Larson, there was even time for a leisurely breakfast and a quiet smoke.[5] The peaceful interlude ended mid-morning when sharp firing broke out to the east.

"extract" from the message he received in return, which acknowledged the information that "Longstreet [is] at Dalton . . . which the major-general commanding cannot believe." It is reasonable to conclude that Minty felt more than a little vindicated.

3   George A. Wilson, "Wilder's Brigade," *National Tribune*, October 26, 1893. See Also: R. H. G Minty, *Remarks of Brevet Major General R. H. G. Minty made September 18th, 1895, at the Dedication of the Monument Erected to the Fourth Michigan Cavalry at Reed's Bridge, Chickamauga National Park* (n.p. 1896), p. 3.

4   OR 30, pt. 1, 922.

5   James Larson, *Sergeant Larson, 4th Cav.* (Southern Literary Institute, 1935), p. 175. Ironically, Larson's mess was the only one that did not get a good breakfast. Foregoing an easy meal for a

The contact was triggered by the collision near Peavine Creek of the mixed battalion riding toward Ringgold under Pennsylvania Capt. Heber S. Thompson of the 7th regiment with the head of Bushrod Johnson's infantry column. With sound tactics and good judgment, Thompson delayed the Rebel advance for some time. According to Confederate Capt. William Harder, leading Company D of the 23rd Tennessee, the initial fighting erupted near Peeler's Mill, after which the Federal skirmishers retired slowly westward. Shortly after the initial collision, General Forrest arrived with his small mounted force and assumed command at the point of contact. Forrest, together with the dismounted troopers from the battalion of Morgan's survivors, reinforced the 23rd Tennessee and steadily pushed the Yankee troopers back.[6]

Forrest's handling of his cavalry at Peeler's Mill is suggestive of his command mindset. His orders were to provide cavalry to lead and screen both Johnson's column and other Rebel forces farther south. That mission went awry from the outset when no troopers were made available for that purpose. When Forrest finally arrived, he was accompanied only by his 100-man escort and Martin's 240 Kentuckians. As a corps commander screening a major movement, Forrest's role was to make sure his men were employed for proper reconnaissance purposes. Instead, he ordered them to dismount and reinforce the infantry skirmish line, fighting his men more like a brigadier or line officer than a high ranking commander in charge of screening Bragg's entire right flank. Johnson had plenty of infantry already—in fact, much more than he needed. Forrest's cavalry could have been more gainfully employed by finding and turning the flanks of Minty's advanced line, or riding behind it to determine what was in Johnson's front. Forrest did neither.

The experienced Minty refused to sit idly by with firing underway. Shortly after 10:00 a.m., perhaps thirty minutes before Forrest arrived, Minty reinforced Captain Thompson with two more battalions, one from the 4th Michigan and another from the 4th Regulars, plus one section (two guns) from the Illinois Chicago Board of Trade Battery. The brigade commander assumed personal charge of the defense. Minty arrayed his dismounted cavalrymen in a

---

more elaborate midday feast, Larson and his messmates were stewing a huge kettle of beef when the alarm sounded.

6 Harder Reminiscences, Combat Studies Institute. This skirmish near Peeler's Mill is discussed in more detail from the Confederate perspective in the previous chapter. The 23rd Tennessee was part of Bushrod Johnson's former brigade, now led by Col. John S. Fulton.

strong defensive position along the crest of Peavine Ridge overlooking a creek of the same name. Once deployed, he awaited developments.[7] Captain Henry A. Potter, commanding Company H of the Michiganders, deployed his men on the left of the Pennsylvanians overlooking their former camp at Peeler's Mill.[8] The 4th Regulars extended Thompson's right flank. Minty's forward line numbered about 600 men and two guns.

Opposing Minty were several thousand infantry under Bushrod Johnson and some cavalry under Forrest. Unsure of the composition or strength of his opposition, Johnson prudently deployed three of his infantry brigades in line, holding one in reserve, and ordered his artillery to engage Minty's brace of cannon. Crossing Peavine Creek took some time, but by the time they reached the creek Johnson's infantry were beginning to work their way around both Federal flanks. After some spirited fighting and a short artillery exchange, Minty implemented a slow but steady withdrawal toward Reed's Bridge.

Minty also dashed off couriers to both Crittenden and Rosecrans reporting the size and strength of the attack. One thing in particular worried him: a dust cloud to the northeast suggested that another Confederate column was heading toward Dyer's Ford, the next crossing site north of Reed's Bridge. Minty had only a small picket force there, and no additional troops to spare. If Rebels crossed Dyer's Ford in strength, they could move unopposed against his left flank and rear, cutting off his brigade from the rest of the army. Minty needed more help. He sent another courier riding south to request help from Wilder.[9]

Johnson's men pushed after the retreating dismounted Federal cavalry with Forrest in command of the advance now comprising his own troopers augmented by elements of the 17th and 44th Tennessee infantry regiments.[10] The rest of Johnson's division trailed within supporting distance. Johnson kept his brigades in battle line, which made for slow going as they negotiated through the wooded and rolling terrain. The methodical Southern advance gave Minty

---

7   Today, this ridge is called Boynton Ridge. There is another Peavine Ridge about one mile east of this location, which should not be confused with the location of the opening fight. See Joseph G. Vale, *Minty and the Cavalry: A History of Cavalry Campaigns in the Western Armies* (Edwin K. Myers, 1886), p. 225. Vale refers to Boynton Ridge merely as "a ridge."

8   Henry Albert Potter, "Account of the Battle of Chickamauga and Wheeler's Raid," Bentley Historical Library.

9   Vale, *Minty and the Cavalry*, p. 225.

10   OR 30, pt. 2, p. 471; and Harder Reminiscences, Combat Studies Institute.

the precious time he needed to fall back and establish a new defensive line near his campsite.

Minty placed his command with care. His camp baggage had been packed up and withdrawn during the fight on Peavine Ridge. Now, with his back to the creek, Minty stationed the 4th Michigan and 7th Pennsylvania north of the bridge, dismounting half of each command as skirmishers.[11] The 4th Regulars were also divided. One squadron was sent with the two guns of the Board of Trade Battery to take up a position southwest of the bridge, beyond where the creek makes a sharp bend to the west. There, where what Minty later described as a "bad ford" crossed the creek, the two cannon were hidden in some brush with the cavalry mounted in line behind them as support.[12] The other two squadrons of the 4th Regulars occupied a piece of high ground on the west (far) side of the creek, overlooking both the ford and the bridge.

These dispositions were nearly finished when help arrived. In response to Minty's appeal, Wilder dispatched Col. Abram O. Miller with his own 72nd Indiana, the 123rd Illinois, and a section of mountain howitzers from Eli Lilly's 18th Indiana Battery.[13] Miller reported to Minty about 1:00 p.m. Worried about his left, the brigade command ordered Miller farther north to guard Dyer's Ford—close enough to see and hear much of Minty's sharply-fought delaying action, but too distant to offer active support. But for a few errant overshots and stinging insects, the detour allowed Miller's command to escape September 18 largely unscathed. "[T]he rebels' shells bursting over us and the Yellow Jackets stinging our horses and us made it any but comfortable," remembered Ambrose Remley of the 72nd Indiana.[14] What Minty could not have known was that no Rebels were moving to cross at Dyer's Ford. The dust cloud that drew away substantial reinforcements from Reed's Bridge was probably kicked up by Colonel Scott's Confederate cavalrymen on their way to Red House Bridge.

About this time, Johnson's infantry arrived to begin the next act of the unfolding drama. Once atop Peavine Ridge Johnson realized for the first time that he faced only a single enemy brigade. He moved to deploy his command for a full attack. The leading brigade under Col. John S. Fulton prepared to

11 Potter Narrative. Bentley Historical Library.

12 *OR* 30, pt. 1, p. 923.

13 *Ibid.*, p. 451.

14 Dale Edward Linville, *Battles, Skirmishes, Events and Scenes: The Letters and Memorandum of Ambrose Remley* (Montgomery County Historical Society, 1997), p. 81.

charge directly for the bridge, while the brigades of Brig. Gens. John Gregg and Evander McNair moved to the right and left, respectively, to assist the attack. Johnson's fourth brigade, Brig. Gen. Jerome B. Robertson's famous Texas Brigade, remained in reserve. Robertson's men were the first of Longstreet's Virginia reinforcements to reach the field. As the infantry moved into position, two batteries of Confederate artillery renewed their fire against the Yankees.[15]

It was at this point in the fighting that Forrest noticed other Federals farther south. Although the record is unclear, Forrest may have believed they were guarding Minty's camp somewhere upstream, and the aggressive-minded general decided to go after it. When Forrest asked Johnson to loan him the 17th Tennessee Infantry for this venture, Johnson acquiesced. When he finally moved out Forrest took with him some 600 men in search of an enemy camp. According to Lt. Col. Watt W. Floyd, the commander of the 17th Tennessee, the column marched about one-half mile south, but "before we got in range, the enemy fled."[16] The consequence of the detour was that Forrest, his cavalry, and the Tennesseans were not available for the subsequent fight for Reed's Bridge.

Johnson was finally ready to attack Reed's Bridge sometime around 2:00 p.m. Fulton's men made straight for the structure, hoping to seize it before the Federals escaped, but ran into stiff resistance from the Union skirmishers and two hidden guns Minty had placed upstream. Minty ordered the mounted elements of the 4th Michigan and 7th Pennsylvania to charge the oncoming Confederates, forcing some of them back in confusion.[17] The rest of the unchecked Rebel line, however, continued driving west and turned both of Minty's flanks, forcing him to repeat the morning's disengagement maneuver and fall back across the creek.

Minty handled the maneuver with substantial finesse, but this time the withdrawal devolved into a bit more of a scramble. The first to leave was the 4th Michigan, which rode across Reed's Bridge. The span was so rickety and narrow that the troopers had to cross in column of twos because four men abreast would not fit.[18] Once across, the Michiganders dismounted and lined the west

---

15 OR 30, pt. 2, p. 472.

16 Ibid., p. 479.

17 James H. Shuster, "Holding Reed's Bridge," National Tribune, August 11, 1910; Vale, Minty and the Cavalry, p. 226.

18 Vale, Minty and the Cavalry, p. 227.

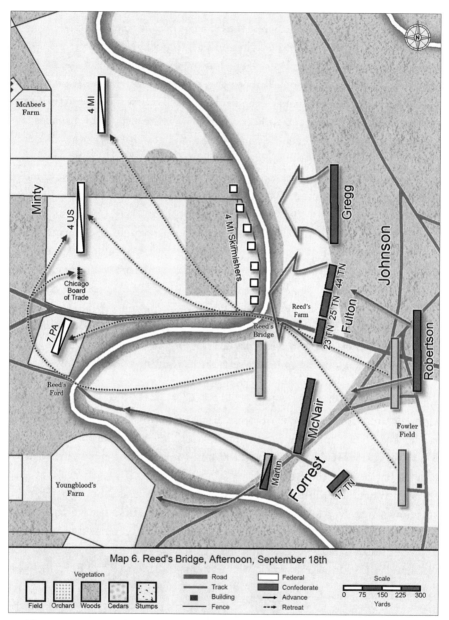

Map 6. Reed's Bridge, Afternoon, September 18th

The contest over Reed's Bridge is notable largely because of the absence of Confederate cavalry. The day-long struggle between Bushrod Johnson's Rebel infantry and Robert Minty's Federal cavalry is witnessed only by a handful of Nathan Bedford Forrest's troopers. Johnson, who was unsure of what he was facing and operating in uncertain terrain, was delayed by the Union cavalry's outstanding stalling tactics. If Forrest's cavalry had secured the crossing the previous day, a fight for the crossing would not have been necessary.

bank of the creek to cover the 7th Pennsylvania's retreat.[19] Once they were across, Minty withdrew the battery and lone squadron of the 4th U.S. back by the upstream ford. The two cannon made it safely to the west bank, rolled back to where the rest of the Regulars had been stationed earlier, unlimbered, and went back into action. The last squadron of the 4th Regulars, acting as rearguard, barely escaped. Commanded by Lt. Wirt Davis, the two troops were preparing to cross at the ford when Davis noticed that the 7th Pennsylvania was jammed up at the bridge and the Rebel infantry was closing in. Wheeling his command around, Davis delivered another mounted charge into Fulton's and McNair's Confederates, who fell back just far enough to allow the Pennsylvanians to finish crossing. Only then did Davis pull his own men back across the bridge. In a final show of bravado, Davis and the last few troopers halted under fire and tore up the bridge railings and planks, hurling them into the creek to float downstream.[20]

The approaching men in gray showed equal audacity. Captain Harder's 23rd Tennessee drove back the 4th Michigan's skirmish line, but the fire was so heavy they could not get across the creek. The captain ordered his company forward to repair the bridge. Tearing planks off the Reed house and barn, the Tennesseans re-floored the span—despite the best efforts of Union sharpshooters to pick them off.

Returning from his venture to the south, Forrest rode upon the scene at the bridge and congratulated Harder and his Tennesseans for their courage before setting out to demonstrate a little daring of his own. The cavalry commander guided his horse across the re-planked bridge and rode to within 100 yards of the Union line, where he halted and coolly surveyed the enemy before trotting back to the waiting Rebels. The display impressed Harder. "He halted, with his accustomed attentive and intensive manner," wrote the captain, "took in the situation of the whole line of the federal[s], while discharge after discharge of grape and canister dashed by him."[21]

With the bridge repaired, Minty's two guns were unable to prevent Fulton's Brigade from crossing. Once on the west bank, the infantry moved north about 400 yards and formed a line of battle facing the Union line only 300 yards

---

19 Potter Narrative, Bentley Historical Library.

20 Vale, *Minty and the Cavalry*, p. 227.

21 Harder reminiscences, Combat Studies Institute.

distant. With Fulton holding the attention of the enemy, Johnson attempted another flanking move. This time he sent Forrest's cavalry detachment and another infantry brigade west toward the ford used earlier by the Federal artillery. They succeeded in reaching the west bank, where they threatened Minty's southern flank and rendered the Federal position untenable.[22] This new threat was developing when Minty received a report informing him that Colonel Wilder, who had been defending Alexander's Bridge farther south all day, had also been outflanked and was falling back to Lee and Gordon's Mills.[23] Faced with encirclement, Minty had no choice but to withdraw. About 4:00 p.m. he sent word to Colonel Miller at Dyer's Ford that he was retreating, and that Miller's men should join him "as soon as possible."[24]

Riding west along the Reed's Bridge Road toward Rossville, the Federal cavalry turned south once they reached the Lafayette Road and moved to join Gen. Crittenden near Lee and Gordon's Mill. Colonel Miller's two regiments of mounted infantry from Wilder's brigade pulled back from Dyer's Ford and followed the same route. September 18 was a long and tiring day for the Rebels. Casualties, although not heavy, were still significant. Nearly 100 Confederates had been killed and wounded in the engagement for Reed's Bridge.[25]

Confederate reinforcements arrived while Johnson's men watched the last of Minty's command retreat past Jay's Mill a few hundred yards west of the creek. The first on the scene was Maj. Gen. John Bell Hood, who was senior in rank to Johnson. Although still suffering from his crippling Gettysburg arm wound, Hood rushed to the field as quickly as possible to take command of Johnson's column (which now included Hood's beloved Texas Brigade).[26] John Pegram's cavalry brigade also made its belated appearance.[27] Exactly what took Pegram's 1,900 horsemen so long to arrive has never been fully explained. After observing the fight at Alexander's Bridge during the afternoon, Pegram broke

---

22 *OR* 30, pt. 2, p. 452.

23 Minty, *Remarks of Brevet Major General R. H. G. Minty*, p. 5.

24 *Ibid.*

25 Neither Johnson nor his brigade commanders reported the September 18 losses separately from those suffered on the 19th and 20th. Only a few units mentioned specific losses in the body of their reports. See *OR* 30, pt. 2, pp. 451-502, for the division reports. Morgan's former cavalry, fighting under Martin, did not prepare a report with losses for this engagement.

26 *OR* 30, pt. 2, p. 452.

27 Minnick, "Reminiscences of J. W. Minnick, 6th Georgia Cavalry," p. 20.

away at some point to join Forrest, crossing the Chickamauga at Fowler's Ford. The total route was not more than a couple of miles, but it took Pegram several hours to negotiate it. As a result, his men contributed almost nothing to either fight.

C hapter 10

The Fight at Alexander's Bridge
(September 18, 1863)

T here is no record of his reaction when he discovered Alexander's Bridge firmly in enemy hands, but William Henry Talbot Walker was not known for his patience or geniality. Walker was a fighter, always ready to plunge into the thick of combat. His old army nickname was "shotpouch," a moniker earned by wounds acquired in Mexico and on the frontier. He didn't just fight with the enemy, however. St. John R. Liddell, a former West Point classmate who served under Walker at Chickamauga, described him as "well known to be a crackbrained fire eater," a verbal quibbler who was always "caviling about something." In the midst of the battle the next day, Walker would argue with D. H. Hill about the tactical situation, and he would die the following spring in the fighting for Atlanta with anger in his heart and a threat on his lips about a perceived insult. On September 18, 1863, the major general's mission was to cross his Reserve Corps of infantry over Chickamauga Creek a couple miles upstream from Reed's Bridge as the second stage of Braxton Bragg's massive envelopment plan. Contrary to Walker's expectations, John Wilder and his mounted infantry were there to see that he did not.[1]

---

1 Arthur W. Bergeron, Jr., "Williams Henry Talbot Walker," in Davis, *The Confederate General*, 6, p. 99. In his Chickamauga report, OR 30, pt. 2, p. 239, Walker wrote: "Before reaching the bridge I was informed I would have to fight for it, as it was held by the enemy."

The previous evening, Wilder sent detachments of Federal mounted infantry to picket the banks of the creek between Lee and Gordon's Mills and the bridge. The rest of Wilder's men camped near the Alexander house on a rise about 650 yards behind the creek.[2] With the bulk of his command concentrated here, Wilder could dispatch reserves to threatened points of his line while the high ground provided the guns of Lilly's battery an excellent field of fire down to the bridge and beyond. That morning (as described in Chapter 8), Wilder's scouts and foragers crossed the creek and moved out into the countryside to the southeast, looking for both Rebels and rations.[3]

About midmorning, Wilder's patrols returned to report their brush with John Pegram's cavalry. There was no immediate threat, however, and the men had time to prepare lunch. When Minty contacted Wilder for assistance, he responded by sending half his command under Colonel Miller to Reed's Bridge, where Minty directed Miller to continue on to Dyer's Ford. Shortly after noon, while Minty's men were battling Forrest and Bushrod Johnson, more Rebels appeared and drove Wilder's skirmishers back across the creek. "Boots and Saddles" interrupted the midday meal.[4]

Initially, only two companies of the 72nd Indiana covered the crossings. Company A's line was centered on the bridge itself, with Company F extending that picket to a ford about a mile upstream.[5] Beyond Company F, part of the 123rd Illinois was assigned to picket the bank from that ford all the way southwest to Lee and Gordon's Mills, a meandering two miles.

Late that morning, a second party of foragers set out from Company A's position, but this expedition was cut short when they also encountered Southern troopers, who galloped after the Hoosiers back toward the bridge. Company A's foragers were scrambling across the span (and in some cases leaping their animals into the creek) when this unidentified body of Confederate

---

2   Wilder Report, CCNMP. This report, dated 1888, is much more detailed than the one found in the *OR*, but in some places is less accurate.

3   Wilder Report, CCNMP; McGee, *History of the 72nd Indiana*, p. 167.

4   Magee, *History of the 72nd Indiana*, p. 167.

5   *Ibid.* West Chickamauga Creek flows generally north to south, with the Federals holding the ground on the west side (the side closer to Chattanooga), and Confederate territory beginning east of the streambed. However, the creek's course is a meandering one, with broad bends and loops, so at times the "western" bank is really the "northern" side of the creek. At Alexander's Bridge, technically speaking Wilder's men defended the "northern" bank, while the Confederates lined the "southern" side of the stream.

cavalry made a hasty effort to storm the bridge. A sharp fusillade of Spencer bullets drove them off. Alerted to the danger confronting them, Company A tore up most of the bridge flooring and used the lumber to build a small lunette in the middle of the road about 100 yards back from the creek bank.[6] They still maintained a skirmish line on the Confederate side of the waterway, but Company A could use the makeshift fort as a final defensive position, if necessary.

Brigadier General Edward Cary Walthall's five Mississippi regiments, part of Liddell's Division, led Walker's column that morning. When firing broke out about a mile from the bridge, Walthall deployed his brigade in a single battle line fronting 600 yards, with his left flank anchored on the road.[7] Rebel skirmishers advanced another 200 yards before the entire brigade stepped off toward Alexander's Bridge. Walthall used the road as a guide, but his line was disrupted when the road curved and his front was forced into a left wheel.[8] The right flank regiment, the 24th Mississippi, found itself running to try and catch up. It fell so far behind and was thrown into such disorder that it took almost no part in the ensuing fight.[9]

Walthall's line extended far beyond the small skirmish line maintained by the Indianans, forcing the last of the Federals to scramble back across the bridge, tearing up the final planks as they retreated. Once across the men tumbled into Company A's hastily erected earthwork. In what must have been an impressive display, the main line of Mississippians emerged into open fields and approached Chickamauga Creek. When the Federals near the Alexander house spotted them, Wilder personally ordered Lt. Joseph A. Scott's section of Lilly's battery to open fire.[10] In addition to the Rebel infantry sweeping forward, Scott spotted Capt. William H. Fowler's Alabama battery coming into action in support of Walthall. He directed his fire against the Rebel cannon.

---

6 *Ibid.*, p. 168.

7 OR 30, pt. 2, p. 271. Chickamauga Creek makes a series of bends between Reed's Bridge and Alexander's Bridge. Reed's Bridge is an east-west crossing, while, due to the winding nature of the creek, the Alexander's Bridge Road crosses the creek from south to north.

8 Robert A. Jarman, "History of Company K, 27th Mississippi," J. D. Williams Library, University of Mississippi.

9 OR 30, pt. 2, p. 277.

10 Joseph A. Scott Reminiscences, Smith Memorial Library, Indiana Historical Society. Scott mistakenly believed that his guns were the first Federal cannon to fire at Chickamauga, but almost certainly the section with Minty holds this honor.

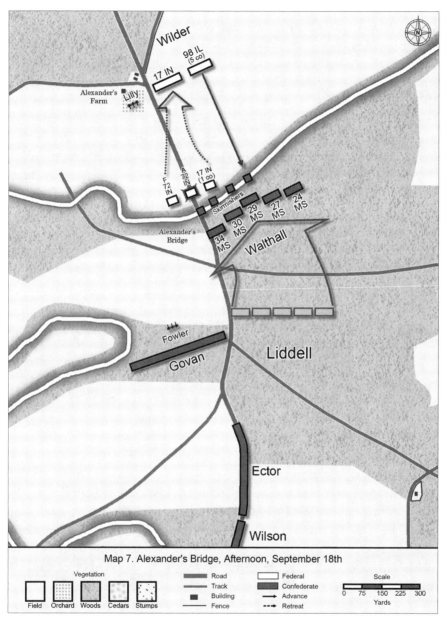

Map 7. Alexander's Bridge, Afternoon, September 18th

Rebel cavalry are also absent in the struggle for Alexander's Bridge. W. H. T. Walker's Reserve Corps of infantry has no success in its effort to drive John Wilder's Federal mounted infantry away from the crossing. After wasting precious time and lives, Walker is forced to move downstream (to the northeast) to find a crossing and outflank the stubborn defensive effort. Wilder, who had sent much of his command elsewhere to support Minty at Reed's Bridge or to watch other crossings, is finally forced to fall back.

While embattled Company A was busy reprising "Horatio at the Bridge," Wilder cast about for troops to help them. The 123rd Illinois and the rest of the 72nd had already departed with Colonel Miller. Half of the 98th Illinois left to replace the 123rd's men guarding crossings all the way up to Lee and Gordon's Mills.[11] The 92nd Illinois, detached to serve as couriers and scouts for Thomas, was still miles to the south at Pond Springs.[12] This left Wilder with only five companies of the 98th and the full complement of the 17th Indiana in line supporting Lilly's artillery. One company of the 17th moved forward as skirmishers on the west side of the road to protect Company A's left flank. Company F of the 72nd was still present and closed up as well, supporting their right flank.[13] These three companies, each armed with Spencer repeating rifles, opened fire on Walthall's approaching Mississippi infantry.

When Walthall's men reached the creek bank, they discovered that was about as far as they were going. The bridge was floorless, and what was left of the structure was swept by Lilly's artillery. Repairing it under fire seemed impossible, and the fast-firing Spencers made up for the lack of Federal manpower. The creek itself, reported Walthall, "was narrow, but deep, the banks steep and impassable."[14] Unable to force a crossing, the Mississippians lined the bank and commenced a prolonged firefight with the Yankees, focusing much of their fire at the Federals in their little wood and earth fort. Major General Walker's job was to get his Reserve Corps across the creek as fast as possible, but Wilder's stubborn defense was complicating his mission. Walker reported that Walthall's fight for the bridge itself was "sharp and short," but the stationary slugfest threatened to consume precious time and eat away at Bragg's rather precise timetable. Thrown into a difficult situation, the unfortunate Mississippians suffered a number of casualties without clearing the bridge or managing to get a sizable infantry force across the creek.

While Walthall's main line traded shots with Wilder's men, enough hardy Southern troops managed to wade the stream to threaten Company A's horses, which were tied to trees while their owners fought. Members of Company F of the 72nd Indiana spotted the movement but could not reach the animals in time

---

11 *OR* 30, pt. 1, p. 458.

12 *Ninety-Second Illinois Volunteers*, pp. 107-8.

13 *Indiana at Chickamauga: 1863-1900, Report Of Indiana Commissioners, Chickamauga National Military Park* (Sentinel Printing Company, 1900), pp. 142-3.

14 *OR* 30, pt. 2, p. 272.

to save them. Instead, the Federals shot down 31 of the 36 Company A's mounts, a cold but necessary decision to prevent the Rebels from capturing live horses.[15]

While Walthall's long line continued laying down a heavy field of fire, the small knots of Mississippians who had managed to wade across found Company A's flank and threatened to turn it. Wilder ordered the men to fall back to the Alexander house. The Southern fire was so heavy the Hoosiers could not leave the lunette *en masse*, so the defenders slipped away by ones and twos, running a gauntlet of minie balls in their perilous flight to safety. Sergeant Joseph Higgenbotham witnessed the intensity of the Rebel fire firsthand when he was shot five times in just 30 yards. The unlucky Federal recovered from all five wounds, but died of disease a few months later at Corinth, Mississippi.[16] To cover the withdrawal from the lunette, Wilder ordered the remaining half of the 98th Illinois forward about 2:00 p.m. to try and drive the Rebels back across the creek.[17]

Despite forcing Company A out of its stronghold, the Mississippians made little additional headway. Only small numbers of Rebels had managed to find a way across the creek, leaving the bulk of the brigade stymied on the far bank. The addition of the 98th Illinois, adding a couple of hundred more Spencer repeaters to the firefight, precluded any serious effort to re-plank the bridge or push more organized bodies of Rebels across the stream's few tenuous crossing points.

Thwarted in his effort to cross quickly and after watching Walthall's Mississippians suffer for as long as two hours, General Walker changed his plans. Instead of forcing his way across Alexander's Bridge, he would find another way over the difficult stream. A local guide led the Confederates to Lambert's Ford about one mile downstream. Walker troops began crossing there. Walthall's Brigade—minus the 105 men who had been killed and wounded in the bloody standoff at Alexander's Bridge—led the way across about 4:00 p.m.[18] Wilder first got wind of the movement a short while later when, about 5:00 p.m., "a picket . . . reported a strong force of rebel infantry in

---

15 Magee, *History of the 72nd Indiana*, p. 168.

16 *Ibid.*, p. 169.

17 *OR* 30, pt. 1, p. 458.

18 *Ibid.*, pt. 2, p. 271.

my rear."[19] Like Minty, Wilder had also waged a brilliant defensive effort, but his only option now was to withdraw or risk annihilation. He sent word to Minty that he was falling back southwest toward Lee and Gordon's Mills.

In later years, a minor veteran's controversy arose over who retreated first: Minty or Wilder. The old soldiers argued the point in print and in person at reunions for years. In an 1888 version of his Official Records report, Wilder claimed Minty's retreat precipitated his own withdrawal, but contemporaneous reports suggest that Wilder reached his decision first.[20] In fact, who fell back first mattered little because large numbers of Rebels had crossed the creek at Lambert's and Fowler's fords, rendering both Minty's and Wilder's positions untenable; neither officer could have held his position.

*   *   *

Because Lambert's Ford proved to be a poor passage for men and wheeled vehicles alike, the crossing was a labor-intensive and time consuming effort. Once they finally crossed Chickamauga Creek, Walthall's Mississippians advanced to the Alexander house, turned onto the Vinyard-Alexander Road, and halted for the night.[21] The rest of Walker's Reserve Corps was still on the Confederate bank of the creek and darkness was fast approaching. Liddell's other brigade under Col. Daniel C. Govan followed Walthall and also halted near the Alexander house. Only part of Gist's Division, which in Gist's absence was being led by Brig. Gen. Mathew D. Ector, managed to cross before darkness made it too difficult and dangerous to continue. Once the crossing stopped, Walker's trains and one infantry brigade remained on the south bank.[22] Walker's Reserve Corps would not finish passing over the creek until after dawn the next morning.

After all the bloodshed and effort, once his troops reached the Alexander house, Walker discovered he had nowhere to go. Bragg's tightly-scripted plan called for Walker to wait for Bushrod Johnson's column to arrive from Reed's Bridge, and then fall in behind it. Given Johnson's delay at Reed's Bridge, even

---

19 *Ibid.*, pt. 1, p. 447.

20 Wilder Report, CCNMP.

21 *OR* 30, pt. 2, p. 272.

22 *Ibid.*, p. 239.

an early success at Alexander's Bridge would have yielded nothing but a longer wait for Walker at the Alexander farmstead. Bragg's orders lacked sufficient flexibility to compensate for unexpected delays.

Johnson also ended the day in some frustration. Once he reached Jay's Mill he found himself supplanted by a stranger. John Bell Hood, commanding James Longstreet's Corps in the absence of its commander, arrived between 3:00 and 4:00 p.m. As the senior officer on the field, Hood was entitled to take command, and he did. Johnson resumed command of his provisional division.[23]

Jay's Mill was about one-half mile west of Reed's Bridge. Two roads diverged there, one led due south to Alexander's Bridge. The other, the Brotherton Road, struck a more westerly direction toward the Lafayette Road. Both routes eventually led to Lee and Gordon's Mills. Hood and Johnson had a minor disagreement about which road to take. Hood overruled Johnson and opted to follow the road south to Alexander's Bridge and meet up with Walker's Reserve Corps.[24]

Once at the Alexander house, Hood's men turned right onto the road leading to the Viniard house, which sat on the west side of the Lafayette Road about one mile and a half north of Lee and Gordon's Mills. Walker's command filed in behind Hood during the march southwest through the woods. The combined column advanced about two miles until, in gathering darkness, they encountered more Yankees.

The Yankees turned out to be Wilder's ubiquitous mounted infantry, who had retreated down this same road after leaving the Alexander homestead. Several hundred yards east of the Viniard house Wilder made contact with Maj. Gen. Horatio Van Cleve's third Division of the Crittenden's XXI Corps. Wilder deployed a line to protect the front and flank of the XXI Corps and was joined there by Minty's command and Colonel Miller with the other two regiments of his own brigade. Crittenden and Thomas Wood, commanding the XXI Corps' First Division, were also present. Wilder did his best to convince a dubious Crittenden of the size of the approaching Rebel threat, and Minty jumped in to add his own report to that effort.[25] Minty also posted his cavalry brigade

---

23 John Bell Hood, *Advance and Retreat* (Blue and Gray Press, 1985), p. 61.

24 *OR* 30, pt. 2, p. 452.

25 Vale, *Minty and the Cavalry*, p. 229.

alongside Wilder's in a skirmish line astride the road leading back to the Alexander house. Crittenden remained skeptical that any Rebels beyond a few cavalrymen were heading toward him, but he did reinforce Wilder's line with two infantry regiments just in case.[26]

This is the line Bushrod Johnson's Confederates collided with about two hours after dark. The collision produced a short and confused firefight that convinced the Rebels to halt for the night. It also ended any doubts Crittenden or his division commanders had about whether Rebel infantry was in their front.[27]

*   *   *

The fight at Alexander's Bridge was an important engagement because it disrupted significantly Bragg's plan to coordinate the turning of Rosecrans' left flank. The head of Walker's column reached the bridge around noon, and Walthall's fight lasted until perhaps 2:00 or 2:30 p.m. The countermarch upstream to find a ford consumed at least another hour and perhaps much longer. Only part of Walker's Reserve Corps would cross the creek that night. (The last brigade and his trains could not resume crossing until dawn on September 19.) In short, Wilder's stout defense cost the Confederates the entire afternoon from the time Walker reached Alexander's Bridge until he paused crossing at dark (roughly 7:00 p.m.).[28]

If Walthall had forced a crossing earlier, his Mississippians would have outflanked Minty's defense farther north at Reed's Bridge much sooner. Alternatively, if Bushrod Johnson's infantry had taken Reed's Bridge more rapidly, Wilder's defense at Alexander's Bridge would have ended hours earlier.

Notably absent in any discussion of the fight for Alexander's Bridge is the role played by Confederate cavalry. In fact, they played no role in the fighting or subsequent turning movement at all, despite Bragg's instructions directing Forrest to lead the infantry, seize the crossings (Alexander's Bridge was named specifically in Forrest's orders of September 16) and generally clear the way for his grand design. The mounted command best positioned to carry out Bragg's

26 *OR* 30, pt. 1, p. 803.

27 Robert G. Minty, "Minty's Saber Brigade" *National Tribune*, February 25, 1892.

28 Text of Walthall's Brigade Tablet, Alexander's Bridge, CCNMP.

orders was John Pegram's. Forrest's subordinate, however, merely informed General Walker that the bridge was held by Federals and then vanished—riding northward on an overly long trek to join Forrest near Reed's Bridge. The logical question to ask is, What could Pegram have reasonably done? The answer is quite a bit—with a little initiative.

The obvious move for cavalry would have been to move some horsemen to Lambert's Ford at midday—even as Walker was deploying Walthall's Mississippians—and cross there while Walthall opened the engagement at the bridge. The Confederates already knew about the ford and regarded it as an alternative crossing site. Walker outlined as much in his report, and even had a local guide. This would have placed 1,600 Confederate cavalry on the west bank of the Chickamauga between Wilder and Minty, in a position to threaten either Federal's flank hours sooner than Walker, who did the same thing crossing at the same ford. Neither Minty nor Wilder had enough troops to cover such a threat and the crossings, and almost certainly would have ordered a retreat rather than risk encirclement. Whether an earlier crossing at Lambert's would have helped fulfil Bragg's plan is debatable, but it would have given him a few extra hours of daylight.

Not all the blame for the delay at Alexander's Bridge can be laid at the feet of the cavalry, but Pegram's passivity raises the question of what more could have been accomplished under the orders that had been issued and the circumstances that he faced.

Chapter 11

The Night of the Missing Southern Cavalry

(Evening, September 18, 1863)

John Bell Hood's and William Walker's men slept that night on the side of the road in a long column stretching back all the way to Alexander's Bridge. Simon Buckner's troops were supposed to move up on Hood's left, but because they spent most of the day waiting for Walker and Johnson to capture the crossings, only one of Buckner's six brigades reached the west bank of Chickamauga Creek before nightfall. Jammed up behind Buckner, Leonidas Polk's Corps remained on the east bank.[1]

Despite the slow progress on September 18, Braxton Bragg still managed to get about one-half of his intended assault force across the Chickamauga, now camped in the woods and fields northeast of Lee and Gordon's Mills. The remainder were closed up on the creek and poised to cross at dawn. No Federals held the Lafayette Road between the Viniard house and Rossville, where Major General Gordon Granger's three-brigade Reserve Corps was camped. Most of the Rebels sheltered in the woods faced only a five-mile gap in the Union line. Bragg, of course, did not know this.

The disposition and operations of Nathan Bedford Forrest's cavalry on the evening of September 18 are unclear. As a corps commander, Forrest should have established a picket line in front of and on both flanks of the Rebel

---

1   OR 30, pt. 2, pp. 77, 357.

infantry column and sent out more wide-ranging patrols to cover the roads running north and west to probe for Union activity. Forrest's command, consisting of John Pegram's Brigade, Martin's Kentuckians, and his small escort (about 2,400 men all told), made camp in a field behind Hood's infantry near Alexander's Bridge.[2] According to Capt. John W. Morton, a commander of one of Forrest's artillery batteries, Hood ordered Forrest to place "scouts and pickets out for the protection of the main body." Morton's assertion may be true, but he was several miles to the south with Frank Armstrong's Division that day and so could not have been a firsthand witness to the exchange.[3]

Henry Clay, a member of Pegram's staff, claims Hood ordered Pegram, not Forrest, to "move out on my right and protect my right flank and ordnance train."[4] The 1st Georgia Cavalry was assigned this task, but where the troopers positioned themselves remains a bit of a mystery.[5] They did not screen Reed's Bridge Road or even stretch as far as Jay's Mill, as subsequent overnight Union movements demonstrate. W. F. Shropshire, a member of the 1st Georgia, later wrote that "our regiment, with Company G, a short distance in advance, was cautiously moving on the road leading by Reeds Steam saw mill, seeking as advance position as possible for the purpose of establishing a picket or skirmish line for the night. On Reaching some 300 yards from [south of] the Saw mill, Company G was fired into by the enemy from ambush." Shropshire went on to note that the regiment fell back another 100 yards, dismounted, and deployed in line. There, recalled the Georgian, "we were not disturbed by the enemy [for the rest of] that night."[6] The distance between the Alexander house and Jay's Mill is about a mile and a half, so if Shropshire's distances are generally accurate, the 1st Georgia picket line was established about one and one-quarter miles north of the Alexander house and at least 400 yards south of the Brotherton Road intersection.

2   *Ibid.*, p. 524.

3   John W. Morton, *The Artillery of Nathan Bedford Forrest's Cavalry* (Marietta, GA, 1995), p. 116.

4   H. B. Clay, "On the Right at Chickamauga," *Confederate Veteran*, Vol. XXI (September, 1913), pp. 439-40.

5   H. B. Clay, "On the Right at Chickamauga," *Confederate Veteran*, Vol. XIX (July, 1911), pp. 329-30. Clay's accounts (same title, published two years apart) makes it clear that at least one company was placed on picket, but he does not say where.

6   W. F. Shropshire Reminiscences, *Confederate Veteran* Papers, Duke University, Durham North Carolina.

Pegram also led a short personal reconnaissance that night in a curious episode that raises more questions than answers. Captain Gustave Huwald, commanding the battery of Rebel artillery attached to Pegram, described the expedition. "During the night of the 18th, our Gallant General Pegram, wishing to reconnoitre, crossed the bridge [Alexander's Bridge] accompanied by his staff and bodyguard, and to his surprise found himself in a lane between two large camps," recalled Huwald. "He addressed a party of soldiers inquiring the name of the command, and was informed that an Ohio regiment occupied one side of the lane, while an Illinois regiment camped on the other side. Without showing alarm or surprise, he turned his horse's head, and recrossed safely Alexander's Bridge."[7]

If Pegram crossed the bridge on both his outbound and return legs of the trip, as Huwald's account clearly states, the Rebel cavalry camps were east of Chickamauga Creek. Curtis Green of the 6th Georgia Cavalry confirmed Huwald's account in this regard when he recalled that "we were ordered back across Chickamauga Creek to camp."[8] Forrest's report merely records that his men camped "on the field in the rear of [Hood's] line near Alexander's Bridge."[9]

A history of Forrest's Cavalry published in 1868 adds a few details as to what some of the Southern cavalry was up to that night. According to that account, Forrest's men captured a party of 30 Federal cavalrymen at Alexander Bridge and re-floored the structure that night.[10] Certainly someone repaired it, because the bridge was used repeatedly the next few days.

Forrest's choice of where to establish his camps, together with Pegram's reconnaissance, raises two questions. First, why would Forrest move all the way to Alexander's Bridge behind Hood's infantry when he should be screening Hood's front and flanks? Camping near Reed's Bridge or in the fields around Jay's Mill offered better locations—especially if he were going to picket the

---

7 Huwald letter, October 7, 1866, Leroy Monicure Nutt Papers, Southern Historical Collection, University of North Carolina.

8 Green, Curtis, "Sixth Georgia Cavalry at Chickamauga," *Confederate Veteran*, Vol. VIII (July, 1900), p. 324.

9 *OR* 30, pt. 2, p. 524.

10 Jordan and Pryor, *Forrest's Cavalry*, p. 314. This source also claims Forrest's cavalry camps were on the west side of the Chickamauga, but the other more reliable evidence cited previously contradicts that assertion.

Brotherton and Reed's Bridge roads, avenues along which Federal troops could easily reach Hood's rear.

Second, how could Pegram ride into the midst of a Yankee brigade without passing through his own picket line? He should have ridden right through the middle of the 1st Georgia Cavalry astride this same road. Surely these troopers would have warned the general about their earlier encounter with the enemy? The 1st Georgia's Shropshire claimed his regiment was sent out early Friday evening, while Huwald's description of Pegram's ride notes only that it was made in the dark, without offering a specific time. If there was a picket line in place when Pegram rode out, it was a very porous one.

Unfortunately, these are the only detailed accounts of the activities of Forrest's cavalry for the entire night of September 18 and the early morning hours of September 19. If Rebel cavalry moved out on the Brotherton Road, or rode up to protect the long exposed flank of the main infantry column along the Viniard-Alexander Road, no record survives. We know that no cavalry except for Pegram's party made their way up the Reed's Bridge Road, for as will be seen, Union infantry moved along it unchallenged. Hood's and Walker's men established their own picket lines to protect their main body, but mounted forces were needed for distant patrolling, an important task left unperformed.

At least part of the problem was a lack of manpower. Forrest had with him only one division of his corps, and that was scattered. Pegram's other brigade under Col. John Scott was supposed to be watching Red House Bridge (where the Old Federal Road crossed West Chickamauga Creek between Rossville and Ringgold, roughly two miles north of Dyer's Ford). In a remarkably bad decision, sometime after dark on the 18th Scott withdrew his command. According to William Sloan of the 5th Tennessee Cavalry, "we left our position at Red House Bridge this morning as no enemy appeared in front of us, and moved two or three miles up the river south, to Gen. Forrest's head quarters."[11] Another Tennessean claimed the brigade moved all the way to Leet's Tanyard, about six miles distant.[12] Colonel Scott makes no mention of any of this in his report, perhaps because by the time he wrote it he realized leaving the bridge

11 Entry for September 18, 1863, William E. Sloan Diary, TSLA. This entry also supports the idea that Forrest's camps were on the east side of the Chickamauga.

12 William Gibbs Allen Memoir, TSLA. Allen claimed that Scott's men spent only two hours at Leet's Tanyard, mostly in their saddles, before moving back to Red House Bridge. If true, Scott's men and horses were in very poor condition for the next day's action.

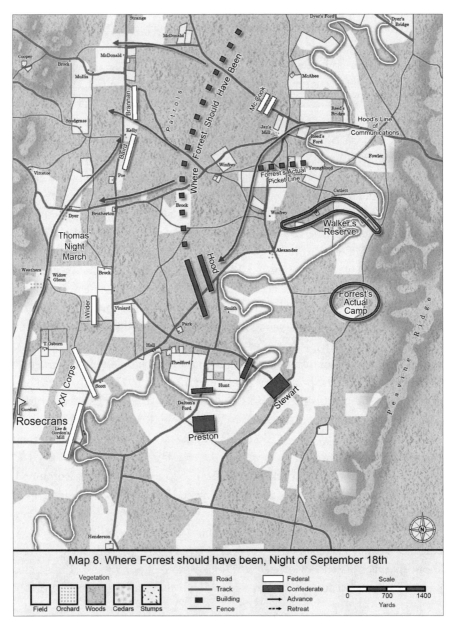

Map 8. Where Forrest should have been, Night of September 18th

After the day's action on September 18, Nathan Bedford Forrest allowed John Pegram's Division to camp somewhere east of Chickamauga Creek near Alexander's Bridge. Unfortunately, this put his cavalry well behind the Confederate infantry. Instead of establishing an extended picket line and launching wide ranging patrols to watch for Union movements that night, his men went into bivouac. As a result, Forrest failed to detect George Thomas' shift to Kelly Field or even Colonel McCook's limited advance to Jay's Mill from Rossville.

uncovered was a serious mistake—even if the Yankees did not take advantage of it. In any case, Scott's men contributed nothing to the security of the army's flank that night.

Frank Armstrong's Division should have ridden up with Polk's infantry corps as Bragg had directed, but confusion and outright incompetence prevented that from happening. D. H. Hill's men shifted north to fill in when Polk moved his infantry in the same direction, only to discover that Glass Mill and Owen's Ford, along with several other crossings, lacked cavalry picket posts. Armstrong's cavalry had charge of these crossings while Polk was there, but now that he was gone and Hill's men had arrived, the crossings were Joe Wheeler's responsibility. When he reached the sector, Hill was startled to find Owen's Ford in Union hands. Concerned that he might be attacked, Hill recalled Armstrong's troopers and informed Bragg of the failure to protect the fords.[13] Armstrong, in turn, informed Polk that he was being recalled. The news irked Polk, who insisted that Hill should call upon Wheeler's men to come up, not Armstrong's men to ride back. Hill shot back that he had yet to see any of Wheeler's people, and then sent a message directly to Wheeler begging for help.[14]

Armstrong was equally frustrated. When he informed Polk that one of his brigades had been recalled by Hill, he also explained that he would no longer be able to fulfill his new orders to screen Polk's movement. "Wheeler is immediately in rear of General H.'s left, and has orders from General Bragg to protect the left flank of the army," wrote Armstrong, whose anger was palpably apparent. "My brigade is not needed there, whilst one of Wheeler's divisions is lying 1 mile west of [Dr.] Anderson's [house] doing nothing."[15]

---

13 OR 30, pt. 4, p. 665. Because this stage of the Chickamauga operation is confusing, it is worthwhile to reiterate the tactical situation to better understand who was where, and what was expected. Originally, D. H. Hill's two divisions (John Breckinridge and Pat Cleburne) defended Lafayette from the west, while Leonidas Polk's divisions (Ben Cheatham and Thomas Hindman) defended the northern approaches near Rock Spring, about halfway between Lafayette and Lee and Gordon's Mills. Polk's line faced both Glass Mill and Lee and Gordon's, both important crossings over Chickamauga Creek. General Bragg intended Polk to shift his line to connect with Simon Buckner, in effect side-stepping both divisions a couple of miles northward. Hill was to do the same, moving his divisions up (north) to replace Polk's men. One of Hill's divisions would march to the vicinity of Glass Mill to replace Cheatham, who in turn would march behind Hindman to support Buckner.

14 *Ibid.*, p. p. 666.

15 *Ibid.*, p. 667. See pp. 664-667 for the entire set of messages.

Wheeler was not overly concerned about Armstrong's problems. William Martin's Division was still patrolling the gaps in Pigeon Mountain and skirmishing with Yankees around Davis's Crossroads, but John Wharton's men had come up from south of Lafayette to rejoin the corps. On the 17th, in response to Bragg's order of the previous evening, Wheeler sent Wharton's men into McLemore's Cove to help Martin harass the retreating Federals. This probe resulted in a skirmish at Gower's Ford between the 4th Georgia Cavalry of Col. C. C. Crews' Brigade, and a brigade of Federal infantry led by William B. Hazen of Crittenden's XXI Corps. Hazen was nearly captured in the fight and escaped only by ducking into a field of standing corn. His infantry drove off the Rebels, killing two, wounding seven, and capturing one.[16] Apparently as a result of this clash, Wharton withdrew his division several miles and camped in the fields around the aforementioned Dr. Anderson's house. His withdrawal uncovered both Gower's and Owen's fords, which triggered Hill's alarm when he found them unguarded.

As General Armstrong complained, after their skirmish on the 17th, Wharton's troopers did virtually nothing much the following day. With most of Bragg's army in motion, and action unfolding across a broad front, Wharton's pair of brigades did not even stir from their camps. A member of the 8th Texas cavalry in Col. Thomas Harrison's Brigade acknowledged that, while awaiting orders he could hear "heavy firing along the lines" on September 18, but he and his fellow cavalrymen did nothing of note themselves. Why Wheeler argued he could not spare these troopers to replace Armstrong is a mystery.[17]

In response to the complaints about him from Generals Hill and Armstrong, Joe Wheeler wrote directly to Leonidas Polk that Bragg had ordered that his troopers "should be used to guard the left flank of the army, and it will therefore be impossible for me to relieve General Armstrong's Brigade."[18] Wheeler's dispatch makes little sense. Hill's Corps *was* the army's left flank, it was now stationed between Owen's Ford and Glass Mill, and by failing to replace Armstrong's men, Wheeler was in fact *ignoring* the very orders upon which he was claiming to rely. Perhaps Wheeler did not know where the army's left flank was on the evening of September 18. But if that was the case, it

16 *OR* 30, pt. 1, p. 768.

17 R. F. Bunting Letter, *Rome Tri-weekly Telegraph*, September 30, 1863.

18 *OR* 30, pt. 4, p. 666.

reflects poorly on his skills as a cavalryman—and the Army of Tennessee's senior cavalryman at that. Wheeler also neglected to explain why Wharton's Division, instead of guarding any flank, spent the day inactive at Dr. Anderson's directly behind Hill's command. Bragg intervened at 11:00 p.m., when he resolved the matter in favor of Polk and Armstrong. The army commander sent an order directly to Wheeler specifying that he was to cover Owen's Ford and Hill's front.[19]

Bragg's order was written so late in the evening, however, that Wheeler's men did not replace Armstrong's command until the following day. Armstrong was supposed to move up with Polk and return to Forrest's command on the night of the 18th. Wheeler's failure to perform as ordered delayed Armstrong for twenty-four hours and guaranteed that his cavalry would not be available to watch Bragg's exposed right flank.

The bridge fights had delayed Bragg's battle plan, but it was not damaged beyond repair. The Army of the Cumberland was still concentrated near Lee and Gordon's Mill—south of the converging Rebel columns—and Bragg had 21,000 infantry on the same side of the creek or poised to cross at first light.

*　　*　　*

Although Bragg could not have known it, Rosecrans' headquarters initially discounted reports of large bodies of Rebels moving from Ringgold. As more evidence amassed, however, Rosecrans could no longer ignore the threat to his left flank. Because of Minty's and Wilder's constant flow of dispatches and updates, Rosecrans was now aware of the danger and intended to do something about it.[20] By nightfall of the 18th, Rosecrans had set in motion Federal movements that would impact how the battle the following day would unfold.

The first decision resulted in the dusk arrival of two brigades under Col. Daniel McCook. This force, part of Maj. Gen. Gordon Granger's Reserve Corps, numbered about 3,000 men and included two artillery batteries. It set off from Rossville and marched almost to Jay's Mill, about one-half mile from Reed's Bridge.[21] The infantry was originally dispatched to support Minty's

19 *Ibid.*

20 Vale, *Minty and the Cavalry,* p. 224.

21 *OR* 30, pt. 1, p. 871.

defense of that crossing. By the time McCook arrived, however, the fighting was over and neither enemy nor friendly troops were anywhere to be seen. Minty had no idea they were coming, nor had McCook been informed of Minty's departure. As a result, McCook knew next to nothing about the overall situation. Unsure of what to do, he halted and made a stealthy camp for the night. The Federals who ambushed Company G of the 1st Georgia Cavalry were pickets from McCook's command. Including as it did both Ohio and Illinois regiments, these Federals were also the enemy John Pegram encountered on his evening ride.

From a Confederate standpoint, their presence was more than alarming. McCook's men—their strength unknown to the Southerners—were well north of Bragg's right flank, and it was an easy march into the rear of Hood's infantry column. McCook was also well positioned to sever Hood's communications with his supply depot back at Ringgold. Hood had only four of his brigades on the field that night and expected several more to join him via Reed's Bridge. Now a Union force of unknown size was blocking that route.

McCook marched his infantry all the way to Jay's Mill without encountering a single Confederate picket.[22] He deployed his regiments astride the Reed's Bridge Road facing southeast several hundred yards northwest of the mill. He also established his own picket line around the mill extending (as we have learned) several hundred yards farther south and east. That night, the Federals demonstrated just how vulnerable the Confederate line of communications was by capturing 22 Rebels from Evander McNair's Brigade of Johnson's Division (now under Hood's command). The haul included a brass band and the brigade's medical detachment.[23] All these Confederates stumbled unwittingly into the Union picket line and were taken quietly. Just before dawn, a detail from the 69th Ohio marched to the bridge and attempted to burn it.[24]

---

22 McCook's men would not have reported Pegram's encounter, since Huwald makes it clear that Pegram escaped without detection.

23 Henry J. Aten, *History of the Eighty-Fifth Regiment Illinois Volunteer Infantry* (Hiawatha, Kansas: n.p. 1901), p. 103.

24 The 69th Ohio was an inexperienced unit, and very nervous about this dawn mission. The Buckeyes piled brush on the floor of the bridge in haste and set it alight, but did not stay to see if the bridge was destroyed. Once the brush was on fire the alarm was sounded and they departed. Little actual damage was done to the bridge. See L. E. Chenoweth to Col. J. H. Brigham, December 6, 1901, Brigham Family Papers, Bowling Green State University Library, Bowling Green, OH, for a description of the event.

It is difficult to understand why this entire peculiar episode played out as it did on this part of the field on the evening of September 18. The Reed's Bridge Road was not some hidden woodland path, but a well-known route listed on every credible map. It was also the shortest route from Reed's Bridge to Rossville, where Union troops were known to be located in strength. McCook's advance should have run into a line of Rebels well short of Jay's Mill. Only Pegram's reconnaissance and the brief skirmish with the Georgians suggest that there was any Confederate effort to patrol the road at all.

However alarming, two brigades of Union infantry from Rossville were not going to seriously disrupt Bragg's plan. The arrival of two Union infantry divisions at the Kelly house, however, was something else altogether. Rosecrans' next decision sent one-half of Maj. Gen. George H. Thomas' XIV Corps to occupy the Kelly farmstead astride the Lafayette Road one mile north of the intersection of Brotherton-Jay's Mill Road and one-half mile south of the Alexander's Bridge Road junction. The movement of troops to the Kelly farm shifted the left flank of the Army of the Cumberland almost two miles farther north. These two divisions, some 11,000 men and six batteries of artillery, marched through the night to arrive around the Kelly place at dawn. The rest of the corps was ordered to follow. When reunited, Thomas' XIV Corps would have 20,000 men with which to hold the door to Chattanooga open. Instead of outflanking the Federals, the Rebels were themselves being flanked.

In addition to the Reed's Bridge Road, two other roads provided important east-west access to the Lafayette Road from the Confederate positions. The Alexander's Bridge Road ran northwest from a point one-half mile south of the Youngblood field to strike the Lafayette Road north of the Kelly farm. The Brotherton Road ran southwest from near Jay's Mill to connect with the Lafayette Road at the Brotherton farm a mile south of Kelly's. Minty and Wilder had withdrawn almost to Lee and Gordon's Mills. That meant that Rebel cavalry had unfettered access to the Lafayette Road along both of these routes. Each road should have been heavily guarded by the Confederates, with patrols ranging to and beyond the Lafayette Road to watch for Union activity. When he arrived at dawn, Thomas sent troops immediately to cover both intersections.[25] No Federal in Thomas' corps reported any contact with Confederate patrols or pickets during that night march. As a result, no reports of a large-scale Federal movement north reached Braxton Bragg.

25 *OR* 30, pt. 1, p. 249.

Rosecrans extended his force beyond where Bragg expected to find it, and his army was that much closer to Chattanooga, but he did so at the expense of a solid front. The Union army had too few troops to cover the entire distance between the right flank of the XXI Corps and the new line established around Kelly field. A large gap remained between the Viniard and Poe fields, a distance of about a mile and a half. This gap would exist for almost the entire day on the 19th simply because Rosecrans did not have enough men to close it. As an inadequate substitute, Col. William Grose's Third Brigade, 2nd Division, XXI Corps, was sent up the road as a roving patrol during the morning of the 19th.[26]

This yawning gap between large pieces of the Federal army was a significant opportunity for Bragg to exploit—had he but known of it. Under his original plan, 21,000 Rebels would have been in position to sweep down on the Union left and rear. When the Union left moved north during the night, those same 21,000 Rebels were left facing the large hole in the Union center. Unfortunately for Bragg, word of the gap never made its way to his headquarters.

If Forrest had pushed cavalry patrols out as far as the Lafayette Road, he would have discovered both General Thomas' overnight movement and the presence of this large gap. At the very least, Bragg would have had a much clearer picture of the Union positions when dawn broke on September 19. It is possible that some patrols or individual scouts moved beyond the lines that night, but there was no systematic effort to find and report on Union dispositions. As far as Bragg's headquarters was concerned, the Union lines had not changed significantly since September 18.

That night Bragg reiterated Forrest's mission for the next day in no uncertain terms, perhaps because of the frustrations and uncertainties that had plagued the mounted arm throughout the 18th. Forrest and Hood rode to army headquarters that evening and arrived there about 9:00 p.m. Bragg instructed Forrest "to develop the enemy on the extreme Confederate right, as soon as possible the next morning, reporting all hostile movements to the nearest commander." Forrest was also, according to a history of his cavalry, "assured of prompt reinforcements, in the event he brought on a general engagement."[27]

Bragg's order triggered Forrest's next collision with Yankees early on the morning of the 19th. But the encounter was not where Bragg expected it to be, and that surprise left him with little choice but to halt his entire advance.

---

26 *Ibid.*, p. 606.

27 Jordan and Pryor, *Forrest's Cavalry*, p. 317.

hapter 12

Forrest Finds a Fight:
Day One at Chickamauga
(September 19, 1863)

Before dawn on September 19, Bragg ordered both Joe Wheeler and Nathan Bedford Forrest to "develop the enemy" on their fronts, essentially repeating his standing orders of the past few days.[1] In the near-term, this translated into immediate work for John Pegram's men. If the Southern cavalry was largely missing in action on September 18, the early hours of the 19th made up for it.

At first light, a messenger woke up Capt. H. B. Clay of Pegram's staff by tugging at his sleeve. Firing was audible from the direction of the 1st Georgia Cavalry's picket line (part of Pegram's Brigade) just southeast of Jay's Mill: Pegram wanted Clay to find out what was afoot.[2] The staffer mounted his horse and rode off to find the pickets engaged near the intersection of the Brotherton and Jay's Mill roads with Union troops that easily overmatched the embattled Georgians. Clay called for reinforcements to drive them back. A squadron of cavalry arrived, followed a short time later by the entire 1st Georgia.

---

1   OR 30, pt. 2, pp. 524; *ibid.*, pt. 4, p. 671. The order to Wheeler survives, dated 8:15 a.m., September 19. The order to Forrest does not, although Forrest mentions receiving it in his report of the battle.

2   Clay, "On the Right at Chickamauga," p. 329.

Forrest was also stirring. The corps leader sent Colonel Scott's wayward brigade back north to Red House Bridge, adding Martin's Kentucky Battalion for good measure. Martin's departure still left Pegram with about 1,900 men, a sizable brigade in the cavalry corps. With Scott's error addressed, Forrest mounted up and set off with Pegram and his brigade.

More command confusion within the ranks of the Confederate cavalry ensued with the arrival of Brig. Gen. Henry B. Davidson. Davidson, who arrived sometime during the night from his former duty station at Staunton, Virginia, was finally on hand to assume command of Pegram's former brigade. According to Captain Clay, however, since Davidson "was handicapped by his want of knowledge of the command," Pegram continued exercising direct control of the brigade.[3] That decision also rippled upward because it left command of the division in Pegram's hands, and leading both organizations simultaneously and well was an impossible task. Most of the men in the brigade were barely aware of Davidson's presence, and continued to refer to Pegram as their brigade commander.

When he determined that the 1st Georgia was making headway against the Federal skirmish line, Pegram reinforced its success by ordering up Huwald's Tennessee battery and some of Rucker's Tennesseans. A quick charge netted a number of prisoners who informed Pegram his men were fighting Dan McCook's infantry brigade. McCook was falling back (Rosecrans had ordered him to withdraw to Rossville), and Pegram let him go. Once the fighting broke off, remembered Captain Clay, Pegram's cavalry "moved to our left, passing an old sawmill (since understood to have been Jay's Mill) and, moving some five or six hundred yards from it, was halted."[4]

While the troopers boiled up some coffee, part of 1st Georgia rode up the Reed's Bridge Road to make sure McCook did not return. Forrest and Pegram conferred about what to do next, called Clay over to join them, and ordered him to take a patrol—once again drawn from the omnipresent 1st Georgia—and reconnoiter west into the woods. Clay and the Georgians rode out about three-quarters of a mile, with early morning birdsongs the only sign of life. Clay

3 Henry B. Clay, "Concerning the Battle of Chickamauga," *Confederate Veteran*, Vol. XII (February, 1905), p. 72. Henry Davidson, it will be recalled, was promoted to brigadier general and ordered to take command of the brigade when Forrest's Corps was created on September 3, 1863.

4 *Ibid.*, p. 72.

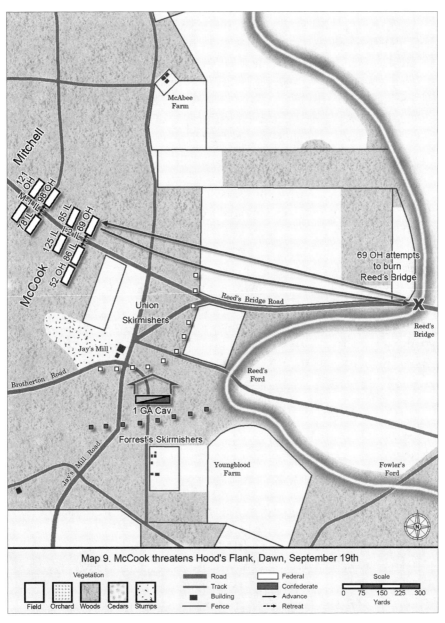

Map 9. McCook threatens Hood's Flank, Dawn, September 19th

The ability of the 69th Ohio to march unmolested to Reed's Bridge illustrates the degree to which Forrest's men failed to properly picket the Rebel right flank. The 1st Georgia's picket line is well south of Jay's Mill, and not alert to the trouble a Union foray against the crossing might cause. McCook's force is small and probably not a strategic threat to Bragg's army, but his presence on the morning of the 19th reveals that the Army of Tennessee's is vulnerable to a Union advance from that quarter.

returned, reported that no enemy was in their immediate front, and stretched out with his head on a tree root for a quick nap.[5]

A lull ensued. The 10th Confederate Cavalry, also part of Pegram's Brigade, was sent westward along a logging trail into the woods to guard the flank Clay had just reconnoitered. To the surprise of everyone involved, the Southerners stumbled into a skirmish line made up of Hoosiers from the 10th Indiana. Behind them was Col. John Croxton's Union infantry brigade, part of George Thomas' XIV Corps. The Rebels threw together a quick charge, but a volley sent them reeling back in disorder.[6]

J. W. Minnich was making breakfast with the rest of the 6th Georgia when the panic-stricken cavalrymen appeared from the west. "[N]one of us thought that there was no enemy within two miles of us," explained the shocked Georgian. "General Pegram's report," shows that he and General Forrest shared in that belief, and that they were as much surprised by the sudden attack."[7] Captain Clay was even more surprised, waking up to find dismounted troopers of the 1st Georgia scrambling to get to their weapons to defend against advancing Union infantry.[8] "[W]here those Federals came from," the captain wondered years later, "has ever since been an unsolved puzzle." His chagrin was well founded, since the Yankees appeared exactly where he had scouted just a few minutes earlier.[9]

With the enemy close at hand, Forrest determined to hold the line and fight. The first thing he did was order Pegram to dismount his brigade and form a line facing the Federals. Next, he requested a brigade of infantry from General Walker's nearby Reserve Corps and then made a hasty appeal to General Polk for Armstrong's long-lost division. Finally, Forrest sent word of the Yankee activity back to General Bragg.[10] News of Union troops much farther north than expected caught the army commander off guard. Bragg halted immediately

5 Clay, "On the Right at Chickamauga," p. 329, and "Concerning the Battle of Chickamauga," p. 72.

6 Anonymous, *Toledo Blade*, October 2, 1863.

7 Minnich Reminiscences, 6th Georgia File, Chickamauga-Chattanooga National Military Park.

8 Clay, "On the Right at Chickamauga," p. 329.

9 Clay, "Concerning the Battle of Chickamauga," p. 72.

10 *OR* 30, pt. 2, p. 524.

the main attack order under which the army was operating and directed Walker to provide Forrest with the requested support.[11]

In hindsight, it might have been wiser if Forrest had simply screened the Union advance to determine the intent of the enemy. Instead, he poured troops into what was a smallish affair and escalated the action quickly into a full-scale meeting engagement, with Pegram's overmatched dismounted cavalry confronting superior numbers of enemy infantry. Unbeknownst to the Confederates, Croxton's large 1,998-man brigade was not alone in those woods. The two other brigades comprising Brig. Gen. John M. Brannan's division were moving to support Croxton, as was another three-brigade division under Brig. Gen. Absalom Baird. Unlike the Southern cavalry, none of these infantry commands was handicapped by the need to keep some of their men out of the fight as horse-holders. The simple fact was that John Pegram was woefully overmatched and the odds against him lengthened with each tick of the clock. If he was going to defend Jay's Mill, Forrest needed heavy reinforcements and he needed them right away.[12]

Until reinforcements arrived Forrest had to hold on with his lone cavalry brigade, which was already weakened by detachments and in some disarray. One gun from Huwald's battery, along with a company of the 6th North Carolina Cavalry, were still guarding Alexander's Bridge. This left Forrest with only three artillery pieces to stiffen a weak defensive line.[13] Part of the 1st Georgia was also absent picketing the Reed's Bridge Road. The 10th Confederate's hasty retreat through the rest of the brigade disrupted not only that regiment but a number of men from other commands as well. When the spooked troopers of the 10th rode wildly for safety through his ranks, a member of the 6th Georgia jumped up and also headed for the rear, shouting, "Boys, this is Hell! I am going for cover!"[14] He was not alone. Others were sure the confusion was a case of mistaken identity. In the 1st Georgia, Private Shropshire heard a number of Confederates yelling, "Don't shoot, they are Longstreet's men!" That notion was soon discarded when the firing grew more

---

11 *Ibid.*, p. 240.

12 See reports of Brannan and Baird, *OR* 30, pt. 1, pp. 275, 400-1.

13 Captain M. V. Moore, newspaper clipping, undated, Martin Van Buren Moore Papers, *Southern Historical Collection*, University of North Carolina. See also Huwald Letter, October 7, 1866. Lieutenant Martin's section consisted of just a single howitzer and was left behind.

14 Minnich, "Reminiscences," p. 23.

intense and the identity of those doing most of the trigger-pulling became clear to everyone on the receiving end.[15]

Notwithstanding the panic that had overtaken part of his command, Forrest calmly called up Huwald's guns and orderd them to deploy on a small rocky ridge about 200 yards west of the mill. Using the three pieces as a focal point, he formed his line around them. The portion of the 1st Georgia still under Forrest's direct control formed the right flank, facing west near Reed's Bridge Road. Next in line on the left of the Georgians was Rucker's Legion, whose left flank connected with Huwald's battery. The large 6th North Carolina Cavalry went into line on Huwald's left, extending the Rebel front southward. The 6th Georgia completed the line of battle, holding the left flank next to the North Carolinians.

These Georgians of the 6th regiment were already badly rattled. When the 10th Confederate came crashing out of the trees, it was these Georgians' whose ranks they tore through, and the stampede nearly routed them in the process. The 6th managed to recover enough to dismount and join the budding line atop the crest of the low ridge. Behind them, the 10th's officers set about rallying their spooked men. The 10th's Confederate's commander, Col. Charles T. Goode, was mortified at the panicked behavior his men had demonstrated and for a while seemed about to quit them in disgust. Slowly but steadily, with his help the regiment was set to rights.[16] A little later, with some order restored, they squeezed into the line between the 6th North Carolina and the 6th Georgia.

The firing line was ablaze with discharging small arms and bullets humming through the ranks like angry bees. To the dismounted cavalrymen Forrest appeared to be everywhere at once, calling out orders here and steadying the troops there. The only hint of nervousness he revealed was when he asked Captain Huwald over and over whether his battery could hold its position. Each time, Huwald assured the general that he could hang on.[17]

With growing and obvious impatience Forrest awaited the arrival of the promised infantry support. Finally, when he could stand it no longer, he turned to Pegram and yelled, "Hold this position . . . until I can bring up

---

15 W. F. Shropshire Reminiscences, Confederate Veteran Papers.

16 Peter Cozzens, *This Terrible Sound* (University of Illinois Press, 1992), p. 126.

17 Huwald Letter, October 7, 1866.

reinforcements!"[18] Pegram's response was a little less certain than Huwald's, but perhaps more realistic: "I'll hold it if I can, General."[19]

For a while, and likely to the surprise of many Confederates, the fighting lines remained largely static. Croxton, a native Kentuckian fighting for the Union, was waiting for his own support to arrive and was reluctant to press home his attack too soon. The action was no less intense for its lack of movement. By this time nearly 4,000 men were blazing away as quickly as they could load and fire. Huwald exhausted nearly all his ammunition, lost most of his battery horses killed and wounded, and later reported that he watched his battery "melt away" as the fight wore on.[20] At some point, his remaining howitzer arrived, summoned from its quiet duty at Alexander's Bridge (though it isn't clear exactly when this piece and its crew joined the action). From his place amid the ranks of the 6th Georgia, Minnich witnessed the battery's plight. After the fight, when he had a chance to walk the ground, the Georgian counted twelve of Huwald's horses dead in one heap and nine in another.[21] Minnich also remembered Forrest's calming presence during the early stages of the action as he rode prominently along the dismounted firing line exhorting, "hold on boys, you are doing nobly. This is an infantry fight you are putting up. Stick to the hill. Take any shelter you can get, only stick."[22] Forrest reassured the embattled cavalrymen time and again that infantry was on its way to help them.

The long-awaited Rebel foot soldiers in the form of Col. Claudius Wilson's Brigade arrived about an hour into the battle. The regiments, Georgians all, were thrown into the fight on Pegram's left in an effort to flank Croxton's Federals from the south. Wilson's 1,300 men drove the Yankees back, but their success was temporary.[23] Baird's reinforcing Federals turned Wilson's flank in the woods, driving him back in turn. While Wilson struggled to keep his command together, a second Confederate infantry brigade under Brig. Gen. Matthew D. Ector arrived. Forrest sent Ector's people northwest along Reed's Bridge Road, moving up behind Pegram to go into action on the cavalry's right

18 Clay, "On the Right at Chickamauga," p. 329.

19 *Ibid.*

20 *Ibid.*

21 Minnick, "Reminiscences," p. 24.

22 *Ibid.*

23 Jordan and Pryor, *Forrest's Cavalry*, p. 319.

flank. A new threat was developing there, as reported by scouts from the 1st Georgia. A second Union brigade under Col. Ferdinand Van Derveer, one of those Croxton had been waiting for, was advancing astride the same road threatening to overlap Pegram's right flank. Ector's men deployed quickly and launched a furious attack against these newly arrived Federals.[24]

Shortly after Ector's advance, Col. George C. Dibrell's Confederate cavalry brigade galloped onto the scene of the spreading combat. Frank Armstrong, his division having finally been relieved by Wheeler's overdue troopers, sent Dibrell's regiments to Forrest as soon as he could, but they had six or seven miles to cover and so were late arriving on the field. Tardy or not, Forrest was delighted to see his old command and ordered them to dismount to help Ector, who found himself overmatched on the Reed's Bridge Road.

Ector's attack against Van Derveer's Federal brigade was not going well. His first charge had been stopped cold with heavy losses when it ran headlong into superior numbers of enemy infantry and artillery. Ector rallied his line and was willing to try again, but he was now worried about his flanks, both of which were exposed. Because Pegram and Wilson were fighting to the south, Ector was most concerned about his right flank. He dispatched Capt. C. B. "Buck" Kilgore to find Forrest and ask him to watch his vulnerable right. "I'll take care of it," the general replied.[25] Dibrell's timely appearance allowed Forrest to respond immediately. Dibrell's men dismounted and hurried across the Reed's Bridge Road to form up on Ector's right.[26]

Ector's angle of advance, however, diverged from Wilson's advance and opened an interval between the two Rebel infantry brigades. At the same time, more of Baird's Union infantry appeared opposite this gap, replacing Croxton's men and moving forward aggressively. Ector now had reason to fear for his other flank. Alone in the woods and watching as his second charge was repulsed, Ector sent Kilgore back to Forrest again. The aide found the cavalryman in the same spot near Huwald's Battery. General Ector, explained Kilgore, was "uneasy about his left flank." Forrest, never a patient man, became

---

24 "Ector's Brigade at Chickamauga," *Mobile Daily Register*, October 14, 1863, and Ector's Brigade Tablet, CCNMP.

25 John Allen Wyeth, *That Devil Forrest: The Life of General Nathan Bedford Forrest* (Louisiana State University Press, 1989), p. 227.

26 Letter from 'OSCEOLA', "Forrest's Old Brigade in the Battle of Chickamauga," *Memphis Appeal*, October 21, 1863.

"furious," recalled the captain. "He turned around on me and shouted, loud enough to be heard above the terrible din . . . 'Tell General Ector that, by God, I am here, and will take care of his left flank as well as his right!' It is hardly necessary," concluded Kilgore, "to add that we were not outflanked on either side."[27]

This story was first published in 1908 and has been related faithfully in every Forrest biography or study thereafter. By the turn of the century, however, Kilgore's memory was either clouded by time or fogged over with admiration for the impressive cavalry leader. Simply put, Kilgore was mistaken. Looming on Ector's left were the lines of Brig. Gen. John H. King's five battalions of U.S. Regulars. These troops, raised for the war but still containing enough pre-war army veterans and a sense of Regular Army discipline to set them apart from the volunteers, were coming into the fight perfectly poised to damage Ector. They spied the Rebels as they were falling back from their second effort against Van Derveer. King seized the opportunity, recalled Union Lt. Henry B. Freeman, by wheeling "the brigade to the left in double time, then forward, striking the enemy in the flank and rolling him up like a curtain."[28]

The Confederates, already disordered from two failed charges, routed when King's Yankees appeared. "[We] found [we] were flanked on the left & commenced falling back in confusion," wrote Pvt. C. B. Carlton of the 10th Texas in a detailed letter home trying to explain how his friend John Templeton ended up a Yankee prisoner. "The boys were scattered pretty badly." When Ector ordered the brigade to march by the right flank, the confusion only increased.[29] Lieutenant Robert Ayres of the 19th U.S. reported that the 9th Texas, "passing along our front from left to right, received our fire, which caused them to break and run and many came into our lines as prisoners."[30] Freeman exulted that the brigade advanced "nearly a mile and captured more prisoners than we had either time or means to care [for.]"[31]

27 Wyeth, *That Devil Forrest*, p. 227.

28 Henry B. Freeman, "At the Battle of Chickamauga," Wyoming Historical Society, Cheyenne, Wyoming, p. 2.

29 "D. G. Templeton, Sir," October 13, 1863, C. B. Carlton letter, J. A. Templeton papers, Simpson History Complex, Hill College, Hillsboro, Texas.

30 *OR* 30, pt. 1, p. 322.

31 Freeman, "Chickamauga," p. 2.

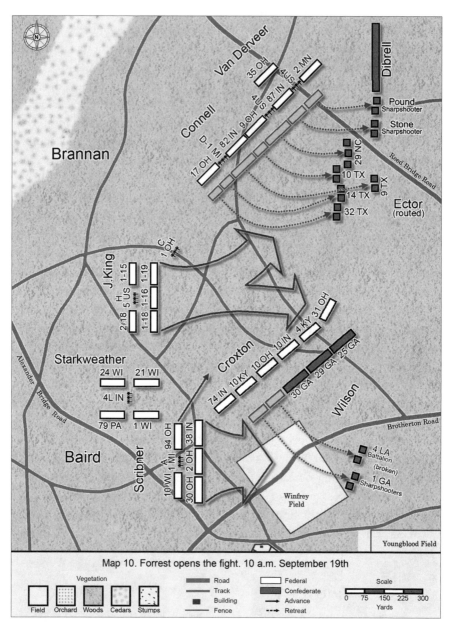

Map 10. Forrest opens the fight. 10 a.m. September 19th

Rather than screening the Union advance, Forrest chooses to engage it by dismounting his men and fighting like infantry. By mid-morning, his outmatched cavalry brigade and the infantry borrowed from Walker's Reserve Corps are in serious trouble. Superior Federal numbers rout Matt Ector and maul Claudius Wilson. George Dibrell's arrival in the midst of the fighting barely stabilizes the line. The escalating fight diverts Bragg's attention from his intended attack to this new worry on his northern flank.

The only troops available to bolster Ector's crumbling line were Pegram's cavalrymen, who were recuperating near Jay's Mill. Either Forrest did not have time to send them forward, or he decided they were already too badly used up to be of any help. In any case, they did not lend a hand. With 527 of his 1,199 men killed, wounded, or captured (some 44%) and his troops scattered from the flank attack, Ector withdrew as many as he could to the east, out of the fight for the rest of the battle. Dibrell's troopers were still in the act of deploying on Ector's right when his left flank collapsed. A trooper in Hamilton's Tennessee Battalion described the moment in a letter to the editor of the Memphis Appeal a month later: "Outflanked and pressed by superior numbers, Ector's gallant Texas Brigade was falling back. We dismounted at Lee's [Jay's] Mill and rushed to their support on foot."[32]

Instead of launching another frontal attack where Ector failed, Dibrell attempted to maneuver. Van Derveer's line (recently reinforced by a battery and two regiments from Col. John T. Connell's Union brigade, also of Baird's Division) faced southeast, perpendicular to the Reed's Bridge Road. Dibrell feinted with a limited force against Van Derveer's front and sent the bulk of his men to work their way around the Federal left flank north of the road. The Federals were too astute to fall for the deception, however, and a quick change of front by part of Van Derveer's men rebuffed the effort.[33] Stymied, Dibrell fell back out of range, leaving a skirmish line facing the Yankees. For a short while the front quieted down. Pegram's troops, who had suffered severely in the morning contest, were held in reserve. They had done all that Forrest had asked of them.

The 19th of September marked an interesting milestone in Forrest's career. On this, the first day of the two-day battle at Chickamauga, Forrest had four brigades under his supervision and it was the first time he directed sizable numbers of infantry in action. Together, the four commands numbered about 3,600 cavalry and another 2,500 foot troops, or about 6,000 all told—as large as any other division in the Confederate army, and probably the single largest force Forrest had commanded in combat thus far. In his report, Forrest noted that "until the arrival of Major General Walker (being the senior officer present) I assumed temporary command of the infantry, and I must say that the fighting

32 Letter from 'OSCEOLA', *Memphis Appeal*, October 21, 1863.

33 Dibrell's Brigade Tablet, CCNMP.

and the gallant charges of the two brigades just referred to excited my admiration."[34]

This initial round of fighting lasted between three and four hours and shattered two Confederate infantry brigades. Both Ector and Wilson lost nearly half of their men. The two cavalry brigades of Pegram-Davidson and Dibrell did not suffer as badly, but were roughly handled nonetheless. According to Pegram, his former brigade lost about a quarter of its strength at Chickamauga, most of it in this fight. Dibrell's losses were lighter. The brigade adjutant reported only 50 casualties for the entire battle.[35] Still, the cavalry was worn out from the morning fight and welcomed a break from the combat.

While Dibrell was attempting to outflank Van Derveer, the infantry battle took on a life of its own. Walker was conferring with Bragg that morning when the expanding fight caught both officers by surprise. When Forrest's first request for help arrived, Bragg ordered Walker to send a single brigade and Wilson was tapped for the assignment.[36] Forrest himself brought up Ector. Despite earlier orders to loan a brigade to Forrest, Walker apparently expected nothing in that direction beyond a heavy skirmish. When the swelling rattle of combat that signaled Wilson's attack on Croxton swelled even further after Ector went in, Walker was caught completely off-guard. The Reserve Corps commander was sitting with John Bell Hood, the latter's arm still in a sling from his Gettysburg wound, when "great was our astonishment . . . to hear the outbreak of heavy firing . . . on our right," recalled Capt. Joseph Cumming.[37] Thomas Claiborne, a member of Simon Buckner's staff, also recalled Walker's "astonishment" when he broke off a conversation in mid-sentence to exclaim, "By God! They are attacking my division!"[38] A hurried discussion with Bragg ensued, followed by orders for Walker to "attack with all the force I had," should the need arise.[39] With orders in hand, Walker and Cumming mounted

---

34 *OR* 30, pt. 2, p. 524. Forrest's report is worth reading to gain a better perspective of how a cavalryman, now elevated to corps level, viewed the battle and his responsibilities.

35 *OR* 30, pt. 2, p. 529. Dibrell's losses are found in *Memphis Daily Appeal*, October 9, 1863.

36 *OR* 30, 2, p. 240.

37 Major Joseph B. Cumming, War Recollections, Southern historical Collection, UNC.

38 Thomas Claiborne Letter, Nashville, Tenn., April 16, 1891, Eyewitness Accounts folder, CCNMP.

39 *OR* 30, pt. 2, p. 240.

and rode north while the other generals dispersed to join their respective commands.

When he arrived at the scene of combat, Walker was dismayed to discover that Forrest had commandeered Matt Ector's brigade without asking permission to do so. He also learned that the Federals were present in large numbers, and both Wilson and Ector were cut up and retreating. Forrest had fed troops into the fight one brigade at a time, managing each crisis in the moment without much regard for a larger battle plan or for Bragg's overall strategy. Despite a legendary temper that verged on "volcanic rashness," Walker passed up the opportunity for recriminations and assumed command.[40] After a short reconnaissance, the Reserve Corps commander rode back the mile or so south to order forward Brig. Gen. St. John Liddell's Division. With Walker's arrival, the battle moved out of Forrest's control.

Liddell's infantry joined the fighting and flanked Baird's Federals. Now it was the Yankees' turn to rout and run through the woods. More Union troops were fed into the battle, pushing Liddell backward. About midday, Bragg dispatched Maj. Gen. Benjamin F. Cheatham's five-brigade division, pulled from Polk's Corps, to support Walker's embattled position. Both sides were introducing troops into the rapidly expanding fight as quickly as they could bring them up to stave off whatever disaster was unfolding. This pattern of back-and-forth commitment and seesaw fighting characterized the battle for the rest of the day.

Cheatham's infantry joined the fight just as Dibrell's attack on Van Derveer was drawing to a close.[41] Bragg intended for Cheatham's five brigades to help Walker, but by the time Cheatham was on hand Walker's Reserve Corps was already out of action. Cheatham's lead brigade under Brig. Gen. John K. Jackson advanced northwest astride the Alexander's Bridge Road and collided with a full Union division from McCook's XX Corps. With two brigades on line, these Federals should have easily outflanked Jackson's narrower front. Forrest, however, spotted the threat and sent a skirmish line of Dibrell's men—now free of the fighting along the Reed's Bridge Road—to cover

40 Walker was clearly irked by Forrest's unilateral seizure of Ector's Brigade, as demonstrated in his report when he wrote, "Ector having also been taken by Forrest without any authority from me. . . ." *Ibid.*, 30, pt. 2, p. 240. For a reference to his "volcanic rashness," see Steven Davis, "A Georgia Firebrand: Major General W. H. T. Walker, C.S.A.", *Confederate Historical Institute Journal*, Vol. II, No. 3 (Summer, 1981), p. 1.

41 Descriptions of Cheatham's fight can be found in *OR* 30, pt. 2, pp. 78, 83-4, 94-5.

Jackson's northern flank. For the moment, the threat passed and the Federal advance was checked.

After an hour's fighting, Jackson was replaced by another of Cheatham's brigades under Brig. Gen. George Maney, whose Tennesseans also slugged it out with the Federals for about an hour until Union numbers began to tell and they were forced to retreat. Private Sam Watkins, serving in the 1st Tennessee Infantry on the right side of Maney's battle line, was present when General Forrest rode up with grim news: "Colonel Field, look out, you are almost surrounded, you had better fall back." Maney tried to disengage carefully, but his infantry fell back in considerable disorder. Dibrell's troopers covered the withdrawal as Maney's men fell back southeast past the Winfrey House. Freeman's Tennessee Battery under Capt. A. L. Huggins deployed astride the Alexander's Bridge Road to provide covering fire and lost several horses repelling a Union advance. Once the Federals drove off the Rebel infantry, they halted and established a defensive front along the west side of Winfrey Field, extending the line south to Brock Field. Dibrell's cavalry opposed them with a dismounted skirmish line on the east side of Winfrey Field.[42]

Maney's disengagement marked the beginning of a long break in the major fighting on the northern sector of the battlefield. Combat continued to rage in the area around Brock Field, about one mile south of the Winfrey farm, until about 2:00 p.m. Bragg committed another division under Alexander P. Stewart to help Cheatham, and Rosecrans upped the ante by sending in all or part of three other Federal divisions, first to try and plug the gap that still yawned wide in his own line, and then in an effort to find and turn the Rebel flank. The Union effort failed when Brig. Gen. Jefferson C. Davis' two brigades slammed into Hood's deployed line of Confederates in corps strength in the woods east of the Lafayette Road about 2:30 p.m.

Davis' collision with Hood expanded the line of battle another two miles or so south all the way to Viniard Field. By this time the battle had become general, expanding from what had started as a sharp fight between Forrest's cavalry and a Federal infantry brigade into a day-long slugfest between seven Rebel and eight Union divisions. From Viniard Field, the engagement crept back north, its center of gravity shifting to the Brotherton farm by late afternoon, and eventually all the way back to Forrest's sector at Winfrey Field at day's end.

---

42 *Ibid.*, pp. 524-5. Sam R. Watkins, *Co. Aytch, Maury Grays, First Tennessee Regiment, or, A Side Show of the Big Show* (Franklin, TN, Providence House Publishers, 2007), p. 109.

The last action on the battle's first day involving Southern cavalry came later that evening as dusk was falling on the smoky fields and woods of North Georgia. This time Maj. Gen. Patrick Cleburne moved forward with his division in the vicinity of Winfrey Field in an effort to break through the Union lines. In a rare example of night fighting, Cleburne launched his attack with Dibrell's dismounted troopers guarding his flank. The fighting was confused and the Confederate tactics were poorly handled, but in the end the Federals fell back. Bloodied, confused, and exhausted, Cleburne's men did not actively pursue and the fighting drew to a close.

The cavalry's involvement in the end of the day fighting was minimal. Morton's Battery, fighting with Dibrell's men, acquired two Federal fieldpieces. The guns had been lost earlier in the day, and fell into Cleburne's hands during the nighttime attack. The new guns were something of a birthday present for Captain Morton, who turned 21 that day at Chickamauga. Morton also lost three horses and a new uniform saved for the occasion—the animals to battle and the clothes to a wayward mule.[43]

*   *   *

As the fluid flanking combat swirled and escalated in the woods beyond Jay's Mill, Col. John Scott dutifully led Pegram's other cavalry brigade north back to Red House Bridge. There, he stumbled into a fight that did not go well at all. "[L]ater in the day [September 19th] we were ordered back again in double-quick time, and found the enemy in possession [of the crossing]," wrote Pvt. Sloan of the 5th Tennessee.[44] The Federals were part of Maj. Gen. Gordon Granger's Reserve Corps, who had orders to block the Ringgold-Rossville Road. Without waiting to do a proper reconnaissance, Scott launched a mounted charge to recapture the bridge. A company of the 2nd Tennessee Cavalry thundered down the road. The lane narrowed and passed through a growth of scrub pine, where Granger's Federals ambushed them. The killing shots knocked ten or twelve men off their mounts and dropped horses to completely block the road.[45]

43 Morton, *The Artillery of Forrest's Cavalry*, p. 120.

44 Entry for September 19, 1863, Sloan Diary. TSLA.

45 Allen Memoir, TSLA.

Undeterred, Scott sent the 5th Tennessee Cavalry to try and flank the Yankees. The 5th located a ford downstream and crossed to the west bank, pushing back the enemy several hundred yards. Emboldened by this success, the Louisiana colonel ordered the rest of his men to dismount and rush the bridge. This effort made little progress, and within a short time both sides settled down into a long range shooting match. At some point a Union battery opened up on Scott's troopers. The artillerists were too close to the firing line, and a number of artillery horses were shot down.

After several hours of fruitless fighting, Col. George W. McKenzie, commander of the 5th Tennessee Cavalry, decided to take matters into his own hands. Thinking the Union battery was demoralized, he ordered his regiment to mount and charge it—even though a line of blue-coated infantry supported the guns. Once again the charge was a bloody failure. Not only did the visible Federal infantry outnumber the 5th Tennessee, but a second line of Yankees waited concealed in a gully at right angles to the attacking Confederates. The mounted Rebels rode directly into a devastating crossfire that quickly emptied saddles and dropped horses to the ground.[46] Scott decided to hold his position and let the fight die away as night fell upon the field.

Questionable leadership plagued Scott's brigade all day. Aside from his decision to abandon the bridge altogether the night before, Scott failed to scout the enemy position properly when he finally returned on the 19th, and was responsible for sending the 2nd Tennessee Cavalry into an ambush along the road. Sloan accused the commander of the 2nd Tennessee, Lt. Col. John H. Kuhn, of being drunk (which might explain why the initial charge was made so rashly).[47] Finally, Colonel McKenzie's equally imprudent decision to charge the Union artillery and infantry line also incurred a number of Confederate casualties with no useful result.

* * *

On the southern flank of the Confederate army, Frank Armstrong (part of Forrest's Corps) was still waiting for Joe Wheeler to show up. That morning, after he sent Dibrell to join Forrest, Armstrong and his remaining brigade continued patrolling the fords and crossings along Chickamauga Creek between

46 Entry for September 19, 1863, Sloan Diary, TSLA.

47 *Ibid.*

John Breckinridge's Division at Glass Mill and Thomas Hindman's Division opposite Lee and Gordon's Mills.[48]

Ordered to distract Federal attention from the fighting farther north, Breckinridge sent a battery of artillery and an infantry brigade splashing across the Chickamauga at Glass Mill. The fighting cost Breckinridge 22 casualties and lasted a couple of hours. Armstrong must surely have been aware of the noisy exchange, but played no role in the affair. When Breckinridge received orders to shift his entire command northward toward Lee and Gordon's Mill he did so, which ended the fight.[49]

Breckinridge's departure coincided with Joe Wheeler's belated arrival. Wheeler was only now undertaking the mission Bragg intended for him to assume two days earlier on September 17. John Wharton's Division was sent to cover both Glass Mill Bridge and Owen's Ford, and was in place by late morning.[50] Since Wharton's troopers had been camped at Dr. Anderson's house since the 17th, only a couple of miles distant, they should have been in place by dawn. Wheeler was still feeling no sense of urgency in carrying out Bragg's orders.

Wheeler employed Martin's Division in a similarly halting manner. Martin's men spent the day at Dug Gap on Pigeon Mountain, about six miles away. After dark, Wheeler finally ordered them to join the rest of the corps.[51] Both commands were still scattered and depleted trying to maintain extended picket lines as far south as Gadsden, Alabama—despite Bragg's order of a week earlier to abandon those more distant posts in order to concentrate near Lafayette.[52] Because of Wheeler's foot-dragging, Armstrong could not leave the army's left flank until late that afternoon, and only joined Forrest on the army's right flank well after dark on September 19.

Some of Wharton's men saw limited action on the afternoon of the 19th. Wheeler, in response to a report of a large Union wagon train rolling out of

48 Jas. A. Lewis Letter, June 19, 1891, 6th Tennessee Cavalry File, CCNMP.

49 OR 30, pt. 2, pp. 197-8.

50 Breckinridge sent his men across the creek at 9:00 a.m. on September 19, and so could not have withdrawn much before 11:00 a.m. OR 30, pt. 2, p. 198. Bunting noted that the cavalry "stood in line for several hours" on the 19th. Bunting Letter, Rome Tri-Weekly Telegraph, November 27, 1863.

51 I. B. Ulmer Reminiscences, ADAH

52 OR 30, pt. 2, p. 520.

McLemore's Cove, closed up his line about 2:00 p.m. on the banks of Chickamauga Creek south of Glass Mill. From there, he later reported, his troopers "warmly assailed their flank, dividing the column and driving the enemy in confusion in all directions."[53] R. F. Bunting of the 8th Texas Cavalry, part of Col. Thomas Harrison's Brigade, had a much different view of the fight. The 8th Texas rode into an open field, threatening to charge the Union train. The 11th Texas Cavalry of the same brigade, meanwhile, dismounted and went in on the 8th's right. Yankee cavalry soon appeared, and "seeing our men exposed, they dismounted, and crossing the creek they crept up through the bushes and opened a heavy fire upon us," explained Bunting. "It was badly planned and we were the sufferers."[54] After taking several casualties during a fight of indeterminate length, Harrison's Brigade retreated about two miles, leaving Company D of the 8th Texas Cavalry to guard Glass Mill Ford. Other troopers picketed the bridge and other sites in between. Bunting blamed Wheeler for the mess: "[I]nstead of sending us alone to that position, his whole force should have been thrown across the creek and hurled upon the enemy, and they could easily have been routed. It is evident," he concluded, "that we have too many commanders and not enough system."[55]

Wheeler's mishandled attack was against Col. Daniel M. Ray's brigade, part of the Cavalry Corps' 1st Division. Ray only had three regiments with him (the 2nd and 4th Indiana and 1st Wisconsin Cavalry), but they proved sufficient to rebuff the effort Wheeler undertook. "The rear of the supply train was attacked by the enemy's cavalry, consisting of about four regiments and two pieces of artillery," reported Colonel Ray. Bringing up the rear of the column was the 2nd Indiana Cavalry, which bore the brunt of the fight when it "formed in line and repulsed the first attack." The Wisconsin and Indiana regiments were sent in support . . . and after a spirited skirmish of about one hour repulsed the enemy and brought the train through in safety." A trooper in the 1st Wisconsin Cavalry recalled that his regiment charged through and scattered a Confederate skirmish line, allowing the Federal wagons to reach the safety of Crawfish Spring unmolested that evening. Ray's report stands in stark contrast to Wheeler's claim that he "warmly assailed" the enemy, divided their column, and drove

---

53 *Ibid.*

54 Bunting Letter, *Rome Tri-Weekly Telegraph*, November 27, 1863.

55 *Ibid.*

them "in confusion in all directions." What is clear is that the wagons made it safely to their destination, and Union cavalry losses were considered "nominal."[56]

When they reached the spring, the Federal horsemen discovered the backwash of the massive battle unfolding just to the north. By late afternoon, field hospitals from seven different Union infantry divisions surrounded the spring and the Gordon mansion, hosting a steady stream of wounded making their painful way from the battlefield. The stately house transitioned from hosting Rosecrans headquarters to use by the surgeons as an operating theater. Blood stains covered the furniture and floors. In order to protect the hospitals and supplies gathered there, the 2nd Michigan Cavalry established a picket line along Chickamauga Creek a mile or so to the east.

One Wolverine patrol trotted out toward Glass Mill. As it drew near the creek, its members discovered a small body of Rebels, probably more 8th Texas men, dismounted in their front. Unhorsing in turn, the Michiganders investigated. "We . . . reconnoitered their position which appeared to be at a mill on the opposite side where the bank had quite an elevation," Pvt. Henry Hampstead wrote in his diary. "We fell back a short distance after sustaining a short skirmish with them, long enough to develop their strength, which appeared to be greater than ours."[57] Night was falling, and both sides ended the light skirmish and fell back to their respective sides of the creek.

* * *

The infantry battle of September 19 spun out of control for both sides, as Braxton Bragg fed reinforcements into the fight one division at a time and Rosecrans matched him unit for unit. Because the battlefield was sprawling, rolling, and largely wooded, neither commander was certain of the other's strength or prepared to launch a general offensive. Bragg was virtually paralyzed with uncertainty. He committed troops as the situation dictated, but only to stave off disaster while he contemplated where to launch the main attack. Rosecrans had a better view and understanding of the enemy, but a large part of

56 OR 30, pt. 1, p. 907; Entry for September 19, 1863, Robert S. Merrill Diary, Carroll College, Waukesha, Wisconsin.

57 Entry for September 19, 1863, Henry Hampstead Diary, Bentley Historical Library, University of Michigan.

his army (McCook's XX Corps) was still marching up from the south to reach the battlefield. And, there was the continuing problem of the large gap in his center between Thomas' XIV Corps and Crittenden's XXI Corps. Rosecrans was well aware of the hole in his line, but he lacked the troops to fill it. By late afternoon the fighting had expanded into a massive bloody slugfest, the action swaying at times back and forth across the Lafayette Road, with neither side able to finish the day with a clear advantage. When darkness ended the conflict, the Lafayette Road served as a rough dividing line between the two armies—an informal no man's land between each side's skirmish lines.

The Confederate cavalry served and fought much better on September 19 than it had the previous day. Some of its organizations suffered severe losses. Many of these came during the periods when the horsemen were mistaken by the enemy as infantry, because they were dismounted and performing the role of infantry—which in turn meant the cavalry was not always fulfilling its mission as mounted troops. Bragg didn't need more foot soldiers as much as he needed more information. Screening and scouting, not infantry charges— should have been the cavalry's main task that Saturday.

Forrest's men bore the brunt of the cavalry fighting on the 19th. Dibrell performed admirably covering Ben Cheatham's exposed flank later in the day, saving Jackson's and Maney's brigades from a more serious reverse. Pegram's Brigade, however, was badly mauled in an action that was clearly avoidable, while Scott fumbled his mission to screen Red House Bridge and suffered needless losses in men and horseflesh. For his part, Forrest continued to perform as if he was still a brigade or division commander rather than a corps commander in charge of Bragg's entire right flank. He made little or no effort to send out more extensive patrols that might report on the overall Union dispositions, a mistake that would affect Bragg's subsequent decision-making.

Wheeler turned in an even less impressive performance. His tardiness kept large bodies of both cavalry and infantry out of the fight. Wheeler's delay in replacing Armstrong kept substantial numbers of Forrest's men cooling their heels when they could have been performing valuable scouting missions. His failure to replace Breckinridge's infantry at Glass Mill kept an entire division out of action for most of the 19th in launching a putative deception effort that failed to fool a single Yankee, and for that matter could have been accomplished by some of Wharton's men that morning. Nor did Wheeler make a serious effort to disrupt the Union movement northward out of McLemore's Cove, or to discern the Federal deployments between Crawfish Spring and Lee and Gordon's Mill.

*   *   *

The battle of September 19 was inconclusive. Each side suffered heavy losses, but neither side was able to gain a decided tactical advantage. The location of the battle lines for both armies were similar to where they had been at the start of the day's fighting, although the Confederate left flank was farther west. For the most part, the Lafayette Road ran through a disputed no-man's-land between the opposing sides. A bulge of Union troops representing Rosecrans' left flank projected well east of the road, where Thomas' forward movement had precipitated the day's action. That projection of manpower was reduced in the early hours of September 20 when Thomas withdrew to a far more compact and defensible position along the eastern edge of Kelly Field (still well to the east of Lafayette Road).

Bragg and Rosecrans spent the night meeting with subordinates and working out new plans. Each expected that the battle would be renewed come daylight.

Chapter 13

Wheeler vs. Crook:
The Cavalry Fight at Crawfish Springs
(September 20, 1863)

Braxton Bragg intended to attack at dawn. His general plan remained the same: strike first from the north and cut Rosecrans off from Chattanooga. A sequence of misunderstanding and incompetence delayed the assault until late morning, when it was repulsed with heavy loss. An equally infamous command foul-up on the Federal side, however, turned the tide of battle when it produced another gap in the Union line. This time, four Confederate divisions poured through under the firm direction of Lt. Gen. James Longstreet, who had arrived from Virginia and been given command of the left wing of the Army of Tennessee. Longstreet's attack swept a third of the Union army off the field and forced the remainder to withdraw that night.

Nathan Bedford Forrest played a secondary role on September 20. His mission remained the protection of the right flank of Bragg's army. Frank Armstrong brought James Wheeler's cavalry brigade north to join Forrest sometime during the night of the 19th, uniting his division and augmenting the cavalry force on Bragg's right to three brigades: Dibrell, Wheeler, and Davidson. Scott's Brigade remained farther north at Red House Bridge to protect that approach to Ringgold. John Breckinridge's infantry division had been engaged down at Glass Mill the previous day. It moved all the way to the extreme right flank and deployed in the woods south of Reed's Bridge Road. Forrest's role included the support of this body of troops.

After their hard fight of the previous day, Forrest decided it was best to leave Davidson's men in reserve and array Armstrong's pair of brigades to watch Breckinridge's exposed flank north of the road. Armstrong dismounted most of Dibrell's and Wheeler's brigades and deployed them in a line extending Breckinridge's right. The 6th Tennessee Cavalry and 18th Tennessee Battalion were retained as a mounted reserve and positioned behind the extreme right flank.[1] At dawn, Forrest selected Dibrell's 11th Tennessee Cavalry to reconnoiter the Federal positions. The Tennesseans rode west, crossing the Lafayette Road north of the McDonald House. Although they did not meet any organized resistance, they did capture a number of Yankee stragglers, many of whom seemed demoralized.[2]

Forrest joined Generals D. H. Hill and Breckinridge in a survey of the Union left flank that morning. The generals were pleased by what they discovered. As Hill later wrote, the flank "was covered for a great distance [only] by infantry skirmishers." Bragg wanted to turn Rosecrans' left flank and shove him away from Chattanooga, and the opportunity to do so still appeared viable.

Breckinridge opened the day's heavy fighting about 9:30 a.m. with a large-scale attack westward toward the McDonald House. Frank Armstrong's cavalry advanced as well, though without encountering any opposition. The infantry thrust scattered the lone Union brigade under Brig. Gen. John Beatty tasked with defending the sector. Two of Breckinridge's three brigades crossed the Lafayette Road and found themselves beyond the northern end of the Union line. Turning south, they attacked the Federal flank. Forrest's men protected their rear during the drive, closing on the Lafayette Road and securing it for about two hours. George Dibrell's troopers captured Union Brig. Gen. John Brannan's divisional field hospital at Cloud Church. The promising beginning of the battle turned against the Confederates when Breckinridge was repulsed by a series of determined counterattacks. His retreat left the Rebel horsemen with no choice but to fall back. "In the midst of a perfect hailstorm of shot and shell, and so enveloped in smoke that you could scarcely see a soldier fifty steps," recalled the 8th Tennessee's historian, "the infantry upon our left gave way, and thus exposed our left flank." It was because of this confusion and

---

1 Michael Cotten, *The Williamson County Cavalry: A History of Company F, Fourth Tennessee Cavalry Regiment, CSA* (Self published, 1994), p. 131.

2 Lindsley, *The Military Annals of Tennessee,* II, p. 693.

heavy smoke that the 8th missed Forrest's first order to retreat, as did Capt. A. L. Huggins' Tennessee battery, which was nearly captured. With no time left to spare, both regiment and battery made good their escape, the latter without the loss of a gun.[3] Dibrell left a small detachment to guard the captured hospital, which was considered a significant prize by Confederates perpetually plagued by shortages of drugs and other medical supplies.

The bulk of Armstrong's mounted brigades retired to take up a line about 1,000 yards east of the Lafayette Road. Armstrong was concerned about three Union brigades at Rossville several miles to the north. Forrest sent John Pegram with Henry Davidson's Brigade farther to the right to watch that approach. While these moves were underway, and Breckinridge's penetration was being thrown back with loss, the main battle shifted south like a rolling barrage, leaving the northern part of the field awash in relative calm.

* * *

The action in the northern sector recommenced about 1:30 p.m. when Pegram dispatched a courier to warn Forrest that fears of a strong Union presence in the vicinity of Rossville were correct: a powerful Union column was marching south from that place. The enemy moved so rapidly it recaptured the field hospital and its handful of Rebel cavalry guards.[4] The Federals turned out to be Brig. Gen. James B. Steedman's two-brigade division of Maj. Gen. Gordon Granger's Reserve Corps, marching to join Thomas' embattled XIV Corps. Left behind without clear orders, Granger and Steedman took it upon themselves to march to the sound of the guns. Their appearance could not have been timelier. Forrest attempted to intercept Steedman by advancing with Armstrong's two brigades and several batteries of artillery. With Rebel cavalry and artillery menacing both their front and left flank, Steedman halted the column and ordered his leading regiment, the 96th Illinois, to form a square. Granger, however, brooked no delay and ordered brusquely that the column get back into motion. Steedman complied and the men hurried south. Forrest's artillery fire, while noisy and annoying, failed to inflict significant losses.[5]

---

3 *Ibid.*, p. 661.

4 Robert Selph Henry, *"First With the Most": Nathan Bedford Forrest* (Mallard Press, 1991), p. 188

5 Charles Partridge, *History of the Ninety-Sixth Regiment Illinois Volunteer Infantry* (Brown, Pettibone and Company, 1887), pp. 178-9.

Granger's troops detoured across fields farther west to avoid the worst of the enemy fire and linked up with Thomas near the Snodgrass House.[6]

Granger's remaining brigade under Col. Dan McCook moved forward to a small hill about 800 yards west of the Lafayette Road. There, supported by a battery, McCook deployed to cover Thomas' left-rear. Some of Forrest's men sparred sporadically with McCook's 2,200 Federals, but the bulk of the Rebel mounted force returned to watch over Breckinridge's infantry flank. Another lull of about two hours ensued. The final cavalry action of the day unfolded between 4:00 and 5:00 p.m., when Rebel infantry made a final attack against Federal breastworks. Armstrong's men advanced alongside, and once again Forrest's men swept across the Lafayette Road—this time to stay. Brannan's field hospital at Cloud Church was recaptured, and a number of Federal artillery pieces abandoned along the road near the McDonald House were also secured. These guns, the debris of batteries that had been wrecked the day before and hauled back to the road to refit, were mistaken for an intact battery by one of Dibrell's men, Sgt. Newton Cannon of the 11th Tennessee Cavalry. Caught up in the excitement of victory, Cannon claimed the honor of being first to lay hands on one of these guns.[7] When nightfall descended on the battlefield, Forrest halted his men along the Lafayette Road.

* * *

John Scott and his cavalry brigade enjoyed a quiet Sunday morning on the 20th at the Red House Bridge while protecting the approach to Ringgold. The Federals were largely gone from their front. Throughout the day, Scott and his troopers had listened to the roar of the large battle a few miles to the south, but orders to move or perform another mission never arrived. That evening, Scott made a cold camp some distance east of the bridge. The enemy infantry Scott clashed with the day before had pulled back toward Rossville on Granger's orders, and were the same troops Forrest engaged en route to join Thomas. Colonel Minty's small Federal cavalry brigade moved up to replace Granger's infantry, but lacked the strength and the orders to engage Scott. Instead, Granger instructed Minty to watch the Ringgold-Chattanooga Road and send out wide-ranging patrols to provide early warning of any further shifting of

6   OR 30, pt. 1, p. 860.

7   Newton Cannon Memoirs, TSLA.

Rebel troops. Minty dispatched men to Graysville and as far west as Chickamauga Station on the Western and Atlantic Railroad without finding any untoward Rebel activity. The only contact between the opposing cavalry came about mid-morning when Minty pushed a detachment as far as Red House Bridge, where he discovered Scott's Confederates in line on the west bank of the creek.[8] The skirmish that followed was light, sporadic and considered insignificant by both sides.

Minty's troopers maintained their watchful posture for the rest of the day until word arrived that the Union army was retreating to Rossville that evening. After dark, Minty began his own gradual withdrawal. The brigade's picket line was so extended that one sergeant and 20 men did not get word of the pullout, and only discovered their perilous situation when someone figured out the rest of their regiment was gone. Despite an anxious night march and almost stumbling into some of Scott's Rebels watering their horses at a millpond on Missionary Ridge, this last wayward detachment of Yankees escaped without loss.[9]

In stark contrast, the action on the southern end of the field near Crawfish Springs on September 20 was one of the larger (and least known) pure cavalry fights of the war. When Breckinridge's Division was ordered to march north to the right flank of the Confederate army on the evening of the 19th, troopers from Wheeler's cavalry replaced them and assumed control of Bragg's left flank. Early the next morning, both of Wheeler's divisions (Wharton and Martin) were concentrated on the east bank of West Chickamauga Creek a mile or so from Glass Mill. Cavalry pickets actively guarded the crossing sites.

Three brigades of Federal cavalry would eventually oppose Wheeler. After safely escorting the wagon train through to Crawfish Springs, Col. Daniel Ray's brigade camped at the springs that night.[10] Colonel Eli Long's brigade, comprised of the 1st, 3rd, 4th Ohio and 2nd Kentucky cavalry regiments, quartered just south of the springs west of the creek near Glass Mill.[11] Colonel Archibald Campbell's brigade—the 2nd Michigan, 9th Pennsylvania, and 2nd Tennessee (US) Cavalry—was assigned the duty of patrolling the creek bank

---

8 *OR* 30, pt. 1, p. 922.

9 James Larson, "Outwitting a Picket Guard," *National Tribune*, September 19, 1912.

10 *OR* 30, pt. 1, p. 907.

11 Thomas Crofts, *History of the Third Ohio Cavalry, 1861-1865* (Stoneman Press, 1910), pp. 112-3.

from near Glass Mill and downstream (northward) as far as Lee and Gordon's Mills.[12] Crawfish Springs was also the site of most of the Army of the Cumberland's hospitals. Seven of the army's nine divisional hospitals were established within one mile of the springs. Until the day before, Rosecrans' headquarters was also located there. Two more Yankee brigades, Col. Louis D. Watkins' cavalry command of Brig. Gen. George Crook's Second Division and Col. P. Sidney Post's infantry brigade from McCook's XX Corps, comprised what can be considered the Army of the Cumberland's rearguard. Both were en route to the springs escorting baggage trains and spent the night several miles south at Steven's Gap on Lookout Mountain.[13]

Dawn was breaking when Companies C and M of the 2nd Michigan Cavalry's Second Battalion eased quietly ahead near Glass Mill through an early morning fog brought on by the sharp plunge in temperature the night before. Fresh from their encounter the previous evening with some of Wharton's Texans, the Wolverines moved cautiously, picketing their side of Chickamauga Creek while alert to any signs of potential danger. Company D of the 8th Texas Cavalry, part of Col. Thomas Harrison's cavalry brigade, was carrying out the same mission on the Rebel side of the waterway at Glass Mill. When one side spotted the other a short fight broke out and the Texans were driven back. Satisfied, the Michigan troopers left some of their own to watch the crossing and fell back to get some breakfast. [14]

Glass Mill was four meandering miles upstream from Lee and Gordon's Mills (about two miles as the crow flies). A low though abrupt hill dominated the east bank of the creek, providing a potential artillery platform, but the west side was almost flat, a gently rising plain consisting of a patchwork of open fields and timber. A large well-tended farm was just north of the Glass Mill Road about 800 yards west of the bridge. One-third of a mile farther north, a farm trail crossed the creek at an unnamed ford. The tranquil setting was about to witness the largest cavalry action of the entire campaign.[15]

As is often the case in combat, an initial outbreak of fighting triggers a response. And so it was that the brief skirmish and repulse of Company D drew

12 R. M. Russell, "Extracts from Journal," General Thomas Papers, RG 94, NARA.

13 *OR* 30, pt. 3, pp. 505, 914-5.

14 Entry for September 20, 1863, Harry Hempstead Diary, Bentley Historical Library.

15 The name of the farmer is unknown.

in the rest of the 8th Texas Cavalry. The Texans arrived while the 2nd Michigan was boiling coffee. A Rebel battery accompanying the Texans unlimbered and threw three or four quick shells into the midst of the Michigan troopers while the Southern cavalry recaptured the mill and established a toehold on the west bank of the creek.[16] Heavily outnumbered by a full regiment of Texans, Companies C and M fell back to the large farm several hundred yards farther west.

Now it was the Yankees' turn to bring up reinforcements. More Wolverines from the Third Battalion of the 2nd Michigan arrived, adding several more companies to the battle line. Reinforced, the Michiganders halted the advance of the Texans and began to slowly drive them back to the creek. The withdrawal stopped when the Rebels reached the trees along the west bank of the stream and used them as cover for a stout line of battle. In the space of two hours, the original skirmish escalated from a few scattered picket shots to a sharp fight between full regiments. It was about to expand again.

The Confederates rushed to commit the rest of Colonel Harrison's Brigade while the Federals moved to reinforce their position with part of the 2nd Kentucky Cavalry from Colonel Long's brigade, plus an unidentified artillery battery, to engage the Rebel field pieces. The Kentucky Federals arrived first, allowing the bluecoats to renew their attack. Things looked bad for the Texans, who were on the verge of being driven into the creek. Just then Harrison's reinforcements in the form of the 3rd Confederate, 3rd Kentucky, and the 4th Tennessee and 11th Tennessee cavalry regiments, along with Capt. B. F. White's Tennessee Battery, appeared. Their arrival reversed abruptly the tide of the fight. Michigander Henry Hempsted remembered with uncharitable disgust as the overmatched Federals recoiled: "Our 'brave' Kentuckians had after a short resistance fled in confusion."[17] With large numbers of Rebels swarming over the creek, presaging another charge, and with their own support evaporating, Hempsted's own 2nd Michigan also fell back—and no less quickly. Glass Mill was now firmly in Confederate hands.

A brief lull ensued as both sides paused for a breather and called for reinforcements. R. F. Bunting of the 8th Texas remembered that just word of the fight was "enough to throw the whole command in motion." Joe Wheeler called up the rest of Wharton's men plus Martin's entire division of two

16 *Ibid.*

17 *Ibid.*

brigades. This powerful mounted force moved up the Chattanooga Road to a spot just east of Glass Mill, where they halted to await developments.[18]

General George Crook arrived with his command at Crawfish Spring that morning and reported to General Mitchell, who directed him "to take post at once in front of the fords of the Chickamauga and hold that point at all hazards." The terrain was difficult for the cavalry. "The only point I could occupy was a thick, rocky woods with heavy underbrush," reported Crook. He ordered Eli Long's entire brigade of 900 sabers out to replace the recently withdrawn 2nd Michigan Cavalry.[19] In turn, the 2nd Michigan was dispatched to rejoin its parent brigade at Lee and Gordon's Mills. The Wolverines were needed there because Maj. Gen. Philip H. Sheridan's infantry division of the XX Corps had been called north the night before to join the main battle, and his absence left that crossing dangerously undermanned.

George Crook did not like what he saw. The career Army officer and veteran Indian fighter was experienced enough to know that terrain often determined the outcome of combat, and the ground around Glass Mill was not to his liking. The woods obscured much of his view, and a distant "juniper thicket" masked the creek itself. When he asked a Wolverine officer where the creek was, the man replied, "damned if he knew." His orders were to protect the crossing, regardless of the terrain or odds he faced, so Crook set about establishing a defense as best he could. He deployed "two lines of skirmishers, one mounted and the other dismounted," with the dismounted men in front. Despite misgivings about the vulnerability of artillery in this rough terrain, Crook ordered his two field pieces—a section of the Chicago Board of Trade Battery—to open fire on the juniper thicket.[20]

Lieutenant Colonel Elijah Watts of the 2nd Kentucky Cavalry, the only non-Ohio unit in Long's brigade, described Crook's dispositions in detail. "General [Colonel] Eli Long . . . placed himself at the head of our regiment, and . . . [moving] . . . by a road leading to a ford on Chickamauga river, we soon

18 Bunting Letter, *Rome Tri-Weekly Telegraph*, November 27, 1863.

19 S. H. Stevens, "Second division Itinerary" CCNMP; *OR* 30, pt. 1, p. 918. Crook's report says he "arrived at Crawfish on the evening of the 20th," but this is clearly a mistake. All related evidence, including General Mitchell's report, which says that "General Crook, with his command, reported about 10 a.m. from Dougherty's Gap," confirms Crook's appearance on the morning of September 20. *Ibid.*, p. 893, 918.

20 Martin F. Schmidt, ed., *General George Crook: His Autobiography* (Norman, University of Oklahoma Press, 1946). pp. 105-6.

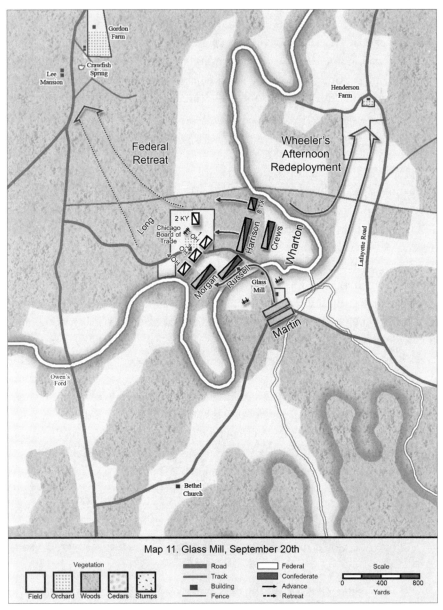

Map 11. Glass Mill, September 20th

Vegetation

Field Orchard Woods Cedars Stumps

▬▬▬ Road
──── Track
■ Building
──── Fence

☐ Federal
■ Confederate
──▶ Advance
--▶ Retreat

Scale

0   400   800
Yards

This fight, which erupts from a picket action early on the morning of September 20, develops into one of the larger cavalry actions of the Western Theater with some 900 Federals facing at least 5,000 troopers from both of Joe Wheeler's divisions. Luckily for George Crook's Federals, a fortuitous bend in the creek limits Wheeler's ability to deploy his men, so it takes some time before Rebel numbers turn the tide of battle. When the Confederates threaten both of his flanks, Crook retreats to Crawfish Springs. Wheeler may have pursued, but new orders divert him to Lee and Gordon's Mills and grant the Federals a temporary respite.

halted and formed line. The 1st Ohio, 3rd Ohio and 4th Ohio dismounted and went into line on our right and advanced skirmishers. At this point the 2nd and 4th Mich[igan] Cavalry passed back from our front. They had been on guard at the ford, but the enemy effected a crossing in spite of them . . ."[21] The Federal cannon moved up the road to a small rise, added Watts, while his regiment of Kentuckians deployed into line on the left side of the guns. "The ground in front of us," he added, "was an old cornfield, ascending slightly from the river; and perpendicular to our left flank was a piece of woodland."[22]

The next move belonged to Joe Wheeler. Bragg's standing orders were to "attack the enemy at every opportunity," and Wheeler intended to do just that. By crossing Chickamauga Creek in force and on foot, he hoped to create a diversion sufficient to convince the enemy that it was another infantry attack. If Rosecrans' headquarters was adequately alarmed, perhaps the thrust would leach Federal reinforcements southward, away from the main battle.[23] Wheeler dismounted Wharton's entire division except for the 8th Texas and sent the cavalrymen splashing across the creek about 10:00 a.m. to resume the fight.

George Guild, who would later become the regimental historian for Lt. Col. Paul F. Anderson's 4th Tennessee Cavalry, remembered the moment Wheeler's orders arrived. "While standing in line . . . we noticed a staff officer ride up to General Wharton. . . . We were ordered to dismount and advance towards a battery that was shelling us. . . . [T]he order was received with cheers," explained Guild, "for the men were chaffing to go forward."[24] Not everyone was as eager as Guild to join the fighting, but only the incautious made that fact known. The men counted off by fives, with every fifth man designated to hold the horses. The count was progressing in Pvt. J. K. Womack's Company F when a "trooper who was number five shouted very distinctly 'bully.'" An angered Lieutenant Colonel Anderson, continued Womack, "said very clearly through his nose: 'Let 'Bully' go into the fight and number four hold horses.'"[25]

---

21 E. S. Watts Report, August 17, 1889, Office of the Adjutant General, Union Battle Reports, RG 94, Box 56, NARA.

22 *Ibid.*

23 OR 30, pt. 2, pp. 520-1.

24 Clipping, 4th Tennessee File, CCNMP.

25 J. K. Womack, "Chickamauga As I Saw It," *Confederate Veteran*, Vol. XXV, No. 2 (February, 1917), p. 74.

Wharton's men attacked Long's dismounted Federal skirmish line while the 8th Texas worked around the Federal left flank. This action triggered a prolonged and intense firefight. "A strong brigade of the enemy's infantry advanced, covered by a heavy skirmish line," was how the 2nd Kentucky's Lieutenant Colonel Watts described the opening of the Confederate attack. "The advance . . . was deliberate and steady, the skirmishers firing as they came, and our regiment responded, checking the skirmishers until they were lost in the main line . . . general firing was [now] opened all along both lines, the 2nd Kentucky pouring a galling fire into them, as did also the board of trade battery."[26]

Private Womack's Company F of the 4th Tennessee was on the receiving end of that fire. "We slowly marched toward the enemy [until] the command 'charge!' came in distinct tones. All went forward with a rush," he recalled. "I could still see the long black hair of Captain [James R.] Lester which seemed to quiver from the Minie balls that filled the air around us. I shall never forget how the enemy, concealed behind trees and logs, poured a volley of leaden hail into us . . . cartridge boxes were shot off, men were wounded right and left."[27] The Federals from Kentucky were not the only ones firing their weapons. Private William Thompson of Company B, part of the 3rd Georgia Cavalry in Col. C. C. Crews' Brigade, was one of those unfortunate enough not to have a horse to hold. As a result, he waded across the creek that morning and into enemy small arms range. "I took four deliberate fires at the old Star Spangle Banner it fell three times but whether it was me or not I don't know," he explained candidly in a letter home.[28]

The fighting intensified when Wheeler ordered in Martin's dismounted troopers to reinforce Wharton's advance. Lieutenant Colonel Tyra H. Mauldin of the 3rd Alabama Cavalry, part of Col. John T. Morgan's cavalry brigade, was ordered "to take my Reg't—on foot—across the bridge to support a battery then in position on the left of the road."[29] Martin's pair of brigades (the other

---

26 Watts Report, RG 94, NARA. Watts mistook Wharton's dismounted cavalry for an infantry attack.

27 Womack, "Chickamauga As I Saw It," p. 74.

28 "Dear Ma & Pa," September 24, 1863, William N. Thompson Letter, 3rd Georgia Cavalry file, CCNMP.

29 3rd Alabama Cavalry Report, Martin Papers, American History Collection, University of Texas at Austin.

under Col. A. A. Russell) navigated the creek and deployed to the left of the road, extending Wharton's line southward to threaten the Union right flank.

Numbers now began to tell. "They drove us back steadily," admitted Crook, "contesting every inch of ground, about 200 yards, where we held our ground." The Federals only had 900 men and a section of artillery to combat two full Southern divisions several thousand strong. When it became obvious that remaining in place risked encirclement, Mitchell ordered Crook "to fall back to the hospital, 1 ½ miles distant." With his orders in hand, Crook ordered his men to retreat.[30]

By this time, the 8th Texas cavalry had succeeded in turning Long's left flank. Texan Robert F. Bunting recalled "charging through a lane and across a camp of the enemy," and "boldly dash[ed] up upon his lines." The dismounted troopers pressed Long's flank "so heavily that he is compelled to flee for safety. Here the fighting was stubborn."[31] Bunting's account was corroborated by Lt. James Thompson of the 4th Ohio Cavalry. "The rebels began to show themselves advancing in regular order & in three columns & as they were pressing us very hard the order was given to fall back but as soon as they saw us giving way [their] Cav[alry] charged us & every fellow tried to save himself," explained Thompson. "Everything skedaddled until [we] got through a skirt of woods."[32]

Several things went wrong all at once for the Federals. Watching the action near the two guns of the Chicago Board of Trade Battery, General Crook realized his flanks were being turned and ordered the cannoneers to "get the battery out of here."[33] As the guns were limbering to leave, the general watched in shock as the 1st Ohio Cavalry mounted in preparation for what looked to be an attack against the oncoming Rebels. Colonel Long intended to launch a

---

30 *Ibid.*; *OR* 30, pt. 1, p. 919. Wheeler's decision to attack dismounted and hopefully deceive the Federals worked to a small extent. In his battle report, General Crook noted, "About 11 o'clock I was attacked by Hindman's division of infantry, a battalion of sharpshooters, and a large body of cavalry." *Ibid.* Thomas Hindman's Confederate infantry were not engaged in this action, and by this time was much farther north about to participate in Longstreet's massive attack. In all likelihood, the Federals knew Hindman's men had been present at Lee and Gordon's Mills on September 18, and may have assumed they were still there on the morning of the 20th. Prisoners and/or deserters from the division may have been taken, or contact might have been made.

31 From R. F. Bunting, *Rome Tri-Weekly Telegraph*, November 27, 1863.

32 James Thompson Diary transcript, 4th Ohio Cavalry file, CCNMP.

33 Stevens, "Itinerary," CCNMP files.

mounted feint, but Crook seemed to realize that the Buckeyes were preparing for a proper attack. With no time to lose, Crook set his spurs and galloped onto the scene, personally countermanding the order. The aborted charge threw the regiment into considerable disorder, and not everyone got the word to halt quickly enough. Lieutenant Thompson of the 4th Ohio witnessed part of the effort and later wrote that "some of the 1st Ohio charged them with the saber but with little effect."[34] General Crook's prompt action saved lives by preventing the forlorn attack from being delivered, but just the act of mounting horses exposed the Ohioans to a ruinous enemy fire that killed and injured many of them. Among the fallen was the mortally wounded Lt. Col. Valentine Cupp, commander of the 1st Ohio.[35] Either Colonel Long's courier garbled the message or Cupp misunderstood, because the move was supposed to be a feint, not a real charge.

With heavy losses, Long's brigade now fell back toward Crawfish Springs and took up a new line very close to the Lee Mansion. Colonel Cupp was brought to the house, and died there that night. During Long's retreat a number of Union prisoners were taken, and some of the Rebels commenced to reap the spoils. John Wyeth of the 4th Alabama Cavalry watched in disgust as a callous Texan stripped the boot from a Federal officer, wounded in the foot. The Texan insisted the boot come off intact instead of being sliced open to minimize the wounded man's pain. "You reckon I'm going to spoil that boot?" spat the Texan contemptuously when other Rebels asked him to show some mercy toward the wounded Yank.[36]

Things might have gone far worse for the Federals, but Wheeler did not pursue all the way to the springs. Just as Crook's men were driven from the field, Wheeler received conflicting orders from his superiors. On the 19th Bragg had instructed Wheeler to guard James Longstreet's left flank. By doing so, he implied that at least a measure of Longstreet's authority extended over

---

34 Thompson Diary, CCNMP.

35 *Proceedings of the Thirtieth Annual Reunion, 1st O.V.V.C.* (n.p. 1909), p. 18. Eli Long's report for the Chickamauga Campaign is not available in the *Official Records*, although an itinerary of the brigade from September 2 through September 30 may be found at OR 30, pt. 1, p. 927. Brigade losses were heavy at 123 men killed, wounded, and missing, and seven officers wounded and one officer (Lieutenant Colonel Cupp) killed.

36 John A. Wyeth, *With Sabre and Scalpel: The Autobiography of a Soldier and Surgeon* (Harper, 1914), p. 248.

Wheeler's troopers.[37] Now, at the height of Wheeler's success over Crook, Longstreet exercised that authority. Shortly before noon, Longstreet's men broke through the Union line at the Brotherton cabin and routed a third of the Union Army of the Cumberland from the field. In an effort to stem the Rebel tide, John Wilder's mounted infantry launched a desperate counterattack, which in turn routed a Rebel infantry brigade.[38] Wilder's advance was reported to Longstreet as an attack by Union cavalry. To counteract the Union horsemen and pursue that part of the Union army fleeing the field, Longstreet sent an aide to find Wheeler and ask for Rebel cavalry support.

Wheeler might have complied with Longstreet's request had he not received an order directly from General Bragg about the same time. Bragg's order instructed his senior cavalryman to ride north a mile or so and attack the Federals found at Lee and Gordon's Mills. Despite two days' fighting and considerable shifting of position by both armies, Bragg was still under the impression that the Union right flank was anchored at the mills: "There his force must be," insisted the Rebel commander in his directive.[39]

37 The full extent of this authority cannot be known, as the original orders do not survive. However, Wheeler confirmed that he did indeed take orders from Longstreet, OR 30, pt. 2, p. 21, and Longstreet, in his memoirs, recalled sending various orders to Wheeler. James Longstreet, *From Manassas to Appomattox: Memoirs of the Civil War in America.* (P. J. Lippincott, 1896), p. 453. However, Lt. Col. Thomas Claiborne, a member of Simon Buckner's staff loaned to Longstreet during the battle, claimed after the war that Longstreet did not know he had authority over Wheeler. Claiborne Letter to Henry Boynton, as quoted in Cozzens, *This Terrible Sound*, pp. 454-5. Claiborne did not explain why, if Longstreet believed this, he sent Wheeler several orders. It is possible that Longstreet's messages to Wheeler were formulated more as requests for support than peremptory commands.

38 This famous incident was the collision between Wilder's Federals and Brig. Gen. Arthur M. Manigault's Confederate brigade, which routed the Manigault's command just at the moment when the Union right wing was fleeing the field. Wilder later claimed he intended to ride through Longstreet's entire command to join General Thomas' embattled Union XIV Corps, which had not been routed. Before he could do so, however, Wilder was ordered off the field by a rather panicked Charles M. Dana, then assistant Secretary of War. Wilder's movement threatened Longstreet's rear just as he was getting ready to launch a final attack on the remaining Yankees, which prompted the call for help from Joe Wheeler. For a detailed description of this action, see Cozzens, *This Terrible Sound*, pp. 394-6. Arthur Middleton Manigault, *A Carolinian Goes to War: The Civil War Narrative of Arthur Middleton Manigault, Brigadier General, C.S.A.* (University of South Carolina Press, 1983), pp. 98-9, provides a Confederate view of these events. Wilder's 1888 report, CCNMP, discusses the attack and incident with Dana. For a discussion of Wilder's proposed move and a detailed map depicting his likely route, see Powell and Friedrichs, *The Maps of Chickamauga*, pp. 190-191.

39 *OR* 30, pt. 4, p. 675.

Wheeler received both of these orders within a short space of time, and their mutual arrival presented Wheeler with a quandary. Should he defer to Longstreet's request in accordance with Bragg's unambiguous instructions of the day before, or should he act upon Bragg's more immediate directive? Wheeler decided to obey Bragg and move to the Mills. Moving on Lee and Gordon's Mills was the logical choice for following either order, since the shortest route to Longstreet's last known position was beyond (north of) the mills anyway, and any Federal defenders there would have to be dealt with as a matter of course.

However, Wheeler's next decision was not as well thought out. His entire cavalry corps was already on the west bank of Chickamauga Creek and, moving overland, no more than about one mile southwest of Lee and Gordon's Mills. Even moving cross-country, it should have been a relatively simple matter to approach the mills from that direction—and possibly take the Union defenders there in the flank. Moreover, Wheeler's command was flushed with success. His cavalry had all but routed Long's Union brigade and his men were exuberant over the victory. Tom Coleman of the 11th Texas Cavalry boasted with pride that this regiment had whipped the 4th Ohio Cavalry, "a brag regiment of the Yankees."[40] Speed was of the essence if Wheeler wanted to capitalize on that success.

For reasons that remain uncertain, Wheeler elected for a more round-about approach. Instead of moving due north, he pulled his entire force back across the creek to the east bank, retraced his steps along the Glass Mill Road almost to Wharton's campgrounds of the night before, and only then turned north on the Lafayette Road to approach Lee and Gordon's Mills from the southeast.[41] Years later trooper John Wyeth defended the move by claiming that Wheeler wasn't aware of Longstreet's success—which was probably accurate—or he would have simply advanced to Crawfish Springs and then turned north, rendering the whole argument moot. Wyeth's account fails to address any of the tactical disadvantages Wheeler's actual route incurred compared to simply moving directly toward Lee and Gordon's Mills from Glass Mill.[42]

40 Tom Coleman Letter, Western Historical Manuscripts Collection, University of Missouri, Rolla, Missouri.

41 Bunting Letter, *Rome Tri-Weekly Telegraph*, November 27, 1863.

42 Wyeth, *Sabre and Scalpel*, pp. 248-9.

Wheeler's decision to move back across the creek consumed a significant amount of precious time. His entire column had to funnel through the creek's choke points at the crossings not once but twice, since Wheeler would have to cross again back to the west bank after he arrived at the Mills. Worse, if the Federals held Lee and Gordon's Mills in strength, the Rebel cavalry would have to force the second crossing under fire. As the fights at both Reed's and Alexander's bridges on September 18 demonstrated, such attacks were costly and time consuming.

Fortunately for the men under his command, all Wheeler lost because of the decision to retrace his steps was time. As his lead elements approached the Mills, Wheeler dismounted most of his command and advanced cautiously to the creek's meandering east bank. When the move met no resistance, at the millpond some members of the 4th Alabama Cavalry tried to keep their feet dry by crossing single file along the top of the dam. Alert to the havoc a single canister round could wreak on such a tempting target, one of Wyeth's officers ordered everyone down into the water. Once across, however, Wyeth discovered "that we could have gone over . . . in perfect safety."[43] Lee and Gordon's Mills was all but undefended; the Federals were already falling back to Crawfish Spring.

Had the Rebels arrived earlier in the day, they would have encountered considerably more resistance. Until midday, Col. Archibald P. Campbell's First Brigade, First Division of the Cavalry Corps—including the pugnacious 2nd Michigan—were assigned to picket the west bank and watch the crossings between Lee and Gordon's Mills and Glass' Mill. Aside from the 2nd Michigan, Campbell's men had thus far remained unengaged. They could have mustered a strong defense of the crossing. When Eli Long's brigade was driven back to Crawfish Spring that morning, and the Federal cavalry lost contact with the Federal main body after Longstreet's massive breakthrough, General Mitchell realized that Campbell's force, now with both flanks unprotected, was vulnerable to being gobbled up wholesale. The Federal troopers retired slowly westward to join the rest of the command in a more compact defensive position near the Lee mansion.

When Wheeler's troopers reached the crossing at the mills, Campbell's main line was already several hundred yards farther west, but a handful of Yankee cavalry were still present as a rearguard. This two-company detachment

43 *Ibid.*, pp. 251.

of the 9th Pennsylvania was commanded by Capt. Thomas McCahan. When he realized that a heavy enemy force (two full divisions) was deploying on the east bank, McCahan sensibly withdrew his handful of pickets as Wheeler's men advanced, scattering no more than a few rounds in their direction.[44] Once McCahan's men rejoined the balance of the 9th Pennsylvania, Campbell ordered the entire brigade to fall back toward the hospitals. The Rebels followed, but did not pursue aggressively.

By the time Campbell's line reached headquarters and reported Wheeler's presence, Mitchell was aware of the larger disaster unfolding to the north and realized he could no longer hold Crawfish Springs. Longstreet's attack had swept all organized Union troops from the field between the springs and Snodgrass Hill, routing them across Missionary Ridge and back toward Rossville. Union stragglers appeared with tales of Rebel hordes close on their heels, and the news alarmed everyone. When Campbell's men retreated past the first of the field hospitals, their retirement only compounded the panic and, fearing capture, some wounded Federals hobbled after them.[45] Even a small Confederate presence at this point may well have induced Mitchell to retreat.

The panic was premature: Wheeler was in no hurry. About 3:00 p.m., General Mitchell dispatched the 9th Pennsylvania north along the old Chattanooga Road with orders to find General Sheridan's infantry division and reestablish contact with the army. The Pennsylvanians traveled about two miles but found neither Sheridan nor any other organized Federal force. They did, however, encounter Rebel infantry and artillery in strength deployed on a rise overlooking the road and blocking any farther move north. The commander of the 9th, Lt. Col. Roswell M. Russell, called a halt and dispatched a courier back to Mitchell informing him of the dire situation. Satisfied he could not rejoin the army via that route, Mitchell ordered the 9th Pennsylvania to return to Crawfish Springs.[46]

And still Wheeler did not press the issue. Sometime during the late morning Mitchell's command was strengthened by the arrival of Col. Sidney M. Post's infantry brigade of McCook's XX Corps, which finally wound its way out of McLemore's Cove. The overall uncertainty of what was transpiring on the

---

44 Entry for September 20, 1863, Thomas S. McCahan Diary, Historical Society of Pennsylvania, Philadelphia, PA.

45 *Ibid.*

46 *OR* 30, pt. 1, pp. 904-5.

battlefield almost triggered a friendly-fire incident when Post's men arrived. Lieutenant Chesley Mosman, marching with the 59th Illinois Infantry of Post's brigade recalled that Yankee cavalry was "drawn up to charge us when [they] discovered by our brigade flag who we were."[47] Post sent the trains he was escorting on to Chattanooga and placed himself at Mitchell's disposal.

With word from the 9th Pennsylvania that the way northward was blocked, Mitchell began evacuating Crawfish Spring around 4:00 p.m. Leading the way were Post's infantry and Long's battered Ohioans, escorting as many of the wounded as could be moved or were still ambulatory.[48] The Federals marched west over Missionary Ridge and then turned north to Chattanooga. Colonel Ray's brigade was next in line, and Colonel Campbell's men brought up the rear.[49] Within an hour Mitchell's ad-hoc column was gone. Wheeler, who had earlier failed to press home a vigorous attack, followed along in the Union wake. By 5:00 p.m. his troopers captured five Union hospitals and about 1,000 Federal stragglers and other oddments.[50]

Wheeler was assessing these captures when another courier from Longstreet arrived bearing a second request—this time in writing—asking that Wheeler come up and support Longstreet's infantry by outflanking the Union right flank near the Vittetoe house, preferably with artillery. Longstreet's infantry wing was locked in a dramatic struggle for Horseshoe Ridge, his exhausted infantry gathering themselves for a final push against equally worn out Union defenders. The big Georgian was looking for support anywhere he could find it. As if to underscore the urgency of his need, a third message reached Wheeler just twenty minutes later repeating Longstreet's request.[51]

Once again Wheeler faced a dilemma. Longstreet's urgent missives were obviously important and well within the bounds of the orders outlined by Bragg the night before. However, the retreating Federal cavalry column should also be pursued as a matter of military course. By this time Wheeler had in his

---

47 Arnold Gates, ed., *The Rough Side of War: The Civil War Journal of Chesley A. Mosman 1st Lieutenant, Company D, 59th Illinois Volunteer Infantry Regiment* (Basin Publishing, 1987), p. 84.

48 *Proceedings of the Thirtieth Annual Reunion, 1st O.V.V.C.*, p. 19; Gates, *The Rough Side of War*, p. 85

49 *OR* 30, pt. 1, p. 912; R. M. Russell, "Extracts From Journal," Thomas Papers, RG 94, NARA.

50 *OR* 30, pt. 2, p. 521.

51 *Ibid.*, pt. 4, p. 675; Longstreet, *From Manassas to Appomattox*, p. 453.

possession a large haul of prisoners and booty to watch over, and men would have to be detailed to secure them. Allocating his forces to all three missions (helping Longstreet, pursuing the enemy, and guarding the prisoners and captured supplies) might well stretch his force too thin. Wheeler needed to prioritize these missions and decide which were the most critical.

Instead of making a firm decision and acting decisively, a curious passivity settled over the Rebel cavalry chief. He had begun the morning aggressively enough with a spirited attack against Eli Long's Yankee cavalry, but thereafter his actions are more difficult to explain. Even though his curious tactical decision to countermarch and approach Lee and Gordon's Mills in a roundabout manner was offset by the Union decision to pull back, Wheeler failed to launch a strong attack against a retreating enemy that afternoon and allowed Mitchell's column to withdraw unscathed early that evening. Nor did he send more than token help to Longstreet. According to George Guild of the 4th Tennessee Cavalry, his regiment rode to join Longstreet and camped near the latter's headquarters that night, but Guild failed to report the timing of that move or whether the 4th participated in any additional action.[52]

Similarly, Wheeler sent only a detachment to follow Mitchell. This produced some light skirmishing but did not (and could not) result in any significant fight or inflict significant damage on the fleeing enemy. In his report, Wheeler explained that "the pursuit was continued till two hours after nightfall, when we retired to feed our horses." Whatever the pursuit entailed, it did little to impress Lt. Col. Russell of the 9th Pennsylvania, whose men comprised the rearguard of Mitchell's retreating column. "Shortly after leaving Crawfish Spring a body of Rebel cavalry made a dash upon my rear guard," reported Russell, "but was instantly repulsed, and I proceeded without further annoyance."[53] Wheeler's "pursuit" cost Campbell's entire cavalry brigade a grand total of four additional casualties.[54]

Wheeler's final decision that evening is equally peculiar. Sometime after dark he ordered General Martin's small cavalry division to guard the captured hospitals and establish a picket line in the direction of Rossville. According to Tom Coleman of the 11th Texas Cavalry, however, Wharton's Division

52 George B. Guild, *A Brief Narrative of the Fourth Tennessee Cavalry Regiment* (n.p. 1913), p. 30.

53 *OR* 30, pt. 2, p. 521; *ibid.*, pt. 1, p. 905.

54 *Ibid.*, pt. 2, p. 178.

"re-crossed the Chickamauga that same evening for [the] purpose of procuring forage." Coleman went on to note, "I will say here I never saw men in such high spirits."[55] In the 8th Texas Cavalry, R. F. Bunting also recorded the move "for corn" back toward their camps of that morning, about four miles to the rear.[56] Instead of preparing to renew the contest at first light on September 21, Wheeler allowed his strongest division to retire several miles to the rear and make camp.

55 Tom Coleman Letter, "Dear Parents and Home Folks," October 3, 1863, Western Historical Manuscripts Collection, University of Missouri, Rolla, Missouri.

56 Bunting Letter, *Rome Tri-Weekly Telegraph*, November 27, 1863.

C hapter 14

The Confederate Pursuit
(September 21-25, 1863)

A s the battle ended on September 20 it was clear to most Confederates that they held the advantage, but it was not immediately obvious that the Federal army had quit the field entirely. Most of the Rebels expected the battle to be renewed at first light, especially on Snodgrass Hill. Dawn, however, revealed that the Federals had retreated. The battle was over, the outcome a Southern victory. How much more could be gained from that victory remained to be seen.

Neither Bragg nor his top commanders were fully aware of the Union movements that night. At about 7:00 p.m. Steedman's Federals, facing Longstreet, disengaged and withdrew initially just to the next ridge line. Later, under the cover of full darkness, they fell back to the new Union line at Rossville Gap, where they joined up with other Yankees from Thomas' lines around Kelly Field and troops who had been driven from the field earlier. The withdrawal left the battlefield eerily quiet, except of course for the haunting cries of thousands of wounded. Late that evening Bragg sent staff officers out to summon Longstreet and Polk to army headquarters. Polk was located after a confusing search, but no one could find Longstreet.[1] Around midnight Polk and Bragg conferred, but decided nothing.

---

1 See Cozzens, *This Terrible Sound*, pp. 513-4, for a detailed discussion of this confusion. Due to the recriminations and acrimony between Bragg and his senior commanders after the battle,

When dawn arrived on September 21, elements of the Army of Tennessee began probing for the missing Yankees. At 5:00 a.m., Longstreet sent Wheeler yet another order asking him to "send forward at once a strong cavalry force, and ascertain the position of the enemy."[2] Like the previous three requests or orders, this one produced the same result: nothing. The bulk of Wheeler's troopers were miles away on the far side of Chickamauga Creek. Unwilling to await and therefore depend upon the arrival of Wheeler's cavalry—perhaps because he had already learned they were not as reliable as the mounted men he had served with in Virginia—Longstreet also ordered his infantry to send skirmishers forward to feel out the Union positions. His infantry was engaged in this task when one of Bragg's couriers finally located him with another request to meet at army headquarters. Replying at 6:40 a.m., Longstreet declined the offer. He sent the same aide back to relay word that he expected the fight to resume momentarily, and so could not leave the front.[3] Shortly thereafter, the first reports from the infantry patrols began to filter back to Longstreet. The front, it seemed, was devoid of the enemy. The news surprised the rank and file of the army. Clarence Malone of the 10th Tennessee Infantry, part of John Gregg's Brigade, wrote that we "all thought that there would be another day of strife, but great was our surprise to awake and find the Yankees gone."[4]

Leonidas Polk's troops were making similar discoveries farther north. Bragg arrived at Polk's headquarters "about sunrise," where he found Brig. Gen. St. John R. Liddell reporting in.[5] Liddell's Division participated in one of the last attacks against George Thomas' XIV Corps the night before, and his troops occupied some of the most advanced Rebel positions around the McDonald house. Liddell's scouts had reported the same information as had Longstreet's: the Yankees were gone. Bragg ordered everyone forward. Liddell recalled that the army commander told him to "push our whole line of

---

accounts of the various meetings between Bragg, Polk, and Longstreet are all contradictory and highly colored by hindsight.

2 *OR* 30, pt. 4, p. 682.

3 Longstreet to Bragg, September 21, 1863, Headquarters and Personal Papers, Folder 10, Bragg Papers, Western Reserve Historical Society.

4 Clarence Malone Letter to "Dear Miss Florence," September 28, 1863, Martha Clayton Harper Papers, Duke University.

5 *OR* 30, pt. 2, p. 34.

skirmishers to the front" and then ordered the rest of the line to do the same. Even Bragg's personal cavalry escort was ordered out.[6]

* * *

Reconnaissance duties are one of the cavalry's primary missions, and while Joe Wheeler was often lax in that regard, Nathan Bedford Forrest was not.

The Tennessean's men were up and moving at 4:00 a.m. on the 21st, well before first light. Forrest ordered both of his divisions (Frank Armstrong's and John Pegram's) to send out patrols in a variety of sectors. Not content to sit at headquarters and wait for the results, Forrest led Armstrong, Dibrell, and 400 of Dibrell's troopers on one of the missions. The column set out due west toward Missionary Ridge, intending to scale the height somewhere south of Rossville. From that point Forrest knew he would have a commanding view of the country. Unlike the infantry, Forrest's troopers found the Federals fairly quickly. Near the foot of the ridge they engaged in a running fight with elements of Col. Robert Minty's Union cavalry brigade, tasked with holding a forward line a mile or so from the gap to prevent just these kinds of efforts. Minty's orders, however, were to avoid a general engagement and if pressed, withdraw to the main line running along the top of the ridge. Forrest, as was his nature, pressed hard.

As the Federals fell back Forrest pursued, touching off a fluid fight. As usual, the corps commander was in the thick of things. A bullet hit his horse in the neck, severing an artery and spraying blood everywhere. Forrest stemmed the bleeding temporarily by sticking his thumb into the wound, an expedient that sustained the animal long enough to finish the chase. When he dismounted, Forrest's horse collapsed and died.[7] The Confederates pressed hard enough to drive Minty's men off to the northwest, which allowed Forrest to lead his small force up to the top of Missionary Ridge.

Forrest's patrol scaled the height somewhere south of where Thomas' infantry line ended, avoiding a direct collision with any more Yankees, and

---

6   *Ibid.*, 35. Bragg's official report was written in December 1863, after he had been relieved of command of the Army of Tennessee, and when criticism of his fumbling the pursuit after Chickamauga was well underway. His tone is accordingly defensive about when and where he ordered a pursuit.

7   Andrew Lytle, *Bedford Forrest and His Critter Company* (Green Key Press, 1984), p. 231.

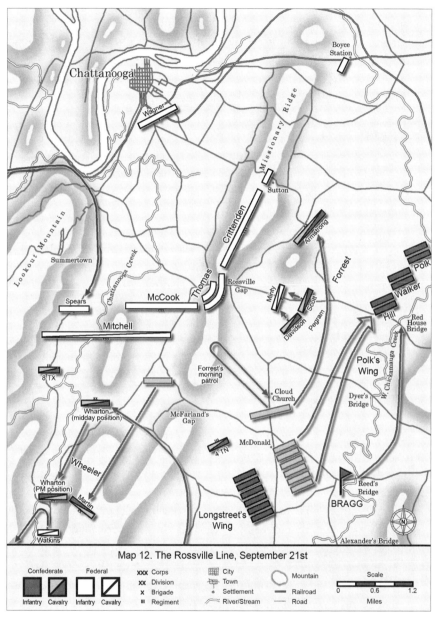

Map 12. The Rossville Line, September 21st

Contemporaries and historians excoriate Bragg for not following up his September 20 victory with an aggressive pursuit by converting tactical success into strategic triumph. Forrest's messages on the morning of September 21 play a key role in their judgment. Rosecrans establishes a powerful new Union line overnight around Rossville Gap, with secure lines of retreat into the budding fortifications ringing Chattanooga. Forrest makes no mention of this line, even though his men found it unbreakable that morning.

reached the crest about 7:00 a.m. Forrest shimmied up a tree to gain a better look at the Union dispositions: Union forces were gathering in and around Chattanooga. The general climbed down and sent Bragg one of the most important messages of the entire campaign.[8] Using a saddle flap as an impromptu writing desk, Forrest scribbled the following:

Genl,

> We are in a mile of Rossville. Have been on the point of Missionary Ridge can see Chattanooga and every thing around. The enemy's trains are leaving going around the point of Lookout Mountain.
>
> The prisoners captured report the pontoon thrown across for the purpose of retreating. I think they are evacuating as hard as they can go. They are cutting timber down to obstruct our passage.
>
> I think we ought to press forward as rapidly as possible.

N.B Forrest
Brig Gen

Lt Gen L Polk
Please forward to Gen Bragg."[9]

This dispatch has served as a key piece of evidence for Bragg detractors—both contemporaries and historians—in making the case that Bragg bungled the pursuit after winning big at Chickamauga. The dispatch, which Polk passed on to Bragg (and at some point reached Longstreet) should have galvanized the Confederate Army of Tennessee into immediate action. The fact that it did not has been hung around Bragg's neck as one of the more significant failings of his checkered military career. And, at first glance, such a conclusion seems an open and shut case.

The information Forrest omitted from the dispatch was more important than what he included. While Thomas' new position atop Missionary Ridge was not intended to be a final defensive line, it was extremely strong. Eight Union

---

8   Jordan and Pryor, *Forrest's Cavalry*, p. 351.

9   OR 30, pt. 4, p. 681.

infantry divisions were deployed there in an arc stretching west to Chattanooga Creek.[10] If Forrest could see the town of Chattanooga and the Union trains in Lookout Valley, he should also have been able to observe Maj. Gen. Alexander McCook's three divisions deployed directly below him to the west, as well as the Federal cavalry in front of them screening the defensive line. Even with the heavy casualties they had suffered during the past two days of fighting, the Union XX Corps still had 10,000 – 12,000 men in the ranks. And they were no longer retreating. Instead, they were deployed in a line of battle astride the valley, facing south, blocking the routes Longstreet would need to use were he to advance on Chattanooga directly.

Turning north, Forrest should have also been able to see at least part of the Union XIV Corps and XXI Corps atop Missionary Ridge—troops that sealed off Polk's direct approach. Instead of "retreating as fast as they can go," the battered remnants of the Army of the Cumberland were standing ready to renew the contest on decent ground of their choosing. Forrest's dispatch made no mention of any of these troops.

With the fateful message sent, Forrest decided to test enemy resolve. He deployed his men in three columns. The 4th Tennessee Cavalry of Dibrell's Brigade was sent west down into Lookout Valley to try and take Rossville from the rear. Forrest personally led Frank Armstrong and James Wheeler's Brigade due north along the spine of the ridge to try and gain a purchase somewhere overlooking the Rossville gap and the village itself. John Pegram's Division, still east of the ridge, would advance along its foot, hopefully paralleling Armstrong's men, and take Rossville from the east.[11] Dibrell's Brigade was held in reserve.

This new movement consumed most of the morning. Minty's Federal troopers screened Thomas' front at Rossville and contested the advance. At first Pegram's men had the easier approach, moving across the relatively flat and open fields north of Cloud Church, but their pace slowed as Yankee resistance stiffened. J. W. Minnich of the 6th Georgia Cavalry was in the forefront for much of the morning's fight. The Georgians first encountered elements of the 7th Pennsylvania Cavalry, which Minnich identified when he picked up

---

10 *Atlas of the Battlefields of Chickamauga, Chattanooga, and Vicinity.* (Chickamauga and Chattanooga National Park Commission, 1895), Map of the battlefield of Chickamauga: movement from Chickamauga to Rossville, September 21, 1863.

11 Jordan and Pryor, *Forrest's Cavalry*, p. 351.

Company H's daybook from a dead Pennsylvania first sergeant.[12] The Rebels continued driving Minty's cavalry until they cleared a small rise about 500 yards from the main ridge. They could go no farther. When the Yankee cavalry retreated through their infantry line, Pegram discovered the full nature of the enemy defenses: they were powerful and well-manned. Unable to make any progress atop the ridge, about 10:00 a.m. Forrest sent Dibrell to reinforce Pegram. The added troopers were not nearly enough to change the tactical equation on Missionary Ridge.[13]

For a time, perhaps an hour or more, Pegram's men clung to the rise, enduring the noisy but largely ineffective shelling of a Union artillery section. A second advance carried the dismounted Rebel troopers to the foot of the main ridge, where they halted and sought cover alongside a road skirting the foot of the heights. The Confederates might have fared much worse had not dense woods prevented the Federals from identifying targets more clearly. Pegram's regiments spent the rest of the day in a loud but largely ineffective and bloodless skirmish that cost the 6th Georgia three killed and nine wounded, but left the Yankees firmly in control of the gap.[14]

Moving through the woods and rough ground of Missionary Ridge, Forrest and Armstrong eventually fell in behind Pegram, either diverted off the crest in order to avoid Federal infantry or because traveling along the narrow wooded spine proved too difficult. About 11:30 a.m., still south of Rossville, Armstrong's column captured a Union observation post atop a tall tree. As the small captured party of Yankee signalmen looked on, Forrest repeated his earlier tree climbing episode and reached the platform. He was now able to survey nearly the entire field. From this vantage point he enjoyed a virtually unfettered view of Chattanooga and the Union forces spread out below him. Behind him, the Confederate army remained in the same basic position it had occupied at the close of the previous day.[15]

Forrest shot off a second message to Polk: "I am on the point as designated, where I can observe the whole of the valley. They are evidently fortifying, as I can hear the sound of axes in great numbers. The appearance is

12 J. W. Minnich Manuscript, 29, 6th Georgia Cavalry file, CCNMP.

13 Lindsley, *Military Annals of Tennessee*, II, p. 661.

14 Minnick, "Reminiscences," *Northwest Georgia Historical and Genealogical Society Quarterly*, p. 28.

15 Jordan and Pryor, *Forrest's Cavalry*, p. 351.

still as in the last dispatch, that he is hurrying on toward Chattanooga. . . ."[16]
Aside from the hint about axes, Forrest made no mention of the fact that his
command had been completely unable to assail the Rossville gap, which
remained firmly in enemy hands.

That afternoon, Forrest sent part of Armstrong's Division around behind
Pegram's men, who were still stuck in front of Rossville, with the intent of
having Armstrong move east and then north to get up on Missionary Ridge
somewhere beyond Thomas' left flank. The move was only partially successful
because after disengaging from the Rossville action, Minty's Federals shifted
northward to meet just such an eventuality.[17] Armstrong's command extended
Pegram's flank, but it could not establish a position on top of the ridge. Both of
Forrest's divisions were stalled in front of Rossville for the rest of the afternoon
engaging in desultory skirmishing. Finally, at 4:00 p.m., Bragg sent new orders
to Forrest: Polk's infantry was moving north and the cavalry was needed to
cover this movement.[18]

Forrest was reportedly disgusted with this order, a sentiment conveyed in a
series of communiqués and at least one face-to-face meeting, though the
various accounts of these incidents are vague and somewhat contradictory. In
one dispatch, Forrest supposedly told Bragg that "every hour was worth a
thousand men."[19] In another, Forrest turned to a staff officer and irritably
demanded, "What does he fight battles for?"[20] In yet a third account, Forrest is
said to have ridden back to Bragg's headquarters, which by this time was near
Red House Bridge, to ask why the army was not pursuing the defeated enemy.
Bragg is said to have replied that it was because his own army had no supplies.
"We can get all the supplies we want in Chattanooga," snapped the
cavalryman.[21] Given that Forrest had been unable to push back or beyond the
Yankees the entire day, his anger at Bragg seems unfair and probably grew in the
telling, goaded along more by the hindsight of the writer than the facts of the
moment.

16 *OR* 30, pt. 4, p. 675.

17 R. H. G. Minty, "Minty's Saber Brigade," *National Tribune*, November 9, 1893.

18 Jordan and Pryor, *Forrest's Cavalry*, p. 352.

19 Hill, "Chickamauga," *Battles and Leaders*, 3, p. 662.

20 Henry, *First With the Most*, p. 193.

21 Lytle, *Bedford Forrest and his Critter Company*, p. 233.

The most fanciful of these tales relates the afternoon's confrontation between Bragg and Forrest. Even if they did meet, the representation of what passed between them is almost certainly embellished. These accounts are also very one-sided. Bragg was at least as disgusted with Forrest as Forrest was supposed to have been with him. Certainly the messages Forrest sent struck a different tone at army headquarters than they had just a few weeks earlier. At the beginning of September, staff officer Colonel Brent described Forrest as "the best cavalry general we have," and Bragg refused to release him for service in Mississippi. Now, just three weeks later, the mood in Bragg's headquarters on that score was markedly different. Diarist Taylor Beatty recorded the arrival of Forrest's most famous dispatch this way: "Forrest reports enemy have burned Chattanooga & fled—the truth turns out that he has never been within three miles of the place & the enemy are still there—having only burned a few houses which were in the way of the guns."[22]

After having been surprised repeatedly the past several days by Union dispositions, Bragg was not about to rush into another large-scale attack without confirmation. Given the heavy terrain, terrible losses, and dispersed organizational nature of the Army of Tennessee, it took until mid-morning for the Rebel commanders to verify that Rosecrans' Federals had departed their immediate front. Longstreet, as noted earlier, was so busy reconnoitering his front in preparation for a renewal of the battle that he did not believe he could take the time to report in person to Bragg's headquarters. Writing to his wife the next day, Leonidas Polk confided that he wasn't sure the Yankees were really gone until 9:00 a.m.—an hour and a half after Forrest sent his first dispatch.[23]

And Forrest was clearly wrong. Instead of "evacuating as hard as they can go," the Federals were only sending their trains and noncombatants across the Tennessee River. Rosecrans' infantry were digging in as fast as they could make the dirt fly. Forrest's own experience at Rossville was a clear sign that this report was, at best, wildly optimistic. His second report confirmed (inadvertently) that the Federals were entrenching for a fight—"They are evidently fortifying, as I can hear the sound of axes in great numbers—not flying in panic." Yet, none of his surviving messages even mention the strong Union position at Rossville that stopped Pegram's advance cold.

---

22 Entry for September 22, 1863, Taylor Beatty Diary, Leroy Moncure Nutt Papers, Southern Historical Collection, UNC Chapel Hill.

23 Leonidas Polk Papers, University of the South, Sewanee, Tennessee.

*　*　*

Nathan Bedford Forrest, however, commanded only one-half of Bragg's cavalry. He can be excused for a lack of professional military training and for his inexperience at corps command. But what of Joe Wheeler, who had the benefit of both?

William Martin's two-brigade division, it will be recalled, spent the night near Crawfish Spring, while John Wharton's two brigades moved several miles to the rear to spend the night in the relative comfort of their former campground east of Glass Mill. At least Forrest had his men close at hand, up before dawn, and scouting and pressing the retreating enemy. Most of Wheeler's men weren't even on the battlefield when the sun broke the horizon on September 21.

Wharton's Division re-crossed Chickamauga Creek early that morning and turned north toward Chattanooga. As he passed through the wreckage of the two-day fight, George Guild of the 4th Tennessee Cavalry took note of one of war's more grisly scenes: a hog running loose alongside the road, an amputated leg clutched in its mouth.[24] South of McFarland's Gap, Wharton's men crossed Missionary Ridge into Chattanooga Valley and turned north again. Soon after, about mid-morning, they collided with Col. David Ray's Federal troopers. The initial picket fire from the 1st Wisconsin and 2nd Indiana cavalry regiments was augmented when the Yankees were reinforced by Brig. Gen. James G. Spears' infantry brigade of Unionist Tennesseans, newly arrived from Bridgeport and Stevenson. As with Pegram farther northeast near Rossville, the appearance of Federal infantry in strength brought Wharton's thrust to a halt.[25] Behind Spears, as noted earlier, were the three divisions of McCook's XX Corps.

While Wheeler was contemplating what to do about this situation, word of another threat from the opposite direction reached him. Martin's pickets reported the arrival of another brigade of Union cavalry trying to reach Crawfish Springs from the south while escorting a wagon train and a large party of semi-invalid Federal sick.[26] Union Col. Louis Watkins' three Kentucky regiments had nearly reached the springs before discovering they were riding

---

24 Guild, *A Brief Narrative*, p. 31.

25 *OR* 30, pt. 1, pp. 884-5.

26 *Ibid.*, pt. 2, p. 521.

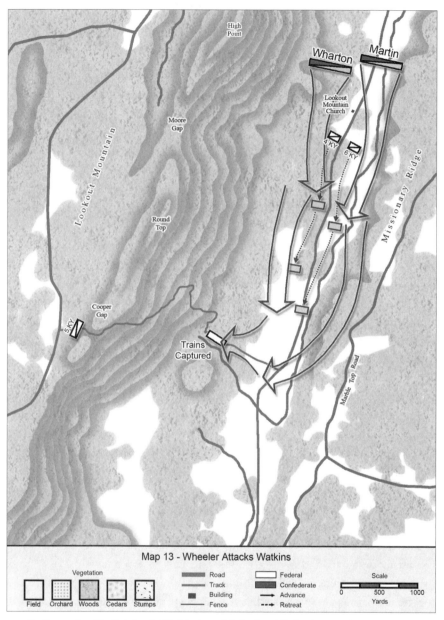

Map 13 - Wheeler Attacks Watkins

On September 21, Col. Louis Watkins' small brigade of Federal Kentuckians is cut off from the main body of the Union army and attempts to find a way into Chattanooga. His men bump into Confederate cavalry. Recognizing a potential prize, Joe Wheeler turns the bulk of both Martin's and Wharton's divisions south to engage Watkins. The result is a running fight southward as Watkins seeks unsuccessfully to hold off the Rebels long enough to get his trains through Stevens' Gap to the crest of Lookout Mountain.

directly into Rebel hands. An alerted Watkins promptly ordered his little column to turn around and head back to Cooper's Gap, from which point it could ascend Lookout Mountain and, using the mountain itself as a barrier, continue on to reach Chattanooga another way.[27] With no viable opportunity against the XX Corps, Wheeler decided to move aggressively against Watkins. Leaving a small force to screen the Federals to the north, Wheeler and the bulk of Wharton's command joined Martin (in all nearly 3,000 Rebels) in rushing south to overwhelm Watkins' small brigade. Once he realized his predicament, Watkins ordered the 5th Kentucky to take the wagons and convalescents ahead while he attempted to hold off Wheeler with battalions from the Union 4th and 6th Kentucky, about 400 men all told. Adopting a Fabian strategy, the Federals retreated slowly toward Cooper's Gap. Wheeler's cavalry repeatedly outflanked them, however, and Watkins' defenders soon fell into disarray. Tom Coleman of the 11th Texas Cavalry, part of Thomas Harrison's Brigade of Wharton's command, described the fight as a "regular wolf chase" lasting several miles. By the end, recalled Coleman, "every one of them [was] taking care of himself the best way he could."[28]

When he reached the foot of Lookout Mountain, Watkins discovered things were even worse than he supposed. The wagons leading the ascent up the road through the gap were moving with agonizing slowness, creating a traffic jam that at any minute threatened to deteriorate into a panicked mess—especially if the Confederate cavalry managed to overtake them. He also expected to find his remaining regiment, the 5th Kentucky Cavalry, holding the foot of the mountain and so able to reinforce his beleaguered line. The 5th, however, had already ridden up through the gap, was on the far side of the traffic jam, and could not provide any immediate help. Disaster, it seemed, was about to envelope the trapped Federals.

According to Watkins, the "enemy's column, flanking on my right, ran in and intercepted a portion of the Fourth and Sixth Kentucky Cavalry, and after considerable slaughter on both sides the enemy captured a large number of prisoners."[29] The 4th and 6th regiments lost more than one-third of their number, including almost 200 prisoners. Fifty-three wagons also fell into

---

27 *Ibid.*, pt. 1, p. 915.

28 Coleman Letter, University of Missouri.

29 *OR* 30, pt. 2, p. 521.

Confederate hands.[30] The remnant retreated through the gap to the top of Lookout Mountain, where they turned north and made for Chattanooga. John Wyeth of the 4th Alabama Cavalry, part of Colonel Russell's Brigade of Martin's Division, thought the affair "was not much of a fight, for we outnumbered them and rode over them just as they had done to us at Shelbyville."[31]

Joe Wheeler embellished his success when he reported that Watkins' command of "nearly 2,000" was "badly scattered," and that he captured 400 prisoners as well as "18 stand of colors and secured their entire train, numbering about 90 wagons, loaded with valuable baggage."[32] Watkins' entire command numbered between 600 and 700 Kentuckians, and without the departed 5th Kentucky counted perhaps 400 troopers, plus the roughly 400 sick from other commands he was escorting. According to Watkins, he lost fifty-three wagons. Wheeler's claim that he captured eighteen stands of colors is inexplicable. At best, Watkins' men would only have stands for the three regiments in their brigade. Perhaps Wheeler was double-counting and/or taking credit for some of the flags captured in the infantry fight. In any case, it was a grandiloquent claim.

Unlike Forrest's messages, Wheeler's reports were still accepted at face value. Taylor Beatty recorded Wheeler's dispatch announcing the success in very different terms from Forrest's—and without editorializing as he had with the Tennessean's message: "Wheeler reports that he has routed the enemy's cavalry & captured over 100 wagons & a good number of prisoners."[33] Wheeler did indeed capture many wagons and prisoners, but he routed only one small brigade—not "the enemy's cavalry." The rest of the Federal horsemen, supported by Spears' infantry, stopped the Rebels cold in their advance on Chattanooga.

Wheeler made one other decision on September 21 that would have larger repercussions during the later siege of the Chattanooga. After Watkins was routed, Wheeler decided not to push cavalry onto or over Lookout Mountain that day. Instead, he ordered his troopers to return to their previous positions.

---

30 *OR* 30, pt. 2, p. 521.

31 *OR* 30, pt. 2, p. 521.

32 Wyeth, *Saber and Scalpel*, p. 253.

33 *OR* 30, pt. 2, p. 521.

*   *   *

The bulk of Union activity on September 21 was not taking place in the Chattanooga Valley but in the next valley over west of Lookout Mountain. In the immediate aftermath of the battle, William Rosecrans' only link with the outside world was the road to Bridgeport and Stevenson, Alabama. That route wandered southwest out of Chattanooga, curved around the head of Lookout Mountain and then carved its way through the valley of Lookout Creek, all the while clinging to the south bank of the Tennessee River. Throughout the 21st and 22nd, Federal wagons rumbled both ways along this road carrying thousands of wounded and non-combatants out of danger and hauling vital provisions back into the city. Rosecrans would need those supplies desperately in the coming weeks.

Always strapped for mounted troops, Rosecrans was hard-pressed to find enough cavalry to guard this traffic flow and still screen the long lines around Chattanooga. The Federal commander also had to be alert to a potential Rebel raid into Tennessee to disrupt the Union supply line farther away from the city, or a strike at the depots of Bridgeport and Stevenson. But in order to do so, he needed yet more troopers to picket the north bank of the river for many miles in order to alert him to any Confederate efforts to cross. Col. Louis Watkins' welcome when he and his battered command finally reached Chattanooga is a good measure of just how strapped for cavalry Rosecrans was in the battle's aftermath. When the beleaguered commander arrived about 10:00 p.m. on the 21st, the army commander refused to allow them time to recuperate themselves or their mounts. Rosecrans ordered the survivors to move the next morning back "up the Nickajack Trace and along the top of the mountain as far as Cooper's Gap" to defend Lookout Valley.[34]

*   *   *

Joe Wheeler's well-executed victory against Watkins' column should have been followed up by a vigorous pursuit of the remaining Kentuckians and wagons up the mountain, and/or an attempt to move a blocking force into Lookout Valley. Inexplicably, he did neither and instead reverted to form. Wheeler left General Martin on the scene to establish a picket line against the

---

34 *OR* 30, pt. 1, p. 154.

Union XX Corps, and ordered General Wharton to ride with his two brigades once again to their former camps east of Glass Mill.[35] The result of these orders placed Wharton's command—nearly twice as large as Martin's and nearly two thirds of Wheeler's entire disposable mounted force—even farther away from the scene of the action. Glass Mill was ten miles to the southeast. For reasons that remain incomprehensible, Wheeler was subjecting his men to an unnecessary 20-mile roundtrip before they could rejoin their comrades the next morning. Martin's small and overworked force of six regiments was left to take up the slack.

Confronted with a resolute Federal army manning an extremely strong position at Rossville, Bragg chose not to make any significant movements on September 21. Instead, he moved his troops off the gory mess of a battlefield, shifting them a couple of miles to the north. Missionary Ridge would continue to divide the two armies. Late that morning Bragg issued orders to his various commanders to begin this move at two o'clock that afternoon. At the same time, army headquarters shifted to Red House Bridge.[36] Bragg's primary goal was to secure his grip on the Western and Atlantic Railroad. With that mission in mind, Polk's Corps was ordered to occupy Chickamauga Station which, after the bridges into Ringgold were repaired, would become the army's main supply depot. Just before dawn on September 22, Thomas pulled the Federal infantry out of Rossville and fell back into Chattanooga. Minty's cavalry and a few infantry detachments screened the movement and acted as rearguard with orders to hold the Rebels east of Missionary Ridge for as long as possible.[37] Once again Bragg and his subordinates were left guessing about the location of the enemy. And once again, the Confederate commander had to order his cavalry to resume one of its primary missions.

* * *

Forrest's entire corps ended the day on the 21st deployed facing Missionary Ridge. On the morning of the 22nd Forrest shifted his command northward to test the Federal deployments in several places at once. In addition to Minty's

---

35 Bunting Letter, *Rome Tri-Weekly Courier*, November 27, 1863.

36 *OR* 30, pt. 4, p. 679. This is the order referred to in the orders Forrest received at 4:00 p.m. on September 21, 1863.

37 Minty, "Minty's Saber Brigade," *National Tribune*, November 9, 1893.

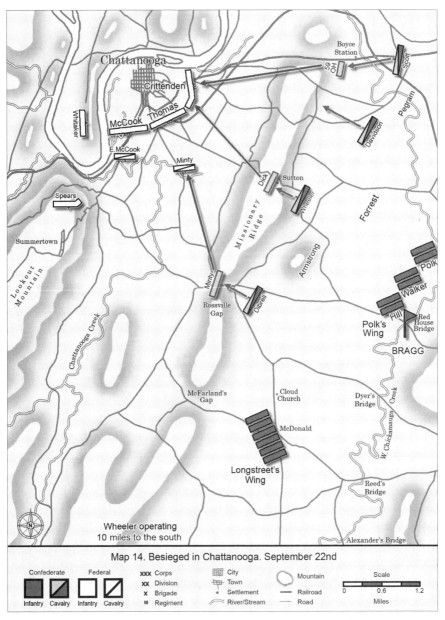

Map 14. Besieged in Chattanooga. September 22nd

Confederate		Federal			
■ Infantry	◪ Cavalry	☐ Infantry	◨ Cavalry		

xxx Corps
xx Division
x Brigade
iii Regiment

City
Town
• Settlement
River/Stream

◯ Mountain
— Railroad
--- Road

Scale
0   0.6   1.2
Miles

Two days after the battle, the Confederates draw tight the ring around Chattanooga. Forrest's cavalry, with both divisions abreast, drive the Union rear guard into the city's defenses. Clashes with Minty's Federal cavalry at Rossville Gap and Union infantry along Missionary Ridge and at Boyce's Station mark the day's operations. By nightfall, only a small Federal force at the north end of Lookout Mountain holds open Rosecrans' final door to the outside world. Bragg has already dispatched Wheeler's cavalry ten miles to the south in contemplation of operations against Bridgeport, Alabama.

troopers at Rossville, more Yankees defended the top of the ridge farther north. Two regiments from Col. George F. Dick's brigade and the 39th Indiana Mounted Infantry were posted to screen the various gaps north of Rossville.[38] Their combined mission was to delay any Rebel advance long enough to let the Union army complete the construction and occupation of the Chattanooga defenses. Forrest's men would spend the bulk of the day sparring with these rear guards, meeting with mixed success.

Forrest placed both divisions (Armstrong and Pegram) side by side facing the ridge. The line ranged from a point opposite Rossville almost to the banks of the Tennessee River several miles north beyond Boyce Station. Armstrong's Division held the left and Pegram's Division the right. On the far left, Dibrell's Brigade faced Minty at Rossville, with James Wheeler operating opposite Dick's infantry on Dibrell's right. Henry Davidson's Brigade of Pegram's Division filed in on Wheeler's right, with Scott's troopers completing the line to the river.[39] This was a broad front for a two-division command, and in many places the line offered little more than thin veneer of pickets. Forrest could expect little infantry support. With most of Bragg's army still on or near the battlefield, the cavalry would be on its own for most of the day.

The first clash came opposite Rossville. Dibrell's Tennessee troopers set out cautiously, well aware of the sharp resistance Pegram had encountered the day before. This time, however, only Minty's troopers held the gap. They fought stubbornly, giving ground slowly, but retreated nonetheless. When the first encounter took place is unclear. Minty recorded "that the sun was well up before the enemy's skirmishers began to feel our position," but by 7:00 a.m. his troops were driven back through the gap and the Federals mounted up.[40] From there, Minty continued his slow retreat, withdrawing his regiments in stages, halting one to fire while the others fell back. For the rest of the morning both sides skirmished on horseback, moving slowly but inexorably north toward the Chattanooga lines. By about 1:00 p.m. the fighting was over and the last of the Federal cavalry had slipped inside the trenches.

While Dibrell was pushing back Minty, another encounter broke out near the Moore house atop Missionary Ridge near the center of Forrest's advancing

38 John H. Rerick, *The Forty-Fourth Indiana Volunteer Infantry: History of Its Services in the War of the Rebellion and a Personal Record of Its Members* (n.p. 1880), p. 99; and *OR* 30, pt. 1, p. 548.

39 Jordan and Pryor, *Forrest's Cavalry*, p. 353.

40 R. H. G. Minty, "Rossville Gap," *The National Tribune*, March 8, 1894.

line.[41] Lieutenant Colonel Simeon C. Aldrich's 44th Indiana Infantry, part of Dick's Federal brigade, erected breastworks covering the road where it crested the ridge. About 10:00 a.m., Southern cavalry drove back the 44th's advance pickets. The Rebels received a nasty surprise, however, when the Hoosiers were reinforced by the 39th Indiana, an infantry regiment from Brig. Gen. August Willich's brigade. Unfortunately for the Rebels, this regiment was armed with Spencer seven-shot repeaters. Now it was the Confederates' turn to fall back. A second stronger attack around noon met with no better results when the Southern horsemen stumbled upon the 44th Indiana's line of breastworks. A well delivered volley sent the troopers tumbling rearward in some disorder. Handfuls of Confederates reappeared on two more occasions in front of the Hoosiers of the 44th, only to be driven off each time. These probes, however, were feints designed to feel out the enemy line, and not serious efforts to dislodge Dick's men. Other Rebels, meanwhile, were working their way onto the ridge around both Federal flanks. By mid-afternoon, both the 39th and 44th Indiana regiments fell back to Chattanooga to avoid being surrounded.[42]

Farther north, where both the Harrison Road and the rail line to Cleveland crossed Chickamauga Creek at the northern end of Missionary Ridge, Lt. Col. Granville Frambes' 59th Ohio (also of Dick's Federal brigade) had a more hair-raising encounter. The Ohioans erected a line of works astride the road about three-quarters of a mile from the bridge and advanced three companies as skirmishers. Frambes' orders from Dick were unequivocal: "hold the bridge over the river and prevent the enemy from crossing." The 2nd Tennessee Cavalry, part of Colonel Scott's Brigade, surprised the Buckeye skirmishers by launching a mounted charge that captured several men and sent the rest scrambling back to the main line, where the Ohioans made a protracted fight of it. Frambes, who recalled the "sharp firing" in his detailed campaign report, ordered the railroad bridge set ablaze if it could not be held while the regiment fought off repeated attacks from Scott's dismounted troopers. Scott's men fought with such determination that Frambes was convinced he was facing "a heavy force of infantry and cavalry." About noon Frambes gave the order to burn the structure, discovered that the Rebels were "moving round my flank,"

---

41 This house was later Bragg's headquarters during the siege and battle of Chattanooga. Rerick, *The Forty-Fourth Volunteer Indiana Infantry*, p. 99.

42 *OR* 30, pt. 1, p. 829.

and informed Dick of the situation and that he "would not be able to hold the place without re-inforcements."[43]

Frambes and his Ohioans held on until about 3:00 p.m., but "neither re-enforcements nor orders" arrived. Left without much choice, "I ordered the pickets to fall back slowly and cover my retreat." The withdrawal to the main Union line closer to Chattanooga proved a harrowing experience. "The enemy effected a crossing above me, and came over the ridge, and was firing on my rear guard from three sides," reported the regimental commander. Using the railroad embankment as an earthwork, and by leapfrogging detachments of his regiment in a splendid example of fire and maneuver, Frambes avoided repeated encircling efforts by the surging Rebel cavalry.[44] Scott's troopers charged several times while Lt. Winslow Robinson's Louisiana battery shelled the retreating Yankees, often at close range. However, the 59th was well versed in skirmish drill and escaped with minimal loss considering the circumstances. In his report, Pegram noted that Scott "was prevented from capturing the regiment entire only by a mistake of one of his own regiments, which fired upon the portion headed by himself."[45]

Certainly Frambes and the 59th had been lucky, escaping only by the narrowest of margins. Unfortunately, Scott's minimalist approach to writing reports reduces our understanding of this interesting affair. His explanation for the long and rather complex maneuvering and running fight on the 22nd was simply, "Here I encountered the Fifty-ninth Ohio Infantry and drove them from their first line of rifle-pits."[46]

Once they had driven Minty's Federals into the trenches, Dibrell's men spent the afternoon probing the new Federal defenses looking for weak spots. Colonel Daniel W. Holman, commanding the combined 10th and his own 11th Tennessee cavalry regiments, rode directly up the Rossville Road until within a few hundred yards of the main Union line. There, under a galling fire, Holman dismounted his men and engaged the Yankees with a battery of artillery, but a

43 *Ibid.*, p. 834.

44 *Ibid.*, p. 835.

45 *Ibid.*, pt. 2, p. 529. Pegram inadvertently listed Col. Henry Davidson as the commander whose brigade engaged the 59th Ohio, but it was clearly Scott's Brigade, as Scott himself corroborates in his own report. It is possible that some of Davidson's men were in the vicinity or participated, but Davidson did not leave a report, and Scott's report is woefully inadequate.

46 *Ibid.*, p. 531.

farther advance was out of the question. Without warning General Forrest arrived on the scene, demanding to know why Holman had stopped. Nonplussed, the colonel reported what he thought Forrest must have seen for himself: the enemy infantry was strongly entrenched and too numerous to attack with a reasonable chance of success. "[T]here must be some mistake in that," Forrest retorted, adding that he "believed he could take Chattanooga with his escort." [47] And the general proceeded to try exactly that, galloping forward with his escort in tow. Forrest encountered the same deadly fire that had rained through Holman's ranks, wounding yet another of his horses and routing the impromptu attack almost before it got started. The hasty effort put an end to any talk of charging into Chattanooga along the Rossville Road.

Seeking another way into the city, Forrest dispatched the rest of Dibrell's men west toward Lookout Mountain. If he reached Lookout's eastern foot, Dibrell could turn north and possibly slip around the Union flank and into Chattanooga via the river route. Of equal importance, the move would also close the logistical lifeline that was the road to Bridgeport. Before he reached the mountain, however, Dibrell ran into James Spears' infantry brigade of loyal East Tennesseans. Spears deployed his men to defend the main road to the top of the mountain, the gap around the northern point, and Summertown at the crest. Also atop the mountain was a detachment of the 15th Pennsylvania Cavalry guarding a Union signal station. From that point the Keystone troops enjoyed a panoramic view of the entire scene unfolding below them.

One of those 15th Pennsylvania spectators was John B. Williams. Initially, the Federals expected Rebel cavalry to appear not from Rossville, but up the spine of the mountain from the south in the direction of Cooper's Gap, and so deployed accordingly. On the morning of the 22nd, however, Williams was back at the northern end of Lookout Mountain. In the early morning light, the view all but overwhelmed him. "Directly beneath our feet, it seemed, lay Chattanooga—an infinitesimal 'city'—encircled by yellow lines of earthworks, which extended unbrokenly from the mountains to the river. An inner circle of dark blue was still more apparent, from which the bayonets and the colors gleamed in the sunlight—as though visibly tipped with the glory of as gallant a fight as any in history."[48] More prosaically, this description also suggested that

---

47 Lindsey, *Military Annals of Tennessee*, II, p. 694.

48 John A. B. Williams, *Leaves From a Trooper's Diary* (Self published, 1869), pp. 72-3.

the Federals were fully entrenched and formed in good order, prepared to defend the city in strength.

Williams' detachment spent the day atop Lookout, watching the approach of the various Rebel columns threading in from the east. They were not directly threatened with attack, however, because Dibrell's troopers did not attempt to clear the summit. Instead, his skirmishers became engaged in a two-front fight with some of Spears' Yankees at the foot of the ridge and the main Union defenses along the Tennessee River.

The Federals were widely dispersed atop and at the foot of the mountain. Spears sent three companies to hold the narrow gap at the point, where Lookout meets the Tennessee River. A regiment and one-half of another were deployed at the crossroads at the foot of the heights. According to Spears, this small force, fifteen companies strong, was pressed by "three regiments of infantry or mounted infantry, and with artillery and cavalry, attacked my line." In fact, the "infantry or mounted infantry" was Colonel Dibrell's cavalry fighting aggressively on foot.[49] The brisk engagement that broke out lasted about ninety minutes, "when the contest in numbers being so unequal, I ordered my command to slowly fall back to a more favorable position on the first bench on the point of the mountain," reported Spears. The "first bench" referenced by Spears was several hundred feet above the valley floor. By the time his men arrived there, Spears' command had lost three killed, nineteen wounded, and two missing.[50]

Dibrell elected not to follow Spears, and instead picketed the road and turned his main attention to the Union lines ringing Chattanooga. Once in place the Tennessee troopers also closed the door to Bridgeport, blocking Federal access to that important supply point. Spears' Federals would remain on the slope and at the top of the mountain for the next two days, effectively sealing off Lookout Valley from the east and north. While no more trains would be leaving the city, at least those trains already en route to Bridgeport were protected from Rebel raiders. The signalmen and the 15th Pennsylvania were cut off as well and spent the night in Summertown. They made free with the local housing and bedded down in unexpected luxury among the featherbedding of the resort hotel located there. The next morning the Federals

49 *OR* 30, pt. 1, p. 885.

50 *Ibid.*

slipped down the mountain via a hidden path, guided to safety by a Union scout.[51]

*   *   *

About 2:00 p.m. on September 22, as Dibrell's fight with Spears was winding down, Forrest met the first of the arriving Rebel infantry under Maj. Gen. Lafayette McLaws. The general led a division in James Longstreet's First Corps and had only just arrived from Virginia, where he served under General Robert E. Lee. McLaws reached Ringgold too late to fight on either September 19 or 20, though some of his men were hotly engaged under Joseph Kershaw, his senior brigadier. With the only fresh infantry on the scene, Bragg assigned McLaws the task of leading the pursuit on September 22. With only three brigades amounting to some 5,000 infantry, however, McLaws was not strong enough to mount a serious attack against the Federal fortifications ringing the city.

Accounts of the meeting between Forrest and McLaws differ substantially. According to Forrest's biographers, that general urged McLaws to make an immediate attack while the Yankees were still demoralized but McLaws declined because he only had orders to picket the Union line.[52] McLaws described the discussion in very different terms. Forrest, he wrote after the war, warned him not to attack because the rest of the Confederate army was still seven miles away. If he assaulted the Federal lines, Forrest continued, McLaws would be "risking the loss of [his] command."[53] Just a few hours earlier under Colonel Holman's astonished gaze, Forrest attempted to storm Chattanooga with nothing but his own escort company. Instead of a discouraged and beaten enemy, he discovered a strongly entrenched and determined line of battle. The affair may have disabused the cavalryman of the notion that the Yankees were still demoralized, and suggests that McLaws' version of the encounter is the more accurate of the two accounts.

Forrest's cavalry corps remained in position ringing Chattanooga for the next day and a half, during which time it was gradually replaced by Rebel

51 *Ibid.*, p. 76.

52 Jordan and Pryor, *Forrest's Cavalry*, pp. 353-4.

53 Lafayette McLaws memoir, Cheeves Family papers, South Carolina Historical Society, Charleston, South Carolina.

infantry. He claimed that he took McDonald's Tennessee Cavalry Battalion and "gained the point of Lookout Mountain" on September 23, but since Spears' Federals were holding that same point on the same day and did not report an encounter with Rebel cavalry that would match Forrest's movements, it is unclear what, exactly, Forrest "gained."[54] Significant skirmishing, however, had sputtered to an end, and by the afternoon of the 24th Forrest's command had moved back to Bird's Mill. After a day's rest and refit, Bragg ordered Forrest to move his troopers to the Hiwassee River on September 25, a shift that presaged a possible move on Knoxville, Tennessee.[55]

* * *

Joe Wheeler's movements during this same period are also not well spelled out. He reported that he returned to Chattanooga Valley on the 22nd, pressing "to within 1 and 1/4 miles of Chattanooga, driving the enemy's cavalry behind his infantry."[56] However, Forrest had Dibrell's men operating in the same area, and they failed to mention Wheeler's presence. In fact, Dibrell's move from Rossville to the foot of Lookout Mountain would have taken him into direct contact with Wheeler somewhere along that route, since he moved across the entire breadth of Chattanooga Creek Valley. No report of any such contact can be found.

The absence of any source on this point is probably because, despite the cavalryman's claim, Wheeler's men played no role in driving the Federals back into Chattanooga. As earlier noted, Wharton's Division began their day on the 22nd all the way back at Glass Mill, fully ten miles from the seat of the action. Additionally, R. F. Bunting of the 8th Texas Cavalry (Harrison's Brigade, Wharton's Division) stated that his command didn't reach their old camps until 11:00 p.m., adding that "all were tired, and on Tuesday morning [the 22nd] did not move very early."[57] When Wharton's troopers reached the field, they did so via the Rossville Gap, which had already been cleared by Dibrell's men. None of Wharton's men came within range of the Union artillery until later that

---

54 *OR* 30, pt. 2, p. 526.

55 Jordan and Pryor, *Forrest's Cavalry*, pp. 354-5.

56 *OR* 30, pt. 2, p. 522.

57 Bunting Letter, *Rome Tri-Weekly Courier*, November 27, 1863.

afternoon, at which time the 8th Texas lost two wounded (one seriously), but encountered no small arms fire at all. This case in point demonstrates the extent of their participation in what Wheeler reported to his superiors as "driving the enemy's cavalry behind his infantry."

Late in the afternoon Wharton's men "fell back a little to rest."[58] After dark, Bragg issued new orders to Wheeler. He intended to thrust Wheeler's entire corps across the Tennessee River to operate against Rosecrans' tenuous supply lines. In anticipation of that move, Bragg ordered the bantam Alabamian to stage his command as far as Trenton, Georgia. That night Wheeler marched his command eight miles to the southwest before halting for a brief rest. Early the next morning, they resumed the long ride.

About midday that Wednesday Wheeler's men halted just short of Trenton. It was there, noted Bunting, that the troopers got a chance to cook a decent meal for the first time in several days. While the bulk of his command was eating and resting, Wheeler sent Colonel Harrison with a hand-picked force of 550 men across Lookout Mountain into Wills Valley to scout for any Union presence, and also to look for places where the corps could ford the Tennessee. Wheeler was still expecting final instructions from Bragg to embark on a full-scale expedition into Middle Tennessee in a grand raid that would decide the fate of Rosecrans' nearly isolated Federals.

At 2:00 p.m., shortly after Harrison received his instructions and volunteers for the advance guard were called for, Wheeler received an entirely different order from Bragg. His entire corps must return north at once "and sweep up Lookout Mountain to Point Lookout."[59] Wheeler set off with an advance guard of 200 men, leaving the rest of the command to follow as quickly as they could. Harrison's reconnaissance would have to wait. Bragg never explained his abrupt change of mission, but almost certainly it had to do with the fact that the Federals still atop the mountain made it difficult for Rebels to operate on the west side of the massive ridge in Lookout Valley, and thus were unable to completely seal off the river route to Bridgeport.

Near dark, Wheeler and his advanced guard reached Summertown, where he encountered the 3rd Tennessee Infantry (US), left there by General Spears the day before. When Wheeler called upon the Yankee Tennesseans to surrender, Col. William Cross, commanding the 3rd, kicked the demand

58 *Ibid.*

59 *OR* 30, pt. 2, p. 522.

upstairs to Spears, who told him to refuse and make a fight of it. The action that followed lasted about an hour and cost the 3rd Tennessee about ten casualties, most of them missing and likely captured.[60] Spears recalled the regiment and just before dawn on the 24th, the Federal general escaped to Chattanooga with his brigade.

With Lookout Mountain now securely under Confederate control, Wheeler received yet another set of new orders. Bragg ordered his senior cavalryman to move to Chickamauga station east of the city, which Wheeler's troops reached on the 25th. Bragg was still convinced a raid against Rosecrans' extended supply lines was the correct plan, but instead of crossing the river below Chattanooga toward Bridgeport, Wheeler was to cross above the city and attack the only remaining land route connecting Chattanooga to Bridgeport through the Sequatchie Valley.[61] With this directive, Bragg effectively abandoned the idea of a direct assault on Chattanooga. Instead, he would starve Rosecrans out.

In practical terms, the Chickamauga Campaign was over. A new phase for the struggle for Chattanooga was now underway.

60 *Ibid.*, pt. 1, pp. 885-6.

61 *Ibid.*, pt. 2, p. 522.

C hapter 15

Failure in the Saddle:
An Appraisal of the Confederate Cavalry

A fter the war, D. H. Hill described Chickamauga as a "barren victory."[1] Despite the routing of nearly one-third of the Union Army of the Cumberland off the battlefield on September 20 and the capture of thousands of men and many artillery pieces, Chickamauga produced only fleeting success for the Confederacy. Two months later, the heavily reinforced Federal army erased the stain of Chickamauga with the stunning climb up Missionary Ridge that knocked Bragg's Army of Tennessee off the high ground. This time, it was the dispirited Rebel army's turn to be driven from a battlefield and back to Dalton, Georgia. The retreat firmly established the strategic objective of Chattanooga as a permanent Union base and set the stage for William T. Sherman's drive south into Georgia the following spring..

The traditional villain of the Greek tragedy that played out along Chickamauga Creek and the hills and valleys surrounding Chattanooga is, of course, Braxton Bragg. And, like the central character in a tragic drama, he made more than his share of mistakes. So did his principal cavalry lieutenants. What follows is a summary of the major errors and questionable decision-making of the Army of the Tennessee's mounted arm.

---

1   Hill, "Chickamauga," *Battles and Leaders*, III, p. 662.

Braxton Bragg's Errors: Real and Perceived

General Bragg's initial deployments along the Tennessee River in early September were unsound, his army too scattered for quick concentration. Bragg's uncertainty about the direction of William Rosecrans' main thrust was exacerbated by the missteps of his senior cavalry leader Joseph Wheeler, whose failure to properly and aggressively garrison his assigned sector on the left of the Southern army compounded Bragg's errors in deployment. Still, Bragg knew or should have known that the only realistic way for a large army to reach Chattanooga from Nashville was via the only railroad that linked those two points. Wheeler's mistakes notwithstanding, Bragg should have been better prepared to meet Rosecrans near Bridgeport.

In a similar vein, the Confederate commander was too easily deceived by Federal feints toward Knoxville. The terrain and sparse civilian population in that area restricted large movements of any kind and supplies in the region by fall of 1863 were sparse at best. His initial order sending John Wharton's cavalry division to the river northeast of the city illustrates the degree of Bragg's fixation with a Federal move there. And yet, Bragg never seriously planned to send cavalry across the river to watch Rosecrans more closely. It was Nathan Bedford Forrest's initiative that send Col. George Dibrell's cavalry brigade to Sparta, Tennessee (some 80 miles north of Chattanooga and between that point and Knoxville), not orders from Bragg. The usually pugnacious Bragg was too willing to surrender the north bank of the river without a fight, which is exactly what he did.

Two significant cavalry movements were undertaken on Bragg's direct orders, both of which exemplified his misuse of his mounted resources. On both occasions the directives duplicated existing efforts and moved Rebel cavalry out of the fight for forty-eight hours at critical moments in the campaign.

The first involved Wharton's move at the end of August (as noted above). Instead of ordering that division to patrol at Bridgeport or Stevenson—where the real Union threat was developing along the railroad leading south from Nashville—Bragg ordered Wheeler to send Wharton to D. H. Hill's front northeast of Chattanooga. It was an odd decision because Forrest's cavalry was already there. It was also a bad decision because it allowed the Federals two full days to cross the bulk of their infantry without opposition at Bridgeport and Stevenson, their only immediate concern was the natural obstacle posed by the Tennessee River.

On September 8, Bragg made a similar blunder by ordering Forrest to send Dibrell's Brigade to Lafayette, Georgia, an area already occupied by Wheeler's entire cavalry corps. Forrest compounded this error by sending Frank Armstrong's entire division and then riding with the column himself. Once again, Bragg's decision weakened severely the mounted forces operating on his right flank to strengthen a front that already had a substantial cavalry presence. Forrest's departure with his best division left only John Pegram's command (which had more than its share of leadership and morale problems) to act as Bragg's rearguard in the face of a vigorous and aggressive Union pursuit. Within twenty-four hours, Bragg had no choice but to reverse this decision and send Forrest's men hurrying to retrace their steps northward. During that period, Armstrong's two brigades accomplished nothing beyond a frustrating series of marches and counter-marches. Both of Bragg's decisions wasted time, men, and horse flesh, demonstrated that he could be easily distracted by one threat to the detriment of another, and reveal a commander who still did not understand how best to use his cavalry.

Not all of the blame for losing Chattanooga can be laid at Bragg's feet, and not all of his command decisions were suspect. For example, Forrest urged Bragg to attack Thomas Crittenden's XXI Corps in the Peavine Valley on September 10, but Bragg chose instead to strike at Maj. Gen. James Negley's division, part of George Thomas' XIV Corps, at Davis' Crossroads in McClemore's Cove. Forrest's partisans point to this decision as evidence of Bragg's unfitness to command, but his basic plan was sound.[2] The attack in McClemore's Cove miscarried only because of the reluctance (and outright insubordination) of some of Bragg's generals (chiefly Thomas C. Hindman) to follow his specific orders. A careful study of the relative positions of the opposing armies makes it clear that Bragg made the correct strategic choice. Negley's command in the cove comprised the approximate center of Rosecrans' attenuated Army of the Cumberland, and a successful strike there would keep the Union army divided and preserve the Confederates' critical advantage of interior lines that were so vital to 19th-century strategy. Moving against either Crittenden or McCook, however, would have required Bragg to turn his back on the other two Federal columns and risk that Rosecrans would unite and attack the Rebel rear. Even though the attack against Negley fizzled, poor strategic thinking was not to blame.

2   Jordan and Pryor, *Forrest's Cavalry*, pp. 306-7.

More problematic was Bragg's decision to suspend the September 17 large-scale turning movement designed to envelop Rosecrans' left flank and drive him away from Chattanooga. Colonel George Brent, who served on Bragg's staff, condemned the decision in his journal that very day.[3] Brent's criticism has merit. By delaying the movement another day, Bragg granted more time to Rosecrans to bring his scattered columns closer together.

Bragg had little choice but to wait because most of his army was out of place and could not have met the stringent timing requirements set forth in the orders. Much of this was Bragg's own fault. After the failure at McClemore's Cove, Bragg sent the bulk of his infantry hurrying ten miles north to Rock Springs on September 12 to support the attack he ordered Leonidas Polk to launch against the Union XXI Corps at Lee and Gordon's Mills. That, too, failed to come off. The next day, September 13, Bragg overreacted to reports from Wheeler that Federals were resuming the advance on Lafayette from the south. Bragg sent those same troops hurrying back to Lafayette, only to discover on the 14th that the Federals Wheeler mentioned were not advancing but retreating. This constant marching to and fro wore down Bragg's infantry, and a pause at Lafayette for a few days was now, to some extent, inevitable to allow the men to recover. If Wheeler's reporting had been more accurate, or if Bragg had not been so quick to react, his infantry would have been in position around Rock Springs on September 17 instead of concentrated at Lafayette ten miles farther south.

In one way the delay worked to Bragg's benefit. A pause of twenty-four hours allowed for the arrival of more of James Longstreet's troops from Virginia, which in turn increased Bragg's numerical advantage over his opponent.

A proper use of cavalry, however, could have erased any advantage the delay provided Rosecrans. While the Confederate infantry needed more time on September 17 to march into position, the cavalry should have already been in position to execute at least part of Bragg's plan. Wheeler, for example, should have ridden up from Lafayette more rapidly, thereby freeing Armstrong to rejoin Forrest on the 17th instead of on the 19th (when Armstrong arrived). Had this simple shift in cavalry taken place, Forrest would have had his full

---

3 Entry for September 17, 1863, Brent Journal. Brent came to despise his boss, so his criticism must be taken with a grain of salt. His observations, however are extremely valuable because of his position on Bragg's staff.

strength on hand to seize the problematic crossings on Chickamauga Creek before the Federals had a chance to properly defend them. Doing so would have avoided the prolonged delaying actions the Federals waged at Alexander's Bridge and Reed's Bridge—gallant defensive efforts that so upset Bragg's timetable when he put his troops in motion on September 18. With his cavalry better positioned and the vital crossings already in Rebel hands, Bragg's mounted troops would have been available to lead his infantry columns when the main movement recommenced.

Instead, what occurred typified the mismanagement of the cavalry that had so characterized Confederate operations thus far. Forrest's Corps was going to take center stage in the next advance simply because his troopers were already in place at Ringgold and Rock Springs. Armstrong's Division, however, was out of place on September 17 guarding crossings farther south of Lee and Gordon's Mills (most notably at Glass Mill). This disposition made sense when Bragg's attention was focused on defending Lafayette from the south and west, as was the case between September 10 and 14. But by the 15th, Bragg knew there was no longer any threat from those quarters. With a new offensive farther north in the offing, Forrest needed Armstrong and Bragg had to know he would need him. But Wheeler's negligence prevented Armstrong from reaching Forrest in a timely fashion. Only Bragg could resolve this problem, and he should have used the time from September 15 -17 to ensure that Armstrong reached Forrest as soon as possible. Armstrong's absence from the army's right flank left Pegram's Division as the only mounted force available to undertake the single and most vital role in the planned September 17 movement. Thus far in the campaign Pegram and his brigades had not performed up to expectations. He would have to divide his division in order to seize the Chickamauga crossings as ordered, and still provide each infantry column with the cavalry support it required. Predictably, none of these things happened. As a result, the daylong delay on the 17th turned out to be a gift of precious time to Rosecrans and a wasted opportunity for Bragg. The burden of this mistake rests with Bragg because he was simply too lax in the oversight of the operations of his mounted arm in general, and of Joe Wheeler in particular.

The delays and slow progress of September 18 frustrated Bragg, but they did not wreck his plans beyond repair. Allowing the Federals to gather in force much farther north than anyone expected, and from that position launch an attack against the army's northern flank on the morning of September 19, was much more serious. The failure to detect the presence of the enemy in that quarter rests with Forrest's failures of reconnaissance and improper picketing on the night of the 18th. Bragg's response to the unexpected crisis was halting and feeble.

When he discovered the enemy was assailing him from the northwest, the Rebel general's impulse was to halt his own attack until the extent of the Federal move could be ascertained. Instead of turning Rosecrans' left flank Bragg spent most of the day feeding troops into a growing fight one division at a time. The Federals responded in kind, and the day's battle turned into an inconclusive slugging match with both sides trading blows to no real result. Bragg's decision was a grave mistake. His army still had the advantages of position, mass, and opportunity over Rosecrans. If Bragg had gone ahead with his intended full-scale attack that morning, Chickamauga might well have been a single day's fight.

The second day's battle was almost more of the same. The infamous confusion between Bragg, Polk, and Hill about orders to attack at dawn on September 20 resulted in a bloody failure that morning, redeemed only by an equally infamous series of misunderstandings on the Federal side that opened a fortuitous gap in the Union line at exactly the wrong place and moment. Through that opening poured Longstreet's powerful column, which swept their part of the field clean of Yankees and nearly drove the Army of the Cumberland from the battlefield. (A full accounting of those errors, and who is to be held responsible, however, is beyond the scope of this effort.)

Bragg has been roundly and universally condemned for not pursuing the beaten enemy vigorously on September 21. A core of his generals comprised his more vocal critics. Unfortunately for history, hindsight has too often clouded considered judgment. Central to any serious examination of this question is— once again—the issue of effective reconnaissance. The axiom that a victorious army is nearly as confused, unorganized, and hamstrung as its defeated opponent held true at Chickamauga. The Confederate Army of Tennessee had fought two long, grueling, and horrendously bloody days of combat that left its confused command structure in a state of appalling disorder. The large and undulating battlefield upon which this combat was waged was heavily timbered and offered limited opportunities for extended viewing in any given direction. As a result, when the sun rose on Monday morning (the 21st), most Confederates expected the fighting to resume where it had left off the night before. Only gradually, after the passage of many hours and after sifting through a series of confusing reports did Bragg's headquarters come to understand that the Army of the Cumberland had abandoned the field. As events would soon demonstrate, the Federals not only disengaged successfully but managed to establish a very strong defensive position on Missionary Ridge at Rossville. Any "pursuit" Bragg could have mounted would have involved renewed frontal attacks against entrenched defenders holding the high ground. Bragg's critics overlook this reality.

The primary evidence in the case against Bragg's failure to launch an aggressive pursuit is grounded in Forrest's dispatches to army headquarters. As discussed elsewhere, these dispatches failed to include several important facts. Forrest's troopers were stopped short by the Federals at Rossville early that morning, but that fact was not reported in either of his messages reproduced in the Official Records. Nor do Forrest's communiqués mention the extensive earthworks the enemy was frantically constructing that day—despite a great deal of other eyewitness testimony that took note of those efforts. In fact, Forrest presented a remarkably inaccurate picture of the actual Union dispositions and intentions on September 21. The Army of Tennessee was quite fortunate that Bragg paid the cavalry general little heed that day. Simply put, the rhetoric against Bragg on this issue does not stand up well to close historical scrutiny.

Nathan Bedford Forrest

New to both regular cavalry operations and corps command, Nathan Bedford Forrest struggled to meet the rigorous challenges of his increased responsibilities. He started well. His initial order sending men to Sparta was a good one, and it corrected one of Bragg's oversights. But once Dibrell was driven out of White County, Forrest's decision to not contest control of the Sequatchie Valley was a significant lapse. From that valley, the Federals could vanish and appear in front of Chattanooga at will, all the time concealing their true strength. As a result, while the bulk of the Yankee army was making for Bridgeport and Stevenson, Rosecrans was able to use a limited force to deceive Bragg into thinking that the main crossing would come northeast of Chattanooga. Forrest was taken in by this deception completely, going so far as to endorse D. H. Hill's misguided plan to cross the river and attack what the Rebels thought was an exposed Union corps on September 4 and 5. Forrest's reports reinforced Bragg's conclusion that Rosecrans would move north of the city first to keep in contact with Ambrose Burnside in East Tennessee, and that the Federal crossings at Bridgeport and Stevenson were just feints.

When the Confederates realized that Rosecrans had turned their left and was in a position to cut their supply line with Atlanta, Bragg had little choice but to retreat south out of Chattanooga. Forrest's responsibility was to protect the exposed rear of the Army of Tennessee. Instead of using Armstrong's experienced division to conduct this sensitive mission Forrest dispatched it south toward Alpine, leaving John Pegram's newly formed and inexperienced command to undertake that critically important task. Instead of remaining with Pegram to supervise the operation Forrest promptly compounded his error by accompanying Armstrong.[4]

Why he did so remains unclear. Armstrong enjoyed good relations with his subordinates, led the most seasoned troopers, and had a proven track record conducting independent operations. Pegram had none of these qualities. He was new to division command, had not proven himself capable of leading a mounted brigade (let alone a division), and his hastily-assembled command was composed of troopers of uncertain training and morale. Significantly, Pegram's relationship with his chief subordinate, brigade commander John L. Scott, remained rocky at best.

An added—and very significant—complication centered on the command structure of the division itself. Until Henry Davidson arrived, Pegram maintained command of both his former brigade and the division. Operating a brigade and division effectively and simultaneously would have been difficult for any leader; Pegram demonstrated time and again it was impossible for him. Finally, if Armstrong ran into any serious trouble south of Lafayette, Joe Wheeler was close at hand and able to take charge of any situation that arose. Forrest, however, tended to go where the action was and if Armstrong was going to undertake a dangerous reconnaissance likely to produce a fight, Forrest intended to be present.

The scope of these errors became obvious almost immediately when the Federals moved aggressively against Pegram. Bragg ordered Forrest to ride back north on September 9 just as his column reached Lafayette. Without time to rest or feed their horses Forrest's tired troopers retraced their twenty-mile round trip. The only thing this unnecessary marching accomplished was to remove Armstrong's men from the scene of action for two days. To his credit, Forrest did not repeat this mistake during the rest of the campaign and for the balance of the month stuck close to Pegram to better supervise his uncertain subordinate.

---

4 Bragg's order to Forrest specified sending Dibrell, but was discretionary in allowing Forrest to take what other cavalry Forrest "deemed necessary." *OR* 30, 4, p. 611.

Forrest's actions were energetic between September 10 and 13, but they reflected his inexperience with corps command and traditional cavalry missions. First, he scattered his brigades, which made it all but impossible for either of his division leaders to control their commands. Next, Forrest cleaved Armstrong's Division in two by sending Dibrell on a scouting mission to Dalton. This left Armstrong with James Wheeler's lone brigade to support General Polk's infantry. Forrest's remaining division was also in a confused state. Its leader, John Pegram, spent all his time with his former brigade while Forrest personally directed Scott's Brigade at Ringgold. In some sense Forrest faced a very difficult situation. There was good reason for him to ride hard on Pegram and direct movements at a grassroots level, but it was also counter-productive. Too often, Forrest found himself in the thick of the action and unable to avoid making tactical decisions better left to others. This, in turn, did little to help Pegram mature as a division commander.[5]

Forrest could and should have: (1) Ordered Armstrong's entire division to the Rock Springs-Peavine Church sector to screen Polk's Corps, and (2) Concentrated Pegram's command at Ringgold so that if a Federal threat there materialized (as it did on the 11th), Pegram would have had both brigades to counter it instead of just Scott's troubled command. Forrest's sphere of responsibility covered an active front fifteen miles wide. This was too much for one general to oversee no matter how capable or tireless he was, and still personally supervise every threatened point simultaneously. This was especially true given the uneven abilities of his subordinates and questionable make-up of some of his organizations. An effective use of his chain of command would have simplified Forrest's task.

The famed raider's personality compounded these problems. Forrest was too often unable or unwilling to resist the lure of personal adventure and/or delegate minor missions. Personally leading his escort on the reconnaissance at

---

5 In June 1863 observers noted that, contrary to his usual custom, Maj. Gen. James (Jeb) Stuart, Robert E. Lee's charismatic cavalry commander in the Army of Northern Virginia, stayed out of the thick of the action during fights at Upperville and Aldie, Virginia. There was a good reason for this. Stuart was now responsible for more cavalry than he had ever led before, and he was trying to develop brigadiers who could assume more responsibility and thus be ready to step up to higher command when needed. Development was important to professional officers, and not just for careerist reasons. Military service is risky and missions must not be allowed to fail because of the loss of a key commander. Forrest understood the need for personal leadership, but he did not fully appreciate how to professionally develop other commanders. Mark Nesbit, *Saber and Scapegoat: J.E.B. Stuart and the Gettysburg Controversy* (Stackpole Books, 1994), pp. 54-5.

Tunnel Hill on the night of September 11, for example, was foolhardy in the extreme. A corps commander had no business conducting such a mission, especially with the divisional chain of command already fragmented and in disarray. If Forrest had been killed or incapacitated, neither division commander knew enough about what was transpiring to assume the reins of corps command in his place, and neither was capable of overseeing a corps— especially in the middle of a campaign. The Tunnel Hill affair was not an isolated incident: on September 18 at Reed's Bridge, Forrest rode alone to within 100 yards of the Union cavalry line under heavy fire; on the 21st he led 400 of Dibrell's Tennesseans against Minty's Federals and had a horse shot out from under him; and on September 22 he brazenly led his escort on a charge against Union entrenchments. While these individual exploits demonstrate Forrest's disregard for personal danger (which his troops found inspiring), they also reflect serious shortcomings as a corps leader, including his inability to delegate authority and his need to always be at the forefront of any action. These episodes of personal bravado came at the expense and neglect of his real duties.

After the infantry failure in McLemore's Cove, it was Forrest who was largely responsible for Bragg's decision to attack Crittenden's XXI Corps at Lee and Gordon's Mill. Forrest first tried to find Bragg and urge him to adopt this course on the night of the 10th, but Bragg was already busy with the Davis' Crossroads affair. Two days later on the 12th, however, Forrest passed information from Pegram to army headquarters that convinced Bragg that the opportunity against the XXI Corps still beckoned. According to Pegram, Federal divisions were scattered between Rossville and Crawfish Springs. This intelligence was wrong. Far from being scattered, an entire Union corps was concentrated across Chickamauga Creek at Lee and Gordon's Mills. General Polk, who was supposedly in a position with sufficient numbers to overwhelm one "scattered" Union division at a time, was instead outnumbered nearly three to one. Forrest was intimately supervising Pegram and Scott at this time, and their reports confirmed his own idea that the Yankees were still separated and so very vulnerable. As a result, he passed their reports up the chain of command without taking concrete steps to confirm the intelligence.

Forrest's performance reached its nadir between September 17 and 19. On the 16th, he was ordered to seize the crossings over Chickamauga Creek. If he had acted promptly, both Alexander's and Reed's bridges would almost certainly have been in Rebel hands by the morning of the 17th and the fighting and delays the following day would have been avoided.[6] However, he did not so act and Bragg's infantry discovered the crossing points in the hands of the enemy when it tried to cross the creek on September 18. Knowing that he did not have the crossings secured, Forrest should have made certain that all three primary infantry columns (one each under W. H. T. Walker, Simon Buckner, and Bushrod Johnson) had the required cavalry support to screen their advances. This requirement was outlined explicitly in Bragg's reissued and updated attack orders of September 18. Forrest did not do that, either. As a result, the unescorted Confederate infantry columns collided with stubborn Union cavalry defenses at both bridges. The sharp and prolonged fighting for each crossing point delayed Bragg's plans for the better part of a day. These actions alerted Rosecrans to the new threat to his left flank and, more importantly, bought the Union commander invaluable time to react to that threat.

Despite Bragg's orders, almost none of Forrest's troopers played a direct role in important events that unfolded on September 18. Instead, the Rebel troopers were sent on peripheral missions or spent the day in transit riding between the moving infantry columns. Colonel Scott began the day at Ringgold, but instead of screening Johnson's infantry he was ordered to ride north and guard Red House Bridge. Pegram started the day with Simon Buckner, provided Reserve Corps commander Walker with only the sketchiest of information about what was going on in front of him at Alexander's Bridge, and then was called away to join Johnson while Walker's infantry was fighting to cross the creek. Pegram's ride north was so slow that afternoon that he did not reach Reed's Bridge until about 4:00 p.m.—well after the fighting there had ended. Forrest's personal whereabouts on the morning of the 18th remains a mystery, and his absence from the front may have resulted in some of these lapses. Forrest reported that he began the day at Ringgold. Thomas F. Berry,

---

6   Union Col. John T. Wilder's Lighting Brigade was ordered to ride from Lee and Gordon's Mills to defend Alexander's Bridge on the afternoon of September 17. Beyond a handful of pickets, Alexander's Bridge was unprotected until Wilder arrived. Quick action by Forrest on the morning of the 17th would have seized the crossing easily. Minty's men were in position near Reed's Bridge a day or so earlier, and would have certainly contested a direct attack, but were extremely vulnerable if outflanked from Alexander's Bridge. In effect, capturing one bridge meant capturing both.

one of the members of Martin's Kentucky Battalion, however, later wrote that Forrest personally reviewed the Kentuckians in their camp at Dalton the night before.[7] The cavalry leader did not join Johnson until 11:00 a.m. on the 18th—after Johnson had already marched his infantry down the wrong road, reversed course, and then collided with the Yankees.

The most significant mistake Forrest made during this period was in failing to secure the right flank of the Confederate army on the night of September 18. His failure to send pickets out on the surrounding road network is inexcusable. As a result, Forrest missed critical Union movements that a routine cavalry screen would have discovered. Just after dark on the 18th, Union Col. Daniel McCook's Federal brigade moved eastward along the Reed's Bridge Road nearly all the way to Jay's Mill, closing off John B. Hood's line of communication with Ringgold.[8] Forrest also missed General Thomas' major redeployment when two Federal divisions of his XIV Corps marched northward to Kelly Field that same night. Missing McCook was bad enough, but the failure to discover Thomas' shift had a direct and lasting consequence on the battle because Thomas opened the combat about dawn on the 19th when he sent those divisions forward.

These reconnaissance failures changed the way the entire battle was fought. Bragg woke up on the morning of September 19 believing that the entire Federal Army of the Cumberland was still well south of his own Army of Tennessee. Thomas' appearance to his north proved a nasty shock. Instead of turning Rosecrans' left flank and driving the Federals away from Chattanooga, Bragg was faced with the uninviting prospect of having to defend his own right flank. He suspended his own flanking operation until the enemy's strength and intentions were more fully developed. As the fighting spread, he fed divisions and brigades of his army into a spreading conflagration very different than the battle he had intended to wage.

By not establishing a proper screen and sending out patrols on the evening of the 18th, Forrest also failed to detect the wide gap in the center of Rosecrans' front that developed as a result of Thomas' move north to Kelly Field. This was perhaps the most significant intelligence oversight of the entire battle. If Bragg

---

7   Thomas F. Berry, *Four Years with Morgan and Forrest* (The Harlow-Ratliff Company, 1914), p. 234.

8   Hood arrived that evening was because of seniority, was now in command of Johnson's infantry column.

had fully grasped that the troops attacking his right flank were isolated from the main Union army, he could and almost certainly would have dealt with Thomas' morning assault very differently. Bragg could have ordered his 25,000 men forward as he originally intended and descended upon Crittenden's exposed XXI Corps flank, or he could have turned, enveloped, and crushed Thomas' two divisions. Brigadier General John Turchin, a Federal brigade commander at Chickamauga, long wondered why Bragg did not advance into the yawning gap in Roscrans' center and believed it was the critical mistake of the campaign.[9] The answer, of course, is because Forrest never informed Bragg the gap existed.

Bragg was no better informed the rest of September 19 or on the 20th. By the morning of September 19, Forrest was busy doing other things. After missing Thomas' march north, Forrest stumbled into an infantry fight at Jay's Mill. When the Federals and Henry Davidson's troopers collided,[10] the wise course was to slowly fall back and screen the Federal advance to determine the extent of the threat and the location of the advancing enemy flanks. Instead, Forrest threw Davidson's cavalry into a dismounted slugfest with a much larger Yankee infantry brigade, thereby negating the true value of mounted troops by stripping away their maneuverability and inserting them into a fight for which they were neither trained to conduct nor suitably armed to wage. When he was reinforced, Forrest compounded his error by repeatedly sending men into the combat one brigade at a time. Predictably, each of these Confederate organizations was mauled badly in the morning's fight. When Dibrell's Brigade arrived, his men were also dismounted and thrust into the battle at a time when Bragg urgently needed effective reconnaissance. Far from clarifying the early Union movements, the Jay's Mill fight only provided Bragg with word that a powerful Union infantry force of unknown strength was attacking his flank from the direction he least expected. It is not surprising that Bragg halted his offensive until he could figure out how much of a threat was looming to the north. This decision, coupled with his failure to drive forward into the hole in Roscrans' front has earned the army commander the indictment of history. This denunciation ignores Forrest's contribution to Bragg's decision-making process. Cavalry provides the eyes and ears for every army commander; Forrest left Bragg blind that morning.

9   John B. Turchin, *Chickamauga* (Chicago, 1888), pp. 63-4.

10   As noted elsewhere in this book, Henry Davidson arrived from Virginia late on September 18 to assume control of John Pegram's former brigade just as the battle was beginning.

The information Forrest is best known for having provided army headquarters came two days later. On the face of it, the two messages Forrest sent to Leonidas Polk on September 21 (which were then passed on to Bragg) seemed perfectly clear. The most quoted of the two was the 7:00 a.m. dispatch, which suggested that the Yankees were in full retreat. The second message, sent at 11:30 a.m., reiterated that idea. In fact, Forrest was wrong each time. Fortunately for the Rebel infantry, these reports were openly questioned at Bragg's headquarters, and with good reason. Rosecrans was not retreating but entrenching, as the fresh mounds of dirt now ringing the city made clear. Tellingly, neither dispatch from Forrest mentioned the strong enemy position at Rossville, despite the fact that Forrest's own men ran up against it there and were easily rebuffed. Bragg was right not to trust Forrest's reports. If he had acted upon them, the Rebel army might well have suffered a very bloody rebuff. On the morning of the 21st, Bragg's most vital need was an accurate intelligence report of the current Union positions. And yet, Forrest failed to report the presence of eight Federal divisions deployed around Rossville—nearly 80% of the entire Union army.

While Forrest made several important mistakes, his instincts often proved to be correct. In stark contrast to the curiously lethargic and detached Joe Wheeler, Forrest was in the saddle at 4:00 a.m. on the 21st and probing the Union lines before dawn. While his interpretation of what he observed was off the mark, he was at least up and moving and trying to do what he thought best to help the Confederate army. His deployment the next day, September 22, utilized both Pegram's and Armstrong's divisions to advance and clear Missionary Ridge, securing important ground Bragg's infantry would need later. Dibrell's advance to the foot of Lookout Mountain denied the Yankees the use of the most direct route between Chattanooga and Bridgeport, a necessary step in the isolation of the beleaguered Army of the Cumberland. His probes of the Union entrenchments on the 22nd revealed where Rosecrans was massing his strength.

All of these actions suggested the Forrest of a year later, at the height of his skills in Mississippi and Tennessee. The Tennessean was evolving from a partisan raider into a more complete cavalry general. At Chickamauga, Forrest was just beginning this metamorphosis.

Joe Wheeler

If Nathan Bedford Forrest's record during the Chickamauga Campaign offers up examples of both high points and low points, Joe Wheeler's record is more consistent. Unfortunately for the Confederates, it was consistently bad. Throughout the campaign Wheeler paid scant attention to his duties and, sometimes, even to Bragg's direct orders. Too often Wheeler was in the wrong place at the wrong time, and he was usually late to boot.

Wheeler's missteps began with his assignment to guard the Tennessee River below Chattanooga at the end of July, a mission he all but ignored. With 7,000 cavalry at his disposal, Wheeler employed barely 500 men to guard 100 miles of river and took the rest of his command deep into Alabama and Georgia.[11] While Forrest spent the month of August patrolling and sparring with Yankees in Tennessee, Wheeler spent it at barbeques and parties.[12] At the end of August, when Bragg discovered the extent of Wheeler's negligence, he ordered his senior cavalry commander to move his command back north with all haste. By that time, however, the damage was done. Left unmolested for a week, the main Federal force crossed the Tennessee River and outflanked the Army of Tennessee's position at Chattanooga. Any attempt to strike Rosecrans in the midst of the crossing was lost.

Even when Wheeler responded to Bragg's orders, he did so in haphazard fashion. Often he scattered his men in small detachments over many miles. While an extensive screen might have been useful in detecting Rosecrans' intended crossing points, once the Federals revealed their hand and the location of the main body, sending Confederate detachments to guard fords and mountain passes as far south as Gadsden, Alabama, was a waste of men.

Even though Wheeler was Bragg's senior cavalry commander, he nearly missed the active part of the campaign and battle at Chickamauga. The bulk of his command only reached the vicinity of the Chattanooga operations through a series of forced marches that shed stragglers and crippled horses that had been

---

11 Bragg's orders allowed Wheeler to send some of his men to the rear to refit, but Bragg did not expect that Wheeler would use the discretionary allowance to withdraw his entire corps.

12 See Thomas W. Cutrer, *The Terry Texas Ranger Trilogy* (Austin, TX: The State House Press, 1996), pp. 206-9. Ephraim S. Dodd's diary documents during this period a brigade officer's ball, a grand barbeque where the Texans presented John Wharton with a new sword, as well as a wedding.

only recently nurtured back to health. The initial problem was triggered by Bragg himself.

On August 29, the army commander sent John Wharton's Division of Wheeler's Corps to reinforce Forrest instead of to strengthen the line below Chattanooga. This error left the 3rd Confederate and 3rd Alabama cavalry regiments alone for the first few desperate days of the campaign. By the end of August, only the 3rd Confederate's 250 troopers were available to patrol Sand Mountain. When the enemy crossed the river, these Southerners were easily swept aside, routed, and demoralized. For several days in early September, Lt. Col. T. H. Mauldin's 3rd Alabama Cavalry, about 300 men, was the only Rebel command available to replace them. Mauldin's task was to defend an equally impossible line atop Lookout Mountain. With the Confederate cavalry dotting the army's left flank only in penny packets, the Federals moved unmolested across Lookout Mountain and occupied Wills Valley with ease.

Bragg's decision was a serious mistake, but Wheeler compounded that mistake by sending the bulk of William Martin's Division 50 miles south to Alexandria, Alabama at the end of July. With Martin's men so far from the front, it was impossible to reinforce the Tennessee River line quickly if a threat developed. When that threat materialized at the end of August with large numbers of Federal troops swarming across the river in boats and on pontoon bridges, Wheeler was in no position to respond quickly.

Wheeler's casual insubordination is best exemplified by his refusal to enter Wills Valley when Bragg ordered him to do so on September 5. Instead of obedience Wheeler offered excuses that revealed a fundamental misunderstanding of the role of cavalry. As far as Wheeler was concerned, protecting Bragg's supply lines was more important than discovering enemy strength and movements. His refusal to implement his superior's orders as written would have justified Wheeler's removal, but Bragg ignored the rebuff.

Two significant consequences flowed from reports filed by Wheeler on September 12-13. Wheeler's belief that he needed to call upon D. H. Hill's infantry on September 13 alarmed Bragg and triggered a stir at army headquarters. Brent noted as much in his journal when he recorded that Breckinridge's men (part of Hill's Corps) "were engaged" with McCook's Federals.[13]

---

13 Entry for September 13, Brent Journal, Bragg Papers. See also Chapter 7, note 17.

In fact, Wheeler collided not with enemy infantry on the 12th but with enemy cavalry. And when he did so, the Federal horseman fell back to Alpine that night. All objective indications suggested that the threat to Lafayette from the south was waning. Wheeler's reports should have made this important point clear, but they did not. As a result, Bragg continued to worry about the threat from Alpine for the next week. As late as September 13, after Davis' Crossroads and after Rosecrans had decided to concentrate his own divided forces, Bragg was still reacting to a perceived threat from Alexander McCook's XX Corps in the south.

Wheeler's September 12 and 13 reports also induced Bragg to send much of his infantry south to Lafayette after he had just hurried this same infantry north to support General Polk in the proposed attack against Thomas Crittenden's XXI Corps. As discussed earlier, this countermarching shuttled two Confederate infantry corps ten miles in the wrong direction (south) just when it was becoming apparent that Bragg's obvious move was to interpose as much of his army as possible between Rosecrans and the city of Chattanooga. In other words, he would need these many thousands of soldiers much farther north.

The result was a needless effort that exhausted the foot soldiers and wasted time that Bragg could ill-afford to give up. By mid-September the army commander was penning orders to Wheeler that were so detailed that a cavalryman with Wheeler's experience and seniority should have felt insulted. These directives instructed him as to the recall of various small detachments and even specified the exact roads Wheeler was to picket. This level of specificity far exceeded Bragg's typical communiqué to a cavalry commander, and suggested as forcefully as anything else that the Confederate army commander believed it was necessary to manage even the minutia of Wheeler's cavalry deployments.

Wheeler proved no less dilatory when Bragg undertook his major offensive effort designed to turn Rosecrans' left flank and sever his communications with Chattanooga. During the opening phase of this move that led directly to the battle of Chickamauga, Wheeler was responsible for the Confederate left flank just as Forrest protected the army's right flank. Since Bragg was massing on his right and planning to make the main attack there, Forrest's mission should have taken priority. Wheeler's job was to close up on D. H. Hill's Corps and protect the Army of Tennessee's rear area, thereby freeing all of Forrest's troopers for their new role. Bragg specifically outlined Wheeler's new mission in Special Orders No. 245, issued on September 16, which instructed Wheeler to "pass through . . . Catlett's Gap, press the enemy . . . and join our flank near Glass Mill."[14]

Nothing went as planned. Frank Armstrong's Division, which was comprised of Forrest's best and most dependable troopers, was delayed two days because Wheeler failed to arrive at Glass Mill as ordered. Without Wheeler's cavalry, Hill had no choice but to retain Armstrong. Wheeler's men were not far away, and Armstrong sent several requests that Wheeler send Wharton's men forward to relieve him. Wheeler refused until Bragg formally intervened with a direct order on the morning of September 19—the day the battle of Chickamauga opened. Bragg's directive settled the matter, but Wheeler's failure to recognize the situation for what it was and then act upon it by dispatching Wharton's men was inexcusable.

Wheeler's judgment did not improve once the battle was joined. His lethargic display in the handling of Wharton's command on the 19th was compounded into gross error when he let Wharton's men fall back two to three miles to their former camps that evening instead of demanding they remain in contact with the Federals during the night. On the morning of September 20 Wheeler overpowered a Union brigade near Glass Mill. Thereafter, when he received orders to move north, Wheeler inexplicably decided to cross back over Chickamauga Creek and ride north along the eastern bank. This required his cavalry to make another attack across the creek at Lee and Gordon's Mills, when he could have taken those defenders in the flank from the same side of the creek since he had already won the west bank at Glass Mill. By re-crossing the creek and undertaking a ride that would likely require a frontal attack, Wheeler assumed unnecessary risks. If Lee and Gordon's Mills had been strongly defended, Wheeler's men might well have been bloodily repulsed. The maneuver also consumed several important hours on the afternoon of the 20th.

Once in possession of Lee and Gordon's Mills and Crawfish Springs, Wheeler seemed content to rest on his laurels. He did not dispatch a strong enough force to work with James Longstreet in his post-breakthrough effort, and he failed to launch a vigorous pursuit after the Federal rout. Instead, Wheeler left Martin's Division to picket the area around Crawfish Springs and once again allowed Wharton's cavalrymen to ride back to their original camps, now a full five miles in the rear.

14 *OR*, 30, 4, p. 657

Wheeler's operations on September 21 were similarly confused and inexplicable. At dawn, while the vital question of the enemy's whereabouts plagued Rebel commanders of every rank, Wharton's troopers were busy riding back to the front and wasting more valuable time. They played no role whatsoever in determining the new Federal dispositions. William Martin's regiments were at least closer to the front and conducted some patrolling duties. Their failure to cross over Lookout Mountain, however, allowed Rosecrans to keep the direct route to Bridgeport, Alabama, open for another very important day. In fact, Wheeler seems to have ignored Lookout Mountain almost completely. On the 21st he made no effort to drive north along the crest and clear the summit of Federals where it overlooked not only the city of Chattanooga, but offered a perfect view of Bragg's movements to any interested Yankee signalmen.

Once Wharton's command reached the Chattanooga Valley that afternoon, his cavalrymen engaged in some desultory skirmishing with Federal cavalry and infantry but accomplished little else. The largest fight developed when Rebel pickets reported the approach of Col. Louis Watkins' Federal brigade from the south as it sought a way into the city. Wheeler shifted virtually his entire command south—away from Chattanooga and the direction the rest of the army was moving—to chase this small Federal column. Later that afternoon, after Watkins was defeated, instead of moving in the direction of Bridgeport or Stevenson, Wheeler once again ordered Wharton's men to fall back to their former camps east of Glass Mill—now some ten miles distant. Why he did so is simply inexplicable.

Because of the distances involved, Wharton's Division was largely absent from the key events of September 22. It was men from Frank Armstrong's Division of Forrest's Cavalry Corps who operated against the Federals that morning, first in the pursuit of George Thomas' XIV Corps troops during their retreat into the entrenchments ringing Chattanooga, and then when Dibrell's Brigade cut laterally across Chattanooga Valley as far as the foot of Lookout Mountain.

On the afternoon of the 22nd, Wheeler belatedly conceived the idea of sending a reconnaissance west of Lookout Mountain. Even though overdue, the move would have helped isolate Rosecrans from his depots in Alabama had it been carried out in sufficient strength. Unfortunately for the Confederates, Wheeler failed to make any effort to secure the crest of the mountain at its northern point before embarking on this new venture. With the northern end of the massive ridge still in Federal hands, Chattanooga could not be cut off from the outside world. A direct order from Bragg finally turned Wheeler's attention to the north end of the massive ridge, but at the expense of sending any force into Lookout Valley.

Wheeler's decisions often reveal a curious bias. Wheeler himself usually accompanied Wharton's command, which left Martin to operate the more independent missions. While this confidence reflects to Martin's credit, it also meant that Martin's men and mounts covered more territory and were much more exhausted than Wharton's troopers. When Wheeler bucked Bragg's orders and refused to send any force into Wills Valley on September 5— Bragg's orders called for a probe to be aggressively undertaken "even at the expense of troops"—it was Wharton's Division that would have drawn the mission. Only Forrest's arrival with Dibrell's Brigade changed Wheeler's mind otherwise. With the Wills Valley reconnaissance back on, Dibrell's men were abruptly recalled. That left Wharton (who had plenty of men for the mission) to face the task alone. Wheeler once again deemed the undertaking too dangerous. The troopers resting at Dr. Anderson's on September 17 "doing nothing" were Wharton's men, marking time after Wheeler refused to send them up to replace Armstrong. Each evening on September 19, 20, and 21, Wharton's troopers were allowed to return to comfortable camps miles in the rear, leaving Martin's command behind each night to picket the battlefield. The impact of this obvious favoritism can be better appreciated with a comparison of the size of the organizations: Martin's Division had only 2,400 men in six regiments and Wharton fielded 4,400 men in nine regiments. Wharton had nearly double Martin's strength. Another way of looking at it is that Wheeler was routinely withholding two-thirds of his cavalry strength when it could have been put to substantially better use.

Wheeler's performance throughout the Chickamauga Campaign was lethargic, argumentative, and often simply unfathomable. His biggest lapse was his repeated failure to provide Bragg with timely information on Union movements. His protest about Bragg's September 5 order to probe Wills Valley demonstrates that Wheeler failed to appreciate just how vital this mission was to the security of the army and for holding Chattanooga. He lacked the aggressive spirit so important in a true cavalry general: he did not vigorously press enemy cavalry during the screening phase, and he did not energetically pursue retreating or routed foes. Throughout this period Wheeler lacked any sense of urgency. His troops were often late to join the fight or execute their assigned missions. His tardy appearances had consequences, and often delayed other movements in turn. As Bragg's dismay with Wheeler's lack of performance grew with each passing day, his orders to his senior cavalryman became more detailed. At times it seemed as though Bragg was instructing a novice in the basic duties of cavalry instead of issuing commands to an experienced corps commander. Even these Wheeler too often ignored.

Reorganization and Recriminations

By October 1863 Braxton Bragg had every reason to be dissatisfied with his cavalry. His decision to consolidate the two corps into a single command following the battle of Chickamauga was prompted by this dissatisfaction. The decision to fuse the organizations meant that one of the two corps commanders had to go. By this time, Bragg's opinion of Nathan Bedford Forrest had changed a great deal from his August assessment that he was a "great strength" to the army. The partisan raider was a bold fighter, brave to a fault, and a magnificent raider—but he was not cut out for conducting standard cavalry operations on behalf of an army. Forrest was an individualistic leader who found it difficult to delegate authority and submit to the inevitable frictions of the chain of army command. He was not ready to take on such a large command, had never had the training or experience to do so, and was unlikely to accept Wheeler as his commanding officer. As a result, by October 13 Bragg signed the order sending Forrest out of the Army of Tennessee. The cavalryman headed for Mississippi and the independent command he had long sought. Given his performance during the recent campaign, removing Forrest and making him available in a role for which he was much better suited was a sound decision.

Removing Forrest, however, left the Army of Tennessee with Joe Wheeler unless Bragg decided to also cut ties with him and elevate another in his stead. The senior cavalryman's performance easily merited demotion or removal. Bragg, however, not only kept Wheeler but increased his responsibilities by assigning Forrest's men to his command. This decision would have implications for the rest of the war because Wheeler remained the Army of Tennessee's cavalry commander almost to the end of the conflict.[15]

15 Joe Wheeler was replaced by Gen. Wade Hampton in early 1865. Hampton, a native South Carolinian who proved to be an exceptional cavalryman, was Robert E. Lee's choice to replace J.E.B. Stuart when that officer was killed in May 1864 at Yellow Tavern. When William T. Sherman's army drove north out of Georgia and into the Carolinas, Hampton was sent south to take charge of Wheeler's demoralized and ill-disciplined cavalry in February 1865.

Wheeler set out to remake the cavalry, and with Bragg's approval brought in a number of younger officers who had distinguished themselves in combat. This move inserted several good leaders into the cavalry's command structure. Two who typified the kind of men Wheeler wanted were Brig. Gen. John H. Kelly and Col. William Y. C. Humes. Kelly was only twenty-three, had attended West Point for three and one-half years before resigning in December 1860 to join the Confederacy, and earned the attention of his superiors with a splendid combat record as an infantry commander. When his appointment to brigadier was approved in November, he became the youngest general officer in Confederate service. He more than proved himself as a cavalry leader under Wheeler. He had less than a year to live and was mortally wounded on September 2, 1864, in a skirmish outside Franklin, Tennessee. Kelly was exactly the kind of cavalryman the army needed: aggressive, intelligent, and inspirational. Humes was a little older, born in 1830, and was a Wheeler loyalist. He was a VMI man, graduating 2nd in the Class of 1851 and had served as Wheeler's chief of artillery prior to his elevation. Humes also proved a good choice for a general's wreath, earning well-earned plaudits in the Atlanta Campaign.[16]

While the reorganization helped revitalize the mounted arm, it also produced a greater degree of personal loyalty among the new arrivals to Wheeler personally. This was the allegiance the young corps commander believed had been lacking among many of his existing and prior subordinates. In the end, the new blood forced several other talented officers out of the cavalry corps.

Bragg's decision to keep Wheeler and effectively promote him without additional rank was a bad decision. If Wheeler had been relieved, a more effective consolidation of the two commands could have taken place, and/or more competent commanders may have been found to assume the reins of each corps. Frank Armstrong was the obvious choice for Forrest's job, as his credible performance during the campaign demonstrated. Either John Wharton or William Martin could have replaced Wheeler. Even though he was the junior in rank of the pair, Martin may have been an especially good choice given his solid performance in August and September. Despite having only six regiments, he capably performed the lion's share of the scouting and screening duties

---

16 For summaries of the careers of these men, see Warner, *Generals in Gray,* pp. 144, 168.

assigned to Wheeler's troops.[17] Any of these combinations would have been far better for the Army of Tennessee than retaining Wheeler and expanding his authority.

Colonel Brent believed his boss made the wrong choice. As far as Bragg's staff officer was concerned, Wheeler should have been relieved and Forrest should have replaced him. The decision to keep Wheeler was "injudicious," he complained in his journal. "Coupled with the existing discontents in the Cavalry it will tend . . . to still further impair its usefulness. Forrest, with many objections, is however the best Cavalry commander in the army."[18] Brent understood Forrest's limitations, but he also grasped Wheeler's greater unfitness for command at that level.

Why then, did Bragg retain Wheeler? The one-word answer is loyalty. In an army rent with dissension among the senior ranks that at times verged on mutiny, Wheeler remained Bragg's faithful supporter. In October 1863, when a number of the Army of Tennessee's generals were preparing and signing a petition to have Bragg removed from command, Wheeler refused to participate, either in writing or verbally. Bragg rewarded him by keeping him in command and increasing his responsibilities.[19] Bragg also elevated Wheeler's hand-picked appointees into command positions.

While command at the corps level proved inadequate, leadership at the divisional level offered a more mixed result. Of the four brigadier generals who commanded cavalry divisions in the campaign, two demonstrated noted ability and proved capable of independent missions, one performed well below par, and one remains a cipher. The two standouts were Frank Armstrong (Forrest) and William Martin (Wheeler). Both men were given the bulk of the independent missions. Armstrong rendered his most notable service between September 9 and 13 when he was screening General Polk's front in the face of the Union advance out of Chattanooga along the Lafayette Road. Several of Armstrong's messages survive within Polk's official report of the campaign. Taken together, they show an excellent cavalryman at work. He consistently kept Polk informed of all the vital elements: the locations of Armstrong's own

17 In fact, Martin would rise to *de facto* corps command later that fall, operating with James Longstreet in the ill-fated Knoxville campaign.

18 Entry for October 30th, Brent Journal.

19 Edward G. Longacre, *A Soldier To The Last: Maj. Gen. Joseph Wheeler in Blue and Gray* (Potomac Books, 2007), pp. 116-7.

men, where the Federals were active, and which forces—both enemy and friendly—were active on Polk's flanks. Despite the absence of one-half of his division, Armstrong established a firm picket line astride the Lafayette Road and harassed Union movements around Rossville. When Polk retreated as ordered, Armstrong carefully screened his withdrawal. Between the 17th and the 19th, Armstrong received orders to hand off his current mission on the army's left in order to join Forrest on the right flank. Armstrong understood the urgency of the directive. His sense of frustration with Wheeler's non-appearance is palpable in his dispatches, but he was too good a soldier to simply leave and expose Hill or Polk to a sudden Union thrust across newly vacated fords.

If Armstrong was the star in Forrest's command, Martin played a similar role in Wheeler's Corps. As noted, Wheeler relied on Martin for the bulk of the missions, and assigned him to all those that required independence or initiative. Martin's troopers were first on the scene as Rosecrans crossed the Tennessee at the end of August, sent ahead while Wheeler and Wharton followed, and while Martin's men were still woefully outnumbered in those skirmishes up through early September, at least they were present. During the days of concentration around Lafayette, Wheeler was constantly at Wharton's side. Martin, by contrast, was assigned missions of much greater independence, first on Lookout Mountain, and then along Pigeon Mountain. Martin turned in his weakest performance before the campaign officially began when he left only two regiments to screen the Tennessee River. More of his troops should have been left to watch that line, and he should not have taken the rest of his command so deep into Alabama to refit. There is not enough surviving correspondence to determine if Martin was even concerned about this weakness, or if he protested to Wheeler about it. Iin any case, the two regiments failed in the important duty of keeping Bragg informed of Rosecrans' actions for the critical first week of the campaign between August 31 and September 2. Wheeler must bear the blame for failing to either reinforce or properly supervise Martin, but Martin failed to use his forces wisely on that occasion.

By way of redemption, Martin's standout moment arrived in McLemore's Cove from September 8 to 12. There, his timely and accurate scouting reports allowed Bragg to glimpse the opportunity the Federals were unwittingly dangling at Davis' Crossroads. Martin also understood the value of accurate information. He sent a steady stream of updates and reports not just to Bragg, but also to both D. H. Hill and Thomas Hindman. When Hindman voiced fears about threats to his own flank, Martin reassured Bragg that those worries were unfounded. Martin's sense of frustration over the subsequent escape of the Yankees was almost as palpable as Bragg's. Writing in 1883, Martin noted that Hindman's "troops were on the ground, and I knew could have attacked, and were eager to do so; I cannot now, nor did I then understand why he failed to move."[20] Once battle was joined on the 19th, Martin's men pulled double duty. With Wharton's Division retiring to its camps every evening, Martin's troopers were left with the thankless and tiring work of picketing and patrolling the lines throughout the night. Perhaps Wheeler simply had confidence that Martin was the more capable commander for these tasks, but constant duty without relief wore down his troops, and there was no excuse for sending Wharton's men so far away each evening.

Unfortunately for the Army of Tennessee, personality conflicts with Wheeler doomed both officers. By 1864, Armstrong decided he could no longer serve under Wheeler and that February requested a transfer to Mississippi. There, he assumed command of a brigade under Brig. Gen. William H. "Red" Jackson. The transfer was short-lived. Three months later he was back under Wheeler's command when Jackson's Division was sent to Georgia to oppose General Sherman's drive on Atlanta. Armstrong and his men did not accompany Wheeler's cavalry eastward when it shadowed Sherman's subsequent March to the Sea, remaining instead with John Bell Hood and the Army of Tennessee.[21] Armstrong eventually ended up back under Forrest's command during the Franklin-Nashville Campaign.

William Martin briefly commanded the Cavalry Corps when it was detached to help James Longstreet during the ill-fated Knoxville Campaign late in 1863, but Martin's tenure there was not crowned with success. Longstreet blamed Martin for numerous shortcomings, some likely beyond his control. By November 1863, the Confederate cavalry was so worn out that its numbers were reduced by two-thirds and the mounts were literally starving. Martin blamed Wheeler for leaving the command in such a sorry state, and further accused him of withholding supplies and replacements. Martin remained at the head of a division into 1864 and served during the Atlanta Campaign. The

---

20 William T. Martin, "A Defense of General Bragg at Chickamauga," *Southern Historical Society Papers*, Volume XI, number 4 (April, 1883) p. 205.

21 After losing the battles of Lookout Mountain and Missionary Ridge in late November, Bragg was officially relieved of command on December 2, 1863. He was replaced by Gen. Joseph E. Johnston, who in turn was also relieved of command at the outskirts of Atlanta in July 1864. John Bell Hood was elevated to replace him.

enmity between Wheeler and himself came to a head on August 14 when Martin did not come up and support Wheeler during an attack on the Union depot at Dalton, Georgia. Wheeler was convinced the failure to act was deliberate and relieved Martin. He was transferred to the familiar dumping ground of Mississippi, where he ended the war.[22]

John Wharton's tenure under Wheeler's command was also coming to an end. Wheeler clearly showed favoritism toward Wharton and his men, and later interactions between the two officers may well explain why Wheeler worked overtime to keep Wharton close. The rift that had begun after the battle of Murfreesboro between Wharton and his commander only grew wider during the Chickamauga operations and would become an inseparable gulf by the end of November 1863.

The final blow came in October when Wharton left the army to travel to Richmond to lobby for what he believed was a long overdue promotion to major general. Rumors filtered back to the Army of Tennessee suggesting that Wheeler was unfit to command the corps, and that he was on the way out. Some believed Wharton was more capable than his superior. Wharton certainly thought so. Wheeler was sure of the source of these comments.

Wharton received his promotion to major general in early November and led his division under Wheeler during the disastrous Chattanooga Campaign. By the time that fateful episode in Confederate history was past and Bragg was no longer with the army, the two cavalry officers were barely on speaking terms. "The truth is, General Wharton allowed his ambition to completely turn his head, as his friend in Congress [Louis T. Wigfall] had assured him that he should command the cavalry of this army," Wheeler complained to the army's new commander Gen. Joseph E. Johnston that December. "This state of things has been going on for some time, the object appearing to be to convince his command that he was their friend, while I was not, and also that he was superior as an officer, &c."[23]

Knowing full well that the Army of Tennessee had been wrecked by too much in-fighting, Joe Johnston determined to raise morale and get it ready to

---

22 Stuart S. Sanders, "Maj. Gen. William Thompson Martin," in Bruce S. Allardice and Lawrence Lee Hewitt, eds., *Kentuckians in Gray* (University Press of Kentucky, 2008), pp. 199-200.

23 Longacre, *A Soldier to the Last*, p. 128; Anne Bailey, "John Austin Wharton," in Davis, *The Confederate General*, VI, p. 123.

fight the following spring. He found the "lack of harmony" within the higher ranks of his army disheartening. For his part Wharton simply wanted out. When he asked Richmond for a transfer to the Trans-Mississippi Theater, Johnston agreed and added, "I cordially approve the application." Wharton left the army in February of 1864 and ended up in Louisiana, where he served capably during the Red River Campaign and eventually assumed command of a cavalry corps of his own. Just before the end of the war on a warm spring day in April 1865, Wharton paid a visit to Maj. Gen. John B. Magruder at his headquarters in the Fannin Hotel in Houston, Texas. An exchange of angry words with a fellow officer followed, and according to one account, Wharton called the officer "a liar." The officer pulled out his pistol and killed the unarmed Wharton on the spot.[24]

Wharton's performance during the Chickamauga Campaign was unremarkable, but in fairness to that officer, Wheeler kept a tight rein on his command and did not allow him to engage in the type of missions that Martin and others performed. The fact that Wharton went on to perform capably on various raids and during the rigorous Red River Campaign suggests he might have excelled as a cavalryman under Wheeler—had the two been able to tolerate one another. Perhaps Wheeler was determined to keep Wharton close at hand so he could keep an eye on what he regarded as Wharton's growing ambitions. If so, this close supervision only exacerbated tensions between the two officers.

Division commander John Pegram did not excel at any level during the campaign. Instead of leading his division he spent most of his time at the head of his former brigade, and by doing so exercised very little influence on Colonel Scott. When an officer is elevated to division command, normal protocol called for him to turn over his former brigade to the ranking colonel. This is the only way for him to focus on his new role and carry out the increased responsibilities of higher command. Instead, Pegram attempted to exercise both jobs at once and succeeded at neither. General Forrest complicated matters by disrupting this chain of command by (1) repeatedly detaching brigades from both of his divisions for other missions, and (2) his tendency to meddle in tactical affairs. In practical terms his interference usurped Pegram, and may have left that officer with little choice but to return to brigade leadership. Whether Forrest did this because he was unable to delegate his authority, could not pull away from the

24 Bailey, "John Austin Wharton," p. 123.

tactical fighting, or because he found Pegram wanting, is unclear. What is clear is that operations between Pegram's former brigade and Scott's command were often disjointed (as displayed in the fighting around Ringgold), and the quality of information Pegram provided was not on par with the intelligence relayed to headquarters by Armstrong or Martin. For example, Pegram filed reports about Union troop movements and dispositions around Lee and Gordon's Mills that convinced Bragg to order General Polk to launch an attack. The reports, however, were rife with errors and Polk knew it. Bragg, however, did not. His anger at Polk for failing to attack on September 13 was largely misplaced, and primarily the fault of John Pegram.

Eight officers served at brigade level, and for the most part they served competently. Most of them had little opportunity to display their individual merits because they often operated under direct supervision of superior officers. As a result, the scrutiny, praise, and blame tend to fall on those officers instead. There are two standout exceptions, one good and one bad, who merit a few sentences in summary.

George Dibrell earned well-deserved laurels in this campaign. He was assigned a number of difficult missions, including the forward deployment at Sparta, Tennessee, in August. Dibrell was the natural choice to go to Sparta since much of his command was recruited there, but he had to fight superior Federal forces far from any support. Ultimately, his men were driven out of the region and fell back to Kingston, but throughout they served as a thorn in Rosecrans' side. Forrest and Armstrong also relied on Dibrell and his men for the bulk of the regular missions. It was Dibrell they dispatched to lead the scout at Alpine when Wheeler refused to follow orders and do it with his own command. It was Dibrell who rode to Scott's aid at Tunnel Hill on September 11, apparently on his own initiative, while returning from a scouting mission near Dalton.

Conversely, John Scott only added to his reputation as an unsuccessful commander. He was surprised at Ringgold on both September 11 and again on September 17. His appalling decision to ride away and leave Red House Bridge undefended on the night of September 18 was grounds for removal, and his handling of the brigade the next morning, when he belatedly attempted to correct that mistake, was equally bad. Scott's adversarial relationship with Pegram meant that the division almost never acted in concert, which served to highlight Scott's own shortcomings. On October 8, 1863, two weeks after the battle and with the taint of failure fresh about him, Colonel Scott resigned his commission and returned to Louisiana. After an apparent change of heart he argued for reinstatement and a new command, to no avail. Scott was later dismissed from the service for neglect of duty and consorting with the enemy.[25]

25 Allardice, *Confederate Colonels*, p. 335.

E pilogue

In the Eyes of History:
Historians Evaluate the Campaign

B raxton Bragg has borne most of the blame for the failures of September 1863, or indeed, for much of what transpired in the Western Theater. He has legions of detractors and few supporters. Despite some obvious military talents and strengths, Bragg's flaws as a soldier and a leader justify much of the criticism historians have heaped upon him. In their haste to condemn Bragg, however, many writers have ignored the fact that he is not the sole reason for the failures of Army of Tennessee in North Georgia.

Thomas Connelly, whose seminal and comprehensive two-volume work on the life-span of the Army of Tennessee is essential reading, repeatedly represents Bragg as out of touch and misinformed at Chickamauga. Connelly chronicles Bragg's initial misplacement of Rosecrans at the end of August and rightly faults Bragg for failing to ensure that Rebel cavalry was in place to cover his front. However, Connelly glosses over the cavalry's egregious missteps.[1]

Connelly is harder on Joe Wheeler than he is Nathan Bedford Forrest, but neither cavalry commander's decisions are examined in any detail. On September 9, as Bragg was seeking to turn and attack the Federals in McLemore

---

1 Thomas L. Connelly, *Army of the Heartland: The Army of Tennessee, 1861-1862* (Baton Rouge, LA: Louisiana State University Press, 1971) and *Autumn of Glory: The Army of Tennessee, 1862-1865* (Baton Rouge, LA: Louisiana State University Press, 1971), pp. 169-70.

Cove, Connelly noted again the problem of poor information. "With two thirds of his cavalry absent," he observed, "Bragg was sorely in need of reconnaissance."[2] Connelly accuses Bragg of simply giving up on September 13 after Gen. Leonidas Polk's failure to attack Thomas Crittenden's XXI Corps at Lee and Gordon's Mills. Connelly correctly notes that Crittenden was not where Bragg thought he was and that the intelligence Bragg received from his horsemen was uniformly bad, but he does so without noting that John Pegram—and by extension Forrest—were responsible for that bad intelligence.[3]

Connelly also fails to chronicle that faulty information was still being provided by D. H. Hill and Joe Wheeler from Lafayette that the Union threat there had not abated. In the same vein, when summing up the confusion of the battle's first morning of September 19, Connelly notes that "Bragg's inability to readjust his plans had cost him heavily," and that he "had never admitted that he was wrong about the location of Rosecrans' left wing." These damning indictments were largely true, but Connelly never mentioned Forrest's failures to keep Bragg informed about Rosecrans' movements and notify him of the gap that loomed large in the middle of the Army of the Cumberland.[4] Connelly is occasionally critical of Bragg's mounted arm in general and especially Wheeler in particular, but it is Bragg who earns the bulk of his censure. Dr. Connelly's work influenced virtually every scholar who has written on this subject.

Bragg fares little better in more detailed monographs focusing on the campaign. Glenn Tucker's *Chickamauga* was the first modern history of the battle. First published in the Civil War Centennial era, Tucker's indictment of Bragg was even harsher than Connelly's. Tucker also portrayed Bragg as out of touch and inflexible. For example, Tucker notes Bragg's surprise at finding Federals on his northern flank, and faulted him for failing to grasp that Rosecrans' center must be weak. "A general of greater mental flexibility might have sensed . . . [that] . . . Rosecrans had a gap . . . in the center of his army."[5] Mental flexibility and the ability to "sense" the enemy are admirable qualities in a general, but for most commanders more mundane tools serve even better.

2   *Ibid.*, 175.

3   *Ibid.*, 188-9. See footnote number 42.

4   *Ibid.,* 207.

5   Glenn Tucker, *Chickamauga* (Dayton Ohio: Morningside, 1981), 151.

Tucker doesn't address the fact that Bragg's cavalry should have provided this information but did not. If there is a lack of mental flexibility evident anywhere, it manifests itself in Forrest's and Wheeler's actions as much or more than it does in Bragg's decisions.

Peter Cozzens is equally hard on Bragg in his 1992 work *This Terrible Sound: The Battle of Chickamauga.* On the advance of Rosecrans' army, Cozzens writes, "Bragg and his generals where wholly unaware of the blue whirlwind rising out of the Cumberland Mountains."[6] On September 4, with the Federals across the Tennessee River in strength, Cozzens describes the atmosphere in Bragg's headquarters as "the same old story with the Confederate high command: sketchy and unreliable intelligence reports, a dazed uncertainty among the generals, and a general lack of will."[7] Cozzens is especially harsh on Bragg on the morning of September 19. The surprise appearance of fighting to the north "unnerved" Bragg, concludes Cozzens, and paralyzed the Confederate attacks for most of the day.[8] Like his predecessors, Cozzens remains silent on the cavalry's role in these various failures. If Bragg's intelligence was "sketchy and unreliable," some or most of the blame rests with the men in charge of gathering that intelligence.

Steven E. Woodworth, author of *Six Armies in Tennessee: The Chickamauga and Chattanooga Campaigns*, also condemns Bragg, though he does so for different reasons. By "August 31 enough information was available to confirm that very large Federal forces were crossing the Tennessee downstream from Chattanooga," explains Woodworth, and this information should have been interpreted correctly.[9] Perhaps this is true, but numerous contemporary sources including Colonel Brent's daily journal paint a very different picture: one of uncertainty and a lack of good reports upon which Bragg could reasonably rely. Woodworth's description of General Polk's aborted September 13 attack on Crittenden also follows the traditional pattern. Woodworth notes only in passing that the Confederate cavalry were mistaken about the Union division at Peavine Church, and he glosses over the fact that most of Polk's supposed numeric superiority—in the form of Simon Buckner's and W. H. T. Walker's

---

6   Cozzens, *This Terrible Sound*, 33.

7   *Ibid.*, 47.

8   *Ibid.*, 129.

9   Steven E. Woodworth, *Six Armies In Tennessee* (Lincoln, NE: University of Nebraska Press, 1998), 66.

Reserve Corps—was still miles away at Lafayette.[10] As for September 19, Woodworth writes, "All Bragg could know by midmorning was that Forrest had run smack into a very powerful enemy force on the army's right rear, where no enemy was supposed to be."[11] It was Forrest's task to screen Bragg's right flank in the first place, a fact left unnoted.

Judith Lee Hallock, Bragg's most sympathetic biographer, is less charitable with Forrest and Wheeler, but unevenly so. In *Braxton Bragg and Confederate Defeat: Volume II* she describes the cavalry movements prior to the Tennessee River crossings as a series of "chaotic" orders from Bragg, without noting why Bragg was scrambling to recover his mounted force.[12] However, she does take Wheeler to task for his strange refusal to enter Wills Valley and, in explaining McLemore's Cove, states that "Bragg's hesitation and lack of confidence . . . may be ascribed in large part to the unreliable information provided by his badly scattered and uncoordinated cavalry."[13] No blame from Hallock's pen flows to Forrest for missing the northward movement of George Thomas' XIV Corps on September 19. Instead, she blames the wooded terrain, observing that on the morning of the 19th, when Forrest discovers the Yankees, "Bragg realized the Federals were not where they should be, and his usual stress-induced pessimism took hold." Hallock's coverage of the Army of Tennessee's cavalry is uneven. Forrest rarely receives so much as a harsh word, while Wheeler is taken to task only intermittently.[14]

The consistent theme of all these works is that it was Bragg who was by turns hesitant and then dogmatic, paralyzed with indecision or too rigidly adhering to outdated plans. There is some truth in this analysis and Bragg bears a great deal of the blame for the Army of Tennessee's stumbles during the first three weeks of September 1863. However, an army commander's decisions are only as good as the information he is provided upon which to act. For Bragg, all too often this intelligence was woefully inadequate to form reasonable,

---

10 *Ibid.*, 75.

11 *Ibid.*, 87.

12 Judith Lee Hallock, *Braxton Bragg and Confederate Defeat: Volume II* (Tuscaloosa, AL: University of Alabama Press, 1991), 50-1.

13 *Ibid.*, 51, 60.

14 *Ibid.*, 67-8.

actionable, conclusions. The bulk of the blame rests with the Rebel cavalry. It was their job to provide Bragg with accurate intelligence.

Of the three commanders who are the primary subjects of this study, Forrest is the one who emerges from the literature all but unscathed. Historians of the battle and his biographers have treated him largely with kid gloves. Forrest biographies lodge most of the blame for whatever mistakes were on display with Bragg. Of the initial river crossing, for example, Robert Selph Henry writes in *First With The Most* that "Bragg had been neatly outmaneuvered." Somehow Henry failed to note that poor, contradictory, and wrong information added to Bragg's confusion.[15] In another instance, Andrew Lytle concludes in B*edford Forrest and His Critter Company*: "The brigades of Hazen and Wagner, still on the north bank of the Tennessee, had left the impression that a corps still remained on the other side. Forrest went to Bragg with a plan to destroy it in its isolation."[16] In fact, this was a scouting failure on Forrest's part (mistaking two brigades for the entire corps). Lytle fails to note why Bragg's headquarters believed there was an entire corps opposite Chattanooga, or how dangerous chasing that illusion could have been for the Army of Tennessee.

Forrest biographers also fail to assign blame on their subject for General Polk's refusal to attack Crittenden at Lee and Gordon's Mills. Several turn Polk into the villain.[17] In his biography *Nathan Bedford Forrest*, author Jack Hurst dismissed the entire affair in one sentence: "Bragg didn't turn north to attempt an attack on Crittenden until dawn of September 13, and then Polk loitered until Bragg had to order him in person to attack."[18] Bragg's misunderstanding of what confronted Polk was the result of defective reports from Forrest and Pegram. Polk's "opportunity" was much less than usually supposed.

Despite Bragg's clear orders, Forrest failed to provide cavalry screens for any of the moving columns for Bushrod Johnson, W. H. T. Walker, and Simon

15 Robert Selph Henry, *First With The Most: Nathan Bedford Forrest* (New York: Mallard Press, 1991), 175.

16 Andrew Lytle, *Bedford Forrest and His Critter Company* (Seminole, FL: Green Key Press, 1984), 198.

17 Henry, *First With The Most*, 179-80; Lytle, *Critter Company*, 203-4; Brian Steel Wills, *A Battle From the Start*. (New York: Harper-Collins, 1992), 133; Lonnie E. Maness, *An Untutored Genius* (Oxford, MI: The Guild Bindery Press, 1990), 164-5.

18 Jack Hurst, *Nathan Bedford Forrest* (New York: Vintage Books, 1994), 134.

Buckner on September 18. This omission is significant because two of these columns ran into serious Union opposition that delayed them and, in turn, disrupted Bragg's plans. Alert reporting by the Federals allowed Rosecrans to shift his own forces to meet the threat, a major move that also went unreported by the Rebels. None of the writers surveyed, however, comment on these lapses. Brian Steel Wills, one of Forrest's most recent biographers, described the day's problems in *A Battle From the Start* as "inevitable delays that constantly seemed to plague the Army of Tennessee's operations [so that] the Confederate offensive appeared doomed to failure."[19] Were these delays really "inevitable?" What steps did Forrest take to ensure that his troopers where in their assigned positions when the day began? Lytle once again blames Bragg: "the general commanding was as a man, who, having eyes, would not see. He neutralized Wheeler in the gaps of Pigeon Mountain, and the scattered condition of his infantry divisions led him to dismember Forrest's Corps to guard the front and flanks of these segments."[20] This comment makes little sense. Bragg was trying to make sure that his "eyes" were in place to find the enemy by having Forrest screen the front and flanks of these columns. Lytle fails to note that Forrest did not accomplish this task.

There are a number of well-known stories associated with Forrest at Chickamauga—all of them praiseworthy. Perhaps the most striking is Captain Buck Kilgore's tale concerning Forrest's repeated promises to protect Brig. Gen. Matt Ector's imperiled flanks.[21] While these exchanges burnish the Forrest legend, none of Forrest's biographers appear to have delved any deeper to discover what actually happened to Ector's embattled brigade. Cozzens, who describes Ector's travails in detail, omits the anecdote altogether, although he does describe Forrest's actions as "masterful," adding that "few generals could both inspire frontline troops and retain a perspective on the larger tactical situation as ably as he."[22] Perspective? Forrest was surprised by a fight at Jay's Mill, failed to grasp the larger threat George Thomas represented on that part of the field, did not discover Thomas' large-scale move northward, committed four brigades one at a time against a larger enemy force, and sustained

19 Wills, *A Battle From the Start*, 134.

20 Lytle, *Critter Company*, 207.

21 See Chapter 12 for this exchange.

22 Cozzens, *This Terrible Sound*, 131.

staggering losses for his effort. (Two of the brigades, Ector and Claudius Wilson, lost about fifty percent of their effective strength.)

A second celebrated and oft-repeated observation comes from D. H. Hill, who witnessed Forrest's dismounted troopers on September 20. "What infantry is that?" Hill asked. "Forrest's cavalry, sir," was the reply.[23] Hill, who had once notoriously scoffed, "who ever saw a dead cavalryman?" was duly impressed. The story is a powerful addition to the Forrest mythology, but the underlying question remains unasked and thus unanswered: Should Forrest's dismounted cavalry have been assaulting enemy lines like infantrymen? Would Bragg not have been better served by having his cavalry mounted and scouting enemy positions and looking for weak spots? Historians should be less credible of tales like this and more willing to probe beyond accepted dogma.

Everyone who writes about Forrest during this period of the war discusses the September 21 message he sent claiming Rosecrans was retreating out of Chattanooga. Most authors accept the story uncritically as yet another example of a great opportunity bungled by Bragg. Yet, it is the absence of discussion on what Forrest did not report—the actual location of the Union army—that is significant.[24] Brian Steel Wills presented a somewhat more critical view of the famous dispatch. Wills does not address the actual Union deployments that Forrest should have been able to observe, but he does note that Bragg might have had reason to not completely trust Forrest's assessment. "Bragg," Wills noted in a footnote and not the main text, "may also have been influenced by the spate of messages he had received the previous year from Forrest concerning Union activities in Nashville. Forrest believed in 1862, as vehemently as he believed now, that the Federals were evacuating the city and urged vigorous action by his superiors. In the case of Nashville, he was incorrect."[25] Now, in front of Chattanooga, Forrest was wrong again.

There are many more biographies and histories of Forrest than those mentioned here, but all strike the same general tone. Jordan and Pryor's *The Campaigns of General Nathan Bedford Forrest and of Forrest's Cavalry* first appeared in

---

23 Henry, *First With the Most*, 183.

24 Maness, *Untutored Genius*, 176-8; Hurst, *Forrest*, 137-8; Lytle, *Critter Company*, 231-3; and Henry, *First With the Most*, 190-3, all describe the incident in a similar manner. Jordan and Pryor, *Forrest's Cavalry*, 350-1, notes that Forrest climbed two trees, one at 7:00 a.m. and a second, fitted out as a Union observation post, at midday. None of these studies discuss the actual Union dispositions or Forrest's failure to locate the bulk of the Union army.

25 Wills, *A Battle From the Start*, 140-2, and see also footnote 50, on p. 399.

1868. It was written with Forrest's permission and cooperation, so it is not surprising that this work, which includes very important details of Forrest's military career, is also uncritical of his actions. Another highly influential nineteenth century work is John Allan Wyeth's *The Life of General Nathan Bedford Forrest*, first published in 1899. Wyeth served in the 4th Alabama Cavalry. He admired Forrest and avoids speaking ill of the man. Most subsequent biographies draw heavily upon these sources, sometimes too credulously.

Joe Wheeler's legacy is less well documented. There are only four biographies of Wheeler worthy of the name, compared to more than a dozen that focus on Forrest. The first was *Campaigns of Wheeler & His Cavalry*, edited by W. C. Dodson and published in 1899. Like Jordan and Pryor, Dodson worked with the subject of his book and his staff. They provided him with documents that allowed Dodson to paint a detailed and positive view of Wheeler's military career. Given all that we know today, it is not surprising that Dodson's work covers the period between August 29 and September 17 in less than one page of text. Wheeler's failure to adequately garrison the Tennessee River is ignored completely. In a work that otherwise makes liberal use of official documents, the orders from Bragg to enter Wills Valley and Wheeler's detailed reply are omitted. The battle of Chickamauga is treated in a page or two and again avoids all forms of criticism regarding Wheeler's leadership. Dodson's book should be viewed more as hagiography than as an objective look at the general.

Similar to Dodson's publication, John Witherspoon Dubose's *General Joseph Wheeler and the Army of Tennessee*, published in 1912, draws on official and personal sources. Dubose also ignores Wheeler's lapses and his work is glowingly positive. Dubose's narrative covers the Chickamauga Campaign even more briefly than Dodson. He ignores the river crossings or Wills Valley completely. Most of the narrative discusses Bragg's movements and the arrival of reinforcements from Virginia. The only description of Confederate cavalry actions between August 29 and September 17 is folded into a single sentence: "In all of the time of the maneuvering of the rival armies, Wheeler and his cavalry, on the Confederate left, guarded that flank for ninety miles southward, while Forrest, with about the same number of men, between three and four thousand, rode through the country toward Knoxville to keep watch there against any movement of Burnside from that direction."[26]

---

26 John Witherspoon Dubose, *General Joseph Wheeler and the Army of Tennessee* (New York: Neale Publishing Company, 1912), 192.

John P. Dyer published a lengthy work in 1941 called *"Fightin' Joe" Wheeler.*[27] Unlike previous works on Wheeler, Dyer discusses the early stages of the campaign in some detail and includes a lengthy defense of why Wheeler could not obey the Wills Valley directive. While mostly positive, Dyer at least offers intermittent criticism of his subject, albeit without much elaboration. Concerning the Federal defeat on September 20, for example, Dyer noted simply that Wheeler rounded up stragglers but "did not strike the fleeing columns in full force."[28]

Some historians examine Wheeler's performance with a more critical eye. While Thomas Connelly reserved his primary ire for Bragg, he also directed substantial opprobrium toward Wheeler. Regarding the river crossings, Connelly noted that "Wheeler must share the blame for the cavalry's misuse, because he had failed to obey orders" by only leaving two regiments to watch more than 100 miles of river bank.[29] When the crisis came, Connelly added, "Wheeler's efforts [to find Rosecrans] were too little and too late."[30] Concerning Wills Valley and Wheeler's flat disobedience, Connelly dismissed Wheeler's excuses as "feeble."[31] Other later incidents garner equal condemnation.

In 2007 and again in 2009, historian Edward G. Longacre published two important and related works on Wheeler and the Army of Tennessee's Cavalry. The first was a full length biography entitled *A Soldier to the Last: Maj. Gen. Joseph Wheeler in Blue and Gray*. Longacre followed this with *Cavalry of the Heartland: The Mounted Forces of the Army of Tennessee*, which examined the history of the army's cavalry. Both works discuss details of the Chickamauga Campaign, though with differing degrees of sympathy toward Wheeler.[32]

---

27 In 1935 Dyer published a 35-page pamphlet on Wheeler's Civil War career and a revised, though much shorter, version of the 1941 publication in 1961 under the title *From Shiloh to San Juan* (Baton Rouge, Louisiana State University Press, 1961). This later work was reprinted in 1992. The 1941 edition remains the most complete.

28 John P. Dyer, *"Fightin' Joe" Wheeler* (Baton Rouge: Louisiana State University Press, 1941), 121.

29 Connelly, *Autumn of Glory*, 164.

30 *Ibid.*, 170.

31 *Ibid.*, 172.

32 Edward G. Longacre, *Cavalry of the Heartland: The Mounted Forces of the Army of Tennessee* (Yardley, PA, Westholme Publishing, 2009).

In *A Soldier to the Last*, Longacre blames Bragg and not Wheeler for the undermanned state of the Tennessee River line below Chattanooga at the end of August. Bragg, argues Longacre, "undoubtedly" laid out the line, not Wheeler; and when Union artillery began to shell the city, "Bragg reacted by hunkering down inside his works."[33] While Bragg specified the distance to be covered, the decision about how many men to commit to that line remained with Wheeler. Longacre mentions that "Martin's Division" was assigned to the job, but fails to note that a mere two regiments were actually sent to do the job. Longacre strikes a similar tone with regard to the order of September 5, in which Bragg directs Wheeler to perform a reconnaissance into Wills Valley "even at the expense of troops." Wheeler, as we know, refused the mission. Longacre argues that by sending a few scouts instead of launching a major probe, Wheeler "acquire[d] the intelligence Bragg needed without the heavy casualties that would have resulted" from following Bragg's orders to the letter.[34] This assessment is simply wrong because Wheeler did not acquire the intelligence Bragg needed.

In *Cavalry of the Heartland*, however, Longacre changes gears and adopts a position closer to Connelly's when he specifically blames Wheeler for these mistakes and others. "Wheeler was primarily responsible for his commander's ignorance," concludes Longacre, who adds that "his cavalry leader's unprofessionalism was a major factor in Bragg's belated decision to evacuate" Chattanooga.[35] Cavalry of the Heartland covers the campaign in more detail, and presumably this increased scrutiny is the reason why Longacre reversed himself. However, neither book examines the impact Wheeler's September 12 clash with George Crook's Federals had in convincing Bragg to move infantry back to Lafayette, or the disruption of Bragg's planning when Wheeler failed to replace Armstrong in a timely manner on September 17.

Unfortunately, very little attention has been paid to the Confederate cavalry below the corps level of command. Of the four cavalry division leaders involved in the campaign only John Pegram has a biography. In the 1993 study, author Walter Griggs points out a number of earlier problems with Pegram's performance but is largely silent about the multiple mistakes he made during the

---

33 Edward G. Longacre, *A Soldier to the Last* (Washington DC: Potomac Books, 2007), pp. 109-10.

34 *Ibid.*, p. 111.

35 Edward G. Longacre, *Cavalry of the Heartland*, pp. 236-7.

Chickamauga Campaign.[36] According to Griggs, Pegram's cavalrymen were "ambushed" at Jay's Mill on September 19. Griggs fails to elaborate how cavalry tasked with picketing and protecting the army's right flank could be "ambushed."[37] Griggs follows the well-worn path of censuring Bragg without also noting the cavalry's contributions (or lack thereof) to Bragg's circumstances or failures. "General Bragg, who did not know how to capitalize on success," opines Griggs, "probably squandered the South's last real hope of victory in the West."[38] Bragg was responsible for much of what went wrong in the Army of Tennessee, but his failure of leadership does not absolve others from their share of the blame.

Frank Armstrong, William T. Martin, and John Austin Wharton have been all but ignored by history, as have all eight brigade commanders. Other than brief biographical essays or references in magazine articles, none of these men have received their due.

*   *   *

Despite grave difficulties, the South fielded a large mounted force that played a vital role in army operations in the Western Theater. As a percentage of army strength, Confederate cavalry in General Lee's Army of Northern Virginia comprised only ten to fifteen percent of its total force under arms during the 1862-1865 campaigns.[39] By contrast, even at Chickamauga with the Rebel cavalry weakened by detachments and his infantry strength nearly doubled by reinforcements, Bragg's cavalry comprised nineteen percent of his total force.[40] Prior to Tullahoma, fully one-third of the Army of Tennessee was mounted. Throughout both campaigns, the Confederate cavalry either equaled or

---

36 Griggs, *General John Pegram*, 75.

37 *Ibid.*, 81.

38 *Ibid.*, 83.

39 The zenith of this strength was probably Gettysburg. According to strength returns for June 30, 1863, General Lee had with him 12,358 troopers out of 79,880 total soldiers, or 17% of his total command. See David A. Martin and John Busey, *Regimental Strengths and Losses at Gettysburg* (Hightstown, NJ: Longstreet House Publishers, 1986), 129, 194. It is interesting to note that Lee's army had been heavily reinforced for the Gettysburg Campaign, while Bragg's army had lost divisions to Ohio and Mississippi.

40 Powell, "Numbers and Losses Study," CCNMP. Bragg's engaged cavalry totaled 13,423 out of 71,194 available troops of all arms, or 18.8% of his total command.

outnumbered their Federal foes. The usual excuse of overwhelming Union strength does not apply here. The reasons for the lackluster Confederate performance are found elsewhere: poor discipline, inadequate training, and a failure of leadership. Chickamauga was the Army of Tennessee's only clear-cut battlefield victory of the war, but it was also a hollow victory, in large part because of failure in the saddle.

$\mathbf{A}$ppendix 1

Confederate Cavalry Strength and Losses

Of all Confederate numbers, cavalry strength remains the most speculative. There are several reasons for this.

First, only a few reports were filed for the Chickamauga Campaign, and those by senior officers. Most were silent on numbers. Not a single Rebel cavalry regimental commander left a report. Those few reports that include Confederate numbers tend to mention detachments and not full unit strengths (which were almost always of greater strength). Unofficial documents such as letters and diaries flesh out a few unit totals, but these are not official calculations. Second, picket duty, courier work, and headquarter escorts complicate matters because these escorts drained a large number of mounted men away from the line units. Whenever possible I have accounted for these escorts separately, but not all of them were reported or even noted by the commands to which they were attached. The result is that it is impossible to track all these minor detachments and come up with accurate numbers for each of them. Finally, the command and organizational structure of the Army of Tennessee's cavalry was undergoing significant changes during the month leading up to the battle. This confusion is reflected in the handful of reports that exist. For these reasons and others, historians have consistently underestimated Rebel cavalry strength at Chickamauga.

Determining the strength of any given regiment or battalion is mostly a matter of educated guesswork, but there are some solid numbers available at the corps and divisional levels. Corps strength returns in the *Official Records* include reports dated July 31, August 10, and August 20, 1863. These three returns represent a determined effort by Braxton Bragg and his staff officers to finally get a coherent and accurate picture of the state of the army's mounted arm and provide very consistent numbers for the overall strength of Nathan Bedford Forrest's and Joseph Wheeler's commands for the month of August.

At the same time, even these reports can be misleading, especially those for Forrest's command. Prior to the arrival of John Pegram's Division from East Tennessee, Forrest's returns only report the strength of the two brigades and two artillery batteries that make up his division, not the additional influx of men added to his responsibilities with the formal creation of his cavalry corps at the beginning of September. A dispute between Bragg and Maj. Gen. Simon B. Buckner further complicated routine accounting matters. Buckner's Department of East Tennessee was subordinated to Bragg's army for tactical reasons, but Buckner continued to administer his department as a separate entity. This command structure quirk meant that Forrest had to report one-half his strength (his own division, now commanded by Frank Armstrong) to Bragg, and one-half of his strength (Pegram's Division) to Buckner.

All of this has confused early historians of the war. One of the first histories of Forrest and his command estimates that both of his mounted divisions numbered only "3,500 rank and file" during the battle of Chickamauga.[1] A number of historians have accepted this figure. In fact, as seen below, Forrest's own division alone was stronger than that, and the troops from East Tennessee under Pegram added another 4,000 or 5,000 men.

The following table shows a solid consistency in the strengths of the cavalry over the month leading up to the battle. The August numbers indicate a slight increase in strength over the July totals, about 5% across the board.

DATE	CAVALRY	ARTILLERY	TOTAL
	Officers / Men	Officers / Men	
Wheeler: 7/31/63	527 / 5,961	9 / 214	6,711

Forrest: 7/31/63	286 / 3,287	6 / 129	3,708
Wheeler: 8/10/63	539 / 6,356	10 / 238	7,143
Forrest: 8/10/63	292 / 3,410	8 / 132	3,842
Wheeler: 8/20/63	495 / 6,377	10 / 260	7,142
Forrest: 8/20/63	290 / 3,450	9 / 127	3,876[2]

EAST TENNESSEE STRENGTHS			
DATE	CAVALRY		TOTAL
	Officers	Men	
7/31/63	425	5,331	5,756
8/10/63	425	5,332	5,757[3]
8/31/63	405	4,825	5,205[4]

Not all of the East Tennessee cavalry units joined Forrest. According to the returns filed on July 31 there were nine regiments, six battalions, two squadrons, and two independent companies of cavalry in the department. Of those, eight regiments and two battalions (which were merged to form a new regiment) were sent to join Forrest. Of the roughly 137 companies comprising the cavalry in

2   OR 23, pt. 2, p. 941, details the strengths of the various units on July 31. See *ibid.*, p. 957 for August 10, and *ibid.*, pt. 4, p. 518 for August 20.

3   *Ibid.*, pt. 2, pp. 945 and 962.

4   Emerson Opdyke Papers, strength return for Pegram's Division, Ohio Historical Society. The date of this return and the classification of the cavalry as Pegram's Division suggest this figure represents only the cavalry that moved with Buckner to join Bragg. If so, the numbers seem high. Since the return does not provide a detailed listing of the composition of Pegram's Division at this time, we cannot know exactly who is and who is not counted in this return.

East Tennessee, 96 companies (70%) merged to form Pegram's Division.[5] Seventy percent of the reported strength for the department on August 10, 1863, is 4,029 officers and men in the units destined to make up the new division. This strength does not include the unit listed as Morgan's Detachment, the two battalions of stragglers and returned men from John H. Morgan's division lost in Ohio the month before. Morgan's Detachment was not organized until August 1, 1863, and not included in either strength report.

Adding these strengths provides a total of 15,287 officers and men available to Bragg just before the battle began, roughly 7,000 cavalrymen in Joe Wheeler's Corps and 8,000 in Forrest's Corps. These figures serve as my departure point for estimating regimental strengths (when unknown) and determining how accurate other reports might be. Admittedly, calculating this figure required some assumptions, but in the absence of more detailed information I believe the above figure is accurate for the middle of August 1863.

Tellingly, Union intelligence also believed it. On September 12, just one week before Chickamauga, a Rebel "Lt. Thomas" of the 3rd Kentucky Cavalry was taken prisoner. He told his captors that "they [Confederates] have their cavalry all concentrated, and about 15,000 of them." This prisoner, reported Maj. Gen. Alexander McCook, "appears to be sincere and honest."[6] The overall strength return for August 31, 1863, reflects 16,248 cavalry officers and men present for duty with the Army of Tennessee.[7] In a letter to Emerson Opdyke after the war, William Rosecrans provided a more conservative estimate of 13,000 cavalry in Wheeler's and Forrest's Corps at the time of the battle.[8]

---

5   See the organizational chart for Department of East Tennessee dated July 31, 1863, in OR 23, pt. 2, pp. 945-6, and compare it to the organization of Pegram's Division in *ibid.*, 30, pt. 2, pt. 20. The 5th and 7th North Carolina battalions, listed separately with six companies each in East Tennessee, were merged to form the new 6th North Carolina cavalry regiment with only 10 companies. The fate of the two remaining companies, if they still existed, is unknown.

6   See OR 30, pt. 3, p. 604. There are more than a dozen men with the last name of Thomas in this unit, and I have not been able to determine which one was captured.

7   See August 31, 1863, summary of strength, Opdyke Papers, Ohio Historical Society.

8   *Ibid.*

FORREST'S CAVALRY CORPS

(189 Companies / 6,553) [Losses: K/W/M = Total]

Companies/Strength

Escort: Jackson's Company[9]
1/67

Frank Armstrong's Division
95/3,486

Escort: Bradley's Company[10]
1/47

James Wheeler's Brigade
35/1,221

Escort: Company E, 6th Tennessee[11]
1/30

3rd Arkansas Cavalry[12]
10/300 [2/2/0=4]

---

9 OR 31, pt. 2, p. 646. Strength on November 7, 1863, at time of transfer to West Tennessee.

10 Richard P. Weinert Jr., *The Confederate Regular Army* (Shippensburg, PA, 1991), p. 38. In a footnote, Weinert cites the company muster roll for June 30, 1863, that shows one officer and 46 men present. In early November the company had 28 men.

11 Ten percent of the regimental strength.

12 OR 30, pt. 2, p. 73. On September 11, 1863, Armstrong reported that he was moving to Reed's Bridge with two regiments numbering 600 men. In the same message he detailed Col. Thomas G. Woodward of the 2nd Kentucky Cavalry to make a scout elsewhere. By process of elimination, the two regiments Armstrong took to Reed's Bridge were the 3rd Arkansas and the 6th Tennessee, with each assumed to have about 300 men. Losses discussed in Calvin L. Collier, *The War Child's Children: The Story of the Third Regiment, Arkansas Cavalry, Confederate States Army* (Pioneer Press, 1965), p. 67.

2nd Kentucky Cavalry[13]
9/427

6th Tennessee Cavalry[14]
9/300

18th TN Cavalry Battalion[15]
6/164

George Dibrell's Brigade[16]
59/2,218 [10/40/0=50, or 2%]

4th Tennessee Cavalry[17]
10/200 [2/16/0=18, or 9%]

8th Tennessee Cavalry[18]
11/300 [3/11/0=14, or 5%]

---

13 Companies A-I. Strength determined by subtracting the known strengths from the 3,740 officers and men reported for this division on August 20, 1863, and then dividing that number by the number of companies left unaccounted for, which provides an average of 47.4 men per company. Multiplying that number by the nine companies in the 2nd Kentucky rounds off to 427 men.

14 *OR* 30, pt. 2, p. 73. See note above for 3rd Arkansas Cavalry. Company E was detached as an escort for the brigade commander. *Tennesseans in the Civil War, Part 1: A Military History of the Confederate and Union Units with Available Rosters of Personnel* (Nashville, Tennessee, 1964), p. 66.

15 *OR* 31, pt. 2, p. 646. Companies A-F. Strength at time of transfer to West Tennessee, November 7, 1863.

16 Dibrell reported 94 officers and 944 men present for duty in January 1864, for a total of 1,038, *OR* 32, p. 2, p. 641, not including Shaw's Battalion or the two artillery batteries. Losses found in *Memphis Daily Appeal*, Friday, October 9, 1863, Brigade Adjutant's Report. No report for Shaw or the artillery.

17 *OR* 30, pt. 2, p. 527. Dibrell's report mentions being reinforced by Col. William S. McLemore and 200 men on August 17. It is not known if the 200 men represented the full regiment or just a portion of the 4th Tennessee Cavalry. Losses found in *Memphis Daily Appeal*, Friday, October 9, 1863, Brigade Adjutant's Report.

18 *Ibid.* The company rolls, NARA, show Companies A-L. L Company assigned on August 1, 1863. Nine companies report 505 officers and men present, mostly June 30 rolls and one from August 31. Company average was 56 men, giving 112 men added back in for the two missing companies, plus five for field and staff, or a total of 622. This strength is speculative, but the overall strength of Forrest's cavalry division on August 10 was slightly stronger than in June

9th Tennessee Cavalry[19]
10/350 [0/8/0=8, or 2%]

10th Tennessee Cavalry[20]
10/474 [3/3/0=6, or 1%]

11th Tennessee Cavalry[21]
10/474 [2/2/0=4, or 1%]

Shaw's Battalion[22]
6/284

Huggins Battery (4 guns): 6-lb. (2) and 12-lb. howitzers (2)[23]
1/65

before the Tullahoma retreat, indicating fairly consistent strengths for this period. Dibrell reported that he had "not over 300 men present" on August 9, 1863, in a skirmish at Sparta, Tennessee. However, Dibrell also mentions sending out many scouts over a wide area and it is unclear how much of the regiment was detached. *OR* 23 pt. 1, p. 848. In his dispatch dated August 18, Dibrell reported that more than one-half the regiment was absent gathering supplies, which would reconcile with the 622 men shown on the rolls. Finally, many Union reports give the impression that several hundred Confederates where foraging all over White County, Tennessee. I have decided that while the 622 figure is likely accurate for how many were with the regiment at this time, no more than one-half were available for combat duties. Losses found in *Memphis Daily Appeal*, Friday, October 9, 1863, Brigade Adjutant's Report.

19 *Ibid.*, 31, pt. 1, p. 550. Dibrell estimates Col. Jacob B. Biffle's 9th Tennessee regiment at 350 strong on November 5, 1863. Losses found in *Memphis Daily Appeal*, Friday, October 9, 1863, Brigade Adjutant's Report.

20 See note for 2nd Kentucky above; 47.4 men per company x 10 companies. Losses found in *Memphis Daily Appeal*, Friday, October 9, 1863, Brigade Adjutant's Report.

21 Companies B-L. Company A transferred to Maj. Charles McDonald's 18th Tennessee Battalion on May 1, 1863. For strength, see note for 2nd Kentucky above. Losses found in *Memphis Daily Appeal*, Friday, October 9, 1863, Brigade Adjutant's Report.

22 The brigade return in *OR* 30 pt. 2, p. 20 shows this unit comprised of Majs. Joseph Shaw's and O. P. Hamilton's battalions, consolidated, along with Allison's Squadron. *OR Supplement*, serial 78, pp. 292-5 shows Allison's Squadron with three companies, A-C., pp. 315-9 indicate that Shaw's and Hamilton's command was the same unit commanded in secession by Hamilton and then Shaw, and likely had three companies (only the muster roll for one company, C, is shown). For strength, see note for 2nd Kentucky above.

23 *Ibid.*, 30, pt. 4, p. 518. The total strength of the two batteries in Forrest's Division was 136 officers and men. When Morton transferred in November, his strength was listed as 71 officers and men. If we subtract that strength from the 136, we are left with 65 for Huggins' Battery.

Morton's Battery (4 guns): 3-in. Rifles (2) and 12-lb. Howitzers (2)[24]
1/71

John Pegram's Division[25]
(93/3,000)

Davidson's Brigade[26]
(55/1,900)

1st Georgia Cavalry[27]
10/295

Admittedly, Morton's strength is from November, well after the battle and the August 20 report, but it represents a known quantity of men serving with Morton at that time. Any alternative estimate is likely as speculative. Dividing the August 20 strength in half, for example, produces a strength of 68 officers and men for each battery, a difference of three men in each unit. Alternatively, Huggins reports 91 total (five officers and 86 men) present for duty in January 1864. *OR* 32, pt. 2, p. 641. Equipment as of November, 1862. *Ibid.*, 20, pt. 2, p. 399.

24 *Ibid.*, 31, pt. 2, p. 646. Strength at time of transfer to West Tennessee, November 7, 1863. Equipment is as described in Morton's memoir, Morton, *The Artillery of Nathan Bedford Forrest's Cavalry*, pp. 176-7. According to a report from May 1864 in *OR* 31, pt. 2, p. 624, Morton had four 3-inch rifles. Morton, however, claims his battery did not have four rifles until two more were captured at Brice's Crossroads in June 1864 and exchanged on the spot for his two brass 12-pound howitzers.

25 A report for August 31, 1863, in the Emerson Opdyke Papers shows 405 officers and 4,825 men present for duty in Pegram's Division, for a total of 5,230. Desertion, attrition, and the exact organization of Pegram's Division at this time make it difficult to tell if that figure reflects only the troops who accompanied Buckner to join Bragg. Regarding losses: Pegram mentioned only that Henry Davidson lost "about one fourth" of his men. *OR* 30, pt. 2, p. 529. The regimental numbers that follow probably underestimate his actual strength.

26 J. W. Minnich of the 6th Georgia Cavalry estimates the brigade as 1,600 or 1,650 strong on the morning of September 19, 1863. It is unclear if this includes the 10th Confederate, nominally part of Col. John Scott's Brigade but serving with Brig. Gen. Henry B. Davidson during the battle. Because the 10th Confederate was not a regular part of the brigade, I suspect it is not included in Minnich's estimate. He was familiar with his unit's own strength on an ongoing basis. I have also estimated Huwald's Battery at 50 men, assuming that Minnich's 1,650 estimate included the battery. Overall, I think this number is likely a minimum rather than a maximum, and using other estimates described below, Davidson's Brigade could have numbered closer to 2,500 men than 1,600.

27 Strength derived by subtracting the known strengths of the other regiments in the brigade and calculating a company average strength for this regiment and Col. E. W. Rucker's men. On October 19, Col. J. J. Morrison reported that his 1st Georgia regiment, plus the 6th Georgia and 3rd Confederate, numbered 1,800 men, or 600 men per unit. Hence, this figure might well be low or not reflect scouting detachments, etc. See note for 3rd Confederate, below.

6th Georgia Cavalry[28]
11/400 [12/72/0?=84]

6th North Carolina Cavalry[29]
10/520 [5/6/18=28]

10th Confederate Cavalry[30]
10/250 [2/11/0=13]

Rucker's Legion[31]
13/385 [37 total losses]

---

28 This is at best an educated guess. Davidson's Brigade reportedly lost about one-quarter of its strength in the battle. J. W. Minnich, in a letter found in the CCNMP 6th Georgia file, reports that regiment's losses at 84 killed and wounded, with no missing specified. A crude estimate of overall losses might be 100, and if we apply the brigade loss ratio of 25% we get a ballpark strength for the regiment of 400 men. As noted above, on October 19, Col. Morrision reported this regiment, plus the 1st Georgia and 3rd Confederate, at 1,800 men, or 600 men per unit, so estimating 400 men here seems a reasonable conclusion. See note for 3rd Confederate, below. The losses stated include light casualties suffered on September 21, 1863.

29 The consolidated 5th and 7th battalions, North Carolina cavalry, numbered 27 officers and 493 men following the consolidation on August 3, 1863. This figure is drawn from the memoirs of Capt. Martin V. Moore.   http://members.aol.com/jweaver301/nc/6nccavhi.htm. For losses, see Jeffrey C. Weaver, *The 5th and 7th Battalions North Carolina Cavalry and the 6th North Carolina Cavalry (65th North Carolina State Troops)* (Lynchburg, VA: H. E. Howard), p. 133. This list is clearly incomplete, and speculative.

30 Strength given as of June 9, 1863, *Macon Daily Telegraph*, June 23, 1863, regimental file, Chickamauga-Chattanooga National Military Park. For losses, see *Columbus Sun*, September 29, 1863.

31 Rucker's 1st East Tennessee Legion was a field organization created by consolidating the 12th and 16th Tennessee cavalry battalions. The 12th had seven companies (A-G) and the 16th had six companies (A-F). Strength is derived by subtracting the known strengths of the other regiments from the brigade total, and then determining a company average. In January 1864, Rucker's Legion reported 19 officers and 171 men present for duty for a total of 190, but this was after hard service and the loss of many horses during the East Tennessee campaign. As a result, a figure about double that seems fairly reasonable for Chickamauga. See OR 32, pt. 2, p. 641. In a postwar 1867 account, Leroy Moncure Nutt estimates the strength at "about 300" in each battalion, which would give Rucker a strength close to 600. Note how this number compares to the estimates of the 1st Georgia, 6th Georgia, and 3rd Confederate regiments, above—all also estimated at 600 strong on October 19, 1863. For losses, see Leroy Moncure Nutt Papers, Southern Historical Collection, University of North Carolina, Chapel Hill, NC. The figure is only given as "37 Killed and wounded." No missing are cited.

Huwald's Battery (4 guns): 12-lb. Mtn. Howitzer (2) and Mtn. Rifle (2)[32]
1/50

Col. John S. Scott's Brigade[33]
38/1,100 [20/80/0=100]

Morgan's Detachment[34]
10/240 [3/7/0=10]

1st Louisiana Cavalry[35]
7/210 [10/42/0=52]

32 Huwald's Battery was armed with two mountain howitzers, and two mountain rifles, which was a 2.56-inch rifle scaled down from a 3-inch piece and mounted on a similar carriage to a mountain howitzer.

33 Colonel Scott's report of the battle claims his strength was 500 men for the entire brigade, including Morgan's remnants. However, Scott also mentions that heavy detachments for patrols and pickets were not counted in this total. Moreover, the brigade's strength reported at the beginning of the month was much higher. If the 500 figure is accurate, then Scott's command suffered catastrophic desertion and straggling in the three weeks between the August 31 muster and the time of the battle, something that is not reflected in the personal narratives and regimental accounts I have seen. By way of contrast, an article in the *Charleston Mercury* dated Saturday, October 10, 1863, states the total for just the 1st Louisiana and 2nd and 6th Tennessee as 590 men, without indicating if this figure includes officers. If we use the newspaper figure, we get a total of some 900 men, or 990 if officers are added. I settled on 1,100 to reflect scouts, detachments, and officers not reported, assuming the figures we have reflect "effectives."

34 In July 1863, a division of Kentucky cavalry under John Hunt Morgan raided deep into Federal territory. Morgan crossed the Ohio River and most of his men were captured. On August 1, 1863, two battalions were formed from the survivors of that raid and detached men left behind. The 1st Battalion had six companies, the 2nd Battalion had four. See *OR Supplement*, Serial 35, pp. 24-5, 52-3. It is unclear whether the two battalions served as a single unit or as individual battalions because the army organization lists only Morgan's "detachment" as serving in Scott's Brigade. In his report, Forrest notes only that these battalions had "about" 240 men. The 1st Kentucky Cavalry shows one man killed at Chickamauga. Since the only portion of the 1st Kentucky present at that battle was in Morgan's detachment, that loss is incorporated here.

35 Company A detached and escorting James Longstreet. Companies E/C detached and escorting John B. Hood's Corps, Army of Northern Virginia. Scott reported the brigade as having 900 men on August 7, 1863, or an average of 300 men per regiment. He lost heavily to straggling on his Kentucky raid in July and early August. *OR* 23, pt. 1, p. 841. Howell Carter, *A Cavalryman's Reminiscences of the Civil War* (New Orleans, LA: The American Publishing Co. 1900). p. 92.

2nd Tennessee Cavalry[36]
10/300 [5/14/0=19]

5th Tennessee Cavalry[37]
10/300 [2/14/0=16]

Robinson's Battery (3 guns): Mtn Howitzer (2) and 3-inch Rifle (2)[38]
1/50[39] [0/3/0=3]

Joseph Wheeler's Corps[40]
(153/6,870)

John Wharton's Division
(94/4,439)

Escort: Company B, 8th Texas Cavalry[41]
1/41

Col. J. J. Crew's Brigade[42]
42/2,125

36 See note above for 1st Louisiana.

37 *Ibid.*

38 Based on relative size of other horse batteries equipped with mountain howitzers. Lieutenant Winslow Robinson's Battery was merged with Wiggins' Battery (under Lt. J. P. Bryant) in October and disappeared from the rolls.

39 *OR* 30, pt. 2, p. 531.

40 As can be seen, reported losses among Wheeler's Corps are few. This dearth of numbers at even the divisional or brigade level makes it impossible to even guess at overall losses in the corps, but it should run to several hundred.

41 Ten percent of the regimental strength given below.

42 Colonel J. J. Crews reported 63 officers and 730 men present for duty for a total of 793 in January 1864. *OR* 32, pt. 2, p. 641. However, this figure includes the 1st and 6th Georgia Cavalry regiments, which were attached after the battle ended.

Malone's Regiment[43]
12/502

2nd Georgia Cavalry[44]
9/600

3rd Georgia Cavalry[45]
10/418

4th Georgia Cavalry[46]
10/605

Col. Thomas Harrison's Brigade[47]
(51/2,273)

3rd Confederate Cavalry[48]
10/550

43 Also known as the 7th/9th Alabama Cavalry. If we subtract the strengths of known regiments from the August 20, 1863, report of the cavalry corps and divide it by the number of companies in the unknown regiments, we get an average of 48.8 men per company.

44 Jim R. Cabaniss, ed., *The Civil War Journal and Letters of Washington Ives* (Tallahassee, Florida, 1987), p. 42. Company G serving as an escort to Ben Cheatham's Division, Polk's Corps.

45 See note for Col. J. C. Malone's regiment, above.

46 Strength given as of August 31, 1863. On September 10, a deserter from the 4th Georgia Cavalry told the Federals that this regiment numbered 300 men. NARA, RG 94, Army of the Cumberland, Summary of Intelligence Received. The 4th Georgia Cavalry reported four killed, 13 wounded, 46 captured, and 17 missing for 80 men total. This includes both the Chickamauga Campaign and Wheeler's October Raid into Middle Tennessee. The vast majority of these losses were suffered in Tennessee. Probably no more than 15-20 were lost at Chickamauga.

47 Colonel Thomas Harrison reported 73 officers and 642 men present for duty (total 715) for January 1864. *OR* 32, pt. 2, p. 641. However, this number includes only the 3rd Confederate and the 8th and 11th Texas regiments because the other units were not in the brigade at this time. The same force here numbers 1,360.

48 Strength given in a Union report via local intelligence gathered by a civilian. Certainly this is not the most reliable way to calculate strength, but the number is not unreasonable. Further, on October 19, 1863, Col. J. J. Morrison reported taking three regiments on a mission across the Hiwassee River (the 1st and 6th Georgia and the 3rd Confederate). On the 19th Morrison reported his strength as 1,800 men, or roughly 600 men per regiment. *OR* 31, pt. 1, p. 14. On November 20 Col. H. B. Lyon reported the 3rd Confederate had 260 effective men (286 officers and men). *OR* 31, pt. 3, p. 722. All Confederate reports, including Morrison's, report

3rd Kentucky Cavalry[49]
10/418

4th Tennessee Cavalry[50]
10/418 [about 40 from all causes]

8th Texas Cavalry[51]
10/412

11th Texas Cavalry[52]
10/398

White's Battery (4 guns): 6-lb. (4)[53]
1/77

---

dramatic straggling and desertion. Morrison's report, for example, reports 1,800 men at the start of his week-long expedition, and just 1,000 at the end of it for a nearly 50% loss. His recorded combat losses were just 14 killed and 82 wounded. This leaves something on the order of 700 men unaccounted for, more than 1/3 of his command.

49 See note for Malone's regiment, above.

50 *Ibid.* For losses, see George B. Guild Scrapbook, 4th Tennessee Report, TSLA.

51 Bryan S. Bush, *Terry's Texas Rangers: The Eighth Texas Cavalry* (Turner Publishing, Paducah, Kentucky, 2002), p. 100. Bush's source cites the strength for the "closing days of August." Company A, Companies C-L, Company B detached on escort duty, above. At the end of the year, Company Rolls, NARA, six companies reported their strength at 168 men as of December 31, 1863. This means average company strength was just 28 men, with 112 men added in for the four non-reporting companies. Adding five more for field and staff yields a total of 285. This strength is likely much too low given the active operations undertaken in October and November during which all the cavalry suffered heavy attrition, not to mention unreported losses in various engagements.

52 Strength derived by comparing the strength for the 8th Texas at the end of August (412) to the known strength on December 31 (285.) That ratio was then applied to the known strength of the ten companies plus field and staff reporting, all for December 31, 1863, for a total of 277. Company Rolls, NARA. Assuming a similar ratio of strength gain and loss, the 277 figure was multiplied by 1.44 to produce an estimated strength for the end of August for the 11th Texas.

53 Three officers and 74 men present for duty in January 1864. While well removed from the battle, this remains the closest hard number I have found for this battery. The Union provost's report on Bragg's order of battle, *OR* 30, pt. 1, p. 232, assembled from prisoner interrogations, lists White's Battery as having six guns. However, the January 31, 1864, report cited above reflects only four guns present. Bush, *Terry's Texas Rangers*, p. 104, lists the armament.

Brig. Gen. William T. Martin's Division[54]
(59/2,431)

Escort: Company A, 3rd Alabama Cavalry[55]
1/34

Col. John T. Morgan's Brigade
(37/1,533)

1st Alabama Cavalry[56]
10/418

3rd Alabama Cavalry[57]
7/279

51st Alabama Cavalry[58]
10/418

8th Confederate Cavalry[59]
10/418

54 Wheeler's report lists Martin's strength as "about 1200 men" but makes reference to at least two regiments that are detached and apparently not reflected in that number. Later in the same report Wheeler mentions that he did not count men who were screening or guarding flanks as part of his effective total. As a result, Wheeler's report is useless for determining actual strength available at the time of the battle. OR 30, pt. 2, pp. 519-22.

55 RG 109, Entry 18, Part 101, Alabama Box 3. Company A reported the same number present on both June and December 1863.

56 See note for Malone's regiment, above.

57 RG 109, Entry 18, Part 101, Alabama Box 3. Six companies reported 235 men present on June 30, 1863, 39 men added in as average strength for Company C (not reported), and five added for field and staff. Companies B-H present. A Company serving as escort to General Martin, Company I (Lenoir) was serving as escort to Maj. Gen. Thomas Hindman. Company K (Halloway) was serving as escort to General Bragg. OR 30, pt. 4, p. 585 indicates that a "detachment" of this command numbered 250 men.

58 See note for Malone's regiment, above.

59 See note for Malone's regiment, above.

Col. A. A. Russell's Brigade[60]
(21/864)

4th Alabama Cavalry[61]
10/418

1st Confederate Cavalry[62]
10/418

Wiggins Battery (2 guns): 2 12-lb. Howitzers[63]
1/28

60 Colonel A. A. Russell reported 65 officers and 724 men present for duty in January 1864 for a total of 789. This figure includes the 1st, 3rd, 51st, and Malone's regiments, Alabama Cavalry, as well as the units shown here.

61 See note for Malone's regiment, above.

62 *Ibid.*

63 This is a figure from January 1864. In June, Captain Wiggins and one section numbering 30 men were captured at Shelbyville. This represented one-half the battery. A year later in 1864, after a number of cavalry transfers, the strength of the battery was listed as 45—30 in one section and 15 in the other. See *OR Supplement*, vol. 14, p. 266. The equipment is an either-or situation. Sometime in April or May the battery received two 12-pound howitzers in place of two of its current complement of four 6-lb. guns. Hence, by June, one section had 6-pounders and one section had the howitzers. When Wiggins and his section were captured, nothing indicates the armament of the guns taken. In his report of his October raid, however, Joe Wheeler wrote that two guns of Wiggins Battery had to be abandoned, and noted that these were howitzers. From this report, it is reasonable to assume that these guns were present at Chickamauga. *OR* 30, pt. 2, p. 725.

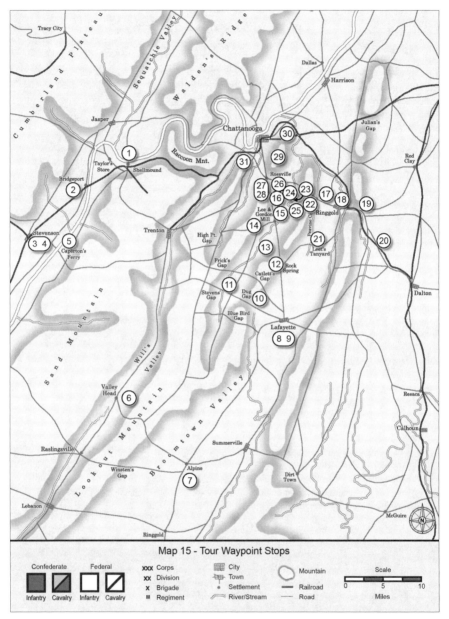

Map 15 - Tour Waypoint Stops

This map outlines the waypoint locations of the various tour stops as they correspond to one another. Note that this map shows the period (1863) road network, and not the modern roads you will be driving. There are 29 different tour stops, and 31 waypoint locations.

A ppendix 2

The Chickamauga Campaign:
A Cavalry Driving Tour

T he geographic area embraced in the narrative includes parts of three states: Alabama, Georgia, and Tennessee. The two armies fought across this broad region in dozens of clashes large and small as each side maneuvered for advantage. This tour has been broken down into three sections to better allow you to explore all or just part of the campaign. Note that most of these sites are not clearly marked and on private property. However, if you follow this tour route, you will always be directed to park on public property or at appropriate set-asides. Please be respectful of all private property, drive carefully, and behave accordingly. In order to simplify the route and reduce driving time, this tour is not sequential. Many of the places you will visit hosted events that took place simultaneously in 1863, some as much as fifty miles apart. As a result, it was not feasible to organize the tour in rigid chronological order.

The first leg of the tour begins just west of Chattanooga at Exit 161 on I-24. (The second and third legs begin at the Visitor's Center of the Chickamauga National Battlefield Park.) The first leg is also the longest part of the tour, and will take most of a day to complete. The second and third legs require about four hours each to complete.

In addition to these driving directions, significant stops or especially hard-to-find locations have been assigned a GPS coordinate waypoint (WP). These waypoints can be pre-programmed into a GPS navigator to facilitate navigation and verify locations. A list of waypoints and their GPS coordinates is provided at the end of this chapter, for ease of programming.

FIRST LEG: STOPS 1 - 13

Stop 1: Shellmound Station/Nickajack Cave
(WP1: Shellmound: 34*59.650 N, 085*36.843 W)

This is the entrance to Nickajack cave, now half-submerged.

Drive on Interstate 24 either east from Nashville or west from Chattanooga. Take Exit 161 and turn west toward New Hope (at the bottom of the ramp) onto Tennessee State Route 156 West. On your right you will see Nickajack Lake. Before the Tennessee Valley Authority (TVA) completed the Nickajack Dam in 1967 (that created the lake), the Tennessee River was much narrower. This was the approximate site of Rankin's Ferry. We are now heading for the site of the Union crossing at Shellmound Station.

Drive 4.5 miles on SR 156 until you reach a shallow cove on your left. The main body of Nickajack Lake is on your right. Directly ahead in the opposite cliff across the cove is the entrance to Nickajack Cave, which today is partially underwater. If you wish to stop, drive .5 miles across the cove and turn left into the Maple View Recreation Area. From there, you can take the short .2 mile trail to the cave entrance and a viewing platform. The recreation area has restrooms and there is a small parking fee. Hours are limited and the area may not be open at all times.

This was the original site of Shellmound Station. On the night of September 2, 1863, Union troops from George P. Buell's First Brigade, Thomas J. Wood's First Division, Thomas Crittenden's XXI Corps, crossed the river on flatboats and landed here. Other elements of the XXI Corps followed, and Wood's division camped here until September 5. Nickajack Cave was an irresistible attraction to the soldiers, many of whom explored its interior. It was not submerged in 1863, and so easily accessible. "There are a great many of our men exploring the saltpeter cave which is quite a curiosity," Lt. Samuel Platt of the 26th Ohio wrote in his diary. "It is said to be thirteen miles in extent. Three soldiers are said to be lost in it since yesterday."[1]

Stop 2: Bridgeport
(WP 2: Bridgeport: 34°56.916 N, 085°42.672 W)

Resume your journey by turning left out of the parking area back onto SR 156 West. Continue 5.3 miles and cross the Tennessee River at South Pittsburg until you reach US Highway Route 72. Turn left and drive south toward Bridgeport. Behind you (north) is the crossing site at Battle Creek, where other troops of the XXI and XIV corps crossed. It is not easily accessible by car and we will not be visiting that site.

After you cross the state line into Alabama, travel one mile farther and exit US 72 at Alabama State Route 277, and turn left to Bridgeport. Go 1.7 miles and turn left onto 7th Street, following the sign toward downtown. Stay on 7th Street until you come to Alabama Avenue and turn left. Follow Alabama Avenue east for several blocks and bear to the left at the first fork. Once you are

---

1 Entry for September 4, 1863, Samuel Platt Diary, Mahoning Valley Historical Society Collections, Youngstown, Ohio.

The Bridgeport train depot.

through that intersection you will see the sign "Historic Battery Hill" to your front and a parking lot with an old train depot to your right. The train depot is now the Bridgeport Area Historical Association. (As of this writing, the association is open Monday, Thursday, Friday and Saturday, 9:00 a.m. to 1:00 p.m. CST, and Sunday, 1:00 p.m. to 5:00 p.m. CST.)

The historical association is the closest public property to the site of the actual crossing at Bridgeport. The railroad tracks belong to the CSX Rail Corporation and follow the historic trace of the wartime railroad. A few hundred yards to the east is the Tennessee River, which is where the actual crossing took place. Note that the crossing site is in private hands and trespassers and relic hunters are not welcomed. The association has some displays and information on wartime Bridgeport.

On September 2, 1863, Maj. Gen. Philip Sheridan's Third Division, McCook's XX Corps, crossed the Tennessee River at this site in support of the construction of a pontoon bridge here. Three days earlier, Jefferson Davis' First Division crossed downstream at Stevenson, which made it possible for Sheridan to cross without opposition. Bridgeport was the XX Corps' main crossing site, with Sheridan's men escorting the corps supply trains across the river over the next two days.

Stop 3: Stevenson Depot
(WP 3: Stephenson Depot: 34*52.086 N, 085*50.398 W)

The Stevenson train depot.

After leaving Bridgeport, drive back out to Alabama SR 277, turn right, and return to US 72. At US 72 follow the signs to enter US 72 southbound toward Stevenson, Alabama. Once on US 72, drive 9.6 miles south to Alabama State Route 117. Turn right onto SR 117and drive north to Stevenson. Once in town, immediately after you cross the railroad tracks, SR 117 turns to the left and becomes Main Street. Turn left, drive one block, and park in front of the Stevenson Depot Museum.

This building was built in 1872 on the ruins of the Civil War-era depot. In August 1863, Stevenson was the major forward depot for Rosecrans' next offensive move across the Tennessee River. Massive supply dumps were established alongside the tracks to hold the needed rations, ammunition, and forage the army required. On August 18, Rosecrans arrived and established his headquarters at a home outside town called "The Little Brick." Most of the Union XX Corps occupied this area about this time, establishing camps along Crow Creek out of sight of Rebel observers on the distant south bank of the Tennessee River. An 1862 Union earthwork was improved and expanded to protect the depot. Later named Fort Harker (after Union Brig. Gen. Charles G. Harker, who would be killed in the Atlanta Campaign the following year), this earthwork became a major Union installation protecting the vital rail line back to Nashville.

Because of its lengthy occupation by Federal troops, Stevenson also became a focal point for Southern Unionists. Pro-Federal refugees flocked here and several companies of the Union 1st Alabama Cavalry regiment were raised here. These men were useful to Rosecrans as scouts for his later operations, as local garrison forces suppressing Confederate guerrillas, and as home guards in northern Alabama. The Depot Museum has displays on local history, including railroads and the Civil War. It is open Monday through Friday, from 8:00 a.m. until 4:00 p.m.

To Reach Fort Harker:

Fort Harker

Leave the depot and drive back east on SR 117 toward US 72. After you cross the railroad tracks you will come to a stoplight. Turn right. The next right you will reach is a gravel road and a small white sign pointing toward Fort Harker. Turn right here as well. The next right is another gravel lane. You will see another small white sign pointing to Fort Harker. Turn right here and drive to the end of the lane. The large earthwork that is Fort Harker is visible just behind the small parking area.

To Rosecrans' Headquarters
(WP 4: The Little Brick: 34*52.418 N, 085*50.148 W)

Site of General William Rosecrans' headquarters at Stevenson, Alabama.

Retrace your route back toward the Stevenson Depot Museum. After you cross the railroad tracks, however, turn right on East Main Street. Drive one block and turn left. This street does not have a visible street sign but it is the next left turn. (As of this writing, a faded sign reading "Ideal Beauty Salon" adorns the storefront on the corner.) Drive one block and turn right onto Adelaide Street. Drive one more block and turn left onto Water Street, and drive another block and turn right onto College Street. You will pass the

Presbyterian Church. Drive one more block and turn left onto Myrtle Place, which makes a ninety-degree turn to the right. You will see the historical marker and ruins for Rosecrans Headquarters called "The Little Brick" on your left.

Stop 4: Caperton's Ferry
(WP 5: Caperton Ferry: 34*50.130 N, 085*48.229 W)

This was the site of Caperton's Ferry Landing in 1863.

Exit Stevenson on SR 117 and drive back toward US 72. After you cross US 72, drive 1.8 miles to the public boat landing on your left. Turn in and park. You are now at the approximate crossing site of Caperton's Ferry. On the night of August 28, 1863, Col. Hans Heg's 3rd Brigade, Brig. Gen. Jefferson C. Davis' First Division, McCook's XX Corps, broke camp on Big Crow Creek and marched to this spot. At daylight on the 29th, Heg's men crossed the river in pontoon boats to secure the crossing and allow Union pioneers to erect a pontoon bridge on this site. Union artillery was hauled down to the river bank and hidden in the foliage to cover the crossing. This precaution proved unnecessary because Heg's men crossed without opposition and surprised only a few Rebel cavalrymen eating breakfast.[2]

From this site you should be able to see Sand Mountain across the river in the distance. Sand Mountain rises abruptly less than a mile from the south bank of the river. Rebels atop the mountain could observe Federal activities from that point. This is why Heg's Brigade did not stop for long on the far bank. Instead, they marched inland and by 10:00 a.m., reached the top of the mountain, where they established a defensive perimeter.

Stop 5: Valley Head
(WP 6: Valley Head: 34*34.138 N, 085*36.932 W)

Valley Head: Winston Place, the site of Union
Maj. Gen. Jefferson C. Davis' headquarters.

---

2 *Military History of Kansas Regiments*, Adjutant General of the State of Kansas (Topeka: Kansas State Printing Co., 1896), p. 121.

Drive back to SR 117, turn left, and take the bridge across the Tennessee River. Once across the river, the road curves to the left and ascends the western face of Sand Mountain. As you drive up, note the views of the Union side of the river that amply illustrate the importance of this terrain. You will be following SR 117 for 26 miles until you reach Winston Springs in the town of Valley Head, Alabama. Note that SR 117 joins with other roads from time to time, so be sure to read the signs carefully.

As you descend the east side of Sand Mountain you enter Wills Valley. This valley was important to the Federals because, unlike the sparsely settled crest of Sand Mountain, it contained good water and forage for the army. Shortly after you enter Wills Valley you will cross over Interstate 59 and reach US Highway 11. SR 117 turns left at US 11. For the next .2 miles, SR 117 and US 11 are the same road, until SR 117 leaves US 11 on the right. Drive about .2 miles and turn to the right, leaving US 11. Make sure you follow the signs and stay on SR 117.

After you leave US 11, continue on SR 117 for 1.5 miles. After you enter the town of Mentone, turn left on Anderson Street and cross the railroad tracks, following the signs to Winston Place Bed and Breakfast. When it is safe to do so, pull over and stop the car. You are now at Winston Springs. The mansion you see is Winston Place. The spring flows in a stone-lined channel through the middle of the historic downtown area behind you. At the time of the war this place was called Valley Head, but is now Mentone, Alabama.

Built in 1835, this plantation was the focal point of Union activity from September 5 to 12, 1863. The house served as headquarters for Brig. Gen. Jefferson C. Davis' division (XX Corps). The troops of his three brigades camped in the fields nearby. General Davis and his wife stayed in the house. The ample spring supplied water for the XX Corps, four brigades of Union cavalry, and the livestock for all these commands. Davis issued orders prohibiting looting on the property because the owner, Colonel Winston, voted against secession in the convention in 1860 and was considered a Unionist—even though both his sons were serving in the Confederate army.

Stop 6: Alpine
(WP 7: Alpine: 34*27.691 N, 085*29036 W)

Alpine Church—all that remains of the small community of Alpine.

Depart Winston Place and drive back to Alabama SR 117; turn left and head south. Shortly thereafter SR 117 begins climbing the west face of Lookout Mountain. As you ascend, on your left you will see Wills Valley below you. At the top of Lookout Mountain, SR 117 turns to the right and you will pass through the modern portion of Mentone, Alabama. Union troops followed this road as they crossed Lookout Mountain and headed toward Alpine.

Leave Mentone. You will cross into Georgia after driving 5.7 miles, where Alabama State Route 117 becomes Georgia State Route 48. Drive another 4.6 miles and you will pass through the small community of Cloudland. Thereafter, SR 48 begins to descend Lookout Mountain on the way to Menlo, Georgia.

The gap through which you are now driving is called Lawrence Gulf. Rebel cavalry contested its passage on September 9. It was one of those passes barricaded by Wharton's men and considered by Joe Wheeler to be impassible to Union troops. The Union 1st Ohio Cavalry fought the Confederate 4th Georgia and 8th Texas Cavalry at the foot of this gap. Take note of the rugged terrain. The historic road ran more directly down the gap to the foot of the mountain, cutting a much steeper descent to the valley floor.

Once down the mountain, SR 48 takes you directly into the small town of Menlo, Georgia. At the stop sign is the intersection of SR 48 and Georgia SR 337. Turn right and head south on SR 337. Travel 1.7 miles from the stop sign until you see a white church on your left. This is the Alpine Presbyterian Church. There is a historical marker in front of the church entitled "The Last Indian Agent," but it does not relate to the Civil War.

Alpine was the headquarters of McCook's XX Corps and Stanley's Cavalry Corps. It represents the deepest penetration into Confederate Georgia by Union troops during the Chickamauga Campaign. Nearly 30,000 Federals camped here in mid-September. From here, Stanley sent Union cavalry north toward Lafayette in order to find both Bragg's Army of Tennessee and George Thomas' XIV Corps, only to be thwarted by Rebel troops closer to Lafayette.

Stop 7: Lafayette, Georgia
(WP 8: Mount Carmel Lane Skirmish: 34*39.836 N, 085*18.788 W
WP 9: Lafayette: 34*42.508 N, 085*16.824 W)

Return north on GA SR 337. When you reach Menlo, you will return to the stop sign at SR 48. Reset your odometer at this point. Do not turn. Instead, continue on Georgia SR 337. You are now heading north through Broomtown Valley and following one of the routes George Crook's Union cavalry rode toward Lafayette on September 13, 1863.[3] Travel 13.7 miles on SR 337 until you pass a small side street on your right called Homer Cagle Road. Travel another .7 miles until you reach the next side street to the right called Mount Carmel Lane. (No tour photo included.) Turn right onto Mount Carmel Lane and, when you can do so safely, pull over. (WP 8: Mount Carmel Lane Skirmish: 34*39.836 N, 085*18.788 W)

In this area (about four miles south of the city of Lafayette) the Union cavalry skirmished with the Confederate infantry of Brig. Gen. Daniel Adams Brigade, John Breckinridge's Division, Daniel H. Hill's Corps. The 9th

---

3   For the other route to Lafayette, take SR 48 east to Summerville, where you will intersect with US Highway 27. Turn left on US 27 and drive to Lafayette. Union cavalry left this route on the night of September 13 because of the stiff resistance mounted by John Wharton's Confederate troopers.

Gordon Hall and Bragg's headquarters marker.

Pennsylvania Cavalry charged up this road and captured enough of Adams' Louisiana infantry to convince Crook that Lafayette was strongly defended. Adams' men were deployed astride SR 337 facing south with the rest of Breckinridge's Division to the east. Nothing remains to mark this skirmish, and this is only an approximate location based on distances reported by the participants.

Continue north on SR 337 until you reach US 27. Turn left and drive one mile until you see the sign for Business US 27. Turn left on US 27 and head north. Just after you pass the old town square, turn right when you reach Wardlaw Street. Look for the sign that marks Joe Stock Memorial Park on the northeast corner of Business US 27 and Wardlaw. In the middle of the park is an older two-story red brick building. This is John B. Gordon Hall. Turn left into the parking lot behind Gordon Hall. This is WP 9: Lafayette: 34*42.508 N, 085*16.824 W.

Gordon Hall was built in 1836 and was a well known local school in ante-bellum North Georgia. At the time of the war it was called the Chattooga Academy, but in 1936 it was renamed after its most famous pupil, Confederate Maj. Gen. John B. Gordon. Gordon served under Gen. Robert E. Lee in

Virginia as a brigade, division, and corps commander, and enjoyed a postwar career as U.S. senator and the governor of Georgia. (Gordon did not have a connection with Chickamauga.) The school served as General Bragg's headquarters while he was in Lafayette. There are several historical markers in front of the school describing Lafayette's Civil War connections and Bragg's time here.[4] There are also markers describing an 1864 action that occurred after the Chickamauga Campaign.

Bragg was here most of the time from September 10-16 while supervising affairs in McLemore's Cove and at Lee and Gordon's Mills. He returned here after Lt. Gen. Leonidas Polk's failure to attack as planned at Lee and Gordon's Mills to rest his army and plan his next move (which was toward Chickamauga Creek). For many years a massive tree known as the "Chickamauga Tree" stood here. According to the legend, Bragg planned the battle in the shade of the tree.

Stop 8: Dug Gap
(WP 10: Dug Gap: 34°44.899 N, 085°20.763 W)

Return to US 27 and turn left back toward the square. When you reach Georgia SR 193, West Main Street, turn right. Travel 7.0 miles west on SR 193. Take special note of the terrain en route because you are now passing through Dug Gap. When you reach the 7.0 mile mark you will see a roadside marker directing you to a Civil War wayside stop. Just past this sign is a gravel lane on your left leading to a gravel parking lot. Carefully turn into the lot and park. Here you will find three signs emplaced by the Civil War Preservation Trust explaining the action that unfolded in this area.

You are now standing in McLemore's Cove. Look back toward Lafayette. You have just driven through Dug Gap, where Patrick Cleburne and his division, along with Bragg and D. H. Hill, waited in vain for Thomas Hindman to launch his attack on September 11. The long low ridge you see is Pigeon Mountain, an eastern spur of Lookout Mountain. If you turn around and look to the west you can see Lookout Mountain in the distance. The Cove ends

---

4 Chickamauga park historians have some doubts whether Braxton Bragg used Gordon Hall as his headquarters. Originally, many of these markers—including the Confederate soldier monument—were in the old town square before it was changed to widen and reroute US 27. At that time, these markers were moved to this location. In 1863, there were a couple of hotels on the square, which would have served as ideal locations for Bragg's entourage.

Dug Gap: These markers represent the farthest Union advance
toward Lafayette from the west.

several miles to the south, where Pigeon Mountain rejoins Lookout Mountain
to form a giant "V." Dougherty's Gap is the southern exit of the Cove, climbing
back up onto Lookout Mountain.

Dug Gap was barricaded with felled trees by Martin's Confederate cavalry,
but as you can see, Pigeon Mountain was not an impassible barrier to a Union
infantry advance elsewhere. Martin warned Bragg on September 9 that he
would not be able to stop a determined Union advance on Lafayette without
significant reinforcements, and that at least one Union division was entering the
McLemore's Cove.

In 1863, the ground upon which you are now standing was between the two
armies. Union skirmishers advanced from the west until they made contact with
the Rebel infantry and cavalry on Pigeon Mountain. Union Major General
Negley, commanding the lead Federal division here, posted his main line several
hundred yards to the west near the actual crossroads. We will now visit that
crossroads.

Stop 8-A: Davis' Crossroads
(WP 11: Davis' Crossroads: 34*45.274 N, 085*22.109 W)

Davis Crossroads: The Widow Davis House.

Turn left out of the parking area and travel 1.0 miles to the next crossroads. This intersection is the junction of SR 193. If you turn right on Georgia SR 341, you will head north toward Lee and Gordon's Mills. The road running south from this intersection is called Hog Jowl Road. Turn left here onto Hog Jowl Road and immediately pull over in front of the wooden historical sign.

The sign explains the tactical situation here in Dug Gap on September 10 and 11, 1863. You are facing Negley's Union line, which looked toward Pigeon Mountain. Another Federal division was present supporting Negley. Hindman's Confederates were supposed to move south down the valley road (SR 341) and attack Negley's left flank while Pt Cleburne's men advanced from the east. As we know, the Confederate attack was never launched.

Stop 9: Rock Spring
(WP 12: Rock Springs/Dr. Anderson's House: 34*49.595 N,
085*14.786 W)

Rock Springs: Dr. Anderson's house.

Turn around and return to the intersection of SR 341 and SR 193. Drive through the intersection and head north on SR 341 for 3.2 miles until you reach Georgia SR 136. Turn right at SR 136 and drive 5.5 miles to US 27. At US 27 (which is also Georgia SR 1) turn left and head north. Drive 5.2 miles to a side street marked as Old Hwy 27 and turn left. (Hint: Old Hwy 27 looks like a frontage road here, angling off to the left. If you miss the first turn, keep driving to the stoplight at Rock Spring Drive, turn left, and drive one block and you will be at Old Hwy 27. Turn right.)

Old Hwy 27 is the original trace of the Lafayette Road before the new US highway was completed. It follows the trace of the historic Lafayette Road toward Lee and Gordon's Mill very closely here. Travel .9 miles until you reach the corner of Old Lafayette Road and Straight Gut Road. The house you see sitting on the southwest corner of this intersection was Dr. Anderson's house, which was present at the time of the battle. (WP 12: Rock Springs/Dr.

Anderson's House: 34*49.595 N, 085*14.786 W) This structure served as one of the locations for the headquarters of Confederate Corps commander Leonidas Polk in the days leading up to Chickamauga, as did Rock Spring Church, which is nearby. The Anderson house is mentioned prominently in reports, dispatches, and private correspondence of the time.

The action in this area was limited, but most of the Confederate army was deployed in this immediate vicinity at some point between September 9 and 16. Lee and Gordon's Mill is a few miles due north, while just to the west is Glass Mill. Both were important crossings over the West Chickamauga Creek. Leet's Tanyard, just a few miles to the east, is where John Wilder's mounted Federal infantry engaged John Pegram's Confederate cavalry on September 12. By September 16, Bragg had shifted his force back to Lafayette, but Rebels would return to this area the next day en route to Chickamauga.

Stop 10: Glass Mill
(WP 13: Glass Mill: 34*51.238 N, 085*16.446 W)

The site where Glass Mill once stood.

From Dr. Anderson's House, keep driving straight on the Old Lafayette Road for 1.5 miles until you reach Glass Mill Road. Turn left and drive another 1.0 mile to the intersection of Glass Mill Road and Old Bethel Road. Turn right (you will still be on Glass Mill Road) and almost immediately you will cross West Chickamauga Creek. Once across the creek, pull over when it is safe to do so.

The sloping open field ahead of you witnessed several actions, including cavalry skirmishes leading up to the September 19-20 battle and a significant fight between Union and Confederate infantry on September 19. This area was the southernmost end of the Chickamauga battlefield, though today it is in private hands. Historical markers describing the action on the 19th once lined this road. This ground was also the scene of the fight between Joe Wheeler's Cavalry Corps and Crook's Federal division on September 20—the largest cavalry action of the campaign.

The original mill sat behind where you are now standing, on the east bank just slightly north of the current bridge. The original bridge was just north of the mill, but the modern road has changed slightly. Note how the ground rises to a low hill on the east bank south of the bridge. This was where the rifled guns of Slocumb's Louisiana Battery deployed to support their comrades fighting on the west bank on September 19. Union and Confederate pickets crossed and recrossed the creek here several times, and the mill was used by both sides for shelter during this period. Some remains of the mill are visible when the water is very low, although this is private property and you must not trespass on it. The men of the 2nd Michigan Cavalry and 8th Texas Cavalry skirmished around the mill early on the morning of September 20.

The open fields ahead of you are where the main action occurred on both the 19th and 20th. At the time of the battle, open timber covered much of the field in front of you. On the 19th, as the main battle of Chickamauga was being waged farther north, Union forces occupied the far side of these fields and Union batteries occupied the slight crests you can see in the distance about 1,000 yards away. Confederate infantry and artillery crossed the creek here and deployed facing west and engaged in a prolonged artillery duel for about an hour and a half (between 8:30 a.m. and 10:00 a.m.). At one point in this action, Maj. Rice Graves, John Breckinridge's chief of artillery, ordered the Rebel gunners of Slocomb's and Cobb's batteries to roll the guns forward by hand in an effort to close with the Union cannon, but Yankee artillery fire was too accurate. A number of men were killed and wounded here, including soldiers in both the Rebel batteries and infantry in the Orphan Brigade, whose men were prone behind the batteries in the fields immediately in front of you in support of the advanced guns.

Wheeler's cavalry arrived on the east side of the creek on the night of September 19. They camped miles away somewhere between where you are now located and Dr. Anderson's house. Wharton's Division returned to this same campsite on both the 20th and the 21st. As you move closer to where the main battle unfolded, please note how far to the rear Wharton's men had to ride after each day's action.

On the morning of the 20th, the 8th Texas was picketing the creek here at the mill and driven back by the 2nd Michigan Cavalry. Shortly thereafter, the 2nd Michigan shifted northward toward Lee and Gordon's Mill (roughly two miles directly north of where you are currently stopped). The Ohio cavalry regiments of Col. Eli Long's Federal brigade replace the Michigan troops and deployed on the far side of this field in roughly the same positions occupied by the Federal infantry and artillery the day before.

The fight attracted Wheeler's attention, and later that morning both his Rebel cavalry divisions (Wharton and Martin) reached this location. They crossed the creek here and at a couple of small fords nearby, driving back the Union pickets. The fighting that ensued was heavy and Wheeler's men substantially outnumbered Long's troopers. The roughly-handled Federals retreated northwest toward Crawfish Spring.

Wharton's cavalry division advanced on the north side of the road (to your right) while Martin's cavalry division advanced in support south of the road (to your left). The 8th Texas Cavalry remained mounted and moved farther to the right in an effort to outflank the Federal line. This advance threatened to capture the Union battery accompanying Long's brigade, and Crook himself ordered the guns off the field. The 1st Ohio Cavalry covered that retreat. This was when the outnumbered Ohioans mounted by mistake in preparation to charge into the Rebel attack. Lieutenant Colonel Valentine Cupp was mortally wounded in the fields in front of you and carried back to the Gordon-Lee Mansion at Crawfish Spring. The Federals were retreating toward Crawfish Spring when Wheeler received Bragg's order to ride north to Lee and Gordon's Mills and attack the Federals he found there.

Stop 11: Crawfish Spring and the Gordon-Lee Mansion
(WP 14: Crawfish Spring: 34*52.227 N, 085*17.583 W)

Modern view of Crawfish Spring.

Continue the direction you were traveling along the Glass Mill Road. This road ends at Cove Road in the town of Chickamauga, which is also Georgia SR 341. Turn right at Cove Road and drive about .25 miles and turn left just beyond Lee High School and park in front of the Gordon-Lee Mansion. Directly across the street from the mansion is Crawfish Spring. Note the cannon and War Department tablets in the yard of the mansion. Across the street you will also see the row of Confederate cavalry monuments lining the street near the spring.

The mansion served as General Rosecrans' headquarters on September 17 and 18, and later as a field hospital. The entire area around you was a massive outdoor hospital, with Crawfish Spring providing the main source of water to the Federals in this area. Wheeler's men captured these hospitals later in the day on September 20 after they had crossed at Lee and Gordon's Mill. You can walk the grounds of the mansion and read the tablets. Today the mansion is owned by the city of Chickamauga. You may contact the manager for tours of the

The Gordon-Lee Mansion, the site of Maj. Gen. William Rosecrans' headquarters.

house, if he's available. There is a phone in a small parking lot closer to the house you can use to connect with the management.

Stop 12: Lee and Gordon's Mills
(WP 15: Lee & Gordon's Mills: 34*52.984 N, 085*16.064 W)

Depart the Gordon-Lee Mansion and drive north on SR 341. Turn right onto 10th Street. After you cross the railroad tracks, the fourth left is Crittenden Avenue. Turn left and drive .8 miles to the next stoplight. Turn right onto Lee and Gordon Mill Road. The next stop light is US 27, which is also Lafayette Road. Do not turn here but continue straight onto the little road that crosses US 27 and then curves to the left. As you follow this curve, you will see various monuments to the Union regiments that defended this crossing on September 19 and 20, as well as more Rebel cavalry monuments commemorating Wheeler's cavalry. If you are not driving, look down the hill to your right and see

Lee and Gordon's Mills as it appears today.

the rebuilt mill below you. Turn right onto Red Belt Road, which takes you down to the mill. If the mill is open, you can park and tour the facilities.

This is a replica of a mill from the 1880s, but you will recognize similarities from period photos. This mill is privately owned but public tours are available. (As of this writing: Tuesday through Friday, 10:00 a.m. to 4:00 p.m. EST; Saturday, 10:00 a.m. to 3:00 p.m., and Sunday, 2:00 p.m. to 4:00 p.m.)

The historic Lafayette Road turned onto what is now Red Belt road and crossed Chickamauga Creek here before turning north again. The modern road (which you just crossed) was moved farther west and now crosses the creek some distance south of this location. At the time of the battle, this mill sat astride the main route between Chattanooga and Lafayette. The mill was another headquarters site for General Polk's Corps, among other troops, and Union infantry occupied this site for about one week before the battle.

After the successful action at Glass Mill on September 20, Wheeler moved his cavalry divisions north and approached Lee and Gordon's Mills via the opposite bank (from the east rather than from the south). The light Union opposition consisted of only a skirmish line, which fell back as Wheeler's divisions approached. By the time the Confederate cavalry arrived it was already late afternoon and the Union troopers stationed here were pulling back in response to the disaster that befell McCook's XX Corps farther north. From here, Wheeler's men rode toward Crawfish Spring.

Stop 13: McDonald House/Visitor's Center
(WP 16: Visitor's Center / McDonald House: 34*56.398 N, 085*15.586 W)

The Chickamauga National Park Visitor's Center sits where the McDonald house once stood in 1863.

Turn right out of the mill parking lot back onto Red Belt Road. Drive up the hill and turn right to return to US 27. Turn right on US 27 and travel .2 miles north. At the next stoplight you will turn right again. If you head straight, you will enter the Frank Gleason Parkway, which is the bypass built to shift the main traffic of US 27 out of the park proper. Shortly after you turn right you will enter the Chickamauga National Battlefield Park. You are now once again following the old Lafayette Road.

Continue north on this road until you come to the sign for the Visitor's Center. Turn left into the Visitor's Center parking lot. The center sits where the McDonald house stood in 1863. Frank Armstrong, one of General Forrest's division commanders, used the McDonald house as his headquarters when Polk's Corps was stationed at Lee and Gordon's Mill. We will return to this site to discuss the heavy fighting that occurred here on September 20. For now it is important to note that this was the northernmost cavalry screen for Bragg's army during the period immediately after the Army of Tennessee evacuated Chattanooga.

This ends the first and longest leg of the driving tour.

SECOND LEG: STOPS 14 - 23

Stop 14: Graysville
(WP 17: Graysville: 34°57.728 N, 085°10.286 W)

When you leave the Visitor's Center, turn left onto Lafayette Road and head north. Drive 1.6 miles until you reach Georgia SR 146, also called Cloud Springs Road. Turn right onto SR 146 and follow this road for 4.3 miles. You will drive under I-75. Drive another .7 miles until you reach the Ringgold Road, which is also the combined US 41 & 76. Turn right onto Ringgold Road.

This is not the historic trace of Ringgold Road (also known at the time of the battle as the Old Federal Road). The route was shifted to accommodate I-75. One mile farther east, the road rejoins the historic road bed. Keep driving and you will cross Peavine Creek. Travel another .25 miles until you see a cross street called Haggard Road to the left (Hassler Drive to the right). Do not turn! Once you pass this intersection begin looking for the Indian Springs Church of God. Once you see the church, continue .25 miles farther until you see Foster Road on your right. Stop anywhere it is safe to do so between Hassler Drive and Foster Road. Usually, the best location is the Church of God's parking lot.

You are now on the approximate spot where the Union 1st Kentucky Infantry was attacked by Confederate cavalry on September 9, 1863. The Federals crossed Peavine Creek (behind you) and, with skirmishers deployed, advanced in column down this road toward Ringgold. The town of Graysville, Georgia, is about 1.5 miles northeast. An unfinished railroad bed ran from Graysville to about this site. Some traces of the bed are still visible, but not

Graysville: This view looks west along modern day US 41
(Ringgold Road) toward Peavine Creek.

readily apparent from the road. Using this railroad bed, two companies of the 6th Georgia Cavalry launched a mounted charge into the flank of the Federal 1st Kentucky Infantry and captured 58 Yankees. General Forrest arrived to witness the end of this action. Other skirmishing continued throughout the afternoon, with the Rebels defending Peavine Ridge. Both sides retired at nightfall, with the Federals retreating to Rossville and the Rebels withdrawing toward Ringgold.

Stop 15: Ringgold
(WP 18: Ringgold: 34*54.922 N, 085*06.469 W)

Continue on Ringgold Road, US 41/76, for another 5.6 miles until you enter the town of Ringgold. At the intersection of US 41/76 and Depot Street you will see the historic Ringgold Depot. Turn left and stop here.

The Ringgold Depot was built in 1849 and witnessed a great deal of action during the Chickamauga Campaign. The depot was the focal point for

Historic Ringgold Depot.

Confederate activity in town and changed hands several times. Because Forrest's men had burned three small railroad bridges just south of town during their earlier retreat from Chattanooga, the depot was not served by the railroad in September 1863. Trains could only approach as far as Catoosa Platform about two miles south. (We will visit the location of the Catoosa Platform later.) On September 11, the town was defended by John Scott's cavalry brigade (Pegram's Division). Opposing Scott was Col. John Wilder's mounted infantry brigade en route to Dalton, about fifteen miles to the south. Scott's Brigade was substantially outnumbered and repeatedly outflanked. The fighting on the 11th was more of a running battle between Ringgold and Tunnel Hill than a set-piece combat. Wilder's men halted for the night near Tunnel Hill. The next morning the Federals returned to Ringgold and then headed southwest. The Rebels reoccupied the town by the 13th.

The next action in Ringgold was on September 17. Confederate infantry was now on hand to hold the town. Several brigades were present by the 17th, including Bushrod Johnson's Tennesseans and the first Virginia arrivals from James Longstreet's Corps: Jerome Robertson's Texans and Henry Benning's Georgians. Scott's cavalry once again picketed the approaches and once again did a poor job doing it. A Union infantry patrol surprised the Rebels on the 17th. Led by Brig. Gen. James B. Steedman, six Yankee infantry regiments and a battery of artillery moved on the town from Rossville that morning. The Yankees reached a hill overlooking Ringgold without any trouble, unlimbered the artillery, and shelled the depot. From where you now sit, this hill was one of those directly to your west back along US 41/76. Having accomplished his purpose and realizing he was outnumbered, Steedman prudently withdrew. That was the last action Ringgold witnessed in this campaign, although the next morning Johnson's provisional division left Ringgold and marched toward the field of Chickamauga to open the battle.

Ringgold Depot witnessed several other historic Civil War events. Andrews Raiders passed here in 1862, only to be caught about two miles farther north when their engine ran out of water and wood. In November 1863, after the battle of Missionary Ridge, Patrick Cleburne's Confederate division fought a rearguard action here in town. His battle line incorporated the depot and the building was heavily damaged by Federal cannon fire. There are monuments to the capture of Andrews Raiders and to the November fighting scattered around town. A number of historic markers also explain Sherman's Atlanta Campaign, some of which you will see alongside the road.

Stop 16: Old Stone Church
(WP 19: Stone Church: 34°54.380 N, 085°04.644 W)

Leave the depot and turn left, heading south on US 41/76 again. Travel 1.7 miles to the intersection of US 41 and Cherokee Springs Road. You will not be stopping here, but take note of the pond just north of the road. In 1863, the Cherokee Springs Resort Hotel stood here, and many Southerners vacationed here before the war to bathe in the springs. Bragg and his wife stayed at the hotel in late August 1863. Bragg, who suffered from a variety of health issues, was recuperating here when he received word of the Union bombardment of Chattanooga. The Cherokee Springs Resort Hotel also served as a hospital for wounded Confederates after the battle of Chickamauga. Continue on US 41 another .6 miles to the intersection of Georgia State Route 2, also known as Catoosa Parkway. On the corner you will see a sandstone church. You can park here.

The Old Stone Church was built in 1849 and also served as a hospital for Confederate wounded. In the open fields on the far side of US 41 is the CSX

The Old Stone Church.

railroad. In 1863, these tracks belonged to the Western and Atlantic railroad. Longstreet's men finished their long journey from Virginia here and rested in these fields. Wooden sidings constructed alongside the tracks in these fields comprised the Catoosa Platform, where thousands of men and many tons of supplies were unloaded.

Stop 17: Tunnel Hill
(WP 20: Tunnel Hill: 34°50.381 N, 085°02.504 W)

Exit the church parking lot and once again turn south onto US 41. Travel south 4.8 miles until you enter the town of Tunnel Hill. US 41 runs over a bridge crossing the railroad tracks below, and just at the southern end of the bridge turn left onto Oak Street. Continue on Oak Street a short distance and turn right at the second turn on Clisby Austin Drive. Drive to the end of the street and you will see a sign for the Tunnel Hill Heritage Center. If you can do so safely, park here. The historic railroad tunnel is sometimes open to

The entrance to the railroad tunnel at Tunnel Hill.

pedestrian traffic, and you can obtain more information about both the tunnel and the Clisby-Austin House at the heritage center.

Wilder's Federals spent the night of September 12 here after driving Colonel Scott's Rebel cavalry out of Ringgold. The Clisby-Austin House, built in 1848, served as a hospital for Confederate Maj. Gen. John Bell Hood after his leg was shattered during the fighting on September 20. It is rumored to be one of the sites where his amputated leg was buried. (In reality, Hood's leg was amputated in a field hospital closer to the battlefield.) According to the rumor, a private was entrusted to carry the leg back to Texas. When he realized the unfeasibility of that plan, he supposedly buried the leg here. The house is privately owned, but during Tunnel Hill's Civil War Days celebration in September it is usually open for tours.

Just south of here on the other side of the ridge is where Forrest attempted his aborted nighttime reconnaissance of Wilder's position. Forrest was slightly wounded in the affair and one of his staff officers was captured. The next day Wilder's men retraced their steps north back to Ringgold to rejoin Crittenden's XXI Corps, consolidating their position at Lee and Gordon's Mills. Tunnel Hill was the scene of fighting in 1864 and there are rifle pits and artillery embrasures scattered in the woods around town.

Stop 18: Leet's Tanyard
(WP 21: Leet's Tanyard: 34*50.271 N, 085*11.502 W)

All that exists today of Leet's Tanyard is this historical marker.

Return to US 41, turn right, and head back north to Ringgold. Drive all the way through Ringgold until you reach GA State Route 151 (also called Alabama Highway). At SR 151, turn left and head south for 3.4 miles until you reach the Mount Pisgah Road, where you will turn right. Drive another 3.8 miles until you come to Nickajack Road on your left and the Mount Pisgah Road that curves to the right. Follow the curve to the right. The next intersection is about 500 yards. There, three roads intersect: Potts Road to your right, Beaumont Road to your left, and straight ahead is the Mount Pisgah Road which changes names to Peavine Road. Park near the historical marker you will see here at the intersection.

You are now at the site of Leet's Spring and Tanyard. This quiet spot was the scene of a pitched battle between Wilder's Federals and Pegram's Rebels.

The route you followed from Ringgold was the one that Wilder took on September 12. Wilder's men were marching down from Ringgold while Pegram's cavalry were riding north. About midday, the Rebels took a rest break here. A fifteen-man Rebel patrol rode up the Mount Pisgah Road and was ambushed by Wilder's men and captured to a man. As a result, no one was available to alert Pegram of the danger.

Shortly thereafter Pegram's men departed the spring, following the route taken by the patrol—and ran headlong into Wilder's column. A running fight chased them back to Leet's. Pegram deployed his men in a defensive position there while Wilder sent several companies to the south to try and flank the Rebel line. Pegram retreated to the large ridge you see just south of you.

This ridge represented Pegram's final position. Wilder tried again to outflank the Confederates but discovered they overlapped his own line. Confederate artillery atop the ridge, plus the concentrated fire of two regiments of dismounted cavalry, drove Wilder's men back. The action lasted about two hours and a number of men were killed and wounded on both sides.

The historic marker does not mention the September 12 fight, but does note that Leet's served as Braxton Bragg's headquarters on September 17 prior to the beginning of the fighting at Chickamauga. Confederate supply trains filled this area at the time of the battle, and it remained an important supply staging area for the Army of Tennessee until September 21 or so, when the army began to move on Chattanooga. In 1864, a number of Federal formations marched through here to kick off the Atlanta Campaign.

If you wish to view the ridge were Pegram's men made their stand, return to your vehicle and at the crossroads turn south onto Beaumont Road. The ridge will be on your left. A quarter-mile south you will see a small road on the left running up the hill named King View Lane. At the crest of the hill you will see a power line pylon. Huwald's Battery, the 6th Georgia Cavalry, and Rucker's Tennessee Legion formed here at the top of the ridge while Wilder's men assaulted from the other side. You are directly behind the Confederate position, which faces east. Please also note that the small road and the power line easement are private property serving the several homes you can see on the slope in front of you.

Stop 19: Peeler's Mill
(WP 22: Peeler's Mill: 34*55.561 N, 085*10.405 W)

Peeler's Mill overlooked this millpond in 1863.

Return to the crossroads. Do not turn on the Mount Pisgah Road. Instead, go straight onto Potts Road and continue north. Travel 2.8 miles to the stop sign and turn left here onto Davis Ridge Road. Davis Ridge Road makes a sharp ninety-degree bend to the left and, .8 miles farther on intersects with Three Notch Road. Turn right on Three Notch Road and drive another 2.7 miles until you reach Boynton Road. Turn left on to Boynton Road. Just after you turn, pause on the side of the road briefly if it is safe for you to do so. This site, now called East Boynton, was once the location of Peeler's Mill. Peeler's Mill was where Union Col. Robert H. G. Minty's cavalry brigade first set up camp on September 17 in order to patrol the roads toward Ringgold and Leet's Tanyard. Note that the waypoint fails to note the exact site of the old mill because the exact site is no longer known. (This was its approximate location.)

Continue west on the Boynton Road. One-half mile farther west you will cross Peavine Creek. It was here that Union pickets first fired on the Confederates of Bushrod Johnson's Division. This initial fire on the late morning of September 18, 1863, marked the commencement of the fighting at Chickamauga. When you cross the creek you will see a low ridge in front of you. The next intersection is now the small community of Boynton, and the road changes names here to Reed's Bridge Road. Continue straight ahead on Reed's Bridge Road as it winds its way over the ridge, which today is called Boynton's Ridge. In 1863, this ridge was referred to as Peavine Ridge (or West Peavine Ridge to distinguish it from the next ridge east of the creek behind you, which is also named Peavine Ridge). The eastern slope of Boynton Ridge is where Minty established his initial line of 600 troopers and two guns about 10:00 a.m. on September 18.

Note that the small town of Boynton and Boynton's ridge are not named for Union Col. Henry Van Ness Boynton, commander of the 35th Ohio and later instrumental in helping to form the Chickamauga-Chattanooga National Military Park. Instead, they are named for Confederate Col. James S. Boynton, who commanded the 30th Georgia at Chickamauga and served as the governor of Georgia after the war.

Stop 20: Reed's Bridge
(WP 23: Reed's Bridge: 34°55.793 N, 085°13.001 W)

On the far side of Boynton Ridge is the intersection of Reed's Bridge Road and Dietz Road. Drive straight on Reed's Bridge Road .33 miles west. Just before you cross the bridge over West Chickamauga Creek, pull over to the side of the road as long as you can do so safely. Just ahead to the right of the bridge is a gravel drive sloping down to the creek. This is public land, so you can walk down to the creek bank.

You are now standing at the site of the original Reed's Bridge. At low water, some of the original timbers for the 1863 structure at the bottom of the creek bed can still be seen. This spot was the center of a great deal of action on the afternoon of September 18. The Federal cavalry retreated across this bridge and a ford upstream (to your left, out of sight around the bend) as Bushrod Johnson's Rebels drove the Yankees back. This is where Lt. Wirt Davis of the 4th Michigan Cavalry paused to rip up the flooring and toss it into the creek in an effort to render the bridge unusable for the Rebels following closely behind him. Captain William Harder of the 23rd Tennessee Infantry tore siding from the Reed house and barn (somewhere behind where you parked) and used the

Original abutments for Reed's Bridge still exist.

wood to re-floor the bridge. General Forrest arrived and trotted across the bridge to examine the Union positions about 300 to 400 yards west of the creek.

Stop 21: Jay's Mill
(WP 24: Jay's Mill: 34°55.834 N, 085°13.736 W)

Return to your vehicle and drive west on Reed's Bridge Road. You will pass several monuments to infantry and cavalry units that fought here. Drive .7 miles farther west until you see the sign for the Chickamauga National Park. Just after you enter the park, turn left onto Jay's Mill Road and head south 200 yards and park in the space provided at the far end of the field.

You are now at the intersection of Jay's Mill Road and the Brotherton Road. A small wooden sign marks the location where Jay's Steam Saw Mill stood at the time of the battle. It was here, on the evening of September 18, after Confederate Maj. Gen. John Bell Hood arrived to take command of Johnson's column, that the Rebels decided to head south along Jay's Mill Road instead of taking the more southwesterly course of the Brotherton Road.

Jay's Mill used to sit upon this site.

Face west toward the tree line on the far edge of the field. There, on the morning of September 19, Forrest and John Pegram's cavalry brigade halted about 7:00 a.m. to water their horses and eat a hasty breakfast after driving Union skirmishers up the Reed's Bridge Road. Rebel patrols wandered into the woods but returned without finding any Federals. Shortly thereafter, the 10th Confederate Cavalry was ordered into the woods as a flank guard and discovered Brig. Gen. John Croxton's powerful enemy brigade. The rest of Pegram's men moved into the field and beyond, reaching a slight slope some distance into the modern woods. On September 19, 1863, this field was much larger because a great deal of the timber had been cut for use at Jay's Mill. The Confederate 10th Cavalry fell back in disorder behind you into the low ground closer to West Chickamauga Creek.

Stop 22: Alexander's Bridge
(WP 25: Alexander's Bridge: 34*54.449 N, 085*13.799 W)

View of Alexander's Bridge from the south bank of West Chickamauga Creek.

Return to your vehicle and drive south along Jay's Mill Road. Travel .8 miles until you reach the intersection of Alexander's Bridge Road and turn left. Drive another .2 miles and you will reach the intersection of Alexander's Bridge Road and the Vinyard-Alexander Road. Note the small rise on the southwest corner of this intersection. This is where the Alexander house once stood. Colonel John T. Wilder established his headquarters here on the morning of September 18, and Capt. Eli Lilly's Indiana battery went into action on this ground. You may stop here and get out if you choose, or continue toward the bridge. Travel another .4 miles on the Alexander's Bridge Road until you come to a small pull-off. The road ends here because Alexander's Bridge is now closed to vehicle traffic. Stop and get out here.

The modern road bed has been raised to avoid flooding, but you can see by the surrounding terrain that it was quite low here and swampy in wet weather. Small markers on both sides of the road memorialize units of Wilder's Brigade. A War Department tablet on the far side of the bridge describes the actions of

Brig. Gen. Edward Walthall's Brigade and its effort to cross the creek here. Company A of the 72nd Indiana defended this site. The earthwork constructed by the Hoosiers with flooring from Alexander's Bridge straddled the road about 100 yards from the bridge. Confederate troops were unable to cross the creek here, but they did work their way across on both flanks and nearly captured Company A's mounts, forcing the Federals to shoot a number of horses to prevent them falling into enemy hands. The fighting was intense and cost Walthall 105 killed, wounded, and missing. Eventually, the Rebels crossed downstream and forced Wilder's men to retreat from this position.

After the fight here ended, Maj. Gen. William H. T. Walker's Reserve Corps marched to the Alexander house, and waited there until Johnson's Confederates passed them and then filed onto the Vinyard-Alexander Road, where everyone halted for the night. Brigadier General St. John Liddell's two brigades camped alongside this road, while the brigades under Claudius Wilson and Matt Ector camped in the fields east of the Alexander's Bridge Road near the creek (these fields are now heavily wooded). By this time Pegram's cavalry brigade had arrived to join Forrest, and his men crossed back over the Alexander Bridge Road to camp east of the creek. Forrest established a picket line on the night of September 18 across the Jay's Mill Road to the north, but it did not reach as far as the mill itself.

Stop 23: Morton's Battery
(WP 26: Morton's Battery: 34*56.508 N, 085*15.111 W)

Turn back around and drive back north along Alexander's Bridge Road. Return to Jay's Mill Road, turn right, and return to Reed's Bridge Road. Turn left on Reed's Bridge Road and head west. One-quarter mile after you turn onto Reed's Bridge Road you will pass monuments to McCook's Union brigade of the Reserve Corps on both sides of the road. These monuments mark the location of McCook's camps on the night of the 18th, and denote where Pegram inadvertently rode into the midst of two Federal regiments. Continue 1.6 miles on Reed's Bridge road until you reach a T-intersection. A side road runs off to your right. On your left is a monument with a statue of an artilleryman on top. Stop here.

This monument was erected by the state of Tennessee to honor the Volunteer State gunners who fought here. Tennessee erected one monument each for the artillery, cavalry, and infantry units that fought at Chickamauga, as

The intersection of Forrest Avenue and the Reed's Bridge Road,
the site of Morton's Battery position on September 20, 1863.

well as individual unit markers for each command. This position also marks the location of Forrest's artillery batteries at midday on September 20. The grassy trail running south from this point into the woods was once a park road known as Forrest Avenue. It follows a ridge that marked the initial deployment positions for a number of Confederate commands before they advanced to the attack on September 20. At midday, Rebel cannon fire from this position forced Brig. Gen. James Steedman's Yankees off the Lafayette Road about 800 yards to your front and across the fields to the Snodgrass house. Red War Department tablets for Morton's Battery and other Rebel artillery units describe the action here.

This ends the second leg of the tour. From here, continue west on Reed's Bridge Road to the Lafayette Road and turn left. The Visitor's Center will be on your right.

THIRD LEG: STOPS 24 - 29

Stop 24: Armstrong Captures the Union Hospital (WP 27: Armstrong Captures the Hospital: 34*57.079 N, 085*15.573 W)

The Tennessee Cavalry Monument marks the area where
Brig. Gen. Frank Armstrong's cavalry captured a Union hospital.

Exit the Visitor's Center and turn left onto the Lafayette Road. Drive north .5 miles into the town of Fort Oglethorpe and turn left onto White Street. Almost immediately you will turn right onto Old Lafayette Road. Drive just a short distance until you are directly behind the Krystal Restaurant. There, you will see the Tennessee state cavalry monument as well as several metal park tablets, both red and blue, explaining the units that fought in this area.

As the Confederate infantry south of your present location advanced westward to attack on September 20, Forrest's two cavalry divisions deployed here to advance alongside them. Armstrong's Division reached the Lafayette Road in this area and captured a Federal field hospital near Cloud Springs Church (a modern version now stands a few blocks farther north). Steedman's division of the Union Reserve Corps, advancing south along the Lafayette Road, drove back Armstrong's troopers and recaptured the hospital. After Steedman moved south, Armstrong's Rebels reoccupied this area later in the day and joined in the final attack against George Thomas' XIV Corps line. Pegram's Confederate division did not advance to this line. Colonel Scott's Brigade remained at Red House Bridge, skirmishing with Minty's cavalry. Today, Red House Bridge is gone but the general location is three miles to the east where the modern Battlefield Parkway (GA SR 2) crosses West Chickamauga Creek. Pegram's other brigade, his former command now under Brig. Gen. Henry B. Davidson, also remained east of here watching Federals near Cloud Springs Church.

Stop 25: Forrest Climbs a Tree
(WP 28: Forrest up a tree: 34*58.888 N, 085*16.902 W)

Looking east toward Chattanooga from Missionary Ridge. Maj. Gen. Nathan Bedford Forrest enjoyed a view similar to this when he climbed a tree to get a better view of what the enemy was doing on September 21, 1863.

Return to White Street and turn left (north) onto the modern Lafayette Road. After you cross Battlefield Parkway, the Lafayette Road once again becomes US 27. From that intersection, travel 2.4 miles until you see a small side street called Georgia Terrace on your left. Turn left on Georgia Terrace and continue up the hill about 200 yards to a sharp right turn. Turn right here onto Clift Drive, which climbs and makes a sharp hairpin turn to the south. You are now on the east face of Missionary Ridge overlooking Chattanooga. Follow this road south until you find a safe place to pull over.

You have now reached the crest of Missionary Ridge at about the location where General Forrest captured a Union tree-based signal station. After the victory at Chickamauga on September 20, Forrest reached this point and climbed to the platform about 11:30 a.m. on September 21 to get a better view of Union dispositions. From there, he could easily see Chattanooga and the Union forces spread out in the Chattanooga Valley immediately to your west. As you can see, today this is a subdivision, so it is difficult to gain the same panorama Forrest enjoyed. This was the second tree-climbing incident for Forrest (he had climbed a tree farther south on the crest of this same ridge).

Stop 26: Rossville Gap
(Note, no GPS coordinate.)

Drive straight on Clift Drive until it ends in a T intersection at Leinbach Road. Turn right on Leinbach Road and travel down the hill to US 27. Turn right (south) on US 27 and take the next left turn on West Crest Road. This intersection is recognizable because of the large Iowa state monument in a grassy area in the middle of the intersection. There is a gas station on the northeast corner of US 27 and West Crest Road. Turn into that parking lot and stop.

You are now on the west side of Missionary Ridge in the Rossville Gap. The high ground you see on both sides of the gap was strongly defended by Federal infantry on September 21. Minty's Union cavalry held the east side of the gap, patrolling and watching for approaching Rebels. Pegram's Confederates encountered Minty's troopers sometime that morning. When Minty's troopers fell back Pegram's men ran into the Union line posted here. For the rest of the day, Pegram's troops skirmished with the Yankees but could not force a passage. Two Federal infantry divisions held this ground, including Maj. Gen. James Negley's command of the Thomas' XIV Corps. The skirmish

Rossville Gap: the Iowa Monument in Rossville Gap.

continued until about 4:00 p.m., when Bragg ordered Forrest to fall back and cover a Confederate infantry movement that would commence the next day.

Stop 27: The Moore House on Missionary Ridge
(WP 29: The Moore House (Bragg Reservation): 35°01.152 N, 085°15.805 W)

Return to your car and turn left onto West Crest Road. This road will curve around until you reach a six-way intersection of West Crest Road, East Crest Road, and Missionaire Avenue. (Note: This route is marked with "scenic route" signs. These signs are white rectangles with a black picture of a locomotive on them and the words "scenic route" written in red. Follow them to reach Missionary Ridge.) Continue straight head and bear to the left onto South Crest Road. You are now climbing Missionary Ridge and will shortly emerge onto the west side of the ridge with panoramic views of Chattanooga on your left. Travel

The Moore House: monuments at the Bragg Reservation on Missionary Ridge.

2.8 miles until you see the sign for the Bragg Reservation. Turn right and park there.

The monuments along Crest Road explain the fighting that occurred here during the battle of Chattanooga (November 23-25, 1863). There were few troops here before the battle of Chickamauga, but this area did witness a skirmish following the battle. Here in 1863 at the Moore house, a road crested the ridge and provided an alternate route into Chattanooga. On September 22, the Union 44th Indiana Infantry erected breastworks here astride the road. The 39th Indiana Mounted Infantry was posted nearby in support, deployed on the east side of the ridge (to your right) as skirmishers. About mid-morning, unidentified Confederate cavalry attacked the Union forces here and even charged the breastworks. They were repulsed. That afternoon, as Federals north and south of them retreated, the 39th and 44th Indiana regiments fell back toward Chattanooga.

Stop 28: Harrison Pike
(WP 30: Harrison Pike: 35*05.125 N, 085*13.617 W)

The bridge over West Chickamauga Creek at Harrison Pike.

Exit the Bragg Reservation, turn right on Crest Road, and head north. Just below the Bragg Reservation you will turn left and cross the bridge over I-24 in order to remain on South Crest Road. Once again, look for the "scenic route" sign. Drive 3.8 miles until you reach a Y-intersection. Crest Road ends here. The street to the right is Lightfoot Mill Road, while on your left is Campbell Street. Turn left onto Campbell Street. After two blocks Campbell street becomes Tennessee State Route 17. Stay on Campbell/SR 17 for another 2.2 miles until you come to a stop light. Turn left onto Addison Street, which three blocks later ends at Harrison Pike at a yield sign. Turn right onto Harrison Pike and drive .4 miles. You will cross a set of railroad tracks and then South Chickamauga Creek. When you can do so safely, pull over here.

This is approximately the area where the 59th Ohio was stationed on September 22 to guard the northernmost approach into Chattanooga from the east. About one-quarter mile farther west is where the railroad crosses South Chickamauga Creek. The 59th Ohio was posted in this area to defend these two bridges (the bridge you are facing and the railroad bridge about one-quarter mile to the west). The 59th was attacked by Scott's troopers, led by the 2nd Confederate Tennessee Cavalry. A protracted fight ensued that ended when the commander of the 59th ordered the railroad bridge set afire and pulled his men back into Chattanooga. The Federals retreated southwest along the railroad embankment, periodically using it as cover to repel Confederate attacks.

In the postwar era, Chattanooga became a major rail center. Today, many more tracks and sidings dominate this area than in 1863. As a result, it is considerably different than when the 59th Ohio and Scott's Brigade struggled here.

Stop 29: Lookout Mountain
(WP 31 Lookout Mountain: 35°00.591 N, 085°20.637 W)

Lookout Mountain: The entrance to Park Point, Lookout Mountain, Tennessee.

Continue north on Harrison Pike, which makes a sharp turn to the east and then another turn to the north, and ends at South Access Road. Turn left onto South Access Road and after driving one-quarter mile turn right onto

Tennessee SR 58. Take an immediate right, which is the ramp to southbound TN SR 153, a four-lane controlled access highway. Be very careful, as traffic here is usually quite heavy. Drive south on TN SR 153 past the Chattanooga metro airport until you reach I-75. Enter the ramp for Southbound I-75 to Atlanta and merge safely into moving traffic. Drive two miles and take the ramp at exit 2 for I-24 westbound to Chattanooga. Travel seven miles on I-24 to exit 178 (US 11 & 41 South). At the bottom of the ramp drive straight across Williams Street to Broad Street, where you can turn left and go south. Follow the signs for US 11 South to Lookout Mountain Parkway. Once on US 11 bear right. US 11 swings to the right and you will come to TN SR 148 on your left heading up the mountain. SR 148 winds around and switches back several times. Follow the signs to Point Park. Once there, park your car. There is a National Park Service visitor's center here with exhibits, a bookstore, and restrooms.

You are now at the point of Lookout Mountain overlooking Chattanooga. Most of the action that occurred here was during the Chattanooga Campaign in November 1863, but as you can see by the magnificent views, this location served as an important observation post for both armies. Bragg had a signal station atop this mountain until he evacuated Chattanooga on September 8. Federals occupied it thereafter. At the foot of the mountain on September 22, Spears' Federal brigade of Tennessee Unionists defended the slopes you just drove up against Col. George Dibrell's approaching Confederates. Here, at the top, John Williams of the 15th Pennsylvania viewed that action and could discern the fresh earthworks Federals were busy erecting around Chattanooga.

The Rebels finally captured Lookout Mountain on September 24, not from below (from the direction you just traveled), but from atop the mountain to the south. Joe Wheeler's Rebel cavalry approached along the top of the mountain and the Federals slipped down the west face along a little-used path, but not before an hour-long skirmish with the Union 3rd Tennessee Infantry. By dawn on September 25, the Union Army of the Cumberland was all but sealed into Chattanooga. The next move belonged to Braxton Bragg.

*   *   *

This concludes the thirty stops of this tour of the primary cavalry operations for the Chickamauga Campaign. There are many other places of significance. Unfortunately, many sites are now too developed and have thus changed so much they no longer retain much meaning for even the most dedicated Civil War students. However, I hope the drive through the countryside of Alabama, Georgia, and Tennessee has given you a greater appreciation of the broad scope of this campaign and the difficult missions the cavalry of both armies were asked to perform.

List of Waypoint Coordinates:

WP 1: Shellmound: 34°59.650 N, 085°36.843 W

WP 2: Bridgeport: 34°56.916 N, 085°42.672 W

WP 3: Stephenson Depot: 34°52.086 N, 085°50.398 W

WP 4: The Little Brick: 34°52.418 N, 085°50.148 W

WP 5: Caperton Ferry: 34°50.130 N, 085°48.229 W

WP 6: Valley Head: 34°34.138 N, 085°36.932 W

WP 7: Alpine: 34°27.691 N, 085°29036 W

WP 8: Mount Carmel Lane Skirmish: 34°39.836 N, 085°18.788 W

WP 9: Lafayette: 34°42.508 N, 085°16.824 W

WP 10: Dug Gap: 34°44.899 N, 085°20.763 W

WP 11: Davis' Crossroads: 34°45.274 N, 085°22.109 W

WP 12: Rock Springs/Dr. Anderson's House: 34°49.595 N, 085°14.786 W

WP 13: Glass Mill: 34°51.238 N, 085°16.446 W

WP 14: Crawfish Spring: 34°52.227 N, 085°17.583 W

WP 15: Lee & Gordon's Mill: 34°52.984 N, 085°16.064 W

WP 16: Visitor's Center/McDonald House: 34°56.398 N, 085°15.586 W

WP 17: Graysville: 34°57.728 N, 085°10.286 W

WP 18: Ringgold: 34°54.922 N, 085°06.469 W

WP 19: Stone Church: 34°54.380 N, 085°04.644 W

WP 20: Tunnel Hill: 34°50.381 N, 085°02.504 W

WP 21: Leet's Tanyard: 34°50.271 N, 085°11.502 W

WP 22: Peeler's Mill: 34°55.561 N, 085°10.405 W

WP 23: Reed's Bridge: 34°55.793 N, 085°13.001 W

WP 24: Jay's Mill: 34°55.834 N, 085°13.736 W

WP 25: Alexander's Bridge: 34°54.449 N, 085°13.799 W

WP 26: Morton's Battery: 34°56.508 N, 085°15.111 W

WP 27: Armstrong captures the hospital: 34°57.079 N, 085°15.573 W

WP 28: Forrest up a tree: 34°58.888 N, 085°16.902 W

WP 29: The Moore House (Bragg Reservation): 35°01.152 N, 085°15.805 W

WP 30: Harrison Pike: 35°05.125 N, 085°13.617 W

WP 31: Lookout Mountain: 35°00.591 N, 085°20.637 W

A ppendix 3

Colonel Alfred Roman's Inspection Report of Joe Wheeler's Cavalry Corps

I n January 1865, Gen. P. G. T. Beauregard sent Col. Alfred Roman of his staff to inspect and report on the condition of Maj. Gen. Joseph Wheeler's Cavalry Corps. Wheeler's men had screened the Army of Tennessee's flanks during Maj. Gen. William T. Sherman's drive southward to Atlanta and shadowed many of the same Federals across Georgia during Sherman's March to the Sea. Wheeler's instructions during the latter campaign were to deny the enemy anything of military value. This directive resulted in an orgy of destruction—some justified, some not. Although Wheeler's efforts did nothing to stop Sherman's march, they did trigger a tidal wave of outrage from Southern citizens against their own cavalry.

Colonel Roman's mission was to evaluate the state of the cavalry corps, determine how accurate the protests and accusations were, and figure out what should be done to fix these existing (and lingering) problems. His report provides the most detailed and damning evaluation of the state of Wheeler's organization. While Roman took pains to excuse some abuses and point out his personal admiration for "The War Child," he concluded that Wheeler was not capable of commanding an independent cavalry corps.

Although Roman's inspection was made some sixteen months after the conclusion of the battle of Chickamauga, the detailed report highlights fundamental problems that were still extant within Wheeler's cavalry corps despite his years of experience in the saddle. These problems should have been addressed long before and would dog Confederate cavalry in the Western Theater for the duration of the war. Complaints similar to those found in Roman's report appear with stunning regularity in letters, diaries, and military documents dating back to the fall of 1863. Why such basic failings of discipline and training were still so prevalent in January 1865 remain unanswered. Roman's conclusion that Wheeler was simply incapable of exercising effective command at such a senior level is especially damning.

Included below is the full text of the report,[1] less a number of statements and exhibits that document the conclusions in greater detail. I did so to provide a better understanding of the state of Wheeler's cavalry, even as late as the end of 1864.

* * *

Military Division of the West
Inspector's Office, January 22, 1865

Inspection Report of Wheeler's Cavalry Corps Made in Obedience to Instructions from Head Quarters Military Division of the West, Dated December 28, 1864

To Colonel G.W. Brent
A.A.G.

Colonel,

Major General Wheeler's command, up to the 16th of January 1865 when I left it, was composed of the following brigades, to wit:

1st Ferguson's Brigade—consisting of the 2nd and 56th Alabama Cavalry, Inge's, Perkins' and Miller's Regiments—commanded by Brig. Genl. S.W. Ferguson with a total exclusive of detached men of 990.

2nd Anderson's Brigade—consisting of the 5th Georgia Cavalry, the 8th and 10th Confederate and the 12th Alabama (belonging to Hagan's Brigade) commanded by Brig. Genl. R.H. Anderson. Total, exclusive of the 12th Ala. And of detached men 704.

---

1   Manuscript Division, Library of Congress, Papers of Alfred Roman.

The 1st Confederate Cavalry belonging to this Brigade is not on duty with it. It is said to be irregularly attached to Major General Forrest's command.

3rd Lewis' Brigade—consisting of the 1st, 4th, 5th, 6th and 9th Kentucky Cavalry, commanded by Brig. Genl. J.H. Lewis. Total, exclusive of detached men, 477.

4th Ashby's Brigade—consisting of the 1st, 2nd and 5th Tennessee Regiments and the 9th Tennessee, commanded by Colonel H.M. Ashby of the 2nd Tennessee. Total, exclusive of detached men, 795.

5th Harrison's Brigade—consisting of the 4th Tennessee Cavalry, the 3rd Arkansas, the 8th and 11th Texas, commanded by Col. Thomas Harrison of the 8th Texas. Total, exclusive of detached men, 945.

6th Dibrell's Brigade, consisting of the 4th and 13th Tennessee Regiments and the 4th Tennessee Battalion, commanded by Col. W. S. McLemore of the 4th Tennessee. Total, exclusive of detached men, 575.

The 10th, 11th, and 19th Ten. Belonging to this Brigade, and three companies of the 4th Ten. Are now with Gen. Hood's Army by order of Maj. Gen. Wheeler.

7th Williams' Brigade—consisting of the 1st and 2nd Kentucky Cavalry, commanded by Col. W.C.P. Breckinridge. Total, exclusive of detached men, 321.

The 9th Ky. Cav. Belonging to this Brigade is absent on duty by order of Maj. Genl. Wheeler, to arrest deserters. Company A of the 2nd Ky. Cav. Is absent on duty as escort to Genl. Williams, by command of Brig. Genl. Robertson.

8th Hagan's Brigade—consisting of the 1st, 3rd, 9th and 51st Alabama Cavalry, commanded by Col. T. Hagan, of the 3rd Ala. Total, exclusive of detached men, 976.

The 4th and 12th Ala. Belonging to this Brigade are detached by order.

9th Crew's Brigade—consisting of the 1st, 2nd, 3rd, and 4th Georgia Cavalry, commanded by Col. C.C. Crews of the 2nd Ga. Total, exclusive of detached men, 1085.

Two regiments of this brigade, namely the 4th and 6th Ga. Are on detached service. The latter, being on Provost Guard duty with Major Messick of the 11th Texas.

10th Hammond's Brigade—consisting of the 53rd Alabama, the 11th Georgia, the 24th Alabama Battalion and Ross' Battalion, commanded by Col. M.W. Hammond. Total, exclusive of detached men, 802.

Divisions as found when the command was inspected

Ashby's and Harrison's Brigades were under Brig. Genl. Hume, Acting Division Commander; Hagan's and Crew's, under Brig. Gen. Allen, Acting Division Commander. Dibrell's and Williams' under Col. Dibrell, Acting Division commander; Harrison's and Lewis's under Brig. Genl. Iverson, Acting Division Commander. Ferguson's and Anderson's Brigades formed part of no division and reported directly to Maj. Genl. Wheeler.

Proposed Organization

I was told by Maj. General Wheeler that as soon as circumstances would permit, his command would be reorganized under order from Dept. Hd. Qrs. And would then consist of three divisions of three brigades each, commanded by Brig. Generals Iverson, Allen and Humes.

This organization, I submit has more than one objectionable feature. In the first instance, it makes division commanders of junior brigadier generals while one of the seniors is held in a subordinate position and placed in the only division (Iverson's) where he could have found a ranking officer. Such proceedings, even when unintentional, as is no doubt the case here, create ill feeling among officers and tend invariably to the destruction of all "esprit de corps" in a command.

If Brigadier Generals Allen and Humes had been regularly promoted to the rank of Major Generals, there would be of course, no objection to the organization about to be effected. But such is not the case. They are junior brigadiers, acting as division commanders, while General Ferguson, the very next in rank to General Iverson, and against whom no charge of inefficiency has ever been preferred, is kept in the background and apparently deprived of his rights.

The main point against the proposed organization is, in the second place, the numerical weakness of almost every brigade and regiment in Wheeler's Corps. When divisions are not larger than brigades, and brigades not larger than regiments, consolidation becomes of the best and certainly the most expeditious of all remedies. It changes nothing in the strength of a command while at the same time, it facilitates discipline and good management. We saw that the total of the ten brigades spoken of in the proceeding pages amounts to 6,670 men, including present with and without serviceable horses. This reduces the average effectiveness of every regiment to about 202 men. Small as is that figure however, it might not be objected to, if all the regiments in the corps really numbered as many men. But it is not so.

I find for example in Ferguson's Brigade the effective total of Inge's regiment is 60 and that of Miller 86. In Williamson's Brigade the effective total of the 2nd Ky. is 94. In Harrison's Brigade the 3rd Ark. Has an effective of 96 only; and in Lewis' Brigade, the 1st Ky. has 89, the 4th Ky. 32, the 6th Ky. 27. In many of these regiments companies are represented by ten, twelve, and, at times, by two or three men only.

While inspecting one of the regiments of Hagan's Brigade (the 9th Ala) Company B was found with one officer and one man, and Company D with one man and no officer at all. The Brigade's Tri-Monthly returns will show the relative strength of each regiment, with the number of absentees, with and without leave. Exhibit D, to which I also refer gives the names of men absent, on detailed service, indicating by whose authority they are so detached, and on what duty.

Organization in two divisions by means of consolidation

I would respectfully suggest that Genl. Wheeler's command be at once organized into two large divisions of four brigades each, and with as many brigadier generals as there would be brigades in the corps.

Evidence has taught us that temporary or provisional assignments are very seldom if ever beneficial to military organizations. They prevent regularity; they destroy unity; they lead to indifference and neglect of duty, both among officers and men. Consolidation would soon give the result sought for; and by using energetic measures to compel all detached men to return to their posts, companies as well as regiments and brigades, would cease ere long to be mere skeletons, mere shadows of commands.

General Officers and Colonels Recommended for Promotion

Should my plan of organization as suggested above meet with the approval of the commanding General and should the officers to be promoted be taken in General Wheeler's command—which perhaps would be preferable—I would then beg leave to recommend the following: Brig. Genls. Ferguson and Anderson as Major Generals, and Colonels Ashby, White, Harrison and Dibrell as Brigadier generals.

General Anderson is a good disciplinarian as well as a gallant officer; and General Ferguson has more system, more military experience than most of the general officers of his years and rank. Both have been brought up as soldiers and would no doubt do honor to their commands.

Colonel Ashby of the Tennessee Brigade is a young officer of high promise. He has in my opinion the best brigade in General Wheeler's Corps. His men look well, their horses and equipments are property cared for, and their soldierly bearing is very satisfactory. Colonel White was in temporary command of Anderson's Brigade when I inspected it. He is evidently an efficient officer, besides being a graduate of West Point.

Colonel Harrison the devoted commander of the Texas Brigade, the "charging Brigade" as it is called, would do better no doubt as a brigadier than as a colonel. His authority would increase and so would his energy. Colonel Dibrell now with General Forrest's old brigade is looked upon as perhaps the hardest fighter in the whole command.

Armament of Corps

The armament of Wheeler's cavalry corps consists of 6,607 fire arms in serviceable condition, comprising 3,896 rifles, 500 carbines and 1,978 pistols. The reports of the different brigade ordnance officers show a deficiency in the whole command of about 1,447 guns, and of about 3,747 pistols. The command has no sabres with the exception of fifty or sixty to be found in Anderson's Brigade. The officers even in most cases have no sabres.

Difference of Calibres:

The arms are of eight or nine different calibres, but mostly of calibres .57 and .54. The consequences is that in many instances ammunition for six or seven calibres is required in the same company.

Captured Arms:

This want of uniformity in the armament which impairs efficiency of the command is due to the fact that it consists largely of guns captured by the men; and it often happens that none but captured ammunition will fit these captured guns.

Calibre should be regulated:

I would recommend that the arms be so distributed in every regiment as to regulate the armament as far at least as calibre is concerned. Some uniformity might thus be obtained.

Accoutrements, deficiency in:

The accoutrements of the command, consisting of 3,772 cartridge boxes, 2,911 cap pouches and 3,000 waist belts are generally very inferior and deficient to the extent of 1,471 cartridge boxes, 1,455 cap pouches and 1,2890 waist belts. This deficiency in accoutrements is a source of great inconvenience.

Waste of Ammunition:

It not only causes much of the ammunition to be damaged and lost, but it also prevents the good soldiers from carrying the required number of caps and cartridges, while it also affords an excuse to others for being entirely un-provided with ammunition.

Horses, Saddles etc.:

With a few exceptions, the horses in Wheeler's cavalry corps are in very serviceable condition. The fact is the men seem to take better care of their horses than they do of themselves. There is however a great want of brushes and curry combs, and the saddles especially those furnished by the government are altogether inferior. Some are now being made in almost every brigade and from what I could judge, they prove to be well conditioned and shaped in such a way as not to injure the horses' backs.

Racing:

Racing seems to be the favorite enjoyment of the men. So long as it does not interfere with their duties or degenerate into gambling habits, there can be no harm in that or any other recreation, which may tend to shorten the tedious hours of camp life. But Brigade Commanders should only allow it as a pass time, or as a reward and not as the main occupation of all men off duty, which at present is pretty much the case.

During my term of inspection, a horse belonging to Hagan's Brigade was killed while engaged in a race; and in the Texas Brigade a man who was thrown from his horse had his head badly fractured and both his arms broken. He was said to be in a dying condition when I left. This would tend to show that the amusement of racing is being carried too far.

Sanitary Condition of the Command:

The general health of the command is very satisfactory. Though camp itch prevails pretty extensively in several brigades. This is due no doubt to the uncleanliness of some of the men, who neglected their persons to a shameful extent. The chief commissary should be made to furnish soap to the Corps, and to make regularly issues of it. Washing of some sort must be encouraged.

Payment of Troops:

The troops were being paid when I inspected them. They had received no pay for the last twelve or thirteen months. No quartermaster funds have been furnished the command since May 1864; in fact not more than $160,000 says Captain Norton, the Chief Quarter Master, for the use of the entire Corps during the whole year 1864. About one million and a half dollars is due in claims for horses killed in action. Much has to be said on that subject. Men are very apt to lose faith in the government when the government is not punctual in the fulfillment of its contracts towards them.

Clothing:

Clothing is very deficient. Captain Norton's report shows that the men are in a very suffering condition, many of them in a ragged condition, and urgently need the following stores: 6,000 blankets, 7,000 suit of clothing, 5,000 hats, 8,000 pair of socks, and some 5,000 pair of shoes.

Discipline, Company Inspections, Ammunition:

Too much familiarity exists between officers and men. Discipline is thereby impaired. It has become loose, uncertain, wavering. Orders are not promptly obeyed. Inspections of arms and ammunition are carelessly attended to by company commanders. They are made weekly and often not at all, when a standing order from Corps headquarters requires that they should be made daily. I found several companies of a regiment just relieved from picket duty (the 13th Tennessee, Dibrell's Brigade) where at least one sixth of the men had not half the ammunition required. Some had none at all. The officers of the companies when I inquired of such gross neglect of duty answered apparently quite unconcerned that "their men had just arrived from the picket lines." As if that fact was not an additional cause of vigilance on their part and stricter obedience to orders issued. When the enemy is near by and we expect to fight him at almost any moment, then is the time that all men have a full supply of ammunition, and that every thing be in readiness for any emergency.

Military Appearance:

The military appearance is bad. The men of Ashby's Brigade and of Anderson's Brigade show to more advantage than the others. They evidently take better care of themselves. They have more pride in their soldierly bearing. Most of the men of the other commands have none.

Roll Calls, Officers of the Day:

Roll calls are neglected. In many cases officers would be at a loss to find a list of their men. The appointment of regimental and field officers of the day is very much neglected. Some few brigades observed the rule but most of them I am informed do not.

There seems to be an independent careless way about most of the officers and men which plainly indicates how little they value the details of army regulations and of tactics in general. I am convinced however that they mean no harm by it; for without a single exception have I found the men as respectful at inspection as they know how to be. They are badly instructed, or not instructed at all. I have no doubt they would make most excellent soldiers if they were in better hands.

Military Court:

I would recommend that a permanent military court be assigned to duty with General Wheeler's Corps, with the organization I have proposed—Two Division—that one military court would be sufficient though judging from what now happens, it would certainly have its hands full. But cases would not be delayed, as they are now, and discipline would thereby gain by it.

Rumors About the misconduct of the Command:

Much has been said and is still being said of the gross misconduct of Gen. Wheeler's men. Their alleged depredations and straggling propensities, and their reported brutal interference with private property have become common by-words in every county where it has been their misfortune to pass. Public opinion condemns them everywhere; and not a few do we find in Georgia as well in South Carolina who look upon them more as a band of highway robbers than as an organized military body.

Exaggeration of Such Rumors:

While I am ready to admit that much truth is hidden under some of the rumors thus brought into circulation yet justice makes it a duty upon me to add that not a little is said about the command which is utterly false. The cry of "mad dog" is here brought in play, bearing with it as usual all the auxiliaries of its well known influence. Statements are daily coming in at General Wheeler's head quarters showing how unfounded are many of these charges referred to. Men, depredators, horse thieves purporting to be of Wheeler's command have been arrested of late, who when confronted have been proven to have never belonged to the corps under whose name they have striven to conceal their misdeeds in order to avoid the punishment they justly deserved.

Bad Men Stragglers Form But a Small Portion of Wheeler's Corps:

I am not inclined to screen the bad men who may certainly be found in Wheeler's Corps as in many others. They have been a disgrace to ourselves and have caused many a brave man and honest comrade to be slandered by the reflection of their shameful behavior. They have created dissatisfaction among other people; they have blasted the good name of their own command, and have thereby injured to no inconsiderable degree the very cause we are fighting for. But guilty as they are the bad men I speak of we must not forget that they form only a small proportion of the corps to which they belong.

Material of Corps Very good:

The material of that corps is the same, the very same as is found in every branch of the Confederate service. It is equally as good as can be found else where.

If discipline is loose in Wheeler's Corps, if orders are not rigidly enforced, if straggling is more than a frequent occurrence, if the men commit degradations, if some of them have stolen horses—I say unhesitatingly that the officers from the lowest to the highest in rank are more to be blamed than the men themselves:

Officers More to Blame Than the Men:

Experience shows that soldiers very seldom forget their duties when officers do not forget theirs.

Cause of Want of Discipline in the Corps:

After having carefully weighed the different reasons which could have brought forth the undisciplined tone and relative inefficiency of Wheeler's command, I have come to the conclusion that these are due:

1. To the negligence and incompetency of many of the company and regiment commanders.

2. To the want of system and good administration in the Commissary Department

3. To the great irregularity in the payment of the troops.

4. To the error of allowing cavalry men to procure their own horses, instead of having them furnished by the government.

5. To the excessive leniency of the corps commander.

I will consider separately in the order just given each of the several heads mentioned above.

Incompetency of Officers:

1. When officers are not personally acquainted with the affairs of their commands, when the colonels have to question their captains and captains their orderly sergeants to answer to most of the questions that are asked of them in relation to their regiments and companies; when so forget the difference between them and their subordinates as to destroy the very semblance of rank and authority, when they seem ashamed to appear soldier-like in their bearing, in their tone of command, and in their daily official intercourse with their men—then I say such officers must be dropped at once as encumbrances, as nuisances, as obstacles in the way of good discipline and I am sorry to say that such I have found to be the case in nearly all the regiments and companies of the command. I would therefore recommend that a board of competent officers (to be selected out of General Wheeler's Corps) be sent to the command for the purpose of examining all regiment and company officers reported as inefficient, and of disposing of them with due regard to the good of the service, and with the least possible delay.

Bad Administration of Commissary Department:

2. The duty of a Chief of Commissary is to be as near to his command as he can. He must direct the course of assistant commissaries. He must see that they precede the troops on a march so as to prepare forage for the horses and food for the men. He must see that they be provided with funds to purchase the supplies required so as to avoid paying farmers with "certified accounts" exclusively and thus alienate their feelings towards the country and the troops. These duties I am informed are not regularly attended to by Major Thomas, the Chief Commissary of General Wheeler's Corps.

Soldiers Will Straggle to Procure Food:

When after a long march men and horses arrive at their camping ground, very often in a starving condition, it is almost natural that if no provisions are made to satisfy their hunger, they should endeavor to procure their food by their own exertions. Private details for forage and for other supplies are then sent out, and men and horses are thus allowed to run about the country in search of "something to eat." This necessarily encourages straggling. Men will buy a pig, a chicken, and pay for them, but on their way back should they come across another pig and another chicken they will kill both and carry them along with them. The blame there lies more with those whose improvidence caused this supposed misconduct

Errors Allowing Men to Own the Horses They Ride:

When a soldier owns the horse he rides, when experience teaches him that though bound to pay for its loss in action, the Government is never ready to do so, that soldier will invariably take so much care of his horse so as to feel at least disinclined to risk him in a battle. That soldier therefore cannot do as good service as if he knew that as many horses as might be shot under him just as many more would the Government give him. And the idea of owning a horse originates almost invariably the idea of trading it for a better one or of selling it for a high price. Horse trading soon creates jockey-ism, and between a jockey and a horse thief there generally is but a slight difference if any at all.

I am aware that the reasons which I here give for the probably causes of loose discipline in Wheeler's Corps exist also more or less in Forrest's and Hampton's commands. I have no doubt they do, for they arise from a defect of organization in that branch of the service, but my knowledge of those two eminent commanders is that they exact more from their subordinate officers; that they make them responsible for the conduct of their men; that they hold them better in hand; and these counter-balance and cancel the other evils complained of.

General Wheeler:

No one admires General Wheeler more than I do. He is a modest, conscientious, industrious officer. He takes a fatherly interest in his command. His activity is proverbial, and is equaled only by his gallantry. But he is wanting in firmness. His mind and his will are not in proper relation to one another. He is too gentle, too lenient, and we know how easily leniency can be made to degenerate into weakness. General Wheeler's men like him, but do not appear to be proud of him. They know he will always fight well, but seem to feel he cannot make them fight as well. The proposition that all able officers are not fit to be efficient cavalry commanders is assuming more and more the proportions of a self evident proposition. The Van Dorns, the Forrests, the Hamptons are not easily found in this or in any other country.

My honest conviction is that General Wheeler would be a most excellent brigade or division commander, but I do not consider him the proper man to be placed at the head of a large independent cavalry corps. Under him and in spite of his good discipline and soldierly qualities, no true discipline will ever be perfect and in his command nor will the whole efficiency of his corps, the entire fighting capabilities of his men, their dash, their intrepidity, be ever fairly and fully developed.

Had I the power to act in the matter, I would relieve General Wheeler from his command, not as a rebuke, not as a punishment, for he surely deserves neither, but on higher grounds, that is, for the good of the cause, and for his own reputation. We have no time to lose at this juncture of our affairs. If we intend to resist we must do it gloriously, promptly and fear no personal dissatisfaction in the performance of our duties. We have too much at stake to hesitate a moment. As to who could be selected to fill General Wheeler's place I am not prepared to say. Others higher in authority must know better.

Respectfully submitted

(signed) Alfred Roman
Lt. Col. & Asst. Insp. Genl.

Appendix 4

Reassessing the
Forrest–Bragg Confrontation

"If you ever again try to interfere with me or
cross my path it will be at the peril of your life."

— *Nathan Bedford Forrest to Braxton Bragg*

The most famous confrontation between Nathan Bedford Forrest and Braxton Bragg was a direct result of the Chickamauga Campaign. Apparently the issue reached a head when Bragg placed Forrest and his men under Joe Wheeler's overall command. That decision, coupled with Forrest's legendary temper and his unwillingness to obey Wheeler's orders, resulted in a fiery face-to-face encounter at Bragg's headquarters. Since the incident is featured so dramatically in every Forrest biography, it is worth recounting here:

Dr. Cowan, Forrest's chief surgeon, had been left in charge of the hospital near Alexander's Bridge, on the battle-field. Having finished his work there, he notified the general that he was ready to report in the field when needed, and in reply received a dispatch directing him to be ready to join Forrest at Ringgold the next day. They proceeded by train to Chickamauga Creek bridge, and rode thence to the headquarters of General Bragg on Missionary Ridge. Dr. Cowan says: "I observed as we rode along that the general was silent, which was unusual with him when we were alone. Knowing him so well, I was convinced that something that displeased him greatly had transpired. He wore an expression which I had seen before on some occasions when a storm was brewing. I had known nothing of the letter he had written General Bragg, and was in utter ignorance not only of what was passing in Forrest's mind at this time, but of the object of his visit to the general-in-chief. As we passed the guard in front of General Bragg's tent, I observed that General Forrest did not acknowledge the salute of the sentry, which was so contrary to his custom that I could not but notice it. When we entered the tent where General Bragg was alone, this officer rose from his seat, spoke to Forrest, and, advancing, offered him his hand.

"Refusing to take the proffered hand, and standing stiff and erect before Bragg, Forrest said: 'I am not here to pass civilities or compliments with you, but on other business. You commenced your cowardly and contemptible persecution of me soon after the battle of Shiloh, and you have kept it up ever since. You did it because I reported to Richmond facts, while you reported damned lies. You robbed me of my command in Kentucky, and gave it to one of your favorites—men that I armed and equipped from the enemies of our country. In a spirit of revenge and spite, because I would not fawn upon you as others did, you drove me into west Tennessee in the winter of 1862, with a second brigade I had organized, with improper arms and without sufficient ammunition, although I had made repeated applications for the same. You did it to ruin me and my career. When in spite of all this I returned with my command, well equipped by captures, you began again your work of spite and persecution, and have kept it up; and now this second brigade, organized and equipped without thanks to you or the government, a brigade which has won a reputation for successful fighting second to none in the army, taking advantage of your position as the commanding general in order to further humiliate me, you have taken these brave men from me.

"'I have stood your meanness as long as I intend to. You have played the part of a damned scoundrel, and are a coward, and if you were any part of a man I would slap your jaws and force you to resent it. You may as well not issue any more orders to me, for I will not obey them, and I will hold you personally responsible for any further indignities you endeavor to inflict upon me. You have threatened to arrest me for not obeying your orders promptly. I dare you to do it, and I say to you that if you ever again try to interfere with me or cross my path it will be at the peril of your life.'"

Dr. Cowan says this whole transaction was so unexpected and startling that he was almost dumfounded. When Forrest refused to take the proffered hand,

Bragg stepped back to one corner of his headquarters tent, where there was a little field desk or table, and seated himself in a camp-chair. He seemed at a loss to know what to do or say in the presence of this violent outburst of rage in one who was so desperately resenting what he considered a systematic and revengeful persecution of himself. He realized that in his stormful mood Forrest acknowledged no accountability to law, civil or military, human or divine, as he stood there towering above him, launching at him this fierce denunciation, and emphasizing each expression of contempt with a quick motion of the left index-finger, which he thrust almost into Bragg's face. The general did not utter a word or move a muscle of his face during this shower of invective from his brigadier. The scene did not last longer than a few minutes, and when Forrest had finished he turned his back sharply upon Bragg and stalked out of the tent towards the horses. As they rode away Dr. Cowan remarked, 'Well, you are in for it now!' Forrest replied instantly, 'He'll never say a word about it; he'll be the last man to mention it; and, mark my word, he'll take no action in the matter. I will ask to be relieved and transferred to a different field, and he will not oppose it.'[1]

Forrest was correct in his estimation. Bragg did not make any formal reference to the incident, no charges were filed, and Forrest was transferred to northern Mississippi at the end of October.

Forrest's angry soliloquy seems so iconic of the man—certainly of the myth that he has become—that it is easy to see why it has been so widely quoted and accepted. Like the role of the Rebel horsemen in the Chickamauga Campaign, romance often obscures real history. A closer examination of this affair reveals a number of problems with Dr. Cowan's version of events regarding both the timing of the alleged confrontation and the temperament of the men involved.

According to Dr. Cowan, he was the sole witness to this verbal barrage and he only told his tale (which includes a long and detailed quote of Forrest's precise language) long after both Bragg and Forrest were dead. His story first appeared in John Wyeth's *Life of General Nathan Bedford Forrest* (1899).[2] Dr. Cowan repeated this story to John Harvey Mathes in 1902 and again for John

---

1   Wyeth, *That Devil Forrest*, pp. 242-44.

2   Wyeth's book has been reprinted several times as *That Devil Forrest*. Unless otherwise noted, references to this work are to the 1989 reprint.

Morton in 1909.[3] No other accounts of this famous confrontation exist. There is not a whiff of it in Bragg's correspondence of the time or in staff officer Col. William Brent's journal. Cowan was not just a member of Forrest's headquarters, but a kinsman to the general and an integral member of the veterans association that sprang up around Forrest's escort and staff after the war. In other words, Dr. Cowan is a very biased witness. So we have a single highly partisan source recounted decades after the event in question supposedly took place. This alone should raise serious questions about the accuracy of the recollection. Instead, this lone account of the confrontation has been embraced widely as part of the Forrest canon.

Thomas Jordan's and J. P. Pryor's *The Campaigns of General Nathan Bedford Forrest and of Forrest's Cavalry*, which was first published in 1868 with the knowledge, complete approval, and full cooperation of Forrest himself, is silent on the entire matter. Jordan and Pryor is the closest thing we have to a Forrest memoir. This "memoir" is not a "tell-all" sort of affair; Forrest's February 1863 confrontation with Wheeler at Dover in February 1863, for example, is also missing. However, Jordan's and Pryor's narrative conflicts with Dr. Cowan's account on a number of other points that cast doubt on his recollection of events.

In his 1909 account, Morton hints that not everyone accepted the story with question. "Some discussion has arisen lately concerning General Forrest's use of such language and General Bragg's submitting to it," writes Morton, "but it seems to be the general consensus of opinion of those who knew both men that the facts are about as here set down." Morton does not offer much more in the way of clarification. He did record that Maj. M. H. Clift (probably Moses H. Clift, a quartermaster in George Dibrell's Brigade) had once questioned Forrest about the incident years after the war and that Forrest replied that "the facts were about as he had heard."[4] Unfortunately, this amounts to little more than vague hearsay. Clift did not specify what "facts" he asked Forrest to confirm or even record what year the two men discussed the incident.

By far the most significant problem with the confrontation is one of timing. When did this insubordinate incident occur? Dr. Cowan does not provide a

---

3 John Harvey Mathes, *General Forrest* (Appleton and Co., 1902), p. 156, and Morton, *The Artillery of Forrest's Cavalry*, pp. 130-1.

4 *Ibid.*, p. 131.

precise date for the meeting, though he places it at the end of September 1863. An examination of events during this period only complicates matters.

On September 24 Bragg dispatched Forrest northeast to investigate intelligence that Federals under Ambrose Burnside were approaching from that direction.[5] Bragg also intended Forrest to cross the Tennessee River at some point and interdict whatever tenuous supply lines Maj. Gen. William Rosecrans still possessed (specifically, wagons moving over Walden Ridge and down through Sequatchie Valley). Instead, Forrest pressed to within thirty miles of Knoxville by the morning of September 25, a decision that provoked a snarling response from Bragg. Brigadier General St. John Liddell visited Bragg's headquarters on Missionary Ridge that morning and recorded Bragg's frustration: "I have not a single general officer of cavalry fit for command!" Bragg raged. "Look at Forrest! I sent him with express orders to cross the Tennessee . . . to destroy [the enemy's] provision trains . . . through Sequatchie Valley, and the man instead . . . has allowed himself to be drawn off towards Knoxville on a general rampage . . . the man is ignorant and does not know anything of cooperation. He is nothing more than a good raider!"[6] Liddell's account was penned in 1866, just three years after the events in question.

Liddell's recollection is substantiated to some degree because that same day Bragg sent an order recalling Forrest and instructing him to turn over all but one of his brigades to Joe Wheeler, who would undertake the Sequatchie Valley raid.[7] Forrest's angry reply was dictated to and written by Maj. Charles W. Anderson, who recalled that among other things the dispatch charged Bragg with "duplicity and lying." When he signed it, recalled Anderson, a grimly satisfied Forrest uttered, "Bragg never got such a letter as that before from a brigadier."[8] Forrest also promised to take the matter up in person within a few days. Bragg, meanwhile, reiterated the order of September 25 with another dispatch three days later insisting yet again that Forrest turn over his command to Wheeler.

---

5   Jordan and Pryor, *Forrest's Cavalry*, p. 354.

6   Nathaniel C. Hughes Jr., *Liddell's Record* (Louisiana State University Press, 1997), p. 150.

7   Entry for September 25, 1863, Brent Journal.

8   Wyeth, *That Devil Forrest*, pp. 241-2. The exact timing of this letter is unclear. It could have been sent after the order of September 25, 1863, necessitating Bragg's follow-up of the 28th, but most biographers place it after the latter communication.

On September 30, Forrest made good his promise to take up the issue in person. Unfortunately, we are left with very different accounts of that meeting. Writing in 1868, Jordan and Pryor note that Bragg assured Forrest "that his old command should be recomposed at the conclusion of Wheeler's expedition."[9] Apparently mollified, and with nothing to do while his troops were with Wheeler, Forrest applied for ten days' leave. Forrest artillerist John Morton, however, explicitly notes that this was the explosive meeting that Dr. Cowan witnessed. If that meeting occurred as Cowan related, Forrest was anything but mollified.[10] The sources do agree that immediately after this meeting Forrest took leave to visit his wife at LaGrange, Georgia, nearly 170 miles distant.

According to Jordan and Pryor, Forrest was at LaGrange on October 5 when he received an order penned by Bragg two days earlier elevating Wheeler to command all of the army's cavalry, which in turn placed Forrest under Wheeler's authority. This was the last straw for Forrest, who was "extremely dissatisfied" with what he viewed as Bragg's betrayal. The cavalryman resigned his commission immediately.[11]

And so the matter of timing raises its head. Dr. Cowan's account (as it appears in Wyeth, Mathes, and Morton) claims Forrest confronted Bragg on or about September 30—after he returned from East Tennessee but before he took leave—and that this face-to-face meeting resulted in an irreparable breech between the two men. Official records and other contemporary diaries confirm that the October 3 order is the triggering event.

Modern biographers resolve this discrepancy by simply moving the confrontation to a later date, which allows for a smoother story uncluttered by available—but contradictory—data. Robert Selph Henry surmises in his 1944 biography of Forrest that the final blow-up must have occurred after October 5 but before Confederate President Jefferson C. Davis arrived to visit the army on October 9.[12] Later biographers followed Henry's lead. A wide variety of authors writing in 1990, 1992, 1993, and 2007 all use Dr. Cowan's account but place the incident after October 5. None of these authors note the timing

9   Jordan and Pryor, *Forrest's Cavalry*, p. 357.

10 Morton, *The Artillery of Forrest's Cavalry*, p. 130.

11 Jordan and Pryor, *Forrest's Cavalry*, pp. 357-8.

12 Robert Selph Henry, *First With the Most*, p. 200.

problems.[13] Only Bragg biographer Judith Lee Hallock caught the inconsistency and observed that Brent's journal is silent about any confrontation during the period in question.[14]

Instead of resolving the issue, however, pushing back the date of the meeting raises new and significant questions. On October 5 Forrest was 170 miles away from the Army of Tennessee. Given the state of the Confederate rail system in 1863, a speedy return to Ringgold was unlikely. Such a journey would have required at least a full day and likely two full days of travel to reach Bragg's headquarters. Henry offers up the most precise timing by placing the face-to-face conflict before President Davis' arrival on the 9th. That solution raises yet another question. Jordan and Pryor note that Forrest's letter of resignation did not reach Bragg until after Davis was present. Are we to believe that Forrest rode the rails to Ringgold, verbally assaulted Bragg, returned immediately to LaGrange, and then wrote out his resignation? For Dr. Cowan there is no discrepancy because he states specifically that Forrest did not offer to resign because he did not want to appear as if he was trying to avoid the consequences of his actions.[15] Jordan and Pryor flatly contradict Dr. Cowan in this case by making it clear that Forrest wrote a resignation letter, and that this letter was the reason President Davis intervened.[16]

In his diary William R. Dyer, a member of Forrest's escort, provides the most detailed contemporary record of Forrest's activities during this period. Dyer does not specifically record the meeting between Bragg and Forrest at the end of September. He does, however, note that on September 30 the escort "returned to Missionary Ridge," which was where Bragg's headquarters was located. Dyer also provides a firm date for when Forrest departed on leave: October 1, which is when "General Forrest went to Atlanta." Between October 2 and 9 Dyer describes only routine duties in the vicinity of Dalton. He mentions President Davis' arrival on the latter date, but does not mention Forrest at all until recording the first rumors of his commander's resignation on

---

13 See Maness, *An Untutored Genius*, p. 182; Wills, *A Battle From the Start*, pp. 144-5; Hurst, *Forrest*, pp. 139-40; and Eddy W. Davison and Daniel Foxx, *Nathan Bedford Forrest: In Search of the Enigma* (Pelican Press, 2007), p. 179.

14 Judith Lee Hallock, *Braxton Bragg and Confederate Defeat*, Vol. II, pp. 130-1.

15 Wyeth, *That Devil Forrest*, p. 244.

16 Jordan and Pryor, *Forrest's Cavalry*, p. 358.

October 10. By the 13th speculation about this abounds. The "camp [is] full of rumors concerning General Forrest's resignation," writes Dyer, including one outlandish story that he would be joining "a privateer vessel." Three days later Dyer dispels all doubt: "Received positive assurance that General Forrest had resigned and was going to raise an independent command." It seems clear that Dr. Cowan was wrong about Forrest not resigning, and Dyer records no evidence of Forrest's presence with the army during this time period.

The manner of the Confederate president's intervention during this period introduces further complications. Davis became aware of the problem when Forrest's letter arrived at army headquarters. In response, Davis wrote to Forrest to ask the cavalryman to join him in Montgomery, Alabama, where Davis was heading after visiting the Army of Tennessee. Davis left the army for Montgomery on October 14, so the letter to Forrest had to have been sent between October 9 and 14. If Forrest was with the army during this time, Davis would have met with him there instead of asking for a meeting in Alabama. The request only makes sense if Forrest is still at LaGrange, southwest of Atlanta, and 100 miles from Montgomery. The two men did meet in the Alabama capital, where Davis agreed to Forrest's request from August 1863 and authorized his transfer to northern Mississippi. He would only be allowed a handful of men: his own escort, Morton's Battery, and McDonald's Tennessee cavalry battalion, about 300 all told. However, Forrest could raise and recruit a new command from men in Mississippi and Tennessee.[17] Bragg had already signed off on this request on October 13 while Davis was still with the army (almost certainly at Davis' urging).

Forrest did not rejoin the army until October 20. Dyer barely mentions Forrest's return, noting only that "Forrest went to see General Bragg."[18] Colonel Brent offers slightly more detail by commenting on the underlying tension between the two men: "Forrest is here and is much dissatisfied. Troubles are brewing in the command."[19] Unfortunately, Brent—who surely knew much more than he wrote—offers no additional details and does not mention any confrontation. Finally, Dyer records one more meeting between Bragg and Forrest on October 30 before the cavalryman's departure for the

---

17 *OR* 31, pt. 3, p. 646.

18 Wayne Bradshaw, ed., *A Member of Forrest's Escort: The Civil War Diary of William R. Dyer* (Wayne Bradshaw, 2009), p. 83.

19 Entry for October 20, 1863, Brent Journal.

long journey to Mississippi on November 2.[20] It is possible that one of these encounters was the confrontation Dr. Cowan describes, but once again the circumstances don't quite fit his detailed description. In Dr. Cowan's account Forrest intends to ask for a transfer (which of course means he had not yet done so), but by this time President Davis had approved the transfer, which was already a matter of record.

One final issue remains to be discussed: temperament. Braxton Bragg was not a moral or physical coward. The idea that he would simply accept such gross insubordination from Forrest (or any officer) defies credulity, especially given other events unfolding during this time. Bragg was embroiled in charges and counter-charges with most of the army's senior commanders. On September 29, for example, he suspended from command Lt. Gen. Leonidas Polk for his failure to attack early on September 20. Within the Army of Tennessee Polk was second only to Bragg in seniority, and he was a close personal friend of President Davis. If Bragg was willing to relieve such a politically well-connected and high ranking officer like Bishop Polk, why would he be intimidated by an angry outburst from Forrest, who had neither rank nor political influence? Dr. Cowan suggests that Bragg's silence was not driven by fear but by a sense of duty. In other words Bragg took the high road when he recognized that relieving Forrest would be "a tremendous loss" to the Confederacy.[21] This, too, does not fit with the evidentiary record. By the end of September Bragg considered Forrest a failure in cavalry command—"nothing more than a good raider," to repeat Liddell's observation. There is no reason to believe that Bragg would ignore such a breach of discipline unless, of course, there never really was a breach of discipline.

*   *   *

After sifting through the evidence I have reached the conclusion that the confrontation between Forrest and Bragg that Dr. Cowan described in such detail never occurred. There was probably an angry exchange between the two men, and it almost certainly took place on September 30 as a follow-up to Forrest's protesting letter. In all likelihood, however, this meeting ended quite differently than related by Dr. Cowan, with a somewhat mollified Forrest who

20 Bradshaw, *Forrest's Escort*, p. 85.

21 Wyeth, *That Devil Forrest*, p. 244.

may have even been apologetic for any angry outburst.[22] This doesn't mean Forrest was content; Colonel Brent's journal demonstrates otherwise. But Brent's record does not offer any details supporting the sort of climactic confrontation Dr. Cowan describes so vividly. Despite the conclusions of many of Forrest's modern biographers, I believe we can dismiss the idea that the Forrest-Bragg meeting occurred after October 5. There is ample evidence that Forrest was not with the army during the time in question and that he did not return until October 20 after his meeting in Alabama with President Davis. Arbitrarily moving the meeting to an early October time-frame makes it easier for biographers to avoid having to deal with annoying internal contradictions, but it does so at the expense of the hard evidence.

Perhaps the confrontation unfolded when and as described by Dr. Cowan. Or, perhaps the infamous confrontation was simply a war story spun in old age by Forrest's former surgeon as he remembered fondly his revered kinsman and commander. Unless additional credible contemporary accounts surface, it is impossible to know with certainty whether this incident really took place.

---

22 This would be in keeping with Forrest's character. His angry comments to Joe Wheeler after the disaster at Dover, Tennessee, were almost immediately followed by an apology, and he is portrayed as very remorseful for having killed Lieutenant Gould in June 1863, despite that officer's attempt on his own life. Forrest had an explosive temper, but he knew it and he struggled to control that aspect of his demeanor.

A ppendix 5

An Interview with Author David Powell

SB: How long have you been interested in the Civil War?

DP: Since I was a teenager. Like most people I read on Eastern Theater battles, especially Gettysburg and wrote a couple short articles on that battle. Later I started reading on the war in the West. The more I read I realized there was more in print for Gettysburg alone than the entire war in the West. The difference is really striking. Chickamauga grabbed my interest, but there wasn't that much available on it. I realized there was opportunity here, and the more I researched, the more I became fascinated by this confusing battle.

SB: What was it about Chickamauga in general that drew your interest?

DP: It was extremely complex and yet so little studied. Many Civil War battles have been written about extensively, and with different points of view. Joe Harsh's take on Antietam, for example, differs significantly from Stephen Sears'. But only a couple books have been written on Chickamauga in the past forty years. There are only a couple worthwhile studies on the entire campaign.

SB: So you wanted to learn more about this battle / campaign?

DP: Yes. The deeper I probed, the more I realized that understanding the battle would require going beyond anything that had been published thus far.

SB: Why do you think it was important to write Failure in the Saddle?

DP: Because how cavalry impacts battles is not well understood. Increasingly, Civil War scholarship is examining and appreciating the role of cavalry in the campaign setting. Once battle is joined, cavalry plays at best a peripheral role on the great fields of the war—but while the armies are maneuvering, the cavalry's role is preeminent. Generals win the laurels for victory and bear the blame for defeat, but they can only be as good as their information allows them to be. Braxton Bragg is not a Great Captain, but it is clear that he was ill-served by his mounted arm in September 1863.

SB: On paper, the Confederate cavalry should have run rings around their Federal opponents during the Chickamauga campaign. Do you agree?

DP: I do agree. Bragg's cavalry had both the numbers and, on the face of it, competent—even storied—leadership. And yet the Federals kept the upper hand for most of the campaign. Bragg was repeatedly given bad information or none at all, and had to make critical decisions based on this intelligence. And so his plans miscarried over and over. Of course, other problems existed within the Army of Tennessee that made things worse, but we might think of Bragg differently today had his cavalry been up to the tasks assigned to it.

SB: How competent was Maj. Gen. William Rosecrans as an army commander?

DP: In my opinion Rosecrans could easily have been in the top tier of generals (and enjoyed a successful political career) except for one or two flaws. He was an excellent organizer, trainer, and disciplinarian. He was a complex strategic thinker. He drafted ambitious plans that embraced wide maneuver and envelopments, and proved that he could execute these plans—most notably at Tullahoma. His physical courage and concern for his men made him wildly popular among the rank and file. And he was not afraid to fight his army.

However, he had a deaf ear politically, and displayed disregard, and even scorn, for his superiors. His relationship with them went downhill after his victory at Stone's River and much of that was his own fault. He was not good at making do with what he had. He meddled on the battlefield. He interfered with his chain of command and failed to let his corps commanders exercise their responsibilities. These flaws, more than any battlefield defeat, doomed him.

SB: What did Rosecrans do right in the battle?

DP: Once he understood the Confederates were not retreating and were planning to spring a trap of their own, he reacted quickly. Between September

14 and 18 he gathered his scattered army and avoided the worst of the danger. When the battle began on the 19th he aggressively supported General Thomas, whose morning attacks disrupted the Rebel battle plan. He grasped the relative positions of the armies more quickly than did Bragg, and he kept looking for ways to find and turn one of Bragg's flanks—and he nearly did a couple times.

SB: What mistakes did Rosecrans make once the battle got underway?

DP: As the battle progressed, he placed too much emphasis on Thomas' sector. He fed so many troops to Thomas that his other two corps commanders became almost superfluous. McCook and Crittenden were not budding Napoleons, but they were reasonably competent. By the morning of the 20th Rosecrans had bypassed them in his chain of command and was managing individual divisions. He did so poorly and with fatal results when the infamous gap opened in his lines at the Brotherton house. This occurred because he was overwhelmed with tactical details, had lost sight of the bigger picture, and had slept little over the past few days and not at all the night before. This lack of sleep seriously impacted his judgment. Of this I have no doubt.

SB: How competent was Gen. Braxton Bragg as an army commander?

DP: On paper Bragg was an ideal commander. Like Rosecrans, he was a good disciplinarian, administrator, trainer, and strategist. He lacked the personal touch, however, and was often at odds with his subordinates. He was incapable of forging a group of individual officers into an effective command team, which proved to be his downfall. His army was rife with suspicion and discontent, an atmosphere that influenced even recent arrivals. As a result, his generals tended to pessimism and defeatism.

SB: Something even John Bell Hood discovered when he arrived on September 18 . . .

DP: Exactly. Hood was stunned by the pessimism displayed by the officers fighting under Bragg. When he remarked to General Breckinridge that "we [will] rout the enemy the next day," Breckinridge demonstrated surprise and jumped up and said he was "delighted to hear so." Hood was from Lee's Virginia army and accustomed to battlefield success. Bragg's officers had no such expectations. The failure to inspire confidence in his officers and men is one of Bragg's greatest failings as a general.

SB: Chickamauga is an important campaign rife with colorful characters, controversy, and hard fighting, and politics. It has one of the best preserved battlefields in the world and hundreds of thousands of tourists visit each year. Why has it received so little attention?

DP: The short answer is complexity. The battle is hard to understand, let alone write about. The battlefield is heavily timbered, and most authors are interested in the Eastern Theater. Few are willing to tackle the tangle of stories that make up the Chickamauga campaign. More works are being written today about Western battles, and this is good news for the study of the Civil War.

SB: Civilian and academic historians pay it scant attention, but the military takes the battle very seriously, right?

DP: Yes. Among military officers, Chickamauga is one of the most widely studied battles of the Civil War. In the 1980s, the Command and General Staff School of the US Army selected Chickamauga as the main focus for their professional development course. Chickamauga has been studied by generations of soldiers from all over the world. A large number of unpublished but readily available theses from this course focus on specific aspects of the campaign from the point of view of professional officers.

SB: What would you like to see done next for Chickamauga?

DP: A new full length study on the entire campaign. The last appeared in 1992 and there is ample room for a new perspective. I think there is room for a volume on each day of the battle, much as we have seen for Gettysburg. There are thousands of untapped archival sources. I believe an entirely new portrait of the battle can be drawn from this wealth of underused resources.

SB: What about Tullahoma?

DP: A scholarly work on the Tullahoma Campaign is also overdue. Rosecrans and the Army of the Cumberland executed this operation at the end of June 1863, and it was the forerunner to Rosecrans' more ambitious undertaking against Chattanooga that fall. But there was no large battle during this operation, so it has been all but ignored. Understanding Tullahoma, especially with regard to logistics, is necessary in order to understand Chickamauga.

Bibliography

MANUSCRIPTS

Alabama Department of Archives and History (ADAH)
    I. B. Ulmer Reminiscences, 3rd Alabama Cavalry file

Bowling Green State University, Bowling Green, OH
    Brigham Family Papers

Carroll College, Waukesha, Wisconsin
    Robert S. Merrill Diary, 1st Wisconsin Cavalry

Center for American History, University of Texas at Austin
    Thomas B. Hampton Letters
    William T. Martin Papers

Chattanooga-Hamilton County Public Library, Chattanooga TN
    Thomas W. Davis Diary (6th Tennessee Cavalry)

Chickamauga-Chattanooga National Military Park, Fort Oglethorpe, GA
    Nathan Bedford Forrest File
    Jas. A. Lewis Letter, 6th Tennessee Cavalry File
    Samuel Pasco Diary, 3rd Florida File
    Powell, David A. *Strengths and Losses of the Union and Confederate Armies at Chickamauga* (unpublished manuscript)
    S. H. Stevens, "Second Division Itinerary." Crook's Staff

Lieutenant James Thompson Diary, 4th Ohio Cavalry file
John T. Wilder Report
Various Park Tablets

Combat Studies Institute, U.S. Army Command and General Staff College, Fort Leavenworth, Kansas
Jason Hurd Diary
William Henry Harder Reminiscences

DePauw University, Greencastle Indiana
William D. Ward Diary and Papers

Duke University
Confederate Veteran Papers
W. F. Shropshire Reminiscences, 1st Georgia Cavalry
Clarence Malone Letter, Martha Clayton Harper Papers

Emory University, Atlanta, GA
W. B. Corbitt Diary
William Cary Dodson Memoir

Georgia Department of Archives and History, Atlanta, GA
William Sylvester Dillon Diary
Frank T. Ryan Reminiscences, Civil War Miscellany File

Historical Society of Pennsylvania, Philadelphia, PA
Thomas S. McCahan Diary, 9th Pennsylvania Cavalry

Illinois Historical Society, Springfield, IL
Edward Kitchell Diary

Indiana Historical Society, William H. Smith Memorial Library, Indianapolis, IN
John M. Bernard Letters, 72nd Indiana Mounted Infantry
Joseph A. Scott Reminiscences, Lilly's battery

Indiana State Library, Indianapolis, IN
William H. Records Diary, 72nd Indiana Mounted Infantry

Library of Congress
    Papers of Alfred Roman
    Rueben S. Morton Diary, John H. Tower Papers, Naval Historical
Foundation

Louisiana State University, Baton Rouge, LA
    John McGrath Papers

Mahoning Valley Historical Society Collections, Youngstown, OH
    Samuel Platt Diary, 26th Ohio Infantry

Minnesota Historical Society, St. Paul, MN
    Robert Burns Letters
    Horatio Van Cleve Papers

Museum of the Confederacy, Richmond, VA
    Army of Tennessee Scout Book, W. T. Holt

National Archives
    Record Group 393
    Part 1, Entry 986 "Summaries of the news reaching
Headquarters of General W. S. Rosecrans, 1863-64"

    Record Group 94
    Returns for XX Corps and Cavalry Corps, Army of the
Cumberland, September 10, 1863.

    Record Group 94
    Captain William E. Crane Diary, 4th Ohio Cavalry, General Thomas' Papers

    Record Group 94
    R. M. Russell, "Extracts from Journal" General Thomas Papers
    John C. Starkweather, "Report of Stevens' Gap" General Thomas Papers

    Record Group 109
    Bushrod Johnson Diary

South Carolina Historical Society, Charleston, South Carolina
    Lafayette McLaws memoir, Cheeves Family Papers

Tennessee State Library and Archives, Nashville, TN (TSLA)
    William Gibbs Allen Memoirs, 5th Tennessee Cavalry
    Newton Cannon Memoirs, 11th Tennessee Cavalry
    Alfred T. Fielder Diary, 12th Tennessee Infantry
    William E. Sloan Diary, 5th Tennessee Cavalry

University of Michigan, Ann Arbor, MI, Michigan Historical Collections, Bentley
Historical Library
    D. L. Haines. *Record of the Fourth Michigan Cavalry*
    Henry Hampstead Diary, 2nd Michigan Cavalry
    Henry A. Potter, "Account of the Battle of Chickamauga and Wheeler's Raid"

University of Mississippi, J. D. Williams Library, Oxford, Mississippi
    Robert A. Jarman, "History of Company K, 27th Mississippi"

University of Missouri, Rolla, Missouri, Western Historical Manuscripts Collection
    Tom Coleman Letter, 11th Texas Cavalry

University of North Carolina, Wilson Library, Southern Historical Collection
    Taylor Beatty Diary
    George Knox Miller Letters
    Martin Van Buren Moore Papers
    Leroy Monicure Nutt Papers
    Gustave Huwald Letter
    Taylor Beatty Diary

University of the South, Suwannee, Tennessee
    Leonidas Polk Papers

Western Reserve Historical Society, Cleveland, OH
    Palmer Collection
    Braxton Bragg Papers
    Benson H. Lossing Papers

Unpublished Theses
    Dudney, Betty Jane. *Civil War in White County, Tennessee.* Master's Thesis,
Tennessee Technological University, 1985

Williams, Coral. *Legends and Stories of White County, Tennessee.* Master's Thesis, George Peabody College for Teachers, 1930. Found online at: http://www.danielhaston.com/history/tn-history/white-county/legends-whiteco5.htm

NEWSPAPERS

Mobile Daily Register
Columbus Daily Sun
Rome Tri-Weekly Telegraph
Toledo Blade
Memphis Appeal (published in Atlanta, Georgia)

GOVERNMENT PUBLICATIONS

The War of the Rebellion: A Compilation of the Official Records of the Union and Confederate Armies Washington, DC, 1880-1901. 128 Volumes.

PRINTED PRIMARY SOURCES

Articles

Clay, H. B. "Concerning the Battle of Chickamauga." *Confederate Veteran,* February, 1905, Vol. XII, p. 72.
———. "On the Right at Chickamauga." *Confederate Veteran,* July, 1911, Vol. XIX, p. 329-30.
———. "On the Right at Chickamauga." *Confederate Veteran,* 1913, Vol. XXI, pp. 439-40.
Frazier, S. J. A. "Reminiscences of Chickamauga," Clipping from *The Lookout,* May 20, 1909. Hamilton County Library, Chattanooga, Tennessee.
Green, Curtis. "Sixth Georgia Cavalry at Chickamauga," *Confederate Veteran,* July, 1900. Vol. VIII, p. 324.
Hill, D. H. "Chickamauga—Great Battle of the West," *Battles and Leaders of the Civil War.* New York, Thomas Yoseloff, 1956. Vol. III.
Larson, James. "Outwitting a Picket Guard," *National Tribune,* September 19, 1912.
Martin, William T. "A Defense of General Bragg at Chickamauga," *Confederate Veteran.* Volume XI, Number 4, 1883.
Minnich, J. W. "Reminiscences of J. W. Minnich, 6th GA Cavalry," *Northwest Georgia Historical and Genealogical Society Quarterly,* Volume 29, number 3, Summer, 1997.

Minnich, J. W. "Unique Experiences in the Chickamauga Campaign," *Confederate Veteran*, Vol. 30, issue #6, p. 222.

Minty, Robert G. "Minty's Saber Brigade: The Part They Took in the Chickamauga Campaign, Part One," *National Tribune*, February 25, 1892.

———. "Minty's Saber Brigade," *National Tribune*, November 9, 1893.

———. "Rossville Gap," *The National Tribune*. March 8, 1894.

Rosecrans, W. S. "Rosecrans' Accounts of Tullahoma and Chickamauga," *National Tribune*, March 25, 1882.

Shuster, James H. "Holding Reed's Bridge," *National Tribune*, August 11, 1910.

Stevenson, William Robert. "Robert Alexander Smith: A Southern Son," *Alabama Historical Quarterly*, Volume XX, 1958.

Wilson, George A. "Wilder's Brigade," *National Tribune*, October 26, 1893.

Books

Aten, Henry J. *History of the Eighty-Fifth Regiment Illinois Volunteer Infantry*. Hiawatha, Kansas, n.p., 1901.

Athearn, Robert G. ed. *Soldier in the West: The Civil War Letters of Alfred Lacey Hough*. Philadelphia, PA: University of Pennsylvania Press, 1957.

Berry, Thomas F. *Four Years with Morgan and Forrest*. Oklahoma City, OK: The Harlow-Ratliff Company, 1914.

Blackburn, J. K. P., L. B. Giles, and E. S. Dowd. *Terry Texas Ranger Trilogy*. Austin, TX. State House Press, 1996.

Bradshaw, Wayne, ed. *A Member of Forrest's Escort: The Civil War Diary of William R. Dyer*. Wayne Bradshaw, 2009.

By a Confederate, *The Grayjackets: And How They Lived, Fought, and Died For Dixie*. Richmond, VA: Jones, Brothers and co., n.d.

Cotton, John W. Lucille Griffith, ed. *Yours Till Death: Civil War Letters of John W. Cotton*. University, AL: University of Alabama Press, 1951.

Crofts, Thomas. *History of the Third Ohio Cavalry, 1861-1865*. Toledo, OH: Stoneman Press, 1910.

Gates, Arnold, ed. *The Rough Side of War: The Civil War Journal of Chesley A. Mosman 1st Lieutenant, Company D, 59th Illinois Volunteer Infantry Regiment*. Garden City, NJ: Basin Publishing, 1987.

Guild, George B. *A Brief Narrative of the Fourth Tennessee Cavalry Regiment, Wheeler's Corps, Army of Tennessee*. Nashville, TN, n.p., 1913.

Hood, John Bell. *Advance and Retreat: Personal Experiences in the United States and Confederate States Armies*. Secausus, NJ: Blue and Gray Press, 1985. Reprint of 1880 edition.

Larson, James. *Sergeant Larson, 4th Cav*. San Antonio, TX: Southern Literary Institute, 1935.

Lindsley, John Barrien. *Military Annals of Tennessee*. Wilmington, NC: Broadfoot Publishing Company, 1995. Reprint of 1886 edition.

Linville, Dale Edward. *Battles, Skirmishes, Events and Scenes: The Letters and Memorandum of Ambrose Remley*. Crawfordsville, IN: Montgomery County Historical Society, 1997.

Longstreet, James. *From Manassas to Appomattox: Memoirs of the Civil War in America*. Philadelphia, PA: P. J. Lippincott, 1896.

McGee, B. F. *History of the 72d Indiana Volunteer Infantry of the Mounted Lightning Brigade*. Lafayette, IN: S. Vater & Co. 1882.

Military History of Kansas Regiments. Adjutant General of the State of Kansas, Topeka, Kansas.

Minty, R.H.G. *Remarks of Brevet Major General R.H.G. Minty made September 18th, 1895 at the Dedication of the Monument Erected to the Fourth Michigan Cavalry at Reed's Bridge, Chickamauga National Park*. Ogden, UT: 1896.

Morton, John Watson. *The Artillery of Nathan Bedford Forrest's Cavalry*. Marietta, GA: R. Bemis Publishing, 1995. Reprint of 1909 edition.

Ninety-Second Illinois Volunteers. Freeport, IL: Journal Steam Publishing House and Bookbindery, 1875.

Partridge, Charles. *History of the Ninety-Sixth Regiment Illinois Volunteer Infantry*. Chicago, IL: Brown, Pettibone and Company, 1887.

Proceedings of the Thirtieth Annual Reunion, 1st O.V.V.C. Columbus, OH: n.p., 1909.

Rerick, John H. *The Forty-Fourth Indiana Volunteer Infantry: History of its Services in the War of the Rebellion and a Personal Record of its Members*. Lagrange, IN: n.p., 1880.

Rowell, John W. *Yankee Cavalrymen: Through the Civil War with the Ninth Pennsylvania Cavalry*. Knoxville, TN: University of Tennessee Press, 1971.

Sheridan, Philip H. *Personal Memoirs of P. H. Sheridan, in Two Volumes*. Wilmington, NC: Broadfoot Publishing, 1992. Reprint of 1888 edition.

Sipes, William B. *The Saber Regiment: The Seventh Pennsylvania Veteran Volunteer Cavalry its Record, Reminiscences and Roster*. Huntington, WV: Blue Acorn Press, 2000. Reprint of 1906 edition.

Stanley, David S. *Personal Memoirs of Major General D. S. Stanley, U.S.A.* Cambridge, MA: Harvard University Press, 1917.

Turchin, John B. *Chickamauga*. Chicago, IL: Fergus Printing Co., 1888.

Vale, Joseph G. *Minty and the Cavalry: A History of Cavalry Campaigns in the Western Armies*. Harrisburg, PA: Edwin K. Meyers, 1886.

Williams, John A. B. *Leaves From a Trooper's Diary*. Philadelphia, PA: Self-published, 1869.

Wyeth, John A. *With Sabre and Scalpel: The Autobiography of a Soldier and Surgeon*. New York, NY: Harpers, 1914.

SECONDARY SOURCES

Atlas of the Battlefields of Chickamauga, Chattanooga, and Vicinity. Chickamauga and Chattanooga National Park Commission, Washington DC, 1895.

Baumgartner, Richard A. *Blue Lightning: Wilder's Mounted Infantry Brigade in the Battle of Chickamauga.* Huntington, WV: Blue Acorn Press, 1997.

Bradley, Michael R. *Tullahoma: The 1863 Campaign for the Control of Middle Tennessee.* Shippensburg, PA: Burd Street Press, 2000.

Civil War Centennial Commission, *Tennesseans in the Civil War.* Nashville, TN, 1964.

Connelly, Thomas Lawrence. *Autumn of Glory.* Baton Rouge, LA: Louisiana State University Press, 1986. Reprint of 1971 edition.

Cotten, Michael. *The Williamson County Cavalry: A History of Company F, Fourth Tennessee Cavalry Regiment, CSA.* Self published, 1994.

Cozzens, Peter. *This Terrible Sound: The Battle of Chickamauga.* Urbana, IL: University of Illinois Press, 1992.

Dodson, W. C. ed., *Campaigns of Wheeler & His Cavalry 1862-1865 and the Santiago Campaign Cuba, 1898.* Memphis, TN: E. F. Williams and J. J. Fox, 1997. Reprint of 1899 edition.

Dubose, John Witherspoon. *General Joseph Wheeler and the Army of Tennessee.* New York, NY: Neale Publishing Company, 1912.

Dyer, John P. *"Fightin' Joe" Wheeler.* Baton Rouge, LA: Louisiana State University Press, 1941.

Fitch, John. *Annals of the Army of the Cumberland.* Mechanicsburg, PA: Stackpole Books, 2003. Reprint of 1864 edition.

Gremillion, Nelson. *Company G, 1st Louisiana Cavalry, CSA. A Narrative.* Lafayette, LA: University of Southwestern Louisiana, 1986.

Griggs, Walter S. Jr. *General John Pegram, C.S.A* Lynchburg, VA: H. E. Howard, 1993.

Hallock, Judith Lee. *Braxton Bragg and Confederate Defeat: Volume II.* Tuscaloosa, AL: University of Alabama Press, 1991.

Hartje, Robert G. *Van Dorn: The Life and Times of a Confederate General.* Nashville, TN: Vanderbilt University Press, 1967.

Henry, Robert Selph. *"First with the Most": Forrest.* New York, NY: Mallard Press, 1991. Reprint of 1944 edition.

Hurst, Jack. *Nathan Bedford Forrest.* New York, NY: Alfred A. Knopf, 1993.

Indiana at Chickamauga: 1863-1900, Report of Indiana Commissioners, Chickamauga National Military Park. Indianapolis, IN: Sentinel Printing Company, 1900, pp. 142-3.

Jordan, Thomas, and J. P. Pryor. *The Campaigns of General Nathan Bedford Forrest and of Forrest's Cavalry.* New York, NY: Da Capo Press, 1996. Reprint of 1868 edition.

Lonn, Ella. *Desertion during the Civil War.* Lincoln, NE: University of Nebraska Press, 1998. Reprint of 1928 edition.

Lytle, Andrew. *Bedford Forrest and His Critter Company.* Seminole, FL: Green Key Press, 1984. Reprint of 1931 edition.

Maness, Lonnie E. *An Untutored Genius.* Oxford, MS: The Guild Bindery Press, 1990.

Martin, David and John Busey, *Regimental Strengths and Losses at Gettysburg,* Hightstown, NJ: Longstreet House Publishers, 1986.

Military History of Kansas Regiments. Adjutant General of the State of Kansas, Topeka, KS: Kansas State Printing Co. 1896.

Nesbit, Mark. *Saber and Scapegoat: J.E.B. Stuart and the Gettysburg Controversy.* Mechanicsburg, PA: Stackpole Books, 1994.

Poole, John Randolph. *Cracker Cavaliers: The 2nd Georgia Cavalry under Wheeler and Forrest.* Macon, GA: Mercer University Press, 2000.

Ramage, James A. *Rebel Raider: The Life of General John Hunt Morgan.* Lexington, KY: University Press of Kentucky, 1986.

Smith, Gen. John C. *Oration at the Unveiling of the Monument Erected to the Memory of Maj. Gen. James B. Steedman.* Chicago, IL: Knight and Leonard, 1887.

Tucker, Glenn. *Chickamauga.* Dayton, OH: Morningside, 1981. Reprint of 1961 edition.

Warner, Ezra J. *Generals in Gray: Lives of the Confederate Commanders.* Baton Rouge, LA: Louisiana State University Press, 1991. Reprint of 1959 edition.

Weaver, Jeffrey C. *The Confederate Regimental History Series: The 5th and 7th Battalions North Carolina Cavalry and the 6th North Carolina Cavalry (65th North Carolina State Troops),* n.p., 1995.

Wills, Brian Steel. *A Battle From the Start.* New York, NY: HarperCollins, 1992.

Woodworth, Steven E. *Six Armies in Tennessee.* Lincoln, NE: University of Nebraska Press, 1998.

INDEX

About the Author

David A. Powell graduated from the Virginia Military Institute (Class of 1983) with a BA in history. He has published numerous articles in magazines, more than fifteen historical simulations of various battles, and is the author (with David A. Friedrichs, cartographer) of *The Maps of Chickamauga: An Atlas of the Chickamauga Campaign, Including the Tullahoma Operations, June 22 - September 23, 1863*. He is currently working on another volume of the Savas Beatie Military Atlas Series, this one on the Chattanooga Campaign. David enjoys leading tours to Civil War battlefields, especially the epic field of Chickamauga. He lives and works in Chicago, Illinois.

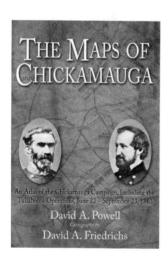

The Maps of Chickamauga: An Atlas of the Chickamauga Campaign, Including the Tullahoma Operations, June 22 - September 23, 1863

David A. Powell (text)
David A. Friedrichs (cartography)

- 126 full page and full color original maps
- Orders of battle with losses
- notes, bibliography, index
- 320 pages

Available at fine bookstores everywhere, online booksellers, and from the publisher.